The First We Can Remember

The First We Can Remember

Colorado Pioneer Women Tell Their Stories

Edited and with an introduction by
Lee Schweninger

University of Nebraska Press | Lincoln and London

The oral and written histories in this volume are used courtesy of History Colorado, CWA Pioneers Interviews, 1933–34. Correspondence between LeRoy Hafen and Anna Florence Robison is also used courtesy of History Colorado, MSS 1458 LeRoy Hafen Collection.

Manufactured in the United States of America

Publication of this volume was supported in part by a grant from The University of North Carolina Wilmington College of Arts and Sciences and Department of English.

Library of Congress Cataloging-in-Publication Data

The first we can remember: Colorado pioneer women tell their stories / edited and with an introduction by Lee Schweninger.
p. cm.
Includes bibliographical references and index.
ISBN 978-0-8032-3515-1 (pbk: alk. paper)
1. Women pioneers—Colorado—Interviews. 2. Frontier and pioneer life—Colorado. 3. Colorado—Biography. 4. Colorado—History—1876–1950. 5. Colorado—Social life and customs—19th century. 6. Interviews—Colorado. 7. Oral history—Colorado. I. Schweninger, Lee.
F781.F57 2011
920.72—dc23
[B]
2011019912

Set in Quadraat by Bob Reitz.
Designed by Mikah Tacha.

for my mom, Alice,
and for my sisters
Mary, Ann, Jan

Contents

Maps

Acknowledgments

I want first to acknowledge the debt owed the many field-workers who recorded these narratives. We all have these women and men to thank for recording—and thus ensuring the survival of—the narratives: M. Amour, W. G. Benneweiss, Elizabeth Cairns, E. E. Carrington, Margaret Fleck, C. E. Gibson Jr., M. B. Gill, B. B. Guthrie, Margaret Merrill, J. Monaghan, Leslie F. Paull, A. K. Richeson, Anna Florence Robison, Leah M. Ryder, A. L. Soens, J. W. Taylor, and Laura White.

I wish to thank the Charles Redd Center for Western Studies for a Faculty Fellowship Award in the summer of 2005 that enabled research travel to the Colorado Historical Society library in Denver. I also received support from a Charles H. Cahill Award and Summer Stipend Award, University of North Carolina Wilmington, grants that made possible a research trip to the archives in the Western History Collection at the University of Colorado at Boulder and the Colorado Historical Society library in Denver. I also thank the Office of the Dean of the College of Arts and Sciences at the University of North Carolina Wilmington for its support of my research and writing by granting a Research Reassignment for the fall of 2005. Each of these grants and awards helped make possible study and research in Colorado libraries.

I want to further acknowledge individually both David Cordle, Dean, College of Arts and Sciences, and Keith Newlin, Chair, Department of English, both at the University of North Carolina Wilmington, for providing financial support to the University of Nebraska Press for the publication of this book.

In addition to the awards, grants, and very real financial support, critical to this project has been the priceless assistance of many different individuals. I would like to express my gratitude to archivist David Hay at the University of Colorado Archives for his aid and advice during my early work there and also to the helpful people on the reference staffs at Norlin Library, the University of Colorado at Boulder, and at the Western History Department at the Denver Public Library. Barbara Dey, Reference Librarian at the Stephen H. Hart Library, Colorado Historical Society, provided assistance both in the library in Denver and through correspondence. The reference staffs in the reading rooms at the Jefferson and Adams buildings of the Library of Congress were also extremely generous with their time and expertise. Once again, Humanities Librarian Elizabeth Peterson at the University of Oregon Libraries has provided me with responses to some very challenging research questions. Also of note have been reference librarians at several public libraries across Colorado. At the Durango Public Library, Nancy McInerney responded to inquiries; at the Boulder Public Library, several years ago I received help from Wendy Hall at the Carnegie Branch Library for Local History, and more recently assistance from Melinda Mattingly, Reference and Collections Manager. I also want to thank the staff members at the Dolores Public Library for their having worked with me as I dug through old newspapers and other records. Special thanks go to Alice C. Odell of Mancos, Colorado, who—from her personal library—provided much of the biographical information about Anna Florence Robison, the field-worker for Montezuma County.

As always, the staff members at Randall Library at the University of North Carolina Wilmington have provided invaluable service. Always extremely prompt and reliable, Sophie Williams and the rest of the interlibrary-loan staff have been indispensable. Sue Cody, Associate Librarian, has been very helpful with research questions.

At the University of Nebraska Press, for their assistance and patience, I want to thank Elisabeth Chretien and Matthew Bokovoy, and especially Sabrina Stellrecht for her help with organizational and other editorial concerns in getting the manuscript ready for the press. In addition, I want to thank Jonathan Lawrence for his meticulous reading of the manuscript from top to bottom. I am also grateful for the many suggestions for improvements from the several individuals who, mostly anonymously, devoted their time and energy to reading drafts of the manuscript, and I am particularly indebted to Melody Graulich for her insightful comments.

A special thank-you goes to Cara Cilano for her unflagging support and encouragement and for her editorial advice all along the trail. I want to offer an extra nod of gratitude to my sister Mary, who—over the past several years on my different research trips to Colorado—in addition to her moral support, often housed me, prepared wonderful meals, and inevitably got me to the bus stop on time at all hours in all kinds of weather. Because they are or have been Colorado pioneers in their own ways, I dedicate this book to my mom and my sisters.

Introduction

I was just thrilled, for the great prairie was one big blanket of pure white snow with here and there a little home like a dot on the whiteness; nothing in sight but the beautiful snow and the sky. Right there I knew I would never be contented until I had a home of our own in the wonderful West.
Nellie Buchanan, Kit Carson County

After an overnight stop during her journey to Colorado in the early 1880s, Nellie Buchanan described her excitement about pioneering in the West. Like the other narrators whose accounts appear here, she was excited about the open spaces, the physical beauty, and the possibility of owning her own home. Like them, she also provided a firsthand, first-person account of her thoughts and experiences traveling to and settling in what became Colorado. The narrators included in this collection told their stories to Civil Works Administration (CWA) field-workers across the state in 1933 and 1934, and these field-workers sent the transcripts of the narratives to the Colorado Historical Society, where they have lain ever since.

As Nellie Buchanan hinted, the attractions accorded the "wonderful West" were many. These narrators believed that the West would offer them, in addition to natural beauty and perceived open spaces, the opportunity to possess their own piece of land; that it held forth the promise of wealth or at least a comfortable living; that it would

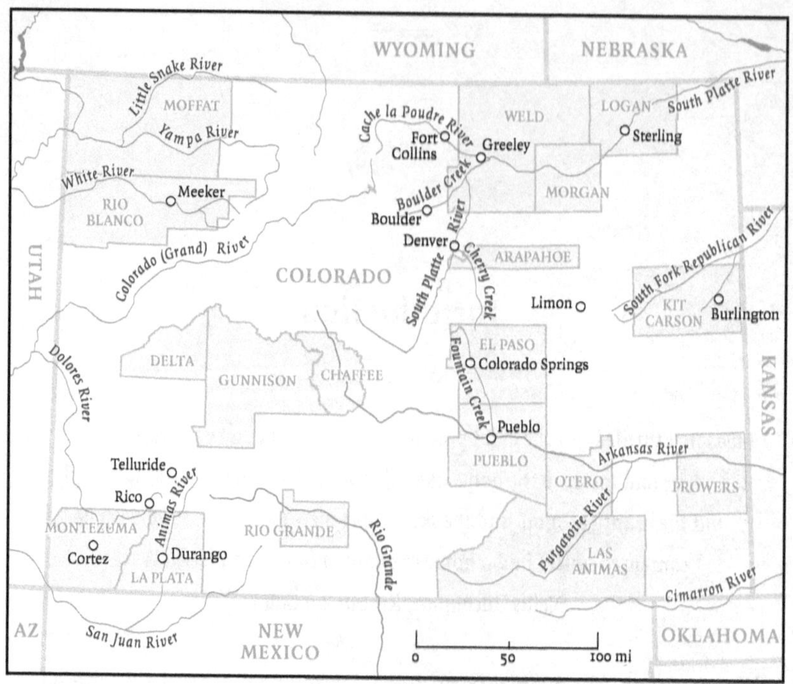

1. Colorado counties represented

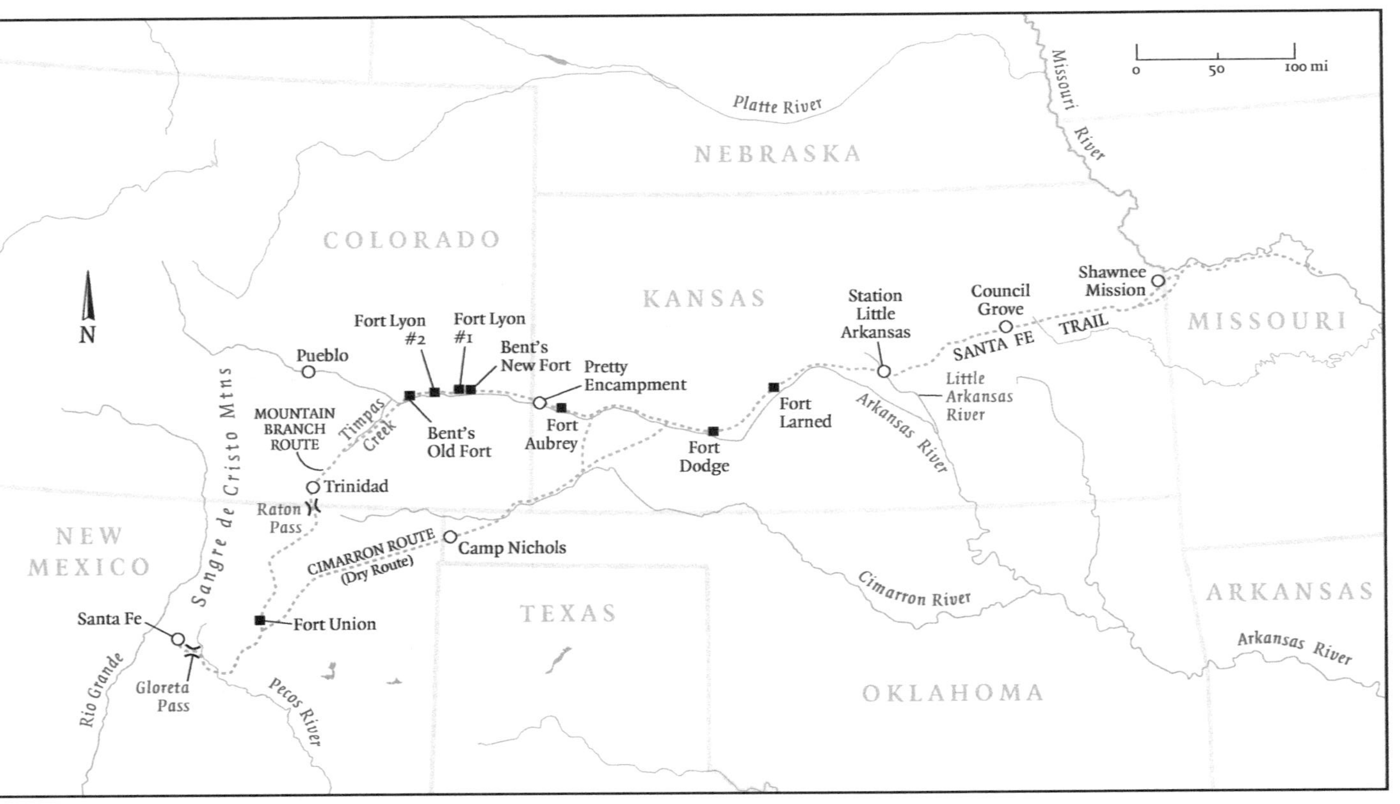

2. The Santa Fe Trail

provide a healthful, arid climate in a place where the entire family would be able to work and reside and thus remain together. As many women recounted, the West also promised adventure and gave them a sense that they were preparing the way for those who were to follow.

Despite the many attractions, however, not all of these women had as favorable a reaction to the West as did Buchanan. Mary Cox of Pueblo County recalled that the prairie she first set eyes on "was the most barren, forsaken country that we had ever seen." Sarah Blakeman of Kit Carson County felt somewhat ambivalent: "I cannot tell you just how I felt when I got off the train in Claremont and looked over the great stretch of prairie. . . . I said to my husband, 'Where have you brought us to?'" In the beginning, she remembered, "I was so afraid of coyotes, and would not step out at night for fear of stepping on a centipede, for I had been told the grass was full of them. . . . And I remember I was afraid of cowboys."[1] Some found it very difficult to adjust, as Jennie Lucas of Weld County recalled: "Mother did not like it here at first. . . . Many times I have seen her walking up and down the river bank crying as though her heart would break."

These recollections of discontent and fear suggest that for these women, homesteading in Colorado was not easy. In *A Place to Grow*, Glenda Riley breaks into three categories the challenges that confronted such pioneer women: the natural environment, personal conflict, and political struggle.[2] These narratives demonstrate the settlers' need to tell their stories about such challenges and thereby to give a shape and a coherence to their pasts. Many expressed their homesickness, and they recalled that they had to survive against pests such as sand fleas, grasshoppers, and locusts. The narrators offered accounts of rattlesnakes, wolves, and sometimes charging longhorn steers. They remembered enduring severe weather: hail, snow, blizzards, cold, floods, and tornados.[3] In many parts of Colorado they faced a severe scarcity of water, and often one of food. Travel to pick up mail and get supplies was difficult and sometimes dangerous. Getting to doctors often put these women at as much risk as did whatever the need for a doctor was in the first place. Schools and teachers were in constant demand, and church services, if held at all, often had to be held in makeshift surroundings.[4] In south-central Colorado there were disputes over land rights, and the narrators tell stories of encounters with marauding miners and squatters, of trigger-happy cowboys, and of attacks by and on displaced or threatened Comanches, Arapahos, Cheyennes, and Utes.

Notwithstanding the stories of hardships and challenges, these women narrators did indeed survive and often did remain on the land they claimed and settled. In many cases they were still on or near their original claims in 1933 and 1934 when CWA field-workers came to their homesteads asking for accounts of their pioneering days. These narratives are thus the stories of survivors; they are the records of those who were successful and who became permanent settlers in Colorado. Unfortunately, there are no narratives of the many women who did not remain; those narratives are not a part of the record, because the would-be narrators were not available to the field-workers in the Colorado counties.[5] Nellie Buchanan remembered one dispirited family returning to the East, and the advice they gave her offered a glimpse of their misfortune: "Man alive, go back to where you came from; go back now while you can, for in a year from now you won't have anything to go back with. Go back before you have to starve." Those who did stay frequently insisted that they played an important role in settling the West. They informed their interviewers, their immediate audience, and ultimately the readers of this volume of what they remembered as important and what they wanted the interviewers to know and believe about their experiences in settling the area.[6]

Naturally enough, these women reported their gratitude and expressed pride in their accomplishments. After all, they often insisted, there were rewards for remaining on the land. As Anna Homm of Kit Carson County boasted, "I have my own little home here on the land

I have lived on for so many years, and I am content and happy." Hattie L. Hedges Trout of El Paso County concluded her narrative this way: "I still live in my little home that was built in 1887—forty-seven years ago. I love it and dear old Colorado where I have lived most of my life and it is my desire to end my days here and be laid to rest with my loved ones in the shadow of Pikes Peak."

The narratives collected here offer intimate glimpses into the general history of Colorado, and such glimpses continue to open new horizons of our understanding of the role of women in the settlement of and even exploitation of the West. As Elizabeth Jameson and Susan Armitage suggest in their introduction to *Writing the Range*, the "West has become less heroic, less pastoral, the cast of characters more diverse, the meanings of the drama more equivocal."[7] The narrators' responses to the landscape and to the Native Americans they encountered, for example, provide us with a better understanding of the cast of characters who had a part in settling the West in very specific contexts.[8]

Civil Works Administration

Beginning in 1933, field-workers collected the narratives of these Colorado pioneer women as a part of the Civil Works Administration project, a program signed into law by President Roosevelt on November 7, 1933. According to Harry Hopkins, the director of the Federal Emergency Relief Administration (FERA), the program was "intended to be a very short program, carrying over the peak of a critical winter. Its chief, original aim was to put four million needy unemployed to work as speedily as possible and to keep them at work for the winter."[9] Of the funds for people that the program promised to put to work nationwide, 6 percent was meant for non-manual projects in such areas as education, arts, and research.

One specific application of the CWA in Colorado—one of over two hundred thousand CWA projects in the United States—enabled professional but unemployed writers, teachers, and historians across the state to interview former pioneers, asking them to talk about their experiences in coming West and settling. According to a January 1934 editorial in *Colorado Magazine*, the State Historical Society of Colorado proposed the survey project, and the CWA approved and funded it: "Workers throughout the state have been selected and are now employed in gathering local historical data. They are interviewing pioneers, gathering printed and manuscript materials of all sorts which relate to local history."[10]

On November 28, LeRoy Hafen, Historical Society historian, museum curator, and editor of *Colorado Magazine*, submitted a proposal requesting twenty-seven field-workers "to engage in gathering local historical material, interview pioneers, gather data and write the history of the founding and early development of towns, leading institutions, and principal industries."[11] These workers were to be paid for a thirty-hour workweek at the rate of either $22.50 (75 cents per hour) or $30.00 ($1.00 per hour) depending on how much travel was involved. The project received approval on December 15, and the following undated letter (probably a template) was evidently sent to the interviewers:

> You are hereby notified of your appointment as a field worker in the Colorado Historical Survey Project, under the Civil Works Administration. This is sponsored by the State Historical Society of Colorado with the undersigned responsible for administration. Twenty-five field workers are being engaged in as many towns of the state. You are to work in ______ and vicinity.
>
> The terms of employment are: $.75, thirty hours per week. The project is to extend from December 1st to February 15th. If you accept the appointment, begin work at once and notify me of your acceptance. Some general instructions and suggestions are enclosed. These cannot have universal application, so each worker is expected to use his or her initiative and adapt methods to the requirements of given situations.

> You are to report to me each week, indicating your progress and sending in completed work.
>
> I am sure that when you get started you will enjoy the work very much. Please accept my best wishes and be assured of my interest and help.[12]

After receiving word that funding for the CWA projects was indeed to be terminated on February 15, 1934, Hafen sent off another proposal on February 19, making the same request for another ten weeks. That proposal received approval on February 26, and the work continued.

Although written instructions or guidelines are missing from the Hafen Papers, one can surmise the typical questions the field-workers asked. Many of the questions were meant clearly to evoke accounts of the respondents' journeys to Colorado and with setting up the households. Also important were questions about establishing schools, post offices, churches, and medical facilities. Interviewers must have also asked about the kinds of work and forms of entertainment that were available. Although they were responding to specific prompts, the narrators typically offered much more than what a mere list of questions would elicit. They offered accounts of their impressions of the land and the people, and they often gave accounts of their own families. Each narrative included here is unique in its account of one particular personal, firsthand response to homesteading in Colorado, and many narratives offer varying accounts of the same event or of similar circumstances, thereby providing diverse historical perspectives.

Writing about the project, LeRoy Hafen proclaimed that it "is one of the most important historical projects ever undertaken in Colorado," in part, he argued, because it would "result in the acquisition and preservation of a vast amount of most valuable historical material" for the entire state of Colorado.[13] Despite the importance of the project, however, it was short lived. In response to its termination, field-worker Laura White, from Pagosa Springs, Archuleta County, wrote to Hafen on April 3, 1934, that she hoped to hear from the State Historical Society:

"they got all the other orders here closing the CWA project. They say down here there is something to take its place. I have registered here for this same work—was that o.k.?" When the CWA was dissolved in March 1934, the FERA continued similar work through the summer and fall of 1934. Upon being reassigned under the new program, Anna Florence Robison, field-worker for Montezuma County, wrote to thank Hafen for the opportunity to continue her work. "Aside from the very real financial help it bids fair to be to me," she wrote, "I have also the satisfaction of doing a thing I love to do. I hereby promise to do my very best at it."[14] But by October, FERA funding was also to expire. Hafen explained to Robinson that since FERA funds would not be available, he hoped to substitute the Professional Projects program in order to continue the research efforts.

Colorado Geography

The history of settlement for what became Colorado is closely linked to the state's physical geography, and the principal physiographic feature is the mountain range that divides the present state roughly down the middle.[15] To the east sprawl the high plains, historically made up primarily of short-grass prairie, the most arid of the mid-continental grasslands. This region is characterized by its small amount of precipitation (often less than ten inches a year), high winds, hail-storms, and limey soil. The blue grama and buffalo grasses native to this area fed the bison, however, and prairie dogs, pronghorns, and wolves also thrived here. Such abundance made hunting attractive, and the land thus sustained many different Native American tribes for centuries. Despite its natural richness, however, in many places this prairie was far too dry for farming, and by the 1880s European American investors had developed the cattle industry, which often resulted in intense overgrazing.[16]

Some early narrators recounted the thriving bison and antelope (pronghorn) herds they witnessed as they crossed the prairie. Elizabeth Harrington described the plenty: "For three days after leaving 'Little Fort Arkansas' we traveled through a moving mass of buffalo. . . . I remember so well how I stood up on our ambulance [covered wagon] as high up as I could get to look at them, and as far as I could see in any direction there was that vast, solid-looking mass of buffalo." Mary Nichols Williams of Gunnison County related that the buffalo "looked like great brownish-black dusty seas, as they galloped along over the plains." She also reported that because the buffalo were so plentiful, the travelers "had no other meat while crossing the plains; and nothing but the best part of the carcass was ever used." She then added that it "seemed sinful to waste the meat that way." Crossing just a decade later, several narrators lamented the scarcity or total absence of buffalo, after the near extermination of bison in North America (by around 1885). Several women reported that they traveled across the plains too late to witness the herds. Elizabeth Lengel, for example, confessed that crossing the prairie in 1886, "I never saw any buffalo." Sallie Cheairs of Logan County related that the "first settlers ate a great deal of buffalo meat as they were quite numerous on the prairie then, but there were none after our coming here."[17]

To the west of the Rocky Mountains lie the great plateaus dissected by such rivers as the Delores, Gunnison, White, and the Colorado (formerly the Grand) and their tributaries.[18] These rivers have carved stunning and sometimes apparently impassible canyons through the sandstone. Much of the plateau's vegetation is semi-desert shrub land mixed with piñon-juniper woodlands. As in the eastern grasslands, cattle grazing was (and remains) an important use of the plateau region. In these high plateaus of the western slope, big game was initially plentiful, especially mule deer and pronghorn. After the frenzy of the mining and the necessity of feeding the thousands of gold and silver miners who arrived ready to pan and pick, however, game became as scarce in the western part of the state as it had become on the eastern prairie. Because of the dryness in the summer and coldness in the winter, the plateaus challenged farmers, but the good lands along the river bottoms and valleys were settled and fully exploited.

Until the discovery of gold in 1858 at the mouth of Dry Creek, the mountains were a barrier that kept white settlement away, long after the Southwest, California, and even Utah had been settled by European Americans. More than the prairies and plateaus, however, it was initially those foreboding mountains that constituted the primary attraction for European American settlers to Colorado; it was in the mountains—first in the streams and placers and then in the mountainsides themselves—that prospectors found gold.

Gold Rush

Once gold was discovered near the confluence of Cherry Creek and the Platte River near present-day Denver in the summer of 1858, the mountains were no longer seen as an impediment to western migration; indeed, almost overnight they became the primary reason for migration.[19] The region—barely populated by European Americans in the 1850s[20]—became a territory in 1861 and a state in 1876. By some estimates as many as one hundred thousand people left the States in 1859 en route to the mountains of Colorado; as many as fifty thousand may have actually made it to the Front Range area during that first year. In a matter of months the tent city of Denver became an urban center, and other towns sprang up all along the Front Range. La Porte, Boulder City, Golden Gate, El Paso, and Fountain City were all early jumping-off points and supply centers for the miners who spread out across the mountains, up the Arkansas River, Clear Creek, and Boulder Creek. Gregory Gulch between Black Hawk and Central City and California Gulch near the headwaters of the Arkansas, just outside of present-day Leadville, were suddenly thriving mining communities. Mrs. Dock Wade of Arapahoe County describes the allure that seeking gold held for her father: "All the rest of his life he followed the occupation of mining. From Denver every day he worked a little farther up stream and a little farther away from home, and finally was so far away that in July 1874 he brought us to Littleton."

The discovery of gold brought the prospectors, but as the narratives here make clear, it also brought the merchants who provided them with food, tools, and other necessities. The mining industry demanded smelters and refineries. As railroads made their way into the state, lured by the prospect of transporting for the mining industry, they brought workers and settlers, and others associated with the business of supporting a mining economy: bankers, dry-goods dealers, grocers, saloon operators, ranchers, and mill workers, for example. Farmers and ranchers found fertile river valleys and huge stretches of grassy parks. Tunneling and digging made irrigation farming possible in dry areas across the prairie and in the southwest. Although the population declined after the height of the gold rush, people continued to come to the area, and subsequent gold and silver discoveries in the southwest promised to bring still more people.

American Indians

The history of pioneering in Colorado is in some ways the history of the subjugation and displacement of certain groups of people by other groups. Certainly, as these narratives demonstrate, European Americans were not the first settlers in the area; they did not migrate into an empty land. Rapid and thorough European American settlement of the state meant specifically the displacement of the Native Americans living in and around Colorado.[21] Indian-white interactions were frequent and often much more complex than a mere history of battles and treaties would suggest. According to Peter Iverson, for example, histories of the American West would do well "to focus more on forms of resistance by indigenous peoples that took place away from the battlefield."[22]

Before the exploration and settlement by European Americans, the Utes traversed much of what is now Colorado.[23] They hunted and traded from the Front Range and Wet Mountains on the eastern slope and west into Utah, and, as the Navajo narrator Mrs. Dan'els of Moffat County reported, the Utes raided Navajo camps in the west. In the southeast Utes occupied lands almost to the Purgatoire River near present-day Las Animas; in the northeast they typically hunted as far into the plains as present-day Greeley. On extended hunting excursions they traveled into eastern Colorado and western Kansas (where they met with resistance from Arapahos and Cheyennes), into the Oklahoma and Texas panhandles, and into northern New Mexico. When Spanish explorers ventured into the mountains in the seventeenth and eighteenth centuries, they found Utes in control of the passes, and later explorers and pioneers made full use of Ute hunting and commerce trails. Emma Amick of Rio Blanco County, for example, told about "going on horseback over the old Ute trail." Today, as many as fifteen streams are called Ute Creek; there are three Ute Mountains, and in Boulder County there is a Ute Peak. There are five Ute Passes, four Ute Canyons, four Ute Lakes, two Ute Gulches, and a Ute Ridge. Despite the ubiquity of such place-names, the Utes themselves were confined to reservations during the nineteenth century. In southwestern Colorado, stretching from the Utah border approximately 120 miles east are the Ute Mountain and Southern Ute Reservations. There are also two large Ute reservations in eastern Utah, Uintah and Ouray.

Many different tribes occupied (or at least traversed) what is now Colorado. In the southwest, Navajos, Pueblos, and Apaches had long been well established, and the Pawnees hunted buffalo in the Republican River area. By hunting in the prairies just east of the foothills, the Arapahos and Cheyennes pressured the Kiowas and Comanches further east. Early battles on the plains—the settlers' militias and the U.S. Army against the Cheyennes and Arapahos, for example—were a means of opening the land for European American settlement.

Nineteenth-century European American newcomers dealt with the mountain-dwelling Utes through treaties, battles, and trade. By the Treaty of 1868 (the Kit Carson Treaty), the Colorado Utes were restricted to the mountains and plateaus in Colorado Territory west of the continental divide and east of the Utah line, an area of about sixteen million acres; this treaty was to be binding "forever." Five years later, the Brunot Treaty of 1873 diminished that specified area by taking approximately four million acres of land that was being grubbed by the miners in the San Juan gold camps. After the Meeker Massacre and the Thornburg battle at Milk Creek in 1879, the U.S. government forced the Northern or White River Utes out of Colorado and placed them in northeastern Utah on the Uintah Reservation, established in 1864. In the southwest, the Southern Ute Agency was established in 1877.

During the 1870s and 1880s the European American settlers in Colorado would have read reports in the Denver newspapers, especially the *Rocky Mountain News*, about the so-called dangerous, treacherous, murderous Utes. Although often exaggerations and sometimes outright lies, the reports carried great force. The newspaperman most responsible for these often inflated or false reports was William B. Vickers, editor of the *Denver Tribune*, but he was supported by Frederick Pitkin, an anti-Indian territorial governor appointed in 1861 by Abraham Lincoln. Headlines such as "Utes must Go!" encouraged and were encouraged by readers thinking of settling or staking claims in the territory. Inevitably the Utes were forced out, and by such means the European American pioneers opened the land for their own settlements. An important additional enticement to settlement of such newly acquired "public lands" came as a result of the allotment of Indian reservations. The 1887 Dawes Act stipulated that any reservation land that had not been allotted to enrolled tribal members became available to non-Indians; that is, after tribal members made their claims of up to 160 acres, "surplus" lands were sold, most often to non-Indian settlers and speculators who could afford such land. The Navajo woman Mrs. Dan'els, for example, referred to how allotment policy allowed her and her non-Indian husband to get Ute land; she related that "We got an allotment where White Rocks Crick joins the Uintah" (in Utah).

The narratives in this collection offer several glimpses into interactions between these different groups. The non-Indian women's responses to the Native Americans they encountered are as various as the narrators themselves. Even the same narrator might express a different attitude at a different moment in the telling of her interactions with particular Native Americans. In some ways the reports of contact with the Utes in the southwestern part of the state bear out Riley's contention that because of clearly demarcated gender divisions of labor among the settlers, European American women "frequently had the opportunity—as procurers of food, clothing, and other domestic goods—to develop a collegial relationship with Indians in their mutual quest for survival."[24]

These narratives do suggest that reactions and attitudes were more dependent on context than on politics or on an attitude toward race in general. When describing Indians while crossing the plains, for instance, the narrators often expressed a sense of fear and hostility. The narrators who had established themselves in communities in the southwest, in contrast, appear to have been much more tolerant than were the women crossing the prairie. Riley argues that perhaps most noteworthy about women's attitudes toward their Native American neighbors was that they were willing "to modify their attitudes toward Indians."[25] Although the narrators never quite admitted that they had usurped another's land, they did occasionally note that violent outbreaks tended to be the fault of European Americans rather than of the generally peaceful Utes.

Several narrators recalled having witnessed actual fighting, while others reported what they heard of nearby or recent attacks on or by Indians. Elizabeth Rule Harrington remembered the time some nearby Mexican cattlemen were attacked: "Screams and cries from the Mexicans drew our attention," she reported, and the "Indians had sprung up from the ground somewhere, evading our pickets, and swooped down into the midst of the Mexicans' cattle, trying to stampede them. . . . The two men were killed and with my own eyes I saw the Mexican lad scalped." Mary E. Hayden, who settled in Pueblo County, recalled crossing the prairie in May 1864. She had heard accounts of bloodshed, and then witnessed the aftermath of an attack. She and the others in her train were warned of the dangers: "They endeavored to have us turn back, telling us of disaster and pillaging ahead, saying all men had been murdered, and women and some eleven children carried off with them."

Besides describing actual, outright battles, the narrators recounted instances when they needed to defend themselves against Native Americans who understood a code of behavior different from their own. Nellie Pollock Snyder reported that one time her mother defended herself by putting a hot iron on a man's face, and Mella McCluer Bohlick of La Plata County told of her mother's act of self-defense: "One day a mean Indian came down and asked for something to eat. We always fed them when they came, but this Indian poured his cup full of sugar, and dumped the rest of it on the floor. Mama said that if she was going to get killed she might as well get it over with, so she picked up a chair and knocked the Indian down."

Historian Dee Garceau-Hagen argues that recent studies of experiences along the westward trails "have conclusively proven that emigrants had far more to fear from accidents, epidemics, and lack of sustenance than they ever had to fear from American Indians."[26] Bearing that out, the narratives in this collection suggest that the fears the women narrators expressed are due as often as not to stories and stereotypes rather than to actual experiences. Mella McCleur Bohlick remembered that her mother's fears were ultimately ungrounded: "Mother often told me that when she first came into the Florida River valley the Indians used to dance on a hill just east of our house and each time she thought that the Indians would come down and kill them." Cynthia Fisher remembered having feared an attack when the men left the train in order to hunt buffalo: "I have often thought what an opportunity the Indians missed of attacking our camp—all of our men out after the buffalo, and nothing in camp but defenseless women and children." Despite her fears, there was no attack, the men returned, and the train crossed without incident. Mary Nichols Williams remembered seeing a dance that terrified her: "During the night, from the Indian camp on the hill, came the sounds of singing. We rose from our beds, and seeing them dancing up and down, and seeing their legs going up and down, silhouetted against the light of their campfires, and the sound of their singing, which sounded awful to us, had an immediate effect upon us, especially upon the new people from Missouri—the women and children were crying and screaming, because they were afraid of being scalped." As it turned out, however, no one was hurt or ever even in danger.

Indeed, Native Americans had more to fear from the settlers than the settlers from the Indians. Some Indians were even subjected to a form of enslavement. As Bohlick described it, for example, one Indian woman who worked as a housekeeper was "property": "When Mother was married, her family gave her an Indian girl as her personal servant. . . . When she died about 1908, she was buried in the family plot. Her stone bears the name 'Trudy' and underneath the word 'faithful.' Father said that word completely described her." The account makes no acknowledgment of the impropriety of such a mistress-servant/slave relationship.

Even though some of these narrators retained biases against Native Americans even into the 1930s, many acknowledged false stereotypes or false blame. Mary D. Hansen reported that when an old Indian man came to her mother for help with a sick daughter-in-law, she noted his anxiety and sadness: "Indians are supposed to have little feeling, but Old Washington and his son suffered pitifully and tried so hard to do what they could for the pretty young girl." In the context of cattle rustlings, Mary Nichols Williams reported that "Everything that was done like this was always blamed on the Indians." Perceiving the U.S. government's unfair treatment of American Indians on the reservations, Mary Hansen maintained that the "only Indian uprisings seem to have been when white people did them wrong." Carrie Smith Dunham of Montezuma County reported that her husband had a similar sentiment: "Mr. Dunham thinks that in almost every case, Indian trouble around this part of the country could have been avoided if the white people had kept their heads instead of losing them. And he was here through the years in the eighties when the worst of it was going on."

In addition to recognizing misperceptions and mistreatment of the American Indians, many narrators reported that their relations were amicable. Carrie Smith Dunham of Montezuma County, an accomplished seamstress, recalled that she once sewed fifty cat skins together to make a robe. She also made gauntlet gloves: "I used to make buckskin gloves for the Indians with my glove pattern, and once they brought me a pair of lovely beaded moccasins." She also remembered that they would come to the farm to buy potatoes and chokecherries: "We had a great many chokecherries down there, and I made much chokecherry butter. The Indians called it coyote medicine and liked it very much. So I traded them coyote medicine for buckskin." Mella McCluer Bohlick told a story about her brother's would-be adoptive mother: "My brother Tim was the first white boy born in what is now La Plata County in February 1876. When he was a baby, a squaw living near us, whose papoose was about the same age as Tim, came to the cabin and wanted to take Tim home with her. Mother said she was afraid to let him go but she was afraid not to so she let him go, and when she went after him she found him stripped naked and painted up like a warrior. The squaw was very good to Tim, took care of him and nursed him the same as her own papoose."

Although many personal relationships between the newcomers and the Native Americans were friendly, there were also of course bloody battles—the best-known of which are the Sand Creek Massacre (1864) and the Meeker Massacre (1879). Nellie Pollock Snyder, the granddaughter of John Chivington, the colonel who led the Volunteers against a settlement of peaceful Indians, defended her grandfather by insisting that he had been misrepresented in the reports excoriating his involvement in the 1864 massacre at Sand Creek. Several narrators also shared accounts of an otherwise essentially unrecorded massacre that took place in Montezuma County in 1885. As they told it, a band of cowboys attacked a group of Ute hunters, and several narrators offered their accounts of the attack and its aftermath. Eva Adams House summarized the event: "When the cowboys killed a hunting party of Indians up at Beaver [Creek] and one got away so that the Indians killed a Mr. Gentner down in the Lakeview neighborhood and shot his wife in the shoulder for revenge, we later had a very bad fright." The explanations for the attack on the Utes camped on Beaver Creek were quite diverse and thus embody an important aspect of history making. At one extreme is Clara Ormiston's contention that the cattlemen wanted the Indians' cattle, and at the other is Dora Pedersen's suggestion that the Utes were "wantonly slaughtering" the white settlers' cattle. The actual reasons for the attack thus remain elusive and open to interpretation, but the fact of the massacre remains.

Western Women's History

The assessments, responses, and recollections these pioneer women narrators offer are an important means of helping to fill out the historical picture of the area that has become Colorado, especially in that the narratives provide viewpoints of women as they recount their everyday lives.[27] Indeed, the inclusion of the voices of these Colorado women has the potential to change the way we view that history. Many historians have long been reconceiving the traditional history of the American West, namely, the history that describes pioneering and community building as a primarily male pursuit and achievement and that finds only a marginal place for women or leaves them out altogether.[28] Susan Johnson begins her discussion of the place of gender in the West, for example, with this: "Of all the regions people have imagined within the boundaries of what is now the United States, no place has been so consistently identified with maleness—particularly white maleness—as the region imagined as the American West."[29] With very few exceptions, discussion of the roles of women, or even the fact of women as a part of that West, long remained absent from histories of the West. Even when a prominent western woman makes it into the historical account—Sarah Winnemucca, Sacagawea, Annie Oakley, or Frances Gummond, for instance—historians tend to avoid incorporating those women's stories into any overarching, dominant national histories of the West. To acknowledge the importance of women's narratives is thus to include women in the telling of history to emphasize the importance of the "actual experience of women of the past," as Gerda Lerner suggests, maintaining that the "true history of women is the history of their ongoing functioning in that male defined world *on their own terms*."[30]

Similarly, in a plea to include women in history making, Julie Jeffrey calls for a history that does not overlook "the experiences of almost half the pioneers crossing the Mississippi."[31] Nearly twenty years later, in 1997, Jameson and Armitage respond to the continuing need to oppose "a national history told from the limited perspectives of the urban East, of public politics and power, of white Americans, and of men." They suggest that "the first steps we needed to take in western women's history were to see the West through women's eyes and to listen to women's words" and "to document the lives of the many peoples who have lived what is now the western United States."[32] In 1998, Susan Armitage and Sherna Gluck write of the need to reiterate this call for inclusion. In the context of women's oral histories, they assert, the issue "is still discover/recovery. There is a world (and I do mean a global one) of women out there, and we've heard from very few of them."[33]

In *Unsettled Pasts* (2005), the editors maintain that "After nearly three decades of increasingly sophisticated work in women's and gender history, popular and academic narratives of the West continue to privilege the masculine."[34] Jameson declares that "History becomes more complex and richer as women are added, and particularly as they are added to narratives of the North American West, a region that has long been seen as 'quintessentially male.'"[35] According to Susan Stanford Friedman, there is an urgently felt "political agenda of women's studies: to engage in the de-formation of phallocentric history and the re-formation of histories that focus on or integrate women's experience."[36]

As historians realize the need for sources from women, they at the same time acknowledge that they should consider not only prominent women but also the voices of relatively unknown or "ordinary" women. The authors of *Western Women: Their Land, Their Lives* (1988), for example, contend that "'anonymous' people *do* affect the historical record."[37] Anne Butler and Ona Siporin drive that point home in their investigation of unique but common women, *Uncommon Common Women* (1996). In *Far from Home* (1989), the editors remind their readers that historians tend to overlook family life and common, daily activities because they write histories of conquests, mining enterprises, and empire building. They are thus "slower to look for the stuff of history in the lives of plain people who wanted not much more than to live in ordinary ways and to build again in a new land the remnant of their old homes."[38] Similarly, Garceau-Hagen has challenged the "exceptional women" approach to women's history: "If historical significance were defined only in terms of exceptional women whose deeds merited biographical study, then the lives of ordinary women would go unexamined." And further, as Jameson and Armitage argue in *Writing the Range*, "Most history begins with the daily acts of ordinary people."[39] Jameson and McManns make a similar point: "National and social boundaries have combined to marginalize most people from history. Histories of nations have often focused on the exploits of public leaders and powerful citizens, thus reinforcing social inequalities by making people with less public power historically invisible."[40] Applicable in this context is Friedman's warning that when looking at women's histories in general, we "run the risk of repeating the same patterns of thought and action that excluded, distorted, muted, or erased women from the master narratives of history in the first place."[41] Harriet Sigerman contends that individual stories "echo the experiences of thousands of other settlers who went West in search of better opportunities and who, facing hardship and tragedy, managed to wrest a bountiful life from the land."[42]

Such repeated statements, spanning the careers of a generation of scholars, reinforce the notion that histories of the West still need to hear from women such as those represented in the narratives collected here: ordinary women experiencing and recognizing the extraordinary in their ordinary lives. The narratives in this collection present many of those daily activities that are a part of home building, going to church, interacting with neighbors, retrieving the mail, getting to and from school. In these ways the women created communities and participated in homesteading, the activities that become the very stuff of history.

As told by ordinary women, these narratives challenge the delimiting stereotypes of pioneer women. The narrators demonstrate that they are multidimensional; they have multifaceted concerns and lives, and they refuse to be reduced to the few roles historians have typically allotted them: sunbonnet saviors, refined and helpless ladies, or "bad," radical, nonconformist women.[43] These are the stereotypes women's historians continue to struggle against and continue to investigate. In *Gender and Generation on the Far Western Frontier* (2007), for example, Cynthia Culver Prescott concentrates on gender roles and argues that "during the time on the trail and early years of settlement, the strains of frontier life made women . . . responsible for many non-domestic, 'masculine' tasks," but these women struggled to reestablish former gender identities."[44] A wider definition of women's roles in the West can thus include women such as Nellie Buchanan of Kit Carson County, a woman who takes care of the ranch herself while raising the children single-handedly as her spouse works in town or is gone for months at a time working on the railroad. It can also include a woman like Lizzie Gordon (Buchanan) of Logan County, who—despite her fears—lives by herself on her homestead and makes a timber claim by herself; and Mary Nichols Williams of Gunnison County, who fishes in order to pay the bills.

In 1979, in the context of further broadening the scope of women's western history, Peggy Pascoe called for "a history of women in the West that is multicultural, cross-cultural, and intercultural." She insisted on the need to see the West as a cultural crossroads where race, class, and gender all played and continue to play important roles. In 1980, Joan Jensen and Darlis Miller referred to Dee Brown's *The Gentle Tamers: Women of the Old Wild West* (1958) in their call for "a new multicultural framework as a focus for western women" that will result in "a more representative history of both men and women in the West."[45] In 1987 Armitage agreed, writing that "Our efforts to reject, revise, and reexamine stereotypes must be multicultural."[46] In *The Legacy of Conquest* (1987), Patricia Limerick also stressed the fact that the West is multicultural and multiracial. Harriet Sigerman, in *Land of Many Hands: Women in the American West* (1997), made the same point, arguing that "By the mid-nineteenth century, the West was the most ethnically diverse region of the United States, a mosaic of people from across the globe."[47] In *By Grit and Grace* (1997) Glenda Riley and Richard W. Etulain argued for the importance of presenting "a variety of early western women, illustrating class status, ethnicity, race, marital status, age, or religious beliefs, all of whom had a hand in shaping the American West," and in *Writing the Range* (1997), Jameson and Armitage considered the ongoing migrations to the West by women of different classes, races, and ethnicities.[48] According to Garceau-Hagen, writing in 2007, "Scholars now think of the American West as a meeting ground of cultures, a crucible of inter-tribal history as well as encounters between diverse races and ethnic groups from other countries."[49]

The narratives collected here include the voices of a few women with a Native American heritage as well as a few who were European-born, but the vast majority of narrators are European Americans, and this demographic is a direct reflection of how the field-workers sought out pioneers according to their own definitions. Thus an important and regrettable lacuna results from the paucity of narrators who do not trace their roots to northern Europe. The absence of such narratives is especially unfortunate in that Hispanic settlement is important to what became Colorado. As Sarah Deutsch demonstrates in *No Separate Refuge*, there was an interlocking of the Anglo and Hispanic frontiers: "It was at this joint frontier that the Anglos arrived in force in the 1880s."[50] The collection is simply limited by the choices the field-workers made in the 1930s. It has become an ethnographic commonplace to acknowledge that ethnographers or field-workers carry certain unavoidable biases into the field with them and that these biases can affect not only the choices they make and how they report their findings, but also how informants respond. As Renato Rosaldo maintains, the field-worker "occupies a position or structural location and observes with a particular angle of vision."[51] Within such constraints, however, these narratives do offer important glimpses from unique perspectives into the history of pioneering Colorado.

Although few non-European American voices are heard for lack of primary material, these narratives nonetheless offer important insights into the study of intercultural relations. Given the frequency with which non-Native women tell of their encounters with Native Americans, for example, we can see that Native Americans were very much a part of the settlement and development of the West. The narratives also demonstrate one of the ways in which the geographical area of Colorado constituted a cultural crossroads. They demonstrate that the West, as Pascoe puts it, "was neither empty nor free and that white Americans . . . were never its only inhabitants."[52] The narratives demonstrate too that these narrators, mostly of Anglo or northern European descent, were on some level at least aware that their neighbors had an earlier claim on the land.

In an ongoing effort to find the meanings of women's role in the West, according to Armitage and Jameson, we must "free ourselves from the all-pervasive masculinity of the popular image of the American West. Until that basic re-vision occurs, we cannot see women in their own right. Authors who write about western women without confronting this most basic reconceptualization fail, in our opinion, to meet the challenge posed by western women's history."[53] In another place, Armitage writes that we do not want the same old violent history of winning the West; rather, we "want to know how people traveled to the West, what difficulties they encountered, how they coped, and how the story turned out in the end. And we want that history of real people to make sense in our lives as westerners today."[54]

A new history, narrated by the women themselves, gives us just what Armitage and others continue to call for. These Colorado pioneer women tell us how they traveled; they detail the difficulties they encountered; they describe how they coped with hardships—sometimes with laughter, sometimes with tears, sometimes with grim determination; and they describe what they hoped for. Some of the narrators relate that they were perhaps afraid of snakes, marauding cowboys, or Indians, but they overcame their fears. Some were brought to tears by homesickness for the places and lives they had left behind, but in time they replaced an old home with a new one. The narratives offer insights into "issues of racial interaction and larger social organization,"[55] for example, and in that they are told several decades after most of the events they describe, they tell us how the story turned out. Mary Nichols Williams of Gunnison County acknowledges the importance of preserving the story of her pioneering for posterity: "Johnny would say, 'Mama, why don't you write a book?'" And Williams recalls having replied: "I wish I had."

Let this collection be a version of the book that Williams and so many other women might have written. This is their book.

A Note on the Texts

This collection reproduces sixty-nine original narratives told by pioneer women to Civil Works Administration field-workers in 1933 and 1934, narratives that offer accounts of pioneering during the last quarter of the nineteenth century. Of the hundreds of narratives that the field-workers collected, I have limited this selection to those told by women and recorded in the first person. Therefore, although field-workers endeavored to record narratives from twenty-seven Colorado counties, only nineteen counties are represented here.

Beyond these two selection criteria, this volume presents the narratives with minimal editorial interference. That is, with only minor spelling or punctuation changes for clarity, the narratives, which vary in length from five hundred to about thirty-five hundred words, are presented here in their entirety just as the field-workers submitted them. Most of the documents come from transcriptions of oral narratives. After transcribing, the field-worker would return the document to the narrator, who would sign it, signifying that the transcription was accurate. A few of the women narrators preferred to write the accounts themselves rather than have them transcribed. A few field-workers also included accounts that had been published in local newspapers or had been presented as papers to pioneer associations or local historical societies. Such instances are noted with the individual texts in question.

As presented here, each narrator is named at the beginning of her narrative, and her name is followed by the name of the county in which she was interviewed and the pamphlet and document number; these numbers identify the document within the Colorado Interviews collection at the Colorado Historical Society. Following this documentation are the location and date of the interview, if provided, as well as the field-worker's name. When available, short biographical notes about the narrators accompany the narratives. As appropriate and to the extent that information has been available, endnotes provide supplementary material, serving to identify places, persons, or events that might not otherwise be clear to twenty-first-century readers.

The narratives cover the major geographical areas of the state, and the arrangement of the narratives is in large measure by geographical region. Each geographical grouping of narratives is headed with a brief introduction that suggests how these particular narratives might be seen to fit into Colorado history in general. As is evident from the narratives, each region offered somewhat different attractions and posed different challenges to the settlers. Narratives from the northwest (although this region was ultimately settled somewhat later than some other parts of the state) offer accounts by a Navajo woman, a woman who refers to herself as of Gosho (Gosiute or Goshute) descent, and two women whose mothers were Shoshone. The collection then turns to narratives of European American women in the mountains and foothills that were heavily settled during the gold rush era. Although these narratives are not restricted to the mountains, this section offers accounts both of some of the miners' experiences and also of the role of those who supplied miners or turned from mining to other, more stable pursuits. Next, the narratives concerning settlement in the Pueblo area describe crossing the prairie, establishing that city, and the urban life and the importance of the smelting and mining industries. Meanwhile, with Horace Greeley's community and the coming of the railroad through the eastern part of the state, settlement began in earnest on the prairies. The narrators here recount the challenges of obtaining water, farming versus cattle ranching, and the importance of the railroads. Finally, in 1873 fresh gold and silver discoveries in the far southwestern part of the state prompted another rush, and settlers pressured the government to obtain Ute and Mexican lands for mining and farming. In such an organizational scheme, some overlap is unavoidable. Not all narrators in the chapter on mountain-area counties, for instance, restrict themselves to discussing mining, nor do all narrators restrict themselves to writing only about their counties or about Colorado. Territories and states such as Utah, Wyoming, New Mexico, and Kansas receive attention as well. The arrangement of the narratives thus suggests the diversity of experience and the importance of interconnectedness in all aspects of the settling of what was to become Colorado.

An appendix includes the correspondence between one of the field-workers, Anna Florence Robison (Montezuma County), and LeRoy Hafen, the director of the program. Their correspondence elucidates to some extent the role of one individual interviewer, and provides some background to her life and concerns as related to her job. It also gives readers insight into the CWA and FERA programs and provides a glimpse of the life of a contemporary of the children of the narrators.

All narratives told by the pioneer women and the correspondence between LeRoy Hafen and Anna Florence Robison are reprinted courtesy of the Colorado Historical Society (CWA Pioneer Interviews: Alamosa, Arapahoe, Chaffee, Delta, El Paso, Gunnison, Kit Carson, La Plata, Las Animas, Logan, Moffat, Montezuma, Morgan, Otero, Prowers, Pueblo, Rio Blanco, Rio Grande, and Weld Counties, 1933–1934, and "MSS 1458 Hafen Collection, Anna Florence Robison Correspondence"). The Colorado Historical Society is the repository and owner of the records.

Chapter 1: The Northwest Plateau

Moffat and Rio Blanco Counties

If you write a book about us, I want to see that book.
Mrs. Henry Harris

To the west of the Rocky Mountains stretches an arid plateau region that includes northwestern Colorado, southwestern Wyoming, and northeastern Utah; the area was home to the White River Utes long before the arrival of European American missionaries, trappers, farmers, and ranchers. The White River Utes and other bands of Native peoples traversed a huge hunting area that included almost all of present-day Colorado as well as eastern Utah and southern Wyoming. Once European American settlement had begun, there was initially some trapping and mining, but for the most part early white settlement in the area devoted itself to cattle and sheep ranching and to farming along the White River drainages.[1]

Between the arrival of European American settlers and 1879, the year of the Meeker Massacre and the Milk Creek Battle, this region was for the most part peacefully occupied by both Indians and whites. During the 1870s, however, the immigrant population had grown to such an extent that the ranchers and farmers were forcing the Utes away from their traditional homelands and hunting ranges. Skirmishes between the new settlers and the Native Americans were the inevitable result.

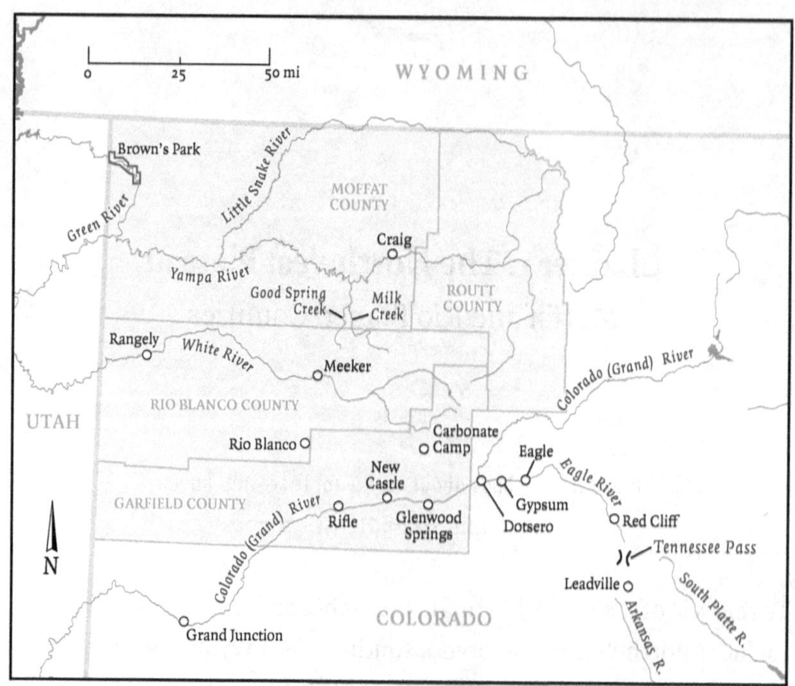

3. The northwest plateau

In 1879, when U.S. troops were ordered onto White River Reservation, the Utes responded by attacking the troop lines on Milk Creek. That same day, fifteen miles away at the agency itself, a group of Utes killed Agent Nathan Meeker and ten others (agency workers and freighters) and also took hostages: Nathan Meeker's wife, Arvilla Meeker; her daughter, Josephine; and family friend Flora Ellen Price with her two children, Mary and Johnnie. The hostages were later released. On Milk Creek, Major Thomas Tipton Thornburgh and a dozen cavalrymen were killed; as many as two dozen more were injured. According to some estimates, thirty-seven Utes died in that battle. After this outbreak of violence at Milk Creek and the agency, the U.S. government forcibly removed the White River band to the Uintah Reservation in Utah.[2]

Of the five narrators from this region, loosely identified by the state's northwest counties but including areas of Wyoming and Utah, four are women of Native American descent. Dan'els identifies herself as Navajo, and Harris notes that her mother was Gosho. The mothers of Madeline Adams and Jennie Reische were Shoshones. Although he does not identify their tribe, field-worker J. Monaghan writes that the sisters Adams and Reische (Reschke) "are Indians to the core." In their specificity, these narratives challenge certain stereotypes of Native American women, thus helping the reader recover a more complete and more valid picture of frontier history. The narratives challenge the misnomer of the word *Indian* as applied to all Native American peoples when the Navajo woman Dan'els, for example, insists on her own tribal identity: "I am not an Indian," she exclaims, "I am a Navajo." Harris, meanwhile, suggests that she has fully adopted European American attitudes toward justice. She recalls that her Gosho maternal grandmother was killed by the army and maintains that she has long wanted to "sue the United States" for having caused that death.

Although these narratives are not limited to the area that was to become Colorado, the entire northwest corner of the state was encompassed by the original territorial county of Summit (1861); that county was later divided into Routt (1877) and Garfield (1883). Rio Blanco (1889) was later carved from Garfield, and Moffat (1911) from Routt.

The field-worker for Moffat County was J. Monaghan.

Mrs. Dan'els, Moffat County [356-20].

Interviewer: J. Monaghan.

Interviewer's note: In real life the squaw in 1934 had outlived her husband [Gran'pa-Dan'els] by almost forty years. At this time she was a typical squaw in appearance. She was five feet tall, weighed about ninety pounds and had a face as brown and wrinkled as an apple that has laid in the orchard all winter, even her tongue and toothless gums were brown. But when she spoke, her mind and her thoughts were those of a white woman. Her speech, although not faultless, was far superior to the average reservation white man. Her life is the story of one brutality after another, yet she tells about it without bitterness and without rancor. For over ninety years she has lived with no advantages, and at ninety she has a calm sweetness and real charm.

I am not an Indian. I am a Navajo. I do not know how old I am but I know I am past ninety, and can still ride a horse with the best of them. Gran'pa-Dan'els always called me "a little bit of a chick."

I would like to go back someday to the place where I was captured. I can see it so plain I would recognize it. There was a big gulch that came out of the mountains and a little prong from the east that joined that gulch. I know it pointed to the east because the sun came out of the head of that little prong every morning. My father and mother and another family camped where the little prong joined the main gulch. Down the big gulch, just a little way, where it went out of the mountain, my gran'mother and gran'father had a little farm. They raised corn and beans and melons. We camped above so we could graze the sheep. There were no white men in the country or no other Navajos that I know about. I was only a little girl, I think about seven.

We lived in an open country with cedars on top of rocky gulches. One morning my father went up on the bluff above camp to get a dead cedar for firewood. He would throw the wood over the bluff into camp. I, and another little girl my age, that belonged to the other family, started off with the sheep. We got to the bend of the canyon where we were out of sight of my mother's camp and not quite in sight of gran'mother's when we heard a funny noise. It was a lot of yipping, just like a flock of wild geese. I often think about that, how it sounded like a flock of wild geese. We should have run and hid but we just stood there. We did not know what it was. In a minute we saw twelve Indians coming with their horses on a big run. The Indians didn't have on no clothes, just moccasins and breechclout. Their bodies were painted black and yellow. They were swinging war clubs. We just stood there and looked at them. They had strings around their heads to keep their hair back. They stopped in a circle around us, tied us up, and rode away yipping like wild geese. The sun was one hand high in the east when they rode away, and it was one hand high in the west when they came back. They had another Navajo girl and two little boys with them and lots of blankets and horses and sheep, and scalps. They put me and the other little girl on a horse, but they kept us tied. We went down past gran'mother's farm and saw her and gran'father lying there with arrows sticking out of them. It must have been in the fall of the year because gran'father was lying in the watermelon patch and the watermelons was ripe. Them Indians took us up on the hill east of gran'mother's farm and built a fire in the cedars. Then they killed some of our sheep—just enough for supper—and threw big hunks of meat on the coals. They ate some of this, ashes and all, like they was hungry, then we started off in the night.[3]

We traveled north four nights and four days. At night we didn't travel as fast as we did in daytime, but we kept going. Sometimes when the grass was good we would stop for a little while to let the sheep and horses eat. The Indians would cook some meat and rest, but they never made camp or went to sleep. We traveled out of the low country up into high country and then back into low country again. We crossed two big rivers. I remember that the water came to my armpits. The Indians crowded the sheep into the water, but they kept swimming back to the same side so they let them go.

Finally we came to the Ute camp. I think that it was on White River, but I don't know for sure. I know that they were White River Utes. When the squaws saw us coming they started to wail and cry. I guess they thought some of their braves were dead. When they found out that none of them were dead, they were happy and got ready for a big dance. I remember that dance.

The men took colored dirt and mixed it with grease and rubbed their bodies. The women put the scalps on the ends of sticks. There was a drum and some singing. The squaws all stood in line and danced back and forth waving the scalps in the air. The men jumped around in a bunch at one side waving their war clubs.

"War clubs" ain't just the right name. They were like slingshots with a loop around their wrists, and the shot was a big rock or something that they never threw, just used it to hit people as they rode past them.[4]

I never liked Indians. They was always moving. They would have a dance and move. Then they would have another dance. Pretty soon they would have a dance and move again. They didn't have nothing to eat but meat, and they cooked it on coals or sometimes they would build a rack of sticks and broil it that way. They did not have no pots or kettles or anything. The White River Utes didn't even have beads in them days. Their tepees were of buffalo skin with the hair scraped off. If they wore any clothes at all it was buckskin. Their summer moccasins were made of buckskin, and in winter they made moccasins out of buffalo hide with the wool on the inside.

I hated the "White Rivers" and ran away every chance I got. I wasn't afraid to be out all night among the wolves and the bears. I'm not afraid now either. There was no place to run except out in the hills, and they always found me and brought me back, but I made them so much trouble that they sold me to Tabby. He was chief of the Uintahs.[5] We still moved around and danced just the same as before.

The first white men I ever saw were trappers who came to Tabby's camp. They had long hair down their backs, and beards. They dressed in buckskin and fur caps in winter. In summer they wore caps the squaws made for them out of willows. Sometimes they wore a handkerchief around their heads in summer like Indians do now. I remember two of them came to camp and stayed at Tabby's tepee. They had a council. I was just a little girl and their names meant nothin' to me, but I have often wondered since who they were. I have heard Kit Carson was in this country, and I wonder if I ever saw him.[6]

The Utes was always afraid of the Sioux. I remember how they used to talk about the Sioux. They went into Sioux country after buffalo sometimes, but they kept a sharp look out.

I think that the Sun Dance is a Sioux dance.[7] The Utes did not dance it when I was with them. In them early days they just had a War Dance, Tee Dance (*Tee-a* is Ute for deer; this dance has died out), and Bear Dance.[8] In the Tee Dance the men joined with the squaws just like "ring-around-a-rosie." They had lots of Tee Dances during the year. They only had one Bear Dance. They think they are dancing like a bear does when he comes out of his den. Old Utes say they seen a bear dance that way once.

Life was better with Tabby than with the White Rivers. We still ate mostly meat, but once we moved west of the mountains to the Mormon settlements and got wheat. Not corn, wheat! The Indians were crazy about that wheat. The squaws used to put it in their open-top baskets with live coals. Then they would shake the baskets so the coals would not burn the willow. They would shake the baskets until the wheat popped. Then they would eat it. After that first taste they would give the Mormons anything for wheat. They used to beg for it.

A bad thing happened at Spanish Fork once. There was no town there then. There was three or four houses at Provo but none at Spanish Fork.[9] The Indians had made camp and were having a Tee Dance. One Indian took his gun and shot his squaw while she was dancing. Then he took his rope and drug her off onto a hill and left her there. He came back to camp and nobody said one word. That's the way Utes are.

If a person died they would dig a shallow grave and make a roof over it and put some food inside. Then they would burn everything he owned and kill his horse in front of the grave. All the time I was with them I never did see Utes bury anybody up in a tree. I've seen tree-graves, but I am sure the Utes never buried nobody that way when I was with them, and I was with them for over six years.

Once we camped on Provo Bench and some strange Indians came into camp. I think they were Shoshones. They talked with the Utes and decided to have a battle. That night the Ute boys and young men got their bows and arrows ready, and next morning off they went. They fought off there somewhere for two days and nobody was killed. Our boys come back without no scalps, but the Utes had a big dance about it anyway.

I remember when the government first gave things to the Utes. They sent a big pack outfit to Whiterocks and gave the Indians flour. I think that was the first flour they ever had. The Utes like flour, but they didn't know how to make bread. We women took feathers and dusted alkali off the ground into baskets and put it in the flour to make it raise.

I used to run away from the Uintahs, same as I did from the White Rivers. I guess that is why Tabby sold me. Two of us girls was sold at Fort Bridger that time.[10] The other girl was Red Jacket Jane. Both her mother and father had died, so the Indians sold her. She used to run away from the whites at Fort Bridger. The Indians would get paid for bringing her back. They would get a sack of flour for returning her. A sack of flour was worth $25 in them days. She did that two or three times. Finally the whites got tired of it and told the Indians they could keep her. After that the Uintahs sold her to the White Rivers. Fort Bridger is where she learned to talk English and how to act in a house. When Meeker was made agent at White River, his wife hired her to help in the kitchen. When Meeker got to quarreling with the Indians, she overheard the family say that the soldiers were coming to kill the Utes because they hadn't done what Meeker wanted. That made them mad and caused all the trouble.[11]

When I was sold to the white people I never did run away to the Indians, not me! Tabby sold me at Fort Bridger to a rebel soldier named Bynum Lane. Yes, Bynum Lane! I think that was his name. You know I have never been to school and I can't read or write, so I can only remember the sound of it. Bynum Lane's wife wouldn't let me go to school. She said that I would get too smart and run away from them. I was at Fort Bridger three years. I must have been about fourteen when I was sold to Bynum Lane and about seventeen when I left.[12]

Bynum Lane was a tie-cutter. Then he got cattle. As soon as he got cattle, he got to drinkin' and his wife quit him. She took her kids and went to her mother's ranch in Weber Canyon. Gran'pa-Dan'els was her father. He was a Mormon. His other wife lived at Wanship, Utah, and I was sent over there. That is where I first saw Gran'pa-Dan'els and he called me "a little bit of a chick."

Gran'pa-Dan'els found some coal in the mountains while he was riding for cattle, and he started to dig it. Brigham Young heard about it and sent him a threatening letter. He said Gran'pa-Dan'els was "desecrating Church property." I was afraid that he would send over a destroying angel. Gran'pa-Dan'els split from the church after that. I remember how he used to laugh and say, "I don't put much stock in a God that won't let a man dig a hole in the ground." But both his wives quit him on account of it.[13]

The church won, and Gran'pa-Dan'els moved down to where Heber City is now and took up a place at the mouth of Dan'els Canyon. He toughed it out there for two years fighting what he called the "grasshopper war." Then he gave up and went to Tintic, Utah, and worked in the mines.[14] That was in 1871. We stayed there three years. Then he wrote to one of his sons in Nevada to come join him, and we all moved to a ranch at Provo. It had changed a lot since I was there with the Uintahs. Gran'pa-Dan'els left us there while he went to hunt gold in the Black Hills, but he didn't find any. We stayed at Provo until after Brigham Young died.

Gran'pa-Dan'els had a lot of growing boys, and he wanted to leave them all a "start," so when Ashley Valley opened for settlement in 1882, he said, "Let's leave this ranch for Dave and go to Ashley and build up a place for Gene and Ben." So we moved over there and by the time Gene was big enough to take over the Ashley Ranch, Gran'pa-Dan'els had spotted a likely location east of Green River on Cub Creek.[15] He had used up his "rights" by now, so he took a squatter's claim in the desert under Blue Mountain. Our cattle summered on the mountain in Colorado, and the first snowstorm would bring them down Cub Crick to the winter range. Gran'pa-Dan'els used to say, "It's only a step from the summer to the winter range."

Our nearest neighbors were the Royle Cattle Company, with headquarters twelve miles away. The Royle boys were New York City fellas, so we had the whole country to ourselves.

Gran'pa-Dan'els built our house under some big cottonwoods. Then he took water out of the crick above the house and planted lucerne.[16] He laid out a mile racetrack around the farm and planted rows of poplar trees from the house to the racetrack, like the spokes of a wheel. No matter how hot the desert was, it was always cool under them trees, and you could hear water runnin'. It was a awful purty place. My boy Al was born there. We lived there three years. One day after my Walter was born, Gran'pa-Dan'els said, "Little Chick, the Utes killed your father and mother. The gover'ment is providing for the Utes. They should provide for you." Then he saddled his horse and rode over to see the agent.

When he came back he said, "Little Chick, Uncle Sam will give you forty acres and a red wagon. Ain't that great? Now we can let Ben have this place and he will be provided for."[17]

So we loaded our things in a wagon and went to the Uintah Reservation. We got an allotment where Whiterocks Crick joins the Uintah. It was in the brush and we couldn't see the mountains, but the grass was good and Gran'pa-Dan'els liked it, so I was happy. That was in 1889. My two girls, Ethel and Mintura, were born there.

Gran'pa-Dan'els died in 1896.

He hadn't been gone long before Superintendent Tidwell called me to the agency. I saddled my horse and went. One-Hair was in the office, and Tidwell said, "One-Hair is chief of the Uintahs and he wants to get married, so I have sent for you."

I looked at One-Hair and said, "You black scoundrel"; then I walked out of the office.

Tidwell called after me, "Look here, little lady, you're only an Indian who can't read or write. You might do worse."

"You may be right," I replied, "but I'm no fool." I never liked Tidwell from that day to this.

A lot of them wanted to marry me in the next few years. There was Provo and Mack and even Tabbywhite's father. I told 'em all, "I don't want another man."

I will never find another man as good as Gran'pa-Dan'els!

On the reservation, as soon as your children are big enough to go to school you don't see them anymore unless they run away, because the gover'ment doesn't want them to go back to their families and learn Indian ways.[18] My children are all I've got, but I told 'em not to run away. Forty acres of land was only ten acres apiece, and that wouldn't support them, so they must learn to make a living some other way. It is lonely, but that is the best thing for them.

I don't like the Mormons on account of the way they treated Gran'pa-Dan'els. Bishop Hatch came over here once and preached to the Indians about having two wives. Critchlow was agent, and when he heard about it he told the bishop never to set foot on the reservation again.[19] The Utes are a bad lot, but they never did have more than one wife at one time.

People don't know how bad the Utes are until they know them real well, like I do. The White Rivers are just as bad as they ever were, only they are afraid now. I remember when an Indian killed the medicine man because he let his son die. The medicine man's relations got excited. I was alone in my tent on White Rocks Crick, and the Indians kept streaming by all day with their rifles. The agent thought there was going to be a battle and said to me, "Aren't you afraid?"

"I'm not afraid," I said, "of any Ute that ever lived." And I'm not. I'm a Navajo.

Last summer I was in the Indian parade at the UBIC [Uintah Basin Industrial Conference]. I put little bells and ribbons on my horse, and he looked real nice.

When I rode up to take my place, there was that old One-Hair. He said, "Huh! Navajo! What you doin' in this parade. You white man."

I told him a thing or two. I can still talk pretty good Ute when I get right mad.

Mrs. Henry Harris [née Reed], Moffat County [356-10].

Interviewer: J. Monaghan.

I was born in Brown's Park, in 1865, and I left there in 1875 when I was ten years old, so I do not remember much about it, but I remember a good deal.[20] I remember Lewis Simmons in his buckskin and another trapper named Boone. I think his first name was Daniel, but I am not sure. There are two Boone draws in Brown's Park.[21] Boone had a cabin on the head of Pot Creek.

I never heard of Fort Davy Crockett.[22] I don't remember any buildings shaped the way you say it was. I do remember that the James Warren place was built in the shape of an ell with another cabin off a little to one side. It was built of round logs with a floor that I always thought was made of hewed logs. The Warren place was not where you say the fort should be. It was on the west side of the river below the mouth of Beaver Creek. I always wondered why Arnold's house was built that way. I'll bet that was the fort.

My father was born in Kentucky in 1811. His father died and his mother married again, and my father left home when he was sixteen years old. He came west with his uncle; Sambo was the name Uncle was known by among the Indians. That is the only name I know for him, and I don't know why they called him that, but they all called him just Sambo.[23] My father's name was Jim Reed. He and Sambo made several trips back to the States for goods to trade with the Indians. Sambo was killed in a big war in the States. I don't know whether it was the Civil War. Wasn't there a great general called Jackson?[24] Well, he was killed then.

They brought their goods on pack mules from the States. I've heard the Indians here say lots of times, the old ones that is, they used to say, "Jim Reed brought Uintahs first butcher knives, first guns, first coffee." They tried to cook that coffee. They thought it ought to boil like beans until it was soft enough to eat. I've heard Father laugh about that. Jimmie Reed also traded Uintahs their first blankets. They were black woolen blankets with a white border. These blankets came in a bolt, and the trader would measure them length for length with tanned buckskin and then cut off the cloth the same length as the buckskin.

My father, Jim Reed, was Pony Express rider from Fort Benton to Fort Bridger.[25] I have read about the Pony Express riders, but I have never read his name. I think they should have his name in the books about Pony Express riders. Father told me they carried no guns when they rode Pony Express. They had the best horses, and the Indians could not catch them, so they did not need guns. Father was hit by an arrow once. I have seen the scar in his back. The arrow lodged in his backbone. Father said the bounce of the pony made the arrow flop up and down so it hurt terrible. He took out his pocket knife and cut off the shaft so it would not flop. When he got to Fort Bridger they pulled out the arrowhead with horse nippers.

Father said that once as he rode that route, he saw something white ahead. It was a long streak of white. He wondered what it was. When he got up to it he saw that it was feathers from featherbeds. Some Indians had raided a wagon train and scattered the feathers and killed the people and burned the wagons. He said that he found a little baby that had crawled up to its mother that lay there dead. Father took the baby and carried it in his buckskin shirt to Fort Benton, where he gave it to a lady. I always said that Father should have got a reward for saving that baby.

When Major Powell, the man with one arm, was getting his display of Indian things, Father went around with him and helped him trade with the Indians.[26] Powell took Father's elk-hide lodge. It was a nice lodge, soft like buckskin but awful heavy when you lifted it onto a packhorse. Yes, he took *my* father's nice lodge. Father died six years ago.[27] He is buried at the school cemetery at Whiterocks.

My mother was Gosho.[28] Her mother, my grandmother, was killed on Bear River. Some other Indians had killed a mail carrier, and the soldiers came to the village my grandmother was in and started to shoot. They killed many Indians, and Grandmother was shot.[29] I always said that we ought to sue the United States for killing my grandmother. That was not right. I think we could get some money from them for that.

I knew Captain Jack. He was a big tall slim-like man. Persune was a small man. He is dead now. Douglas looked exactly like that woman. She is his daughter, and she was carved out of him with a butcher knife. She is deaf so she can't hear us speak.[30]

If you write a book about us, I want to see that book.

Emma Daum Amick, Rio Blanco County [342-77].

Interviewer: J. Monaghan.

I was born in or near Fond du Lac, Wisconsin, on April the 8th, 1868, the youngest of seven children. Later my family moved to Russell, Kansas. A number of years later we moved to Independence, Kansas, in Montgomery County. Lived a few years in Elk City, Kansas, but moved back to Independence, where my sister and myself were attending high school. As my father sold his business and went to Leadville, where three of my brothers had been for some time, in February 1882, the rest of the family also went to Leadville, Colorado.

In July 1884 my father, John Daum, brother Henry, and myself started from Leadville, going by way of Tennessee Pass to Red Cliff, over Battle Mountain in a covered wagon, with White River Valley and Meeker as our destination. We ferried across the Eagle River, part of the load at a time, and swam the horses across behind the ferryboat. We crossed a mountain pass they called Belly Ache Mountain, and we thought it well named by the time we were over it. When we arrived at Dotsero, crossed the bridge over Grand River, going, as it looked, straight up the mountains toward Carbonate Camp.[31] We took half the load as far as Willow Springs. They called it six miles. They were long miles. We then went back to Dotsero for the rest of the load. We decided the rest of the way up to Carbonate Camp was just as steep as the first few miles were, but the scenery was grand and to look off down in the deep canyon below, and see tiny objects moving, at times, was very fascinating.

When the people at Carbonate Camp sighted us, they all came to meet us, as they had not seen anybody but the mail carrier for eight months. Only one woman had remained in the camp all winter, the postmaster's wife, Mrs. Price. They were all looking for some freighter to bring them supplies, as they were running low on food products. We thought we were on top of the world. There was a post office, saloon, and a number of other buildings, not many of them occupied, as most of the population had left before they were snowed in. Mr. Price made drawings of the place when the snow covered all the houses, and only the stovepipes and trails they dug out from their doors were visible. They used snowshoes and skis to go out to cut the trees down for wood and snake them close on piles to cut for firewood. All the woodpiles still had snowbanks underneath them. The drawings were very nicely done, and very interesting to look at. Mr. Price had made his wife a work box and birdcage, out of cigar boxes, cut in the smallest pieces, shaped in diamonds, et cetera, polished and glued on a foundation; they were beautiful. When asked if it did not take lots of patience, Mr. Price said anyone would have the patience to mold bird shot if they had to spend a winter up there.

Next we started down the mountains toward the South Fork Canyon of the White River. There were no roads, so the going was very steep down, and very rocky for a long way, until we reached what we might call the White River plateau. Just before entering the South Fork Canyon, we had to ford the river many, many times, and as the river is very rocky, with many boulders, which at times were very difficult to avoid. We came to a very steep hill, not very long, but which ended with not much more than a wagon length at the bottom, to the riverbank. A party before had attempted to let their wagon down by ropes tied to a tree at the top of the hill, but broke down, and packed their horses on through. Father and Henry cleared the road as best they could, but it was difficult and dangerous to make so short a turn without turning over. However, Henry made the attempt and succeeded. He then threw his hat in the air and shouted "Hurrah! We made it." That canyon echoed and re-echoed, and frightened most of the wild animals within hearing out of their haunts and hiding places, even the little squirrels scampered away.

Later we crossed the river again, the steep grade being on the opposite side of the river. After going up the steep bank a ways, we struck solid rock and the horses could not get a foothold, so we propped the wheels of the wagon with rocks, for if it went back it would go over a cliff into the river, then took the horses and hooked them to the end of the wagon tongue, so they were where they could stand and get a firm foothold. I was told to get a persuader, in the form of a switch, and use it on one of the horses, which I did. They did not need much persuading, as they were a good steady pulling team.

Late one evening we came to the river, where we wanted to cross, before dark, when just below we saw a bear under a tree. As we went closer she disappeared, but up in the tree were three little cubs, and they looked so cunning way up there, at a safe distance. We crossed the river, which was a difficult crossing, and by the time they rode back across it was too dark to see. The next day we were stuck in a swampy place, and it took us all day to get out, so our camp was not far distant from where we had camped the night before. About a mile or little more from the mouth of the canyon, we drove in the middle of the riverbed, and followed it down until we came out into the valley of the South Fork of the White River. It was a very hazardous ride. A little farther on, we met Charlie Smith, an old hunter and trapper well known on the upper White River for many years. And yet with all the seeming hardships, we paused at times to note the beauty of God's wonderful creations, and the wild creatures we saw from time to time in their native haunts paused to look at us, then disappear from sight.

We landed at what is known as the old "LaKamp" place on the third day of August 1884. We went on to Meeker, but came back, and Father located on North Elk Creek, joining the old Eugene Gully place on the river bottom, at the mouth of Elk Creek. My brother Henry and I soon returned to Leadville, going horseback over the old Ute Trail. I rode all the way with just a saddle blanket cinched on my horse, riding, as was the custom at that time, sideways. It was a wonderful trip, and we arrived in Leadville in time for the opening of the fall term of school.

Henry returned to White River to remain with Father, and Andy Belott, who was located on Piceance Creek, returned with him.[32]

The next summer Henry returned to Leadville, by way of Meeker, New Castle Stage Route, and by way of Glenwood Springs, where they had a ferryboat to cross the Colorado River, at that place, and brought my mother and myself to the ranch on North Elk Creek, where my father was engaged in farming and stock raising.[33] Cattle prices at that time were nearly as low as at the present time. At that time, nearly all produce was freighted into Meeker by way of Rawlins, Wyoming, with horses and wagons, and the prices were high. A few years later the railroad was built through and down the Colorado River, and the town of Rifle came into existence. Then the stage line and freighters did their hauling between Rifle and Meeker.[34]

At the time of the late Ute Indian War, the Indians were camped a few miles above the mouth of Elk Creek, on the hills above Big Beaver Creek. The sheriff and his posse attempted to arrest an Indian for breaking the game laws, and so the trouble began. The Indians packed their squaws and families and started them back to the reservation under the cover of night. The buck Indians were then supposedly to be on the warpath. The officers followed them down the river, and some soldiers were sent in to help. They had a fight with the Indians, miles below Meeker. One man was killed and several slightly wounded. But the stories and excitement were highly exaggerated, and many of the citizens were panic stricken. Two of my brothers in Leadville (Andrew and Lawrence) heard of the outbreak, took horses, and started for the ranch, thinking the worst I guess, riding all night and arriving at the ranch. Father and Mother were still there and persuaded them to go down to Meeker, for protection and safety. But after being there a day, none of us could see that there was any danger at the ranch, and stock and everything needing attention, we went back to the ranch and stayed there. We did see a lone Indian crossing above our place and once in the hills, but supposed he was scouting around.

The boys then wanted to go deer hunting. I went along. After we went up in the hills we separated, and Andy and myself took the lower trail. It being his first trip in those hills, I led him to a deer lick and there were seven elk. He took a shot and killed one. We returned home in a short time. The other boys did not get in until late evening, without anything, and did not want to believe in our success, until they saw the proof.

As soon as the war cry died out, I returned to Leadville with my brother Lawrence to visit my sisters. We rode from Elk Creek, over the hills to New Castle and Glenwood Springs. We met Dr. Hughs, who was also returning from the Indian War. Rode to Gypsum the next morning, in time to catch the train for Leadville, Lawrence riding on through with the horses. Gypsum was as far as the D&RG [Denver and Rio Grande] Railroad was completed at that time, building on down the Colorado River, later.

The town of Meeker derived its name from the man by the name of Meeker that was massacred a few miles below where the town of Meeker is now located.

A number of years ago the game warden from Garfield County came over here to arrest some Indians for violating the game laws.[35] They were camped up in the Nine-Mile-Hill section. He took the sheriff and deputy and went up and brought them to Meeker and pitched their tents and camp in the park, in the center of town. Drove their horses off in a pasture out of town. There was a little Indian boy about three or four years old, and the people seemed to delight in taking that child any toys they could buy and gay calico for the squaws to make themselves dresses. And they were enjoying it all. The Indians put up a bear hide to pay for their defense, and they were turned loose. There was some dispute over the bear hide, but the judge walked off with it. The game warden was not satisfied over the decision, so he decided to take them to Glenwood Springs for trial. The officers here refused to help him take them out of this country, but he obtained help to take them out. So they took the Indians and all their camping outfit, and started for Glenwood Springs. After they had gone a ways out on the government road, the Indians made a break across the hills, scattering their paraphernalia all over as they went. One buck Indian was all they held back. They took him on to Glenwood Springs, and he was treated so nicely over there, that when they turned him loose he did not like to leave, as he was enjoying his vacation immensely.

In later years, after the Meeker bank robbery, there were a great many letters of inquiry received concerning the description and identity of the young man (one of the robbers) killed at that time, fearing it was a relative. One mother wrote to Mr. Amick, thinking it might be her son, as she had never heard of him since he had left England as a boy, a few years previous to the robbery.[36]

Madeline [Baker] Adams and Jennie [Baker] Reische [Reschke], Moffat County [356-51].

Interviewer: J. Monaghan.

The first we can remember we were living in a two-story house on Clear Creek. Father had some cattle there.[37] We went back to that house in the nineties and it was still standing, but we were afraid to go upstairs.

Father had been over on Snake River when he was working for the fur company. He decided to settle there, and in April 1873 we packed all our belongings in a wagon and set out. We had the team and one saddle horse and some cattle. We came by way of Laramie. There were two men besides Father in the party. This was after Mother died. We girls drove the cattle most of the way on foot, but we took turns riding the horse. One of the men would most always help us. We didn't go very far each day, and when the feed was good we would camp for several days. We arrived on Snake River on the fourth day of July 1873, and we've been right here in the same place ever since.[38] We would be a lot better off if we had stayed on Clear Creek.

There were not many people on Snake River when we arrived. Perkins had a store just west of Dixon.[39] It was east of the Snake River bridge on the north side of the river, in the meadowland under the cottonwood trees. Perkins was a short, heavy-set man with a pocked face. He was a smart man, but he died broke. He deeded his property to his wife, and she wouldn't give it back to him. The Utes came from a long ways to trade with Perkins. He sold them whiskey, but never enough to get them drunk. He never had any trouble with the Indians.

There were lots of cattle in the country at that time with big, long horns. Mr. Reader had a big cow ranch on Snake River. Father had cattle too. There were lots of sheep in the country when we came. But the sheep never went on the south side of Snake River until later. Then the cowmen over in Colorado ran them back.

Father never objected to the sheep. He said that they did not hurt the range any more than the cattle did. Both of them will hurt the range if there are too many of them. There was no trouble between the sheep and cattlemen on the Wyoming side of the line. The reason for that was that there are more streams in Colorado than there are in Wyoming. Little cattlemen took up ranches on all these streams, and they did not want the sheep around them. In Wyoming there were no little ranches. It was all open country, big flats, and the sheep were there as soon as the cattle were. Father sold his hay to a sheep man, Mr. Massey, once, and he has not got his money for that hay yet. It was Massey's Mexican herder who shot Mrs. Adams's husband.

Father used to talk about his early experiences, but you can get that in Mumey's book.[40] It is in there better than I can remember it. Most of the things in that book are right, but some of the stories have been stretched a little. The writer left out one thing altogether that I know about. Father was with the soldiers on White River during the winter of 1879. Mumey doesn't mention that.[41]

When Meeker was killed we girls were frightened and went to Rawlins. We came back to Snake River after a few weeks, and Father was gone. He had left a man on the ranch to do the chores. This man told us that Father had gone to White River to scout for the soldiers.

Before he left, Father divided his furs with his partner, Bible-Back Brown. Father's half of the beaver and mink skins was stored in the second story of our cabin, and stolen before spring. We were living underneath them all the time. That man working for Father must have stole them because he was the one who howled about it the most. Bible-Back Brown died at Reader's ranch between 1890 and '95.

Father had a gun explode in his hands before we knew him. It took off one of his thumbs and broke his jaw. The scars showed the rest of his life. When Father's things were sold at auction, I bought his gun for $2.50. He had made it over. I know that he rebored the barrel to a larger size.[42] I bought his clock too. There it is. Then I have this picture of Father, Major Oakes, and Bill Clark. I think his first name was Bill. That's Major Oakes sitting down in the chair. Father is standing at his right with his big pipe in his mouth. That young man on Major Oakes's left is Clark. He was a dentist in Denver. My mother made him those buckskin clothes. He thought they made him look wild and woolly and he wanted to have his picture taken with Father and Major Oakes, and there they are. That picture was taken in Denver.

Chapter 2: The Mountains and Foothills

Gunnison, Rio Grande, Chaffee, Delta, Arapahoe, and Alamosa Counties

I think the pioneer women of that day did their share in keeping things going and in developing the country.
Anna Lee Fulcher Clarkson

Although not all of the counties included in this section are mountain counties, each of the narratives included here concerns itself to some extent with the details of traveling to, traveling through, settling in, and mining in the mountains of Colorado. Taken together, they offer a broad overview of the European American settling of the state, and as they make evident, after the gold rush of the 1860s had played itself out, many homesteaders turned to farming, ranching, and trading for their livelihoods.[1] Although many finally did stay put, it also becomes clear from these narratives that many of the pioneers moved frequently before settling in Colorado, and once in Colorado they continued to move frequently. As Virginia Scharff suggests, perhaps it is time we "stopped envisioning women's history as a narrative chiefly about attempts to establish geographical stability (what might be called 'home on the range'), and begin to accord itinerancy the historical importance in western women's lives that the record suggests is necessary."[2] Many of the narratives in this section corroborate Scharff's contention.

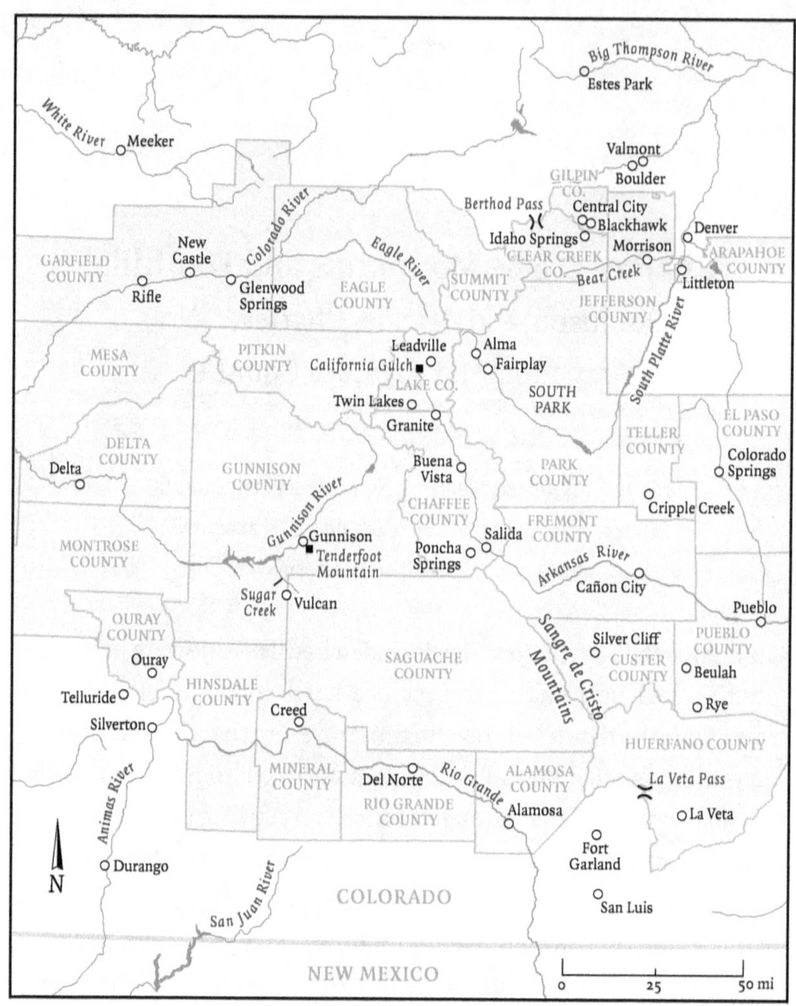

4. The mountains and foothills

As with the northwest area of the state, new settlement in the mountains and on the prairies inevitably brought conflict with the previous inhabitants, and these narratives offer several different views of and accounts of interactions with Native Americans. Two narrators refer to the Meeker Massacre or the Milk Creek Battle, for example, and several express their fear. Although Mary Nichols Williams seems to share the general fear of Indian attack, she recalls good-natured encounters with many individual Native Americans, mentioning, for instance, a dance in which one of the dancers "wore a good-sized mirror suspended by a string around his neck. Very often he'd stop dancing, lift the mirror and admire himself, then resume his dancing, with more activity than ever." Elizabeth Harrington recalls witnessing an attack on a group of Mexicans with their cattle as she was crossing the prairie, yet later in her narrative she gives several accounts of the Utes' peaceful interactions with the white settlers. In the context of the U.S. government's payments to Utes for their land, she confesses that "if I had been an Indian I would have felt as he did—ready to fight for a 'square deal.'" These narratives demonstrate that despite the stories of bloodshed and accounts of actual battles, many women encountered Native Americans on a casual, almost daily basis and tended to get along—at least on a superficial level—sharing food, for example, and exchanging cultural information.

The field-workers for these counties were Margaret Flick (Gunnison), Laura C. Mason-White (Rio Grande), E. E. Carrington (El Paso), J. W. Taylor (Delta), Leslie F. Paull (Arapahoe), and C. E. Gibson Jr. (Alamosa).

Mary Nichols Williams, Gunnison County [350-68].

Interviewer: Margaret Flick.

I was born in Carroll County, Missouri, March 3rd, 1851. My maiden name was Mary Nichols. I was only fourteen years old when I married

Thomas Williams. He had been a soldier, and we were married at the close of the war. He was a northerner; my folks were southerners, and I used to have much fun teasing him about being a northerner. He'd joke me, too, about being a little rebel.

Our first child was born in Missouri. Then we got the westward fever and moved to Kansas, in a covered wagon in company with many other emigrants; it wasn't safe in those days to start alone anywhere, on account of the Indians. Along the Kaw River all we saw was buffalo. They wouldn't cross in back of the wagons, but would gallop along in front. So many of them, looked like great brownish-black dusty seas, as they galloped along over the plains. We had no other meat while crossing the plains; and nothing but the best part of the carcass was ever used. It seemed sinful to waste the meat that way.

My second child was born in Kansas. My husband got work helping to build the railroad, then moving westward. And, again, we moved west. Times were awfully hard in Kansas, anyway, so of course we didn't like it any too well there. So again our covered wagon was fitted out, to move west, as the laying of the rails progressed. I had a boardinghouse for the men; that is, I cooked for thirty of the construction gang using my wagon for a pantry, and the men ate at long board tables with benches on which to sit. We had tin dishes, and I had a good stove, which made my work much easier. We got our provisions from the freight wagons. Again our chief article of diet was buffalo meat. I cooked great wash-boilers full at a time. The men who killed the buffalo could skin them in a jiffy, and if the buffalo was old, nothing was saved but the hide. The young animals made good meat. The skinners just left the carcasses where they were killed, and the part that was not used soon smelled badly. Sanitation was not known in those days. But the bad smell was a part of camp life, so we endured it as best we could.

The Indians were seen nearly every day at a distance; they never came close in daytime, but at night would ride around on their ponies, and in among the grazing stock, to try to stampede them. Ours never happened to get away, as the stock was carefully guarded by a night herder.

When we left Kansas my husband had a fine team of horses, which he traded for a team of big oxen. I didn't like it because he traded our beautiful horses. These oxen weren't too well behaved, as all oxen aren't alike, and would get loose and run with the buffalo. After Mr. Williams had to hire two men to catch them a few times, and be unable to work until they were caught, he was glad to trade them off and get another nice team of horses.

When we'd be moving camp, the oxen would behave as long as my husband walked and drove them, but when he got tired and would get into the wagon to ride, the oxen would run away. They wouldn't hurt anything because there was nothing to hit. The plain was almost as smooth as a floor, but their running was vexatious. A team of oxen was worth $200. A team of horses, $300 to $350.

I remember how the great loads of buffalo hides looked, as drawn by long strings of oxen: they bounced along over the prairie, on the way to market. This was about the only thing that was produced that was of marketable value. We burned dry buffalo chips for fuel; no oil stoves, no electricity, no coal or even wood was to be had in those days. But the buffalo chips were a part of life, as was everything else mentioned above. One nice thing was there never was any scarcity of fuel.

We lived in this manner until we and the railroad arrived in Pueblo, which was just a small place then.[3] The city offered us our pick of lots if we would build, but Alma and Fairplay were booming. We moved there. After staying in these camps about three years, we got our covered wagon out and started to Del Norte, and from there went to Durango, following the railroad into Silverton.[4]

On the way over we were accompanied by two other families who had just come out from Missouri. The wagons this time were drawn by mules, and they were greatly afraid of the Indians. We could always tell when an Indian was near; the mules would smell him, and then it would be all the driver could do to control them. When the mules were lariated and picketed to graze, and the Indians were around, sometimes they'd break loose.

One time while we were camping between Del Norte and Durango at the river's edge where the berries were plentiful, and the children were picking them, some Indians came and told us to move on, that this was a deer run, and they wanted to hunt. We were camped for the night, and because the berries were so nice, we hated to move on, and as my husband thought the Indians weren't hostile, we decided to move on the next day. During the night, from the Indian camp on the hill, came the sounds of singing. We rose from our beds, and seeing them dancing up and down, and seeing their legs going up and down, silhouetted against the light of their campfires, and the sound of their singing, which sounded awful to us, had an immediate effect upon us, especially upon the new people from Missouri—the women and children were crying and screaming, because they were afraid of being scalped—which was great enough to cause us to move on, yet that night, and you may believe, we weren't long in breaking camp.

My husband and son Johnny hauled ties from the sawmill to the railroad construction gangs.

As we were going into Silverton it was winter, and roads were cut through the snowbanks. I was so afraid, and told my husband I hoped they wouldn't be that way when we came out again; but they were. The snow gets very deep there. Robbers were bad, and hold-ups were numerous. I cut holes in the mattress and hid my money inside, then put the stuffing back and carefully sewed up the holes. We had a big white bulldog named Blanco, and his growl scared away more than one robber. Somehow, thieves fear a dog worse than a gun.

While on this job Indians were again numerous. I ran a boardinghouse, and during the day, while my husband and son were at work and the little children and I were at home alone, the Indians would come and beg food. They always wanted "a biscuit." As flour was ten dollars a cwt,[5] I didn't like to give them biscuit. They would get off their ponies and come into the house and make themselves at home. I was frightened nearly to death and sent the children running for a Frenchman who lived near. He came and told them to get out. He talked Spanish to them, and showed them his guns, two .45 Colts. But they weren't much afraid, and finally he told them he'd write Chief Ouray a letter and tell him.[6] He told them that they'd promised to be peaceable, and if Ouray knew how they were acting he'd make trouble for them. That did the work.

They liked to sing and dance. One big buck wore a good-sized mirror suspended by a string around his neck. Very often he'd stop dancing, lift the mirror and admire himself, then resume his dancing, with more activity than ever. It is funny to look back upon, but I couldn't appreciate the humor of it at the time. These Indians were on their way to Pueblo to collect the money due them from the government. They didn't wear anything but breechclouts and moccasins, with bells and beads for ornaments.

One time when we were living near Durango, our six cows that we had brought from Fairplay with their calves were driven off. We supposed the Indians did it, and we hired Mexicans to find them, but without result, and we later thought that perhaps the Mexicans got both the stock and the pay for trying to find them. Everything that was done like this was always blamed on the Indians.

At the time of the Meeker Massacre we lived in Del Norte.[7] Everyone was scared to death. We knew Ouray and always liked him.

While on the railroad construction job, and living in tents, skunks were numerous. They often came into the tent while the men were eating, and there was no way of shooing them out. They were treated with consideration; usually we would put a piece of meat on the end of a stick and hold it up in front of their noses and thus coax them out.

After the railroad job was done we went back to Del Norte, where Rose, my youngest child, was born, making us a family of six children, as three others had been born at different places in our travels.

Hearing of the Gunnison boom, we next made our way there. Mr. Williams fitted up a brickyard, where he burned brick. He hauled his own lime, likely from the Lime Kiln Gulch, or Grafflin Gulch, near where Already, the ranch belonging to Raleigh Flick, is now situated, east of Tenderfoot Mountain. His yard was here in West Gunnison, probably near the old C&S [Colorado and Southern] roundhouse. He furnished brick for the first brick schoolhouse, and also some used in the building of La Veta Hotel.[8]

When Bob Lewis ran La Veta Hotel, I used to fish for him. It was not unlawful to catch fish to sell in those days, and I could make two or three dollars a day that way. My favorite bait was willow flies, and I think it must have been a favorite with the fish, too. Once I caught a big trout that weighed over eight pounds down by Cooper Rocks. My little girl Rose was with me, and she spread my apron in the shallow water after I had played it for a half hour, and when I got the fish on the apron she gathered the apron and ran to the dry land.

Mr. Lewis had the fish mounted, and it was in the window of La Veta Hotel for a long time. It was no trouble to catch fish in those days, and none were small. I still like to fish, but the last few summers I've been unable to.

Our chief amusement was dancing. We didn't have any time for amusement while crossing the plains, but after we were settled at Fairplay and Alma, and later at Durango and Del Norte and other places, we attended many dances.

My husband was quite a musician; he brought his violin—fiddle it was called in those days—from Missouri. We saved that from the fire in Kansas. And he was always in great demand to play for the dances. He usually received from ten to fifteen dollars for one night's playing. We'd begin dancing early and dance all night and sometimes a part of the next day. We always fixed big suppers with everything to eat. When my husband got old, he did not care for the violin, and finally sold it to George Jaynes, who kept a secondhand store in the Big Rock building at 901–03 West New York Avenue.

After we moved here to Gunnison, my husband and W. S. Bitto became great friends because they were both old soldiers and had served all during the Civil War. My husband was from Ohio. He talked a great deal about Sherman. I do not have any of his papers because we had a fire when we were in Kansas and nearly everything we had was burned. I had so many pictures and such nice bedding that I had brought from Missouri.

When the Vulcan boom came, we moved there.[9] Again, I kept boarders. My husband worked in the mines and prospected for himself. My son Johnnie died there. He was working in the mine and contracted pneumonia and didn't last but a few days. He was a good boy; I miss him yet.

I used to tell the children stories about my experiences with the Indians, and our early life in the West. Johnny would say, "Mama, why don't you write a book?" I wish I had; I've forgotten so much.

In 1900 we took a dry-land homestead on Sugar Creek.[10] We may be called pioneers, too, in the sense of being dry farmers. We always had a good garden, a nice crop of potatoes, and some grain.

My husband died there in 1916, and is buried at Vulcan beside Johnny. I lived there until about seven years ago, when I was compelled to sell it. James McConnell buying it. I love this place, and would like to be there yet.

But two of my children are living: my oldest, Mrs. Fannie Milner, of California, mother of Claude Clay, who lives here in Gunnison; and my youngest, Mrs. Rose Smith of Gunnison.

Hattie Buck Williams, Rio Grande County [367-23]. January 2, 10, 1934.

Interviewer: Laura C. Mason-White.

Interviewer's note: The home which Mr. and Mrs. Williams have called RoSeWild, the initials of the name which are in capitals for the initials of Mr. Williams, has been made very beautiful by the work of Mrs.

Williams's hands, both in painting and needlework. Her paintings are scenes from the nearby mountains, such as Wagon Wheel Gap, Creede, and scenes up on Clear Creek.

I was born January 8, 1866, on the old Kurtz Ranch, between Littleton and Morrison on Bear Creek, Colorado.

My parents were, mother, Cynthia S. Kelsay; and father, Robert E. Buck; and here I shall have to go into the Kelsay history a little before resuming the story of the Rio Grande Valley.

The J. S. Kelsay family left New Jersey in 1852, no doubt by way of the Ohio River, and resided for about seven years in southern Illinois. Grandfather J. S. Kelsay came to Central City, Colorado, in May of 1859, just ahead of the great stampede for the Pikes Peak district.[11] Will Buck, our father's cousin, came with Grandfather Kelsay. They were in Central City eight months; meantime, Grandfather went back to Illinois and brought the family in 1860. Grandmother became very homesick and went back very soon to return with my mother, who was Cynthia Kelsay, her daughter, and my father, who was not in very good health, and they thought he would regain his health in this western climate. They brought my oldest sister, little Ida, back with them to Central City. This was in the year 1862. Little Ida died from the effects of the whooping cough, October 2, 1863. My brother Henry Oscar Buck was born October 27, 1863.

Among some of the places in which my father worked was the Bobtail Mine at Central City. The family lived at Cold Spring, about five miles out of Black Hawk in 1864.[12]

Moved to Platte Valley near Littleton, Colorado, in 1865, and rented and lived on the Sanford Farm northwest of Littleton.

Then in 1866 they resided on the Kurtz Ranch on Bear Creek between Littleton and Morrison, the place where I was born. For several years my grandparents continued to reside in Central City and Blackhawk, where he conducted a butcher shop and my grandmother a millinery shop—then they moved and homesteaded four miles from Boulder at the head of Gregory Canyon, now called Chautauqua Canyon. Mr. Gregory of Central City fame made a road from Central City to Boulder, called Gregory Road, and this is the place of which I am speaking.[13] My grandparents also kept a stopping place for travelers, and farmed this homestead. This was probably the year 1870. They and their younger son, Lafayette, resided here. During the year 1870 Grandfather Kelsay died, leaving Grandmother living on the homestead for a time until she bought a home in Boulder, where she resided until 1886 or 1887, when she bought a little home in Denver.

My family—my father and mother and we children—during the year of 1868 lived on the Peter Magnus place about two miles west up the Platte, from the old John Lilley and Joe Bowles farms, where Father's last illness occurred. He was taken to Denver to be near a physician and died at the Bell House December 7, 1868. Mother and the family continued to live on the Magnus place through that winter and the next summer, then Mother kept house for the two bachelors, Dick Hussy and Charlie Montgomery, near Littleton, about where Petersburgh now stands.[14] This brings us to about 1870 when she and Uncle Jim Kelsay rented the Fox place on the Platte. They did not stay there very long when Mother secured through the then county commissioners of Arapahoe County the position of matron of the county hospital; Joe Bowles and John Lilley were two of those who secured this job for her, and another man whose name was Bound. It was at this time that she sent my brother Oscar to school in Denver. I was with my grandmother Kelsay up on Gregory Road near Boulder. In 1874 Mother went to Boulder to keep house for my uncle Newt Hockaday, who had been elected sheriff of Boulder County.[15] Mother put Brother and I in the schools at Boulder at this time. She remained in Boulder until 1885, when she came to the San Luis Valley, where she became the wife of Howell Davis, March 17, 1885, in Alamosa. They were married by the Rev. Joe Gilchrist.

Mr. Davis was a stockman of the San Luis Valley who had come from South Park in the year 1874, bringing with him his herd of cattle, which he had gradually developed into the prize bunch of Herefords. These were sold in 1906 to Henry McNeil, of Monte Vista.[16] He took out and recorded the cattle brand D which is one of the oldest recorded brands in this part of the state.

My mother and Mr. Davis established for themselves a most picturesque home under the cliff north of Del Norte, near the head of the Rio Grande and Saguache Canal where they resided for twelve years.[17] Here she cultivated the old-fashioned flowers, roses, iris, peonies, the native columbine. Hers was the first floral culture in the valley to any great extent, and people came there from miles away to find out how flowers could be grown to such extent in this altitude.

After my grandmother Mrs. Kelsay became too old to care for her little home in Denver, she came to the home of my mother and stepfather, Mr. Davis, which had been established in Monte Vista in 1898, after their residence on the river near Del Norte, where Grandmother died in 1901. My mother passed away at this same time, as did my uncle Jim Kelsay, all within a few days of each other, in Monte Vista.

When my family came to the valley, I of course accompanied them, and in the year 1885 I started school in the Presbyterian College of the Southwest in Del Norte. I was the first graduate of that college, and the only member of that class who got through. I graduated alone, but the other members who started out with me in the class were George S. Darley, who afterwards became minister in Alamosa; Eva Cleghorn; Maude Dobson; Cora Campbell, who afterwards became Mrs. Samuel Thompson, a doctor; Millie Campbell, afterwards became Mrs. Will Mallett; Annie Franklin, afterwards Mrs. George Seibert. All had married or took up careers before time to graduate but me. The Rev. Goodell from Illinois was the professor of the college at that time.[18]

I taught for four years in the college after graduation. Then I filed up on a homestead in 1887, which land lies just east of the Soldiers and Sailors Home; after the prescribed three years I made final proof. I then took up a preemption adjoining the homestead, and in the due course of time I made final proof on that too.

In 1897 I married Robert S. Williams, who had come from Iowa in 1877 to the upper Rio Grande district and had been a resident of Colorado since that time. We were married by the Rev. Blaisdale and have resided in the San Luis Valley continuously ever since. We came to RoSeWild, our present homestead, in 1909. RoSeWild is the ranch Mr. Williams filed up on in 1890, and we are perhaps the only landowners in the near vicinity who are still living upon land just as it was, just as the title was issued to them by patent.

We have a wonderful view of the Sangre de Cristos on the east of us, and the San Juans on the west, with the Saguache Range to the north, and on the south we can look upon the Hilltop Mountain in New Mexico.

Anna Lee Fulcher Clarkson, Rio Grande County [367-18]. December 18, 1933.

Interviewer: Laura White.[19]

I was born in Council Bluffs, Iowa, January 3, 1868. My father, Silas Redmon Fulcher, the pioneer of this article, was born in Boone County, Missouri, April 24, 1824, shortly after Missouri had been admitted as a state. My mother was born in Schuyler County, Missouri, in 1824. She and my father married August 26, 1844, in Schuyler County. My father was teaming for the government at the time of the Civil War. They moved from Missouri to Iowa, where they resided until 1872, when they came to Colorado, taking all the family but one with them. Our uncle Milt Robinson, my mother's brother, had already moved to Boulder County, Colorado, from Iowa, and for that reason when my father and family came to Colorado, they came directly to Boulder County, near

Valmont, at a place known as White Rock Mill.[20] The children were Tom, John, Mary, Millard, Ira, Etta, and Anna Lee, myself. Mattie, the oldest, remained in the East.

White Rock Mill got its name on account of the great quantities of pure white sandstone hills and boulders all over that section of the country. This mill was a real flour mill, and Mr. John Carnahan was the proprietor.[21]

Early in 1873 my father and the two oldest boys, Tom and John, left the rest of us at White Rock Mill and set out for the San Luis Valley. They crossed over La Veta Pass, came down to Fort Garland, and from there to where Alamosa now stands, although at that time the little settlement there was called Wayside.[22]

They came west, up the river from Alamosa about eight or nine miles and took up a hay ranch on the south side of the river. The Hank Dorris family came a few years later and settled on a hay ranch on the north side of the river, directly opposite that of my father's. The family of John Shock came from Central, Missouri, 1874, settling on the south side of the Rio Grande, just around what was called Fulcher's Bend. The Louie Widman family had already settled a little farther west on the river, as had the Johansens, and these three families—Widmans, Johansens, and Fulchers—were the first pioneers in that particular section in 1873.[23]

My father and the boys—Tom and John and Millard—homesteaded four hay ranches in a continuous body of land, and theirs was the original filing on this land from the government. When they had taken up these ranches, they went up into the hills on the west side of the valley, over on the Piedra Valley and went up into one of those little draws or gulches and built the first log cabin there, in which they lived when they were taking out posts (cedar) and quaking-aspen poles for the fences for these four ranches. Those cedar posts which were put into the ground in 1873 are still in a good state of preservation after these sixty years of usage. Of course, the pole fences are gone and barbed wire has taken their place. This little gulch was named Fulcher's Gulch and has carried that name for a number of years until the forest service renamed creeks and gulches. They built three log cabins on the ranches, and these cabins had dirt roofs and dirt floors for several years.

After they had finished a cabin for us to move into, my father and the boys came back to Valmont after the rest of the family, the teams and supplies and furniture.

Before he left the valley that time, Father noted that the only flour the people who lived there had to use—there was quite a scattered community of Mexicans living in the valley then—was a very coarse black stuff that was milled out by sheep and goats tramping it. Now, we didn't have much of this world's goods to take with us, so he loaded up the wagons with thousands of pounds of pure white flour from the White Rock Mill—and it was real white flour too—so my mother was the only woman down there who could have nice white bread. We didn't sell any of it either, and it was a good thing, I guess, for there were many times when we had nothing but black coffee and bread for our meals. We had no milk for some months, and when the men would be gone to Del Norte (our nearest post office and supply station) for several days at a time, our food would run very low.

We used both oxen and horses for our wagons in making the trip over. Among other things that we brought—though we were not allowed to take much furniture crossing the mountains, for once or twice we had to unload and climb a hill and load again—was my mother's carpet loom, and we wove our own carpets and those for our neighbors for years. We made our own soap too, using wood ashes for lye—this makes a very strong soap, but it gets the dirt. I have helped my father mold bullets many times; we made both the cartridges and large bullets. My father was a great hunter and in the wintertime supplied our table with meat. This reminds me that we had a candle mold too; it was about twenty-four inches long and was a twelve-candle mold.

We used cotton wick, and tallow for the making of the candles, and I have made many dozens during my childhood. The cotton wick is the same as is used these days for the tufted bedspreads the fancy-work departments of the stores are exhibiting so much.

Father engaged in freighting from Pueblo to Del Norte for a few years, and he furnished nearly all the hay for the contracting firm of Carlyle, Orman, and Crook when they were building the Denver and Rio Grande Railroad into the valley. The railroad came to Alamosa in 1879. Hay was worth between thirty-five to forty-five dollars a ton those days. This was the only way we had of making a living, as all those ranches along the river were hay ranches. We had cattle too later on. Brother Ira was in with Father in the hay and freighting business. A hay baler from Fort Garland used to make trips through the country and set up on the ranch and bale up all the hay. Jim Lowery was the man who owned the baler at that time. A family by the name of Kent lived at the Wayside station, kept a little store and the post office in the same building.

When the family came from Missouri, they brought with them a very fine mare, a single-footer; we called her Old Kit.[24] She stayed with us until she died. When Father came back to Valmont after the rest of the family, we had a beautiful black stallion colt, her baby, to fetch along, with the rest of the belongings and possessions. After he was old enough to ride, he became a sort of ferryboat for all the neighborhood. Any number could ride him, and he was sure-footed, never making a misstep when he had the children on his back. Whenever Mrs. Dorris wanted to cross the river, and visit the Fulchers or others on the south side, she would just come out the door and call to us, or put up a signal, and I would put the bridle on Bill, and we would ferry Mrs. Dorris over. Or if mother or any of us wanted to go to the Dorrises, Bill was the ferryboat across the Rio Grande.

In 1874 the family of Mancil Garrett moved from Missouri to the San Luis Valley. Now, Mrs. Mancil Garrett was Sarah Ann Fulcher, my father's sister, so that connects the Garretts and Fulchers. The Garretts were headed for the La Jara, but crossed La Veta Pass and came in by Fort Garland to Wayside, the same as we did.[25] From Alamosa they went south to the La Jara meadows. My father had no idea these people were coming to the valley, but when he was on one of the trips to Boulder County, one evening he was camped out on the road, probably near the pass, and after he had unhitched the horses, and made his camp for the night, he discovered he had neighbor campers, although the night was getting dark. He could not see their faces very well, but he imagined he heard a voice he hadn't heard for some years. So he walked over to the other camp to investigate. He found he had actually heard the voice of Mancil Garrett, his brother-in-law, who with his family were en route to La Jara. He told my mother afterwards: "I just knew that was Manc's voice."

The Robert S. Neeley family—three boys, Perry, Charlie, and James, and Jennie—came to Alamosa in 1897, some of them settling there, and James after some years, going on up the river to where Monte Vista now stands, and took up some land. My brothers sold their holdings on the river to Rob S. Neeley later on. One brother, T. G., after having experienced a couple of cold winters in Wyoming and Colorado, decided to go back to Missouri, marry, and settle down there.

I want to say something about the first school I attended in the valley. It was in 1878 or 1879, there was a little log schoolhouse built across the river from father's place on land that belonged to John Shock. The equipment was primitive, and the second teacher we had was a little on that order too, but the first teacher was a Mr. Marcy (C. W.), a little, dark-complected man of about thirty-five, who boarded with us. We seemed to do pretty well under his teachership, but I was rather young. Then the second teacher we had was Wayne Starbuck; he did the best he could, but his equipment, to say the least, was pretty slim. The benches were hewn out of logs, and the large desk that we used to have to stand up to write on was a huge slab of wood fastened up to the side of the wall, like a shelf, on one side of the room, and we had to stand up to do what writing we could. The pupils were the three Dorris girls, Kate, Jennie, and Hattie (who in later years became Mrs. William H. Adams);[26] the Shocks, Ada, Carrie, and Josie, and it seems to me there were two boys in this family, but were perhaps too young to go to school when I did, and then there were Perry and Charlie Neeley, me, and my two brothers, and part of the time my sister Etta, and the two Rutherford girls. Perry and Charlie Neeley and I used to ride horseback across the river to get to school.

I remember when we came to Colorado, and passed through Denver on our way to Valmont, my first impression of Denver was indeed a very poor one. We had heard so much about it, and my sister and I kept looking out of the back of the covered wagon and saw only a clump of log buildings; we were much disappointed. Of course, there were some larger buildings, but we did not see them at first, and our first impression was not much.[27]

In 1876 an event happened that stands out in my memory, and that was the first big dance given in the valley. I have told you that our cabins had dirt floors, but as soon as it was practicable, floors were put in, and we had just put in a new floor in our largest cabin. Whether the dance was given in celebration of the new floor or the fact that Colorado had entered statehood is not clear in my mind, only I know that night I was allowed to dance with anyone who would ask me, and I danced a lot, because I was so small. Well, there were several people at this dance who afterwards became of some importance to the state of Colorado. A young man, rather slight of build, wore a little mustache, and had blue eyes, and a fancier of fine horses, although his occupation was cowboy, he still loves to ride, came over from Alamosa way, and his sweetheart and her sister. That was Billy Adams and the Ottawa girls.[28] Then there was Bert Sanford; I am not sure, but he stole Billie's girl that night. Then from the Piedra side were the Hockers, and Heilmans, and some of the Laricks and McOlloughs. Sigel Heilman was teaching school at that time, but he afterwards became county superintendent of Rio Grande County. Old man Babe played the violin, and he did his own calling too. Whenever anyone did not make the right change in the square dances, and we danced mostly those then, he would stop playing and go down and straighten out the couple, show them the right change, and then the music would go on. We had other players too; one Lucero from up near Del Norte was a wonderfully fine violinist.

My brothers Tom and John left the valley, having sold out to the Neeleys, and went to Durango in the early eighties, and a few years later my brother Ira followed and went into the cattle business there. Then he took up a ranch on the La Plata, and finally went into the sheep business over there. My father engaged extensively in the cattle business in the late seventies, and our old brand taken out years ago was the I X L.

I left the valley in 1884, going to Durango for a couple of years, and then to other towns in the San Juan, coming back to Durango in the nineties. In 1893 I went to Rifle, where in 1895 I married George E. Clarkson, who was an old settler of Aspen.

Father came to live with me in 1892, after the death of my brother Ira. He lived with me fourteen years, until the time of his death in 1915, at the ripe old age of ninety-one years. My mother came to me in Rifle in 1896, and stayed two years. She passed away at my sister's home in Durango in March 1911.

My daughter was born in January 1898, now lives in the East. After my husband's death in 1923, I came to Denver where I have since resided.

I nearly forgot, I would like to add something about the first milk cows we had on the Fulcher place. There was a Sam Bailey of Texas fame, came in there about 1875 with a large herd of Texas longhorns—and they were LONGHORNS and no mistake, and poor and scrawny. My father took those cattle—there were about fifteen hundred head of steers and cows—on the shares for five years; that is to say, he got one-half the increase of the herd for his pay, for the care of them.

The first milk we had was from some of these old cows, and this is the way we got it. My two brothers rode into the corral, one of those high, round pole corrals common to the times. One could rope a cow around the horns, while the other tied the hind legs to keep her from kicking, and my mother milked them. They would fasten the cow securely to the fence, otherwise mother would not have been safe, and where do you suppose father was? On the top pole of the fence bossing the job. It took a good big lariat rope for the horns, because they were indeed spread.

I wanted to add this to my statement because I think the pioneer women of that day did their share in keeping things going and in developing the country, and it mostly fell to the women of that time to do the milking. Of course, mother made butter, and had a very primitive churn at first, but when we had a store churn, that was loaned to all the neighboring ranches during the week.

I remember on one trip to Del Norte to market the butter; we went into the old Windsor Hotel there, and there was an old colored cook who had made some of the nicest doughnuts I had ever tasted; and being hungry and having driven about twenty-three miles, I accepted them and ate plenty. When I got home I told my brother about them, and he proceeded to make fun of me because the cook's hands were so black. This bantering had the opposite effect on me this time, and I defended my colored friend against heavy odds, believe me, and they didn't tease me anymore about those black hands, and he had an idea the doughnuts ought to have been black too.

Elizabeth Rule Harrington, Chaffee County [346-20].
Interviewer: Margaret Flick.

Life started with me, as far as recollections go, when I was eight years old and my mother died. My father, Matthew Rule, had gone to California in 1849 and was on his way home at the time of my mother's death. Mother, with her family of children, had been left well provided for in Kansas City. At that time Kansas City was not much more than a steamboat landing. As my mother's health failed, her father took us to his farm some eighteen miles north of Kansas City to care for us. Word was sent Father of Mother's rapid decline, and he hastened home. Hoping to make the trip faster by boat than overland, he took passage on a sailboat from San Francisco. Shortly after sailing, they were becalmed and delayed three weeks. Finally they reached the Isthmus of Panama. Crossing this neck of land in a chair strapped to the back of a hired native, he reached the Atlantic coast and sailed for Havana; thence to New Orleans, and then up the Mississippi and Missouri Rivers, reaching home just one week after my mother had passed away.

My father, broken-hearted and discouraged, left for the West again in 1860, putting me in a young ladies' seminary, where, under the care of the principal, a Presbyterian minister, Professor Scott, I received regular schooling and religious training. This early training has stayed with me through life.

The Civil War came, and the school arrangements were broken up. My father, who was in California Gulch, sent for me to come to him with a cousin and his family who were starting West to find a new home.[29] My cousin Thomas Rule, known to me as Uncle Tommie, was a Baptist minister who had lost all his fortune during the war. So towards the end of May 1865, with ox teams and prairie schooners, and quite a herd of cattle, we started out to cross the plains, with a desire of retrieving our lost fortunes in the West. Kansas City was a western terminal for the railroads, and all who traveled west went as we did.[30] Thence we journeyed southward through Westport, four miles south of Kansas City, which, with its numerous warehouses, was then the outfitting point for most of the immigrants going westward to Salt Lake, Santa Fe, and Taos. In our party there were my cousin and his wife, his two sons and three daughters, a daughter of Colonel Boone, then Indian agent for the Cheyennes, her husband and two children and myself, besides the old family cook—a darky known as Aunt Hanna, and her children.[31] Old Aunt Hanna refused to part from us, even though freed, saying, "Masser Thomas, all de freedom I wants is to be wid you—if you don't provide for me to ride, I'll walk and follow." Poor faithful old soul! Little did she realize what a "walk" it would have been. That year the travel was exceedingly heavy, and the main route was along the Arkansas River, over what is now called the Santa Fe Trail. There was a constant stream of white-topped wagons—some going West to settle, others freighting for the government, bringing in supplies to the military posts.

We traveled along without any incidents until we came to the Little Arkansas Fort, a fort built to protect the immigrants from the hostile Indians, the Kiowas and Comanches; from there to Bent's Old Fort we were continually harassed by the Indians.[32]

On reaching Little Fort, Arkansas, we were detained ten days, waiting for enough wagons to come along to make up an outfit that would justify the government sending a military escort. An outfit consisted of from 100 to 250 wagons. An escort would accompany an outfit from one post to another; then we would be given another escort, which saw us safely to the next post, while the first escort looked after outfits going east, which usually were freighters.

When we came to the Indian country, we also came to the land of the buffaloes, for they were the food of the Indian. For three days after leaving Little Fort, Arkansas, we traveled through a moving mass of buffalo, which were emigrating from the northeast to the southwest. I remember so well how I stood up on our ambulance as high up as I could get to look at them, and as far as I could see in any direction there was that vast, solid-looking mass of buffalo. They were not frightened by our wagons, but passed between them whenever they found an opening. When we camped for the night, they kept on, and all through the night you could hear their constant tramp.

We women of my cousin's family rode in what was called an ambulance, a schooner fixed up with as many comforts as possible for the women. There were seats in the ambulance in the daytime which were lifted out at night and our beds made up. When we first started out we older girls were allowed to ride horseback, but once we entered the Indian country my cousin forbade it. The tongue of our ambulance was fastened to the wagon which my cousin drove, and I remember the merriment we had when a little young buffalo jumped over the tongue of the ambulance, raised as it was from the ground.

At Fort Larned we were given an escort of forty men—well mounted—who took us as far as Fort Dodge.[33] We left the river and took what was called the Dry Route, to shorten the distance by a half day's travel. Besides, it was the best road during this wet season. After leaving Fort Larned some twelve miles or so we were traveling up a large arroyo and stopped for the noonday meal. Now, we did not carry firewood with us, and in this part of the plains there was none to be had; nevertheless, we had our three hot meals a day, the fire being built of buffalo chips. When we later came to the woods and the men brought firewood to old Aunt Hannah, she began to sputter and gave orders: "Go get me some of dem buffalo chips—none of dem green cottonwoods singing for me."

You can imagine what a sight our white city of 250 white-topped wagons made. The wagons were always drawn in a semicircle, or V shape, so that when necessary the cattle could be corralled in this enclosure, and this defended them from the Indians.

Across the gully, almost opposite us, were some Mexicans with their cattle grazing nearby. Two Mexican men and a Mexican boy were herding their cattle. I had just finished my dinner and had picked up my book, Mrs. Hemans's poems, to read.[34] You know we could not carry many books with us, but how we did treasure the few we could tuck in here and there in our ambulance. Screams and cries from the Mexicans drew our attention. The Indians had sprung up from the ground somewhere, evading our pickets, and swooped down into the midst of the Mexicans' cattle, trying to stampede them. Our troops rushed to their rescue and drove the Indians off, but the two men were killed, and with my own eyes I saw the Mexican lad scalped. He had rushed into some tall grass and tried to hide in it, but an Indian spied him, and leaning off his pony, he grabbed him by the hair and cut the whole scalp off. We women hurriedly tore up some clean sheets and ran to the poor lad and offered our services to the surgeon who worked over him. The boy was still alive, but a terrible sight, with head of dripping blood. The men were wrapped in blankets and laid in the ground. A rude cross was erected, and candles burned that night over their graves.

We did not go farther that day, but no one slept that night. All feared a second attack from the Indians, and when I would look out into the night I could see the candles burning there on the graves. It was a melancholy, weird sight that made a lasting impression on me.

Taking the poor Mexican lad along with us, we started onward the following morning. After traveling some several hundred yards we drew up out of the arroyo and there before us lay the plains as level as a floor. The wagons were bunched up, as many as eight abreast, to prevent the Indians making a charge and dividing our forces. We had traveled along perhaps for an hour or so when we observed Indians to the rear and in front of us. They would approach just out of gun reach and tempt our guards to charge against them. As it was, our escort did not dare give chase or attack either those in front or in the rear, for then they would have left the caravan unprotected.

Finally we reached Fort Dodge, near sundown, the Indians following and annoying us to within a mile of the fort. We remained there several days, waiting for an escort. We left the Mexican lad there. He recovered and later went to his home in Mexico.

Traveling in our outfit was a wealthy merchant, Tom Boggs, a schoolmate of my cousin's wife, and hence our families visited back and forth when we camped for the night. Tom Boggs had married the daughter of a very wealthy Mexican, Bovino.[35] One of Bovino's daughters married Maxwell, who came into possession of the Maxwell Grant, through his wife. Tom Boggs was very fond of fine horses and had with him on this trip a strawberry-roan, thoroughbred racehorse. The Mexicans were inveterate gamblers, and Boggs won many a "pile" with his Kentucky thoroughbreds against the Mexican mustangs. Mrs. Boggs's nephew, who had been in school in the East, was returning with them. The boy came down with typhoid fever, but was improving as we all thought, when one night in his delirium he mounted this racehorse and rode off and never was seen again. We waited a whole day, hoping for his return. Our guards could not leave us and search the country for him. We moved on. Five days later the horse dashed into our camp. Dried blood on his flank led us to believe that the Indians had killed the boy while the horse had escaped.

Many are the stories we heard about the prominent people who went up and down the trail and those who had settled in the new country.

Russell and Majors were well-known freighters, supplying Salt Lake, Santa Fe, and Taos. Majors was known as a very religious man and made all his wagon bosses, drivers, et cetera, sign a contract not to use profane language—a thing he finally found out was impossible for a man to do and drive oxen. He then presented each boss with a Bible and ordered no traveling on Sundays. The oxen really needed the rest. The men used to call it signing their souls away to work for Majors and Russell.

Solomon Young was a neighbor of my grandfather, and he went to Salt Lake and opened up a store with a Mr. Byers.[36] Brigham Young, hearing of Solomon Young, went to see him, and Solomon, in order to humor Brigham, helped him trace out that they were distantly related, and so Brigham became a good customer of Solomon's, often visiting in the store.[37]

Young and Byers had brought in a shipment of straw hats, the first in Salt Lake, and the string of straw hats in the store created considerable excitement, especially among the boys. Brigham was making one of his visits in the store when a lad came in and Brigham said: "Give the boy one of those straw hats." Solomon did so, and charged the hat to Brigham Young. Soon another lad came in: "I'd like one of those straw hats," he piped. "Whose boy are you?" Solomon Young asked. "Young's," the lad replied. "What Young's?" "Brigham Young's," said the lad. "Well," said Solomon Young, "who is that man standing right over there?" pointing to Brigham Young. The lad gave a look. "I don't know," he replied. Well, Brigham didn't know him either, but he said: "Give him a hat, and charge it to me."

We continued our journey along the Arkansas River, finding many beautiful camping spots. Frequently the valley would widen out a half to three-quarters of a mile. One afternoon on a very hot, calm, dry day we climbed to the top of a bluff along the river, from which we could see for miles over the level plain. While standing on top of the bluff, we observed a company of some fifteen or twenty cavalry troops mounted on fine, well-groomed steeds. Deliberately they rode along in a northeast direction. Looking farther, we saw a beautiful lake of clear water, along whose margin grew high grasses and weeping willows, with now and then a stately pine tree. When the cavalry reached the lake they rode right into the water, and the horses drank and drank as if ever so thirsty. We could even see the ornaments on the browbands of the horses as they stood knee deep in the water. We could see the soldiers turn their heads in conversation with each other, and while we stood there beholding this realistic scene, all in an instant soldiers, horses, lake, and trees vanished, nothing but the bare plains remaining, and then we realized it was only an optical illusion, a mirage.

Reaching Bent's Fort, we camped there for several days. At last, on the twenty-fifth day of August we reached Pueblo and located there for the winter. My father met me there. Pueblo then consisted of a few log huts with flat mud roofs. One only had a shingle roof—the dry-goods store of Thatcher Brothers.

My cousin's stock cattle we turned loose on the mesa, south of Pueblo, and grazed them over the grounds that are now occupied by the Pueblo Steel Works. In order to while away the time, for we were so homesick, we girls would ride our ponies and look after the stock and round them up. Another pastime for us young people was to secretly play a game with cards. My cousin would never have sanctioned a deck of cards being in his home, nor have allowed us to play, but the deck was there, and the harmless game went on just the same. It is my opinion that the deck of cards in the early pioneer days saved many from sheer desperation, and I feel like saying suicide, it being the only amusement that many had to while away the lonely evening.

I stayed in Pueblo one winter with my cousin, and for some of us it was a gay winter of parties and dances. We were young and happy and without responsibility. One dance in particular lingers in my memory as being so characteristic of our social life. It was no hardship to go eighteen or twenty miles to a party, and this one was at Jude Henry's ranch near Boone.[38] I can still see the promising young men of the day—John Thatcher, O. P. Baxter, Lou Branum—as they swung their partners in the gaily festooned hall.[39] We always danced till daylight to a Mexican violin and a banjo.

Sometimes I think how crude and simple was our life, how different from the life in the seminary, and on my grandfather's farm, yet with it all, there was true courtesy and genuine hospitality.

In those days, the westerners were afforded much pleasure whenever an easterner alighted from a stage coach, especially if he took the form of a dude. Perhaps a little of the same amusement still prevails in the West. Ian Hicklen, who married a third daughter of the wealthy Bovino, and who owned a large tract of land on the Huerfano River, often laughed as he told his story of one easterner dude who was obliged to stop and seek shelter for the night at his ranch. It had been a hard winter for the pioneers, and the table lacked the delicacies that perhaps the "dude" had been accustomed to in the East. Nothing was plentiful that winter but frijoles, and on the table for supper was a large bowl of frijoles, and a bottle of pepper sauce. The beans were offered the easterner, who refused a helping of them with an upturned nose and the comment that he didn't ever eat beans. "Very well then," came back Hicklin, "just help yourself to the pepper sauce." What a roar Hicklin could produce from his listeners as he took off to perfection the tone and manners of the dude.

The following spring, 1867, I came on up towards Cañon City, where I met and married my husband, O. E. Harrington. In the days before the war he had gone from Kentucky to New Orleans, from there into Texas, and in 1860, with a company of twenty-two men, had driven sixteen hundred head of cattle from Texas on up into Colorado, entering near Las Animas, then following the Arkansas River to Cañon City, wintered in that neighborhood. Here they divided up the stock, and he drove his share of them on up to California Gulch, where he found a lively market for them.

It was in 1867 that we were married and went to Twin Lakes to the mining camp, Dayton, then flourishing county seat of Lake County.[40] Things were brisk and rustling there then, with three hotels, and needless to say, several saloons. The Westons were in charge of one of the hotels. Later, when the camp went down, they took up land near Buena Vista and built their present home on its site the year Colorado became a state. Later a slice was taken off Lake County and formed Chaffee County, and Buena Vista became the county seat. The mining excitement went to Granite of Chaffee County, and the courthouse followed, making it a county seat of Lake County.

We then moved to Granite.[41] Near Granite, where Clear Creek empties into the Arkansas, was a thriving mining settlement called Georgia Bar, nearly all the miners being Georgians.[42]

It was in 1868 that we located in Adobe Park, taking up a preemption claim of 360 acres. This was ten years before there was any Salida. The present site of Salida was a soapweed park.

Our first home was a cabin built where the country farmhouse now stands. This ground was later sold to the county, and we built the home that now stands on the Harrington Ranch, in 1880. Twenty-nine years we lived in this house with only one death, my father's, no births, and no marriages. Our land also included Fairview Cemetery. This land, eighty acres, was sold to the Fairview Cemetery Association, and one-half foot of water was included. This was the only cemetery within miles that had water rights.

These were years, you must bear in mind, before there was a railroad into the valley.[43] We went to Centerville to a little store for minor supplies.[44] The stock of that store could have been hauled off in one white-top wagon. Twice a year, spring and fall, we made trips to either California Gulch or to Cañon City for supplies. It was quite an event in our lives, for days before starting there was cooking to be done to last on the trip. We packed up, as if starting overland, for there were no hotels to stop in over night. We camped. It took two whole days to reach Cañon City.

Being the only woman for miles around us, it is needless to say that there were times when I longed for women companionship. There was always plenty to be done to keep me busy, for those were days when many necessities were made in the home. We made our candles out of deer tallow, for that made a much whiter, finer candle than beef tallow, and it was no effort to get a deer in those days, as they ranged the foothills then.

In the spring of 1875 we put in forty acres of wheat. That may not seem to many as an abundance of wheat to plant, but when we consider that we were working new ground and paying ten cents a pound for seed, you can imagine how we looked forward to our wheat crop. It grew beautifully and was so promising, so tall that it hid me when I walked through it. Then, on the fifth of August we noticed a heavy dark mass hanging in the sky and approaching. Later, as the mass hung over us, the grasshoppers began to drop and drop, covering the earth. The plague was upon us. All the wheat was destroyed, the cabbage all eaten, and the crops of the whole valley literally eaten up. They deposited their eggs, and the years of 1876–1877 were fruitless. Many abandoned their claims, having no stock to carry them through. Food values were high. We have sold many a pound of butter for a dollar. Don't get alarmed over undue profit; on the other hand, we paid from twelve to twenty dollars a hundred for flour, sixty cents a pound for coffee, et cetera.

Every fall the Indians, Uncompahgre Utes, gathered in our valley, coming for their annuities from the government, which were dispensed by the Burnetts on their ranch near Poncha.[45] One of their favorite camping posts, as they came down the river, was opposite our ranch where the Ohio and Colorado smelter now stands. They often had with them buckskins to trade or sell, or to gamble. The squaws prepared the buckskins, but the men disposed of them. Many a time we have watched their horse and pony races, which they indulged in while waiting for the day to come to "get their presents." The annuities were paid in October, but they began to gather in our neighborhood in August. Each Indian taking part in the race would have his buckskins and trophies, or whatever he could lay his hand upon, in a pile out in the road where the race was to take place. The loser had his pile carried over and placed on top of the winner's pile. Then the loser would go rummage for more things to wager. A great deal of shouting and yelling, with such yells as only Indians can give, accompanied the start and finish of the racing and the bickering that followed.

Yes, the Indian was friendly, though at times troublesome.

One October we went to Burnett's ranch to see the Utes receive their presents from Governor Hunt, as they said.[46] For their land they received flour, sugar, dry goods, blankets, trinkets, old uniforms left over from the war, and so many head of cattle. Now, the government's instructions were to pay the Indians with cattle, that you could call cattle, allowing a reasonable price to be paid for them. It was not much wonder that the Indians were dissatisfied and angry that day, for the cattle were cheap Mexican scrubs—all head and horns. The flour was the cheapest and poorest to be had. Nothing came up to their expectations. Someone was robbing them; the Burnetts had nothing to do with the providing, they simply stored the things for the government. Shavano, the war chief, was present and was very angry.[47] If things had been left to him, there would have been a fight or massacre. I am afraid if I had been an Indian I would have felt as he did—ready to fight for a "square deal."

However, Ouray, the chief, was a fine-looking man, dressed up in a U.S. officer's uniform, but with a red blanket thrown over his shoulders. The government men kept him appeased with presents and promises, and he addressed his tribe for an hour, cooling and calming them. How I wish I could tell you what he said! It must have been a wonderful address from the effects it had, for they departed in peace. I remember they were given some axes, which they turned over to the squaws, they having no use for them. One poor squaw came running into Mrs. Burnett's house, crying: "Me no Governor Hunt's present." Throwing back her blanket, she showed us a string around her neck with an open-end thimble dangling on the end of it. That was her present, which was "no present" to her.

Shavano and Ouray were brothers-in-law, both being educated in the Sister School in Mexico. Both could read and write the English language. Shavano always stood when he prayed, but Ouray always knelt as his religious Catholic training taught him.

Our valley was nothing more than a pioneer's settlement until the approach of the civilizer—the railroad. Both the Atchison, Topeka and Santa Fe [AT&SF] and the Durango and Rio Grande [D&RG] Railway Companies desired to build into the valley by way of the Royal Gorge. (Cleora was laid out by the AT&SF Railway as their townsite, but after considerable litigation and almost a pitched battle between the Rio Grande and Santa Fe forces near Cañon City, the D&RG won out in the courts, gaining control of the right of way through the Royal Gorge. The following year it extended its lines into the valley and Salida was selected as the new townsite.)[48] Captain Blake, after whom the Blake Block is named, was the first postmaster.[49] Shortly afterwards, the railroad company established its shops here, and it rapidly developed into the flourishing town.

Poncha was a well-established town long before either Cleora or Salida came into existence.[50] James True came into the valley from Colorado Springs in 1874, bought the McPherson claim, laid out the town of Poncha, and opened up a general store.[51] A man by the name of Jackson built the Jackson Hotel; Davenport started a lumberyard; other stores followed, and soon there was a prosperous town. When the railroad was built into Poncha in 1880 it was the most promising town in the valley, and it looked for a while as if Salida might be moved up there. After the railroad was continued over Marshall Pass, however, the town gradually declined, and Salida gained the ascendancy.

A fire destroyed most of the town in 1882, and it has never recovered.[52] It continued to decline until now there is left only a general store and a few dwellings.

Mary R. Goff, Delta County [365-19].

Interviewer: J. W. Taylor.

My name is Mary R. Goff, [I] was born in Morgan County, 1860. Am a cousin of Jeremiah Rusk, first secretary of agriculture.[53]

My father's family came from there to Osage County, Kansas, in 1870 and preempted land on the Sac and Fix Agency and erected the first sawmill in that county and the section lines were not surveyed.

At ten years of age, I went to school in a schoolhouse twelve by fourteen, no desks, the room was crowded. The next year we went to a school in the room of a house built for Indians, a three-months' term in summer and the same in winter. In those schools I finished the eighth grade and then attended a school for one year where higher branches were taught. I then attended the first teacher's institute in the county and received a second grade certificate to teach and the next year a first grade. I taught for three years at this place, then married in 1871. The country teachers received twenty-five dollars per month.

We came to Lander, Wyoming, where my husband was foreman for a big cattle company. We moved to Meeker, where I taught the first school in Rio Blanco County, length of term three months, salary thirty dollars, which exhausted all the money. There were but five pupils in this school, the girls all named Maud.

My husband carried the mail from Meeker to Glenwood for two years, carried it on horseback. It took three days to make the trip; he stayed at the Gersons' ranch each night gone. Then he bought horses and sold them again in Aspen and other mining towns. He established a trading post at Meeker and bought hides of the Indians and whites, who slaughtered so many deer that Colorado passed a law that green hides could not be shipped from the state.[54] Then he established a trading post down the White River a few miles from the Colorado line where he established a lucrative trade with Indians for hides and furs for ten years. He established this post in 1893.

The government had stocked the Uintah Agency with cattle; Mr. Goff bought and shipped those cattle.

Our relations with those Indians, they were principally Colorow's renegades.[55]

These Indians always came to our post just after their payday, and they would stay for weeks and gamble. Cowboys would want to gamble with them, which my husband would not allow. Fifteen miles above us was a whiskey joint where they obtained whiskey, where after selling it they would not permit them to drink it there; this made trouble for us for two years as they many times under its influence became dangerous.

In the fall of 1887 an event occurred that might have caused another massacre at Meeker. These Indians had the privilege of hunting deer and elk each fall in the mountains above Meeker. An Indian was accused of stealing a horse. The sheriff went to arrest him with a posse. It was afterward ascertained he had not done so, and the Indians refused to give the horse up. The sheriff tried to force them, the young bucks were so angry that the sheriff came to Meeker without the horse, and it was afterward proved that outlaw white men put up a job to run the Indians out in order that they might steal their horses and sheep which they drove with them on those hunting expeditions. Everyone was alarmed; the Indians massed twelve miles down the river, the governor sent in Major Leslie with the militia with the assistance of citizens of Meeker; a battle here occurred in which one white man was killed and a dentist, Doctor Dumont, was shot through the ribs but finally recovered.

Chipeta and her brother had a home fifteen miles below our post, and owned cattle, horses, and sheep, and through his dishonesty this woman lost her part in the property.[56] When Ouray died, he had a thousand dollars in gold which he had kept for her which was the amount she had expended in this enterprise.

When Chipeta came to the post, she came to our place and visited with me; she was very sociable and enjoyed talking with me. One night Colorow's old followers got drunk and became dangerous. Chipeta made them leave the premises.

The Utes claim that my son is the only white man that can speak the whole Ute language; he was forty-nine, March 3, 1934. I am sending a picture of Indians who belong to Colorow's old band.

Henry Wildhack, [of] Meeker, can verify this.

Mrs. Dock Wade, Delta County [365-12]. January 15, 1934, at Cedaredge, Colorado.

Interviewer: J. W. Taylor.

My name is Mrs. Dock Wade. I was born in Kansas in 1852. I came from that state to Colorado in 1876 and arrived at La Veta. I and my husband together with William Haney and family, Henry Holliday and family, arrived here the twentieth day of June. We were out of money, which we had to have to pay our way through the toll gates in order to reach Ouray so our men all having ox teams, two yoke to the wagon, hired to a sawmill company for a month to haul logs to the mill.[57]

After this we traveled by way of Fort Garland and Del Norte over Wagon Wheel Gap to Lake City.[58] Part of the road was almost impassable; the men had to drive the oxen, we women drove the cows on foot. At Lake City we stopped a month, and my husband and Henry Holliday rode over the Horse Thief Trail to Ouray to find a route over which we could pass with our teams. They found the route impassable, but while absent they explored the Dallas Valley and the beautiful park below Ouray. This land was south of the south line of the Uncompahgre Ute Reserve. They believed the land to be fertile and easily watered and great prospects for the future mining prospect for Ouray to become a great mining center where all products of the farm could be sold.

So we three families immigrated to that part of the country. To get there we traveled over dangerous roads. Our two yoke of oxen went over a cliff; one ox was killed.

We arrived at our destination at last and took up 160 acres of land on the beautiful Dallas Creek, seventeen miles from Ouray, built a log cabin in which we wintered; the weather was so mild that our cows and oxen wintered on the hillsides. Mr. Wade had to leave me here during that winter seventeen miles from a neighbor or settlement all alone with my little five-year-old daughter and a six-weeks-old baby boy. He was gone ten weeks. I chopped my wood and tended the stock. His earning enabled us to put out a crop of potatoes, beans, cabbage, turnips, parsnips, and onions which we sold in the fall of '77 in Ouray.

One night during that winter I was aroused by the bellowing of our only cow; I took up a rifle and arriving at the corral, I found her thrown down by a mountain lion, which soon would have killed her, but I shot the beast and saved the cow and have the animal's hide, which is made into a rug.

One day I was hoeing in our garden when a band of Utes led by the renegade Washington, meanest of his tribe, rode up to our cabin and demanded food and my last sack of flour.[59] I stood them off with my rifle, my little girl and baby being behind me. The renegade insisted on taking the food, and I do not know what would have happened had not Henry Holliday, William Haney, and Mr. Reed arrived on the spot which caused the Indians to leave.

We here made success of farming, but my husband, through speculation and gambling in mining stocks, lost out. In 1900 we moved to Delta County.

Ada B. Sittser, Arapahoe County [358-34]. March 12, 1934.

Interviewer: Leslie F. Paull.

I was born in St. Louis, Missouri, in 1869. My father's name was John C. Johnston. He was then engaged in buying and shipping horses and mules. Most of these went to Chicago, which was then a very rapidly growing city. But then came the great Chicago fire in October 1871. After that the demand for horses and mules became so small that he abandoned it.

In 1873 he brought his family to Denver by way of Cheyenne. Having no other occupation, he began washing gold in the Platte River. All the rest of his life he followed the occupation of mining. From Denver every day he worked a little farther upstream and a little farther away from home, and finally was so far away that in July 1874 he brought us to Littleton.[60] We lived in the house which still stands at number 255 North Curtis.

Soon after we came to Littleton, he turned to prospecting in the mountains. He was too restless to stay long in one place. He located and established many claims, but never did much in the way of development. Instead, he sold out for what he could get, which was often a very small sum in proportion to the value.

He joined the Cripple Creek boom in 1889 and was for some time in partnership with J. C. Mitchell there.[61]

The opening of the Klondike took him to Alaska in 1899. He came back with more than three thousand dollars' worth of gold mostly in nuggets. I still have the leather pouch in which he transported a part of this gold.

During his long periods of absence his family remained in Littleton. There were nine of us children. I began to go to school when I was five years old. My first teacher was Miss Clorinda Cornell, who afterwards became Mrs. Cole.

In 1886, I was married to Charles W. Sittser of New York. In 1902 Mr. Sittser became the first county clerk of the present Arapahoe County.

Julia E. [Purcells] Cozens, Arapahoe County [358-31]. March 14, 1934.

Interviewed by Leslie F. Paull.

I was born in Peru, Indiana, in 1851. My father's name was James Purcells, a clergyman. We moved to Illinois in 1863.

I came to Colorado to stay with my brother's family. That was in 1880. He had come to Silver Cliff, Custer County, some time previous in the attempt to recover his health.[62]

In Silver Cliff I met Clark Z. Cozens, and in 1882 we were married. In May 1883 we came to Littleton. Mr. Cozens was a carpenter by trade, and during the five weeks we spent there he built a dwelling house on Main Street. It is now a store, Henri's Jewelry Store.

About this time my husband caught the mining fever. He had a brother, William, who owned a hotel and health resort at Fraser. From there, with another brother, Nelson, we went to Williams Fork to try a hand at mining. My husband was sick some of the time, and the mine did not prove very successful, so at the end of summer we moved to Denver, where he resumed his trade of carpentry.

In 1885 we returned to the neighborhood of Littleton, where we bought twenty acres on Dutch Creek, where the Lathrop Turkey Farm is now. We lived there for fifteen years. Mr. Cozens continued to work at his trade and built or helped to build many Littleton houses.

We did not really make a business of farming. Rather, the ranch contributed to our support. About half was kept in alfalfa. We had an orchard and a garden, including strawberries and currants. At one time or another we had from one to five cows, together with chickens; our butter was twenty-two cents a pound, and the same for a dozen eggs.

Most of our activities centered in Littleton. We did our trading there, a large part at J. D. Hill's Store. We went to church there. My two older children were born in Denver, the two younger on the ranch. As they began to go to school I took them to the Littleton school in the morning and went after them in the afternoon.

In 1900 Mr. Cozens built the house which I now occupy. In 1906 he was appointed postmaster of Littleton. He died in 1908, and my daughter, Jessie, served out his term and was reappointed for another term.

HOUSEKEEPING ON WILLIAMS FORK

In the summer of 1883 my husband and his brother Nelson determined to do some mining in Grand County. Some time earlier, and before we had met each other, Mr. Cozens had been there and built a log cabin.

He said that even while he was building it, he had a feeling that he would bring a bride there.

We were in Littleton when the decision was reached. We proceeded to Fraser by way of Denver, Idaho Springs, and over Berthoud Pass. We went from Fraser, up St. Louis Creek, and over to Williams Fork on horseback. My husband insisted on my riding sidesaddle, which, over these rough trails, I found most uncomfortable.

The cabin had but one room, but by means of a curtain of blankets I secured some privacy. All of the cooking I did in an open fireplace. The chimney was made of stone, but the floor of the fireplace was of earth.

Equipment was very limited: a tin bucket, a Dutch oven, a long-handled frypan, tin plates, and tin pans constituted the major part. I was laughed at for slipping in a few teacups and some silverware.

Supplies were also limited in variety. We had flour, ham and bacon, coffee, canned milk and a few other canned goods, white sugar, salt, and dried apples. Very rarely we had potatoes. These supplies came from Georgetown by way of Fraser. Of course the boys secured an ample supply of venison and trout, one or both of which we had daily. We were at too high an altitude for wild fruit, although there was considerable farther down. I do not recall having other game than venison. I was not very fond of it but could eat it. It was always fried, as was the fish. As a rule the meat course was bacon or ham for breakfast, venison for dinner, and fish for supper.

The men chopped the wood and built big fires in the fireplace, so that by the time I was ready to prepare a meal there was a large supply of hot coals. There was some sort of hook in the chimney-place on which to hang the bucket in which we made the coffee. We put the coffee in cold water from the creek, and when it boiled up the second time, we considered it done.

Every meal we had hot biscuits baked in the Dutch oven. Flour, water, bacon fat, and salt made excellent biscuits; we saved the milk for the coffee. The Dutch oven was excellently adapted for baking in a fireplace. It was made of heavy cast iron, with a heavy lid, and stood on three short legs. A handle on the lid enabled me to remove it when hot by means of an iron hook which was kept for the purpose. The oven was placed on a bed of hot coals, and hot coals were placed on the lid. When I baked biscuits or dried apple pie in it, the pan fitted so snugly that I often burned myself trying to pry it out with a knife.

There were brown bears about, and they were not pleasant animals to meet. My brother-in-law went out one morning to trail the horses that had been turned out at night to graze. He had no weapons with him, and a bear treed him and held him there for some time. He got down when the bear wandered away. He ran all the way to the cabin, arriving there in an almost breathless state.

Mrs. William Stewart, Alamosa County [349-25].

Interviewer: C. E. Gibson Jr.

I came to the valley in a wagon in 1878, with my father. In '79 I married William Stewart, who had a ranch on the Rio Grande about a half mile above the mouth of the Conejos.

Mr. Stewart had settled there about 1874 and built a ferryboat, which was used a great deal during the high water of the spring and early summer. I can remember the soldiers from Fort Garland crossing on the boat many times. Mr. Stewart had been a sailor in his youth, which probably explains his interest in the ferry. When he first came to Colorado, he freighted from Pueblo to the San Luis Valley.

The Rio Grande was very different then from now-days and, during the high water in the spring, flooded great stretches of country. We had to lay in enough provisions to see us through the spring, as there was no way to leave the ranch during flood season, except by boat.

Later we ran a store at the ranch and did quite a business with the Mexicans of the old town of La Sauces, which was about a mile and a half south of us.[63]

A man by the name of Dexter bought land and put together a large ranch just to the south of us. He lost it in a gambling game to Bob Austin, who ran a large gambling palace in Denver. Mr. Austin built a fine house and a large barn on the place, and it was the scene of many gay parties of folk from Denver and elsewhere.

I rode horseback a great deal in my younger days, and believe I was as good a hand as most of the cowpunchers. And speaking of cowpunchers, many people seem to have the idea that they were a rough, wild lot. I was around them very often, and ate and worked with them, and never saw one that was not a gentleman, at least while there was a woman present.

My favorite horse was a high-strung half-breed Arabian, which I called Smitty, after the man from whom I got him. He was mighty smart, and well knew the business of handling stock. One time I was driving a workhorse to the ranch from the pasture across the river. The horse bolted as he crossed over, and trying to head him, Smitty stepped into a hole and threw me into the river. He paid no attention to me but went on, herded the workhorse through the barnyard gate, and then returned to the river for me.

Mary Jane Cole, Alamosa County [349-4].

Interviewer: C. E. Gibson Jr.

Father had written to a friend of his who was already in the valley about the opportunities there, and had received such a favorable reply, that on May 26th, 1879, we loaded up our belongings and started west. There were two big wagons with four horses each, and two smaller wagons, with only one team apiece, and a number of loose horses. We had the haying machinery, mowers and rakes, the household goods, and our clothes. The trip was really a lark, and we all enjoyed it, though at Dodge City we were rather nervous when some very rough looking men admired our big Missouri mules. It was rather a relief when we had traveled several days journey from there and still had the mules. We were scared again going through the Indian country in western Kansas, but nothing happened to us.

During the day we mixed the bread in a large tin bucket, let it rise, and then would bake it when we camped for the night. As soon as a stopping place had been decided on, the stove was set off, and the children scurried around for wood or buffalo chips. In the morning we made only enough fire to get a light breakfast so the stove would not be too hot to load. Each of the family had a chair, and Mother and I had a bed in one of the wagons with a spring and mattress.

The day before we left we had a batch of baby chickens hatch, and we took them along. Each night their box was opened and they would run and pick around, perfectly at home. They grew so fast during the six weeks we were on the road that their box had to be enlarged several times. We also had a six-weeks-old colt along, which our neighbors had said would never stand the trip. He did get sore-footed, and we made him some moccasins out of an old pair of shoes. Every two weeks we laid over a day and did the family washing, even scrubbing our chairs and cleaning everything just as if we were at home.

None of us had seen the mountains before, and our excitement was intense when one day far in the distance we saw a low blue line along the horizon. From day to day these grew until at last we reached Pueblo and could see mountains north and south as far as the eye could reach, with Pikes Peak looming white in the haze to the north.

We went through the town of La Veta and camped in the canyon below the Muleshoe curve. While we were there a train came over the pass, and in awe we watched it crawl along the edge of the cliffs, wondering if our friends in Missouri would believe that railroads could be built in such impossible places. There were two tollgates on the Veta Pass road, one on the other side and one at Placer on this side.

On May tenth we camped on the east side of the river, across from

Alamosa. I stayed in camp, but the boys crossed on the railroad bridge which was planked over, and came into town. When they returned they reported it was a pretty tough place, with every other building a saloon.

The next day we went on up the river, crossing near either the Shocks or Dorris Ranch and continuing on south. It was south or west of what is now La Jara that we came to a natural open meadows, and here we camped. All summer we mowed, raked, and stacked hay, moving as the cooler fall weather came on to a small unfinished log cabin, which we chinked and made habitable, on Spring Creek. We had to keep an eye on our loose stock which grazed close by where we worked. When a covered wagon came by the horses would look up, take a few more bites, and then start following after it, as they had been in the habit of doing for the six weeks we were on the road.

In the late fall Father bought a baler, baled the hay, and had no trouble disposing of it to the freighters, at thirty dollars a ton, which, as it had cost nothing but the labor, made a profitable summer. We then moved back to the Rio Grande and Father bought the preemptions on John and Tom Fulcher adjoining the ranch where Al Cole lived.

That winter Father made a trip to the mountains and brought back some wood from which he made a loom. It was the first in this country, so far as I know, and people from miles away brought in rags and we made carpets for them. We were not very impressed with the industry of the people; they didn't bother to raise gardens. I guess we fell into their ways ourselves pretty quick, for the best garden we ever raised was the first year we were on the ranch.

In 1881 Al Cole and I were married. Al raised hay and grain, and in the fall and winter baled hay all over the valley. Adam Shellabarger, Steve Kinney, the Dickey Brothers, Pat Wilkins, and later Billy Adams were some of the men for whom he baled. One time he freighted a load of hay to Leadville which brought him $125 a ton.

In 1891 we opened a store in Alamosa in the Manders block, but a little later, feeling the rent was too high, we bought a piece of ground from Sandy Oliver and put up the building where the Mt. Blanca Drug Store is now located. Here we handled hay, grain, groceries, and some dry goods.

Chapter 3: The South

Pueblo, Otero, El Paso, and Las Animas Counties

This was a terrible year, and I often wonder just how we managed to survive the intense cold, the lack of food, and the great discomforts which our log house afforded.
Cynthia Fisher

At the conjunction of the Arkansas River and Fountain Creek, the site where the city of Pueblo now stands, the men in Zebulon Pike's 1806 expedition into Colorado built a breastwork of logs for shelter and protection. In 1840 the hunter, trapper, and guide Richens Lacy Wootten, known as Dick Wootten, perhaps best known for his building a toll road over Raton Pass, reputedly established a buffalo farm in the area to provide eastern zoos with exotic western bison. Situated at the confluence of two rivers, Pueblo became an important stopping point for travelers. Francis Parkman, author of *The Oregon Trail* (1849), visited in 1846, and explorer and mapmaker John Frémont stopped over in the 1850s. Although a substantial fort was erected in 1842, it was the smelting, coal, and steel manufacturing businesses beginning in the 1880s that made Pueblo Colorado's "second city." With the Colorado Coal and Iron Company, later the Colorado Fuel and Iron Company (CF&I), producing steel, including rails for the railroad industry, the city's success was ensured.[1] Between 1880 and 1890 the population

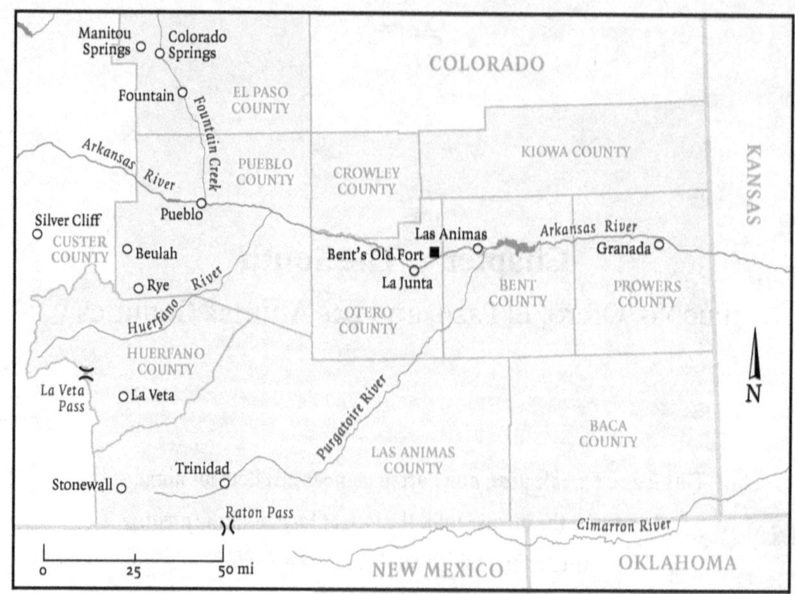
Manitou Springs
Colorado Springs
COLORADO
Fountain
EL PASO COUNTY
Fountain Creek
Arkansas River
PUEBLO COUNTY
CROWLEY COUNTY
KIOWA COUNTY
KANSAS
Silver Cliff
CUSTER COUNTY
Pueblo
Beulah
Las Animas
Arkansas River
Granada
Bent's Old Fort
La Junta
Rye
River
Huerfano
BENT COUNTY
PROWERS COUNTY
OTERO COUNTY
HUERFANO COUNTY
La Veta Pass
La Veta
N
BACA COUNTY
Purgatoire River
LAS ANIMAS COUNTY
Trinidad
Stonewall
Raton Pass
Cimarron River
0
25
50 mi
NEW MEXICO
OKLAHOMA

5. The south

grew from three thousand to twenty-four thousand. Established in 1861, Pueblo County was one of the original seventeen territorial counties in Colorado, with the community of Pueblo as the county seat. El Paso County, established in 1861 and named for "the pass," Ute Pass, was also one of the original seventeen territorial counties. Las Animas County was carved out of the originally huge Huerfano County in 1866, and Otero County, earlier a part of the Cheyenne and Arapaho Indian reservation, was established in 1889.

The eight narratives from these counties demonstrate an interesting progression from the early prairie crossings to daily life in a well-established city. The narratives provide pictures of the western migration from perspectives of the several different women whose early concerns were naturally enough with the dangers of crossing the prairie and with the hardships of the first years after arriving on a homestead. Later narratives describe life in the growing city, nightlife, and social clubs—even the establishment of a city park becomes a topic of importance for one narrator. Marion Russell describes the itinerant life she led as a child before crossing the prairie with her mother and brother, paying their way by boarding other travelers. Mary Hayden gives a vivid account of an attack on her wagon train, and then describes coming upon Bent's Fort in the middle of the night: "Buildings were still burning and everything was ablaze; the night seemed as bright as day. Across a threshold lay the bodies of two men, scalped; beside them a dog howling piteously." One narrator, Nellie Pollock Snyder, mentions the November 29, 1864, Sand Creek Massacre, in which a group of Colorado Volunteers, led by the narrator's grandfather, John Chivington, attacked a settlement of peaceful Arapahos and Cheyennes. Snyder offers a defense of Chivington, reporting that "the tribes of Indians were at that time all hostile" and that the "Santa Fe Trail was literally running with blood." Of that hostility, however, she gives no specific account.

Unlike some other narrators who expound on the beauty of the frontier landscape, these women's attitudes tend for the most part to converge in that they describe the land and the weather as harsh and forbidding, more as distraction or impediment than as inviting beauty. Mary Hayden describes the weather and the frozen mule teams she sees as she crosses the prairie. Cynthia Fisher bemoans the swampy areas, the muddy creeks, and difficult crossings. Even the tall grass is a nuisance. After arriving and establishing a farm, she laments that the severe weather and grasshoppers destroy her crops. Underlying Mary Cox's account is her disappointment with the landscape in general. She describes the West as "the most barren, forsaken country we had ever seen." She attributes the death of her father to the hard work of homesteading, and she declares her homesickness: "Often I wished that I had never left Cincinnati." Cynthia Fisher describes crop damage and a woeful lack of food. She also she recalls that at one point her husband had no shoes. In contrast, Ana Dillon and Mary Cox recount the development of the city, describing their work in hotels and the celebrations in the streets. Dillon's account is especially entertaining given her descriptions of corruption at the city dog pound and the occasional riotous behavior of some of Pueblo's residents.

Field-workers for these counties were A. K. Richeson (Las Animas), Leah M. Ryder (Otero), Elizabeth Cairns (Pueblo), and E. E. Carrington (El Paso). Anna Florence Robison, working primarily in Montezuma County, also contributed with an interview concerning Otero County.

Mrs. R. D. Russell [née Marion Sloan], Las Animas County [359-9]. Trinidad, December 16, 1933.

Interviewer: A. K. Richeson[2]

As early as 1852 with my mother, Mrs. Sloan, and my brother, William, I came the Cimarron Route to Santa Fe and Albuquerque.[3] In 1860 we again came from the east but through Trinidad and over the Raton Pass to Santa Fe. In 1871, having married Richard D. Russell, I came to Stonewall, Colorado, west of Trinidad, to live.[4] At that time we thought we were settling upon government land, but this later was decided by the courts and the government to be part of the Maxwell Grant.[5] However, by purchase and deed I acquired the 160 acres my husband had homesteaded for my own in 1902.[6]

I was born January 27, 1845, at Peoria, Illinois. My father, William Sloan, an army doctor, and mother, Eliza St. Clair, came from Orangeville, Ohio, in Trumbull County. My father died while I was very young, and it was Mother's determination to join her folks then in California. With this purpose in mind she sold her jewelry and started out, but we never reached California.

My only brother, William H. Sloan, was with us in these travels. Afterwards he was a Baptist Missionary in the western part of this country. He was later sent to Mexico and India.[7]

In 1848 we went to St. Louis, and it was here at the age of three that I was lost. A large Negro found me and restored me to my mother. My mother was married again, and we went to Fort Crawford in Wisconsin. My stepfather was in some way connected with the army, but not as a soldier. From here we went to Fort Snelling some six miles from St. Paul, Minnesota.[8] In 1850 my mother left her second husband and determined to go to California.

While at Fort Snelling I can remember a treaty made between the Chippewas and Sioux Indians. It seems as though the Chippewas came to the fort for protection, since the Sioux had broken a treaty. The soldiers placed cannons between the two tribes. After the new treaty was signed the Indians staged a huge dance in the hills nearby, and this was visible from the fort. My memory was good at this age I presume on account of the ever present danger.

In 1850 we—Mother, Brother William, and myself—came to Independence, Missouri. The following year my mother while at St. Jo heard that a government train was to set out for the West.[9] By furnishing board for three army officers, we were given transportation. It was while in Independence that we boarded with Dr. Twining at the City Hotel. He was an uncle of Jesse James.[10] Also I can remember the burning of tar barrels for disinfectant against cholera prevalent at that time.

When we were leaving Leavenworth in August 1852, my mother's kitchen stove was left behind (on the prairie) because it would not fit in the wagon. We went by the Cimarron Route to Santa Fe, New Mexico. The train was a government one, but a citizens' train under the leadership of F. X. Aubrey accompanied us. The wagon master for our train was Mr. Hamilton. We reached Santa Fe after passing Fort Mackay on the Arkansas River in the later fall of '52.[11] Mr. Aubrey took a packtrain on, but since there were no wagons we could not go, and he promised to take us with him on his next trip. However, when he returned in '54, he was killed. The assistant editor of the paper in Santa Fe put a joke in the paper about him. Major Weightman was the editor and they met in a saloon. Under the influence of liquor they quarreled and Weightman taking Aubrey's gun killed him. Weightman was later acquitted of the crime.[12]

In the spring of '53 we went to Albuquerque and stayed at Carr's Ranch, one-half mile from town. Colonel Ed Sumner—afterwards General—during the Civil War lived here also.[13] My mother had a mahogany box, eight by twelve inches, in which she kept her money and jewelry. This box was stolen, and she found her letters in a ditch back of the house. A Mexican lad who worked for Lieutenant Sturges—later General—had been put up to the job by some soldiers. Sumner showed her where her watch chain was buried under a soldier's tent. This chain and her letters were all that she recovered. In 1854 we returned to Santa Fe, where my mother kept boarders for the next two years. Then we returned to Westport Landing, Kansas City.[14]

In 1860 we left Westport Landing to return to Santa Fe. This time we decided to come a northern route over Raton Pass.[15] Soldiers under the command of Colonel Crittenden were going to California.[16] We camped on the Picketwire River near Trinidad.[17] I can remember that then there were no houses where Trinidad now is. It was here that my brother traded ammunition for venison.

When we were living in Santa Fe, I went to school at the Convent of the Sisters of Loretto.[18] Mother Madaglen was in charge. Some of the sisters were Ann Joseph, Joana Rosana, and Monica Katheryne. Two of these sisters and Joana were sent in 1863 to Denver to open a convent there. I have my bill from the convent to my brother. Board and tuition was $35.00, washing $4.80, bedding $2.40, guitar lessons $9.00. This bill was for a period from April 25 to July 15, 1852.

It was during the Civil War in 1865 that I was married to Richard D. Russell. He had enlisted in Colorado D, first serving at Fort Union under General Carleton.[19] He also served under Colonel Alexander, who was in charge of the soldiers sent to Trinidad during the Indian uprising of 1865. Lieutenant Russell was of Company H at Fort Union.[20]

Orders were given in May 1865 for Kit Carson to march eastward along the Santa Fe Trail, which passed Fort Union, and to establish a cantonment for the protection of the wagon trains and stages along this route to the end of the railroads in Missouri and Kansas. I did not go to this new port of defense until two weeks after the troops left Fort Union. I was then twenty years of age.

Kit Carson, who marched from Fort Union with his regulars and selected the site, would not let me make the initial trip in May, although I begged that I might accompany my husband and laughed at the dangers. It was perhaps two weeks later that upon the soldiers' arrival at Cedar Bluffs that he ordered Lieutenant Russell to proceed with some wagons and an escort to Fort Union. It was on his return that I accompanied him to this new Camp Nichols.

On our arrival in June 1865, we lived in army tents until our houses were completed. The latter consisted of stone walls, built one-half underground and one-half aboveground. Logs held up a dirt or mud roof. There were about three hundred soldiers at Camp Nichols under Colonel A. H. Pfeiffer.[21]

It was an imposing sight to watch the arrival of a long procession of covered wagons with their massive clanking wheels and high bodies, to listen to the cries of men, to follow the wagon leader as on horseback he rode up and down the line urging forward the tired animals. They had a reason to be tired, for some of these wagons carried as much as five thousand pounds. Also very interesting was the watching of them making camp as sunset heralded the approach of nightfall and great danger from the Indians. Invariably the wagons were placed in a circle, and this took quite a long time for oxen move very slowly.

The fare at Fort Nichols consisted of hardtack, bacon, beans, beef, flour, sugar, and coffee. There were no vegetables or even dried fruit. Once in a while some canned fruits and foods were brought in, and these sold at a very high premium. Our only stoves were Dutch ovens.

Carson was a short man, slow of speech, and very quiet in his manners. His English was crude. The last time that I saw him was as he, leading his horses, stopped at our tent, the morning he set out for Fort Union and leaving us, to bid me good-bye, and again to warn me not "to go out thar," pointing off to the Santa Fe Trail, as the Indians might get me.

In 1866 Mr. Russell was mustered out of the army as a captain. We moved to Tecolote, eleven miles from Las Vegas, New Mexico. There he was in the mercantile business.

We moved to Stonewall, Colorado, in the fall of 1871; this land was known as St. John Valley, named after Don Juan Gutiérrez.[22] George Storz, also from Tecolote, followed us shortly before Christmas. Mr. Storz set up the first gristmill, the first fish hatchery in Colorado, and the highest fruit-bearing orchard, elevation 7,600 feet. Before our arrival Mr. Stoner had a log cabin next to the wall, but had abandoned it.[23] We were the first settlers, and daughter Ella (Mrs. J. E. Coe), born in 1872, was the first child to be born in that region.[24]

Other settlers coming shortly after we did were Frank Chaplin; John

Donohue a blacksmith; Billy Bourroughs, now with Branson-Griswold Hardware, Trinidad; Mr. Fielding; John and Anderson Duhling, 1882 and 1886; Mr. Burnet; Fisher; Frank Kerr; R. R. Pooler; J. P. Coe; Torres; and Vallijes.[25]

We thought that we were settling on government land, and received our papers from the land office in Pueblo. The north boundary of the Maxwell Grant as we knew it was the crest of the Raton Mountains. Thus all the water draining south towards the Canadian River was claimed by Maxwell.

In years to follow, the purchasers of the Maxwell Grant claimed the northern boundary to be Fisher's Peak, and thus all of the Stonewall country. With their influence and money they were able to win out in the courts. My husband lost his life on August 25, 1888, defending his home. O. P. McMains worked for the settlers but to no avail.[26]

After the trouble D. D. Finch went to Mr. Shunberg and asked him to give me a clear title to our homestead. They gave me a deed to eighty acres, and after two years they allowed me to pay the government the price of $1.25 an acre for the other eighty acres. This was in 1902. Mr. Chaplin received $1,200.00 for his improvements on the land. Anderson Duhling paid $3.60 an acre for his. Torres and Vallijes bought their lands.

My children were:

Hattie—buried at Fort Bascom, New Mexico
Kate—Mrs. Harvey, Folsom, New Mexico
George Russell, Trinchera, Colorado
Ella—Mrs. J. E. Coe, La Veta, Colorado
Harold D. Russell, Stonewall, Colorado
Oliver E. Russell
Marion—Mrs. (Lige) E. A. Duhling, Trinidad, Colorado
Charles Clifford, deceased
Richard Raymond, deceased

Hattie L. Hedges Trout, El Paso County [345-11].

Interviewer: E. E. Carrington

Interviewer's note: A story of other years in Colorado Springs and the Pikes Peak region, written from memory by Hattie L. Hedges Trout for the El Paso County Pioneer Association and presented to them Tuesday evening, October 10, 1933.

I came to Colorado with my parents and sisters in September of 1866; came in a stagecoach with four big fine horses which were changed for fresh ones every ten miles, all the way. They would have the horses all harnessed ready to hitch on when we stopped, then away we would go for another ten miles.

Lunches could be obtained at the stage stations but were very high-priced. A cup of tea or coffee would be one dollar.

We had lovely weather and a nice trip. It took seven days and nights to come from Quincy, Illinois, where we lived, to Denver. We were quite tired after the long journey. My father was not very well, that being one reason for our coming to Denver; also he had a brother here who urged him to come and try Colorado climate. He was greatly benefited and lived to be nearly eighty-five years old.

There was not much of Denver at the time. We lived in a little house near where the Union Station now stands.

Higher Prices Then: Everything was very high-priced those days. Flour was ten dollars per hundred; quart cans of fruit or vegetables were fifty cents per can; soap, twenty-five cents per bar, and everything else according. Day board was ten dollars per week, and later in the season when snow came they paid one dollar per hour for shoveling snow from walks and streets.

We lived in Denver about two years, then came to Colorado City in 1868.[27] There were very few houses here at that time and none in the

Colorado Springs or Manitou—just a slab shed over the soda spring.

We came here in the stagecoach from Denver and stopped at an old frame hotel that stood on the corner of Colorado Avenue and Twenty-eighth Street, where the home of the Stockbridges now is located.

Those were very exciting days as the Indians were on the warpath here.[28] People for miles around came and brought their families for protection from them, and we were forted up in the old Anway house which was located at 2618 West Pikes Peak. As I remember, it was a log house with stairway going up the outside. It still stands but has been remodeled and sided up and painted so no one could recognize it now.

We were with others in the fort while my father with other men stood guard on the hill north of town.

We were living here when the three boys were killed by the Indians near where the Antlers Hotel now stands. They were herding cattle when they were watched by the Indians from the hills. The oldest of the boys was young Everhart. I believe he was twenty-one years old. The Robbins boys were much younger. They were brought here and laid out in the old log building which was the first statehouse. It was located on the north side of Colorado Avenue between Twenty-sixth and Twenty-seventh Streets. I can just remember of going with my sister to see the bodies, as everyone was flocking there so horrified and grieved over it. Oh, they were a terrible sight, scalped and speared, and they had placed their guns to their eyes and blew them out, and faces and necks all powder burnt. Even after all these years I dread to recall the awful sight, for at that time I hid behind my sister after a horrified glance at them.

Oh, those were terrible times for everyone, so filled with fear and dread. The Indians also stampeded stock. The trail where they crossed Sand Creek east of Colorado Springs with the stock they drove away was a mile wide.

Different tribes of Indians scalped differently. Some just took a very small round piece of the scalp; others took all over, just leaving few hairs in front of the ears.

The Indians at that time attacked an old man by the name of Baldwin but found he had been scalped before so left him to die as they thought, but he lived many years after that and finally met death falling into a vat of an old slaughterhouse.[29]

After some time we moved to Pueblo and later to Wet Mountain Valley, three miles south of Rosita.[30] My father helped dig the first prospect hole there, which I believe never developed anything to the company who were interested in it. While living there we had another experience with the Indians. My father was working in a livery stable in Denver as there was no employment for him at home, so Mother and we three children were living there on the ranch alone. The nearest neighbor was over a mile away.

One day an Indian came galloping up on his horse and stopped and asked Mother for biscuit. She gave him all she had; then he looked at my sister, who was fourteen years old at that time. He said, "Nice squaw. You give me squaw; I give you fifty buckskins for squaw." You can imagine the fear of my mother, thinking he might take my sister anyway. He said to Mother, "You got man?" She said, "Yes, back here." She was afraid to let him know she was alone, but after awhile he got on his horse and rode away. What a relief to us, but Mother lived in fear and dread until my father came home.

After a time we moved to Cañon City, then to Pueblo for a time, then we moved to a ranch on the divide, fifteen miles northeast of Palmer Lake, where I met and was married to Mr. Trout, January, 1, 1880. After a few years there we went to Denver on a farm six miles west of Denver, then September 15, 1887, we came back to Colorado City.

Very lively times here then as the Colorado Midland had built their road through to the Western Slope.[31] Everyone was at work and happy; no depression here then. We had to live in a tent until we built our home at 713 South Twenty-fifth Street. There were no houses to rent. Men were employed in the Midland shops days, and we could hear hammering all times of the night, building their houses to live in.

Anthony Bott was called very benevolent and was called the "Poor Man's Friend." He and many of the pioneer residents have gone to their last reward, which, if just, will be great. Clem Kinsman, another pioneer who had lived here most of his life, in speaking of Colorado City one time, told me somehow he could sleep better if he laid down in the shadow of Pikes Peak. He, too, has passed away.

Anthony Bott's log house, where he lived in Indian times, still stands. It is located just a few blocks west of my home on St. Anthony Street. They say there are portholes in it so they could protect themselves from the Indians by shooting through them if they came here.

I still live in my little home that was built in 1887—forty-seven years ago. I love it and dear old Colorado where I have lived most of my life, and it is my desire to end my days here and be laid to rest with my loved ones in the shadow of Pikes Peak.

I am a member of the El Paso County Pioneer Association and the Half-Century Club, and I enjoy their meetings and look forward with pleasure to them and the reminiscences of the early days of the pioneers of Colorado City and Colorado Springs.

Mrs. Will Mattingly, Otero County [360-3].

Interviewer: Leah M. Ryder

Interviewer's note: Mrs. Mattingly was a daughter of Mr. and Mrs. George Spane, and came with them to Colorado in the early seventies in a covered wagon. They went first to a ranch near the present site of Beulah. Mrs. Mattingly was very small then and only knows of the pioneer days in Colorado by hearing her mother and father speak of them. That first winter was very severe, and once when Mr. Spane was out hunting a snowstorm arose and became so intense that it prevented his return to the ranch. Mrs. Spane and the small children were "snowed-in" for eighteen days, and to keep their cow from starving, Mrs. Spane cut

> open a mattress and fed the cow the corn shucks with which it had been filled. A year or so later Mr. Spane moved his family to Pueblo, where he secured employment for a railroad company, and in 1875, when the Kansas Pacific Railroad was in the course of construction to La Junta, he was sent to that point to work, and moved his family there. Later Mrs. Spane's mother, Mrs. Nancy Wickham, and her other daughters came to La Junta from Kansas, and operated a boardinghouse here. Mrs. Mattingly's memories date from the time the Spane family moved to La Junta. At that time the town was very small, only consisted of a few buildings, and at first they had to get their supplies from Pueblo. They lived in part of a store building.

The schoolhouse then seemed a long distance from town, across the prairie, and the children always took their lunch. We sat on logs and used dry-goods boxes for desks. In those days there were no playground activities or athletics upon which the excess energy of the boys could be expended, and the chief pastime among the boys was fighting. The girls had no playthings, and most of our play time was spent outdoors playing the rough games with the boys, and we all became regular tomboys. Game was plentiful then and occasionally wild animals ventured near the town. Once a skunk came into the schoolroom. The boys killed it, but the struggle to do so resulted in school being dismissed, and we had a vacation for a while. When a regular school was built, we had desks and seats.

Nellie Pollock Snyder, Otero County [360-32].

Interviewer: Leah M. Ryder

> *Interviewer's note:* The manuscript of this was given to me for copying by Mary Randall Hindman, Rural Route, Cortez, Colorado. Perhaps you [LeRoy Hafen] have this material elsewhere, but I include it in case you do not. The explanations which head the manuscript are Mary Hindman's.

This essay was submitted by Mary Randall-Hindman, a granddaughter of Sarah Chivington, in June 1933 and was awarded first prize by the judges of the Colorado History Essay contest of the Colorado Federation of Women's Clubs at Denver in July 1933.

"Recollections of the Pioneer Life of Sara Chivington Pollock, The First White Woman to Gaze upon the San Juan Basin."[32] Told by Nellie Pollock Snyder.

My grandfather Colonel John M. Chivington was one of the very early pioneers of Denver. He was commander of the military district of Colorado at the time when the state was called Jefferson Territory.[33] He held a pastorate in Denver, was a Methodist minister. He was coroner of Denver at one time, was also a charter member of the Masonic lodge, and was at one time grand master of the same. He was called the Hero of Glorieta and is supposed to have saved the West for the Union in the battle of that place with Southern troops in the Civil War.[34]

Colonel Chivington was very unjustly misrepresented in reports sent in to Washington after the battle of Sand Creek, these reports being original with some officers in the army and caused by military jealousy. Those who are interested in learning the true facts of this battle and results of the military investigation of the same may find the true facts in the book *The Indians of the Pike's Peak Region*, written by Irving Howbert of Colorado Springs, who served in the army in those days and was personally acquainted with the military men involved on both sides.[35]

To go on with pioneer incidents, Colonel Chivington's daughter Sarah became the girl-bride of Thomas Pollock in 1860 at Denver. Thomas Pollock was in command of a wagon train bound for the Southwest in quest of adventure and exploration preparatory to settlement. She was only sixteen years old on starting on that memorable trip, the happenings of which she was never able to forget. It was her wedding trip and a more colorful one than a girl of today would care to take. She was the first white woman in southwestern Colorado in the section that is known today as the San Juan Basin.

They left Denver with a large wagon train, and of that train there was nothing left except two yoke of oxen when they returned about two years later. I do not know how many graves were left in those lonely hills. I have heard her tell of men killed in their beds under the wagon in which she was sleeping. The tribes of Indians were at that time all hostile, and they never knew when the war whoop would sound.

I have heard her tell many things of that trip, of the dreadful winter and the terrible storms. She was at one time nearly frozen to death, and they cut to pieces the wagon boxes to make wood for fire to keep her warm. She told me she saw my father drive his men around the wagons and whip them with a black-snake whip to keep them moving so they would not freeze to death. Several times on that trip they were compelled to take the wagons to pieces and lower them over cliffs and bluffs.

She told me of her first impressions on seeing what is now Pagosa Springs. I later looked at that little town and big boiling spring and tried to picture to myself how that camp of white men and one woman must have looked in that lonely and dangerous country when they never knew from one moment to the next when they must fight for their lives. It is a lovely place now, even after so-called civilization has robbed it of much of its original beauty. What must it have been in all of its wild glory?

Mother said they had a laugh at one of the men who thought that nice hot water hole an ideal place to launder his shirt—a woolen one. Of course it simply fell to pieces when he took it out of the spring—no small loss at that time, I assure you.

Later on, this party was for some time with Baker's party in Baker's Park, where the town of Silverton now stands.[36] She told me also of their camp at Baker's Bridge up the Animas Valley above the present city of Durango, where in later years they settled on a ranch, and it was here she spent her last days, also raised her two children, a boy, Louis, and a girl, Ruth, by her second husband, William Girardin, whom she married some years after my father's death in 1876.

My father, Thomas Pollock, located in that vicinity first with the purpose in mind of starting a town, and in fact did organize a town either there or on what is known as Cascade Creek—I am not sure which.[37] I am told that an old town-book corroborates this story, but I do not know this positively. One of Baker's men whom Mother knew well is buried a few miles from Rockwood. His grave is between Castlerock Spring and the old beaver lake.

I have seen this grave, as it is on a ranch that my oldest sister and family later lived on. The grave of a poor cowboy who was hanged in Silverton is there also. I knew his sister when I was there. I have stood by that pretty little lake and watched beaver and thought what a wonderful country it must have been in those early days.

To go on with my story, the Utes and the Navajos were fighting among themselves. It was the last big fight between those two tribes, and the Utes had whipped the Navajos to the San Juan River for good. The Utes had in the course of the war captured four little Navajo children and were going to burn them alive. My father felt that he could not stand that, so he bought the four children. He gave sixteen hundred dollars in money and goods for them. He gave three of them to army friends. I understand one of the little girls was given to an army colonel and later killed by Indians with all his family near Colorado Springs. I do not know whether this is true or not, as I have no proof of it.

My parents kept one boy. He was named John Milton Pollock and was raised to manhood in my father's family and was given the same love and care that was bestowed upon the white children of the home. I do not remember him so very well. I just have a dim recollection of him as a tall, dark, handsome boy over six feet tall and straight as an arrow.

To resume, my father was out of supplies and must have food and bedding and other needs for that long, hard trip back to Denver; so he left my mother in charge of the Navajo chief and started on that long trip, going first to Santa Fe, New Mexico. He was gone three months, and my mother stayed behind, a hostage held by those dark, sinister people. But they were good to her. Only once was she molested. She was ironing one day, a flat iron being one of the "luxuries" she had been able to bring along, when a young buck walked near her and spat contemptuously. Her Chivington blood rushed to the surface at the insult, and before she took time to consider, she shoved that hot iron in his face. In a moment the realization of her act came over her, and she thought "Now all is lost." But, strange to say, the Indians hooted the foolish boy out of camp.

The Santa Fe Trail was literally running with blood. No wagon train got through without fighting. Pearly Watson was my father's guide to Santa Fe. He was afterward stage driver on the old Rico stage line and later turned stage robber.

After my father's return from Santa Fe came the long, hard trip back across the mountains to Denver with danger all the way. My oldest sister was born in Denver shortly after the trip and was named Jessie Fremont Pollock, being named for Colonel Frémont's wife.[38]

My people were close friends with the Frémonts, Kit Carson, and Buffalo Bill Cody. My mother told me of visiting in the Carson home at Taos, New Mexico.

My father was among the first peace officers of Denver, was in fact I think the first sheriff of Arapahoe County.

My mother accompanied my father back to Springfield, Ohio, to visit his people in later years. In all, she made the trip across the plains four times in wagon trains. My father served through the years of the Civil War. I have my father's commission now, signed by President Lincoln, and treasure it highly.

During my father's period as peace officer in Denver, he was compelled to kill the outlaw Steele on the streets of Denver, and years afterward the rest of the Steeles sought revenge for the deed.[39] It saddened my father's life, my mother said. The gang thought to kill my mother would hurt him most. My mother's sister, Jane Chivington, who had married Charles Ottoway, an early pioneer of Alamosa, looked much like my mother. Both women had nursing babies at the time, and one evening Jane was sitting near a window holding her baby. She heard a voice say "There she is," and she dropped to the floor just as a shot was fired through the window. I have seen the powder stains on her breast. Her child, Will, the baby, carried the powder stains on his face to his grave.

My people participated in the gold rushes of Clear Creek, Black Hawk, and Golden. And then they and the Ottoways moved to New Mexico. My father engaged in placer mining and made a big stake for the day and age. Then we came on to Del Norte. I was born in Loma, a little town across the Rio Grande from Del Norte. My parents stayed here for some time, engaged in stock raising. My father was peace officer here also, was an early member of the Masonic lodge here. He owned a blacksmith shop and a butcher shop, was doing well. But the lure of gold pulled him on, and he moved on toward the San Juan.

He was one of the first men to advocate lead mining in the West, and for years he came into the hills. When Silverton was first built, he moved his family there, and in 1876 he died in Howardsville near Silverton.[40] During the time he was making trips to Silverton, he was freighting supplies, and among his wagon trains was a wagonload or two of whiskey. A team died, and the wagon broke down. So as it was the thing needed least in his train, he cached the liquor. It is buried somewhere in those mountains today. What a find it would be in these days of prohibition! It would cause a stampede equal to a small gold rush.

During this stay in Silverton, my sister stayed all night with a girlfriend, and coming home next morning early on her way past a saloon, she was horrified to run into a hanging man. He had been hanged the night before and had not been taken down.

In 1877 after Father's death, Mother decided to come back to the San Juan Basin, and she never left it again. The Ottoways moved to Alamosa, and thus came the final parting of the ways for these two pioneer sisters.

Mother's grave is near the old homeplace in the Animas Valley, near what is now known as Pinkerton-in-the-Pines.[41] She died in 1900, having lived one of the most colorful, picturesque, and truly pioneer lives in early Colorado history.

Mary E. Hayden, Pueblo County [344-18].

Interviewer: Elizabeth Cairns

Interviewer's note: Mrs. Gallup read Mary Hayden's account before the Southern Colorado Pioneers' Association on June 28, 1918, just two weeks after the pioneer had died.

After coming to Pueblo from Emporia, Kansas, in the fall of '63, urgent business matters necessitated my return in the spring of '64. Leaving Pueblo March 20th, in order to catch the stage from Santa Fe to Bent's Old Fort, we resumed our journey from there April 1st and reached the camping place, known to all travelers as Pretty Encampment, where we stopped for the night.[42] During the night we were awakened by a high wind; sleet and snow fell without cessation for forty-eight hours; everything about us was stark and stiff. We managed to kindle our fire with fuel of the plains, and ate with great zest our only rations, bread and bacon.

On our way again next day we passed train after train of wagons, mules, and oxen in their tracks frozen stiff.

We reached Council Grove the ninth of April, and the first of May, having my younger sister with me, we were ready to return. While we were waiting, news came of the depredations and slaughter from Indians beyond Fort Larned.[43] A coach with passengers and drivers en route for Santa Fe had been held up by the Comanches, and all hands killed, coaches burned, mail sacks cut open and the contents strewn to the winds, in consequence of which the coach following had been detained at Larned. Transportation during these two weeks seemed impossible to secure.

In company with the Cheyenne interpreter, John Smith, who, through government orders, was trying to reach the tribe to use his influence to pacify, we left Council Grove the tenth day of May.[44] The first day out we experienced no difficulty. The second day we began to pass trains that were concentrating and traveling four to six abreast, with scouts ahead, all well armed. The second evening we reached Cow Creek and there found all the settlers fleeing, all their teams hitched to their wagons.[45] Great excitement prevailed. Asking our destination, and on finding it was Fort Larned, they endeavored to have us turn back, telling us of disaster and pillaging ahead, saying all men had been murdered, and women and some eleven children carried off with them. Uncle John said he was obliged to go on, that immediately following a raid was the safest time to urge ahead. So we hired a fresh team and decided to make Larned by daybreak. However, it was midnight before we reached Big Bend.[46] Buildings were still burning and everything was ablaze; the night seemed as bright as day. Across a threshold lay the bodies of two men, scalped; beside them a dog howling piteously.

Uncle John, well, didn't believe the stories, but they were only too true. I began to grow fearsome, and each bush seemed to take the form of an Indian. I exacted a promise from John Smith, that if the Indians came to despoil he would end our existence then and there. He promised, but my sister said, "Oh no! don't shoot me, I will hide under the seat." But we reached Walnut Creek—Charles Wratch's place—without molestation, worn out from lack of sleep, and were much relieved to get within the shelter of the fortification.

The place was filled with thousands of buffalo robes, on some of which we slept. Charles Wratch furnished a fresh team, and taking a

Kiowa scout with us, we arrived at Larned about noon. The agent for the company had detained the coach immediately following the ill-fated one. A coach from Kansas City came in after a few days with orders to proceed and requisition on the commanding officer for escort, which was given us to the number of twenty-five. With four coaches filled with passengers bent on going through and six baggage wagons, we began our long trip over the dry route. The first two days, no danger seeming imminent, we were congratulating ourselves, but had counted without our host. Scouts were out ahead; a gunshot told us of the approach of Indians. The wagons were corralled and all preparations were made for battle. The soldiers were placed to the best advantage. War whoops were followed by bareback Indians, riding all around us, and intermittent arrows pierced the mules in the corral. Finding us so well prepared they retreated, but followed us over and over again. The last day we reached to top of the hill, and once again stretched before us Pretty Encampment. The view ahead struck terror to our hearts. It was now an Indian village, tents and wigwams, replete with some three or four hundred Indians. While we were gazing in astonishment, we saw a team leave the encampment and come out to meet us. On nearer approach someone exclaimed, "Why, it's Barnum himself," and with him was Dan Hayden. We found the Indians friendly; they were Left Hand's band of Arapahos.[47]

The balance of the day and part of the night was spent in trying to cross the Chicosa, which was rampant from heavy rains and difficult to ford.[48] We reached Fort Lyon about midnight, Bent's Fort next day, and from there we went ahead into Pueblo.[49]

It was not long after until all the tribes of the plains and mountains were involved, and all outlying settlements threatened. Pueblo was soon filled with refugees. The citizens built a big log block house with loopholes and a lookout on the hill where constant watch was held. We experienced no disturbances, but many were killed between Denver and Pueblo.[50]

The following summer we danced away our cares to Ed Cousin's fiddling.

Today we are not the same number. The two Barnums, Tom and Lewis, Ed Dorris, Billy Booth, George Sears, George Hall, Ott Wineca, Governor Hinsdale, Pete Dotson, Rock Cofer, all have joined the silent majority.[51]

But in the midst of our summer pleasures we were kept busy building embankments against the Arkansas, which flowed back of our kitchen doors on Santa Fe Avenue. While we were busy thus, John Thatcher was hoarding up in the coffee barrel, with a shot bag for a small purse, while Dan Hayden's cash was generally found in the bean sack.

Cynthia Fisher, Pueblo County [344-13]. January 5, 1934.

Interviewer: Elizabeth Cairns

We came from the state of Kansas in '73 and made our home about four miles above the present Rye, Colorado—up on the side of Greenhorn Mountain. I was born and raised in North Carolina, and if I remember correctly I will be eighty-seven this next September, for I was born in the year of '47. In North Carolina I was used to the luxuries of the "South," and I had never had to do anything in the line of work, for we had colored help. However, all of this changed when I became married. Our first home was in the state of Kansas, in Miami County, which is about fifty miles from Kansas City. Miami County in those days was about the last outpost of civilization—a few houses, a few families made up the community. We stayed here, all of the time the frontier moving farther West, and the country in the near vicinity gradually building up to city-like dimensions.

Conveniences and luxuries were unknown in Miami County; why, we had nothing but a treacherous water hole from which to get our water. I used to have to send Flora, then but two years old, after the water. I would give her a pail and send her for the water, hoping that she would return safely. The water was in an ugly, gaping hole in the ground, and into this we had to dip the pail to draw up the water. I sent Flora for I was unable to go myself, and her father was often out in the fields working, or away from the farm selling our meager crops. In the part of Kansas in which we lived the land was unusually low and marshy. One of the family would just get over an attack of the "chills and fever" when another one would take down with it. We had no medicine, or knew nothing of the new methods for fighting this sickness, and many of my friends died during the frequent attacks of chills and fever. Many times, prolonged attacks of chills and fever resulted in consumption.

When Flora was four years old and Frank was two, we started for the "West." A neighbor of ours, a Mrs. Graybeal, was ill, and everyone thought she was going into consumption. Her husband was anxious to take her to a higher altitude in hopes that her health would be benefited. He talked to both my family and others in the country, and it was decided to make up a wagon train to travel west. We left Kansas in May in 1873, and with all of our possessions and all of our cattle we started on our long trip. There were fifteen wagons in our train, and several men who acted as guards. The trip was both hard and dangerous. We all felt afraid of an Indian attack, but it was never our misfortune to have any trouble with the Indians. I do remember one time on that trip when we all got a terrible fright. We were traveling along and on the hills in front of us we could see a cloud of dust, and what looked to us like a whole tribe of Indians on horseback. A cry of alarm went up through the whole train, and preparation for an attack was in order when several of our scouts returned to tell us that what we thought to be Indians was nothing more than a herd of buffalo. Almost all of the men left our temporary camp and went to stampede the buffalo, in hopes of getting some of the young calves. I have often thought what an opportunity the Indians missed of attacking our camp—all of our men out after the buffalo, and nothing in camp but defenseless women and children. The men went wild over the hopes of getting buffalo meat, and apparently forgot the danger of the Indians. I know that I was greatly relieved when the men returned with their kill and we started on our way again.

I will never forget the many streams that we had to ford, creek beds running bank to bank with muddy waters. I can see the horses plunge down into the water, not at all sure that the water would not carry them and their load on downstream. Many times we had to plow our way through the low flat places which were covered with mud, and such things as these I have mentioned made the journey all the harder and slower. In some places, especially along the water, the grass grew very high, almost as high as the bed of the wagon. The cattle traveled very slowly, and we had to stop many times to let them graze. With a good horse one could travel about twenty-five miles a day, but with wagons and a lot of slow cattle we didn't begin to make as good a record as this.[52]

After we had been out on the trail about six weeks, Mrs. Graybeal became so weak that Mr. Graybeal thought that the train had better separate and half of them go on, the other following with all of the cattle and the rest of the supplies. We decided to go on with the Graybeals, so left the other families and continued our trip. Without the cattle we were able to make much better time, and finally reached our destination. We settled on the Greenhorn, about four miles above Rye, Colorado.[53] Here we had a rude log house—dirt floors, sod roof, and a fireplace. Our home was along the side of a beautiful little mountain stream. We had no money, and there was absolutely no way of earning money, for Rye was hard to reach. This was a terrible year, and I often wonder just how we managed to survive the intense cold, the lack of food, and the great discomforts which our log house afforded.

We decided that our best crop should be potatoes, for potatoes brought a higher price than did other products. My husband had no shoes, and with winter at hand we decided to sell some of the potatoes. I groveled out the biggest potatoes and filled a small wooden pail with them; then Mr. Fisher took the potatoes to Rye, where he exchanged them for a pair of shoes. I thought that we would let the rest of the potatoes mature, and then sell them at Rye, but my plans were interrupted as a big hailstorm came and ruined everything that we had, including the potatoes. The next year we had a crop of corn beaten to a pulp by hail, and had all of our other would-be crops eaten up by the grasshoppers.

One time Mr. Fisher took a pail of potatoes to Walsenburg, and there sold the potatoes for two calico dresses for me. Of the greatest pride were these two dresses to me. To have two dresses at one time, and these both of calico, placed me on a high level among the people of the frontier. Almost all of our clothing was made by hand—hand woven and handmade. To have two calico dresses was almost heavenly. It took Mr. Fisher four days to make the trip to Walsenburg and back.

One winter when we were especially hard up, Mr. Fisher had to go back up on the mountainside where there was dead poles—the poles left standing after a forest fire—and bring them down to the house. From the house he hauled the timber to Crow, where he exchanged the poles for food for us to eat.[54] These poles were used to mark off the boundaries of people's land, for such a thing as barb wire was unknown.[55] The land was fenced in by these poles, and it was years before wire fences were erected.

Many times we had nothing to eat for days but potatoes and chokecherries. The chokecherries we had gathered during the summer months and had dried them. This was about all of the fruit known in Colorado at the time; occasionally we would find wild raspberries farther up in the hills, but one almost had to have a horse to ride to these places. Some of the other parts of the state were more fortunate in finding other kinds of berries, but these two kinds were about all that grew around Rye. We practically lived on venison, and I never was sicker of anything in all of my life than I was of eating venison. But at times, when we were unusually hungry even venison tasted mighty good.

In later years we were able to afford a barrel of apples, and the children would steal them upon every occasion that they got—so hungry for fruit were they. I had to divide the apples evenly among us, and dole them out upon rare occasions only. Butter brought a good price when one could take to market their supply, but this was hard to do as it took so long to go anyplace. I often made butter, but with about half as much effort as is put into its making today. Mr. Fisher fixed a box out of the stream where I could put the butter to harden, and after the crock was full if he took it to Crow he could get a good price for his efforts.

We had a workhorse and a pony, but because we were unable to get hay for the horse, he died. We fed him wheat, and the chaff in the wheat killed the poor horse. The pony we traded in to a neighbor for his "gentle-riding" horse, but this trade proved to be a bad one for the gentle horse was a bronco, and threw you off every time you tried to ride him. We finally checked his spirit enough so that he could be ridden, with some difficulty however. Perhaps our cow, which we were able to afford after several years, was our most valuable possession; more than once the milk and butter that we had kept us alive and from starving. Flour was a true luxury, and one time Mr. Fisher exchanged a wagon bed two feet high, three feet wide, and about eight feet long full of shelled corn for a sack of flower. In the sack was one hundred pounds, and in addition to all of that corn, he still owed the storekeeper some cash for the flour.

To get a doctor to come out to the country to attend anyone who was sick it was necessary to ride to Pueblo. When you came after the doctor you had to see that he also got home, and the average fee charged for his services ranged between five and ten dollars a trip. So the patient had to be very ill to have medical attention. Many stories are told of how horses were run to death in an effort to reach the doctor in time to be of help to the sick person.

Anna Dillon, Pueblo County [344-45]. January 20, 1934.

Interviewer: Elizabeth Cairns

Interviewer's note: Mrs. Anna Dillon, 207 Midway Avenue, has lived in Pueblo for a period of over fifty years. She has been in the state for fifty-two years. When Mrs. Dillon was twenty-one years old, her family, according to custom, picked out an eligible young man for her and asked that she marry him. Rather than marry this man, Mrs. Dillon packed up all of her belongings, leaving her native land, Bavaria, Germany, and came to America. She was acquainted with a family in New York, also had a brother in Blackhawk, Colorado; but other than these two she knew no one. She was unable to speak any English, and upon reaching this country found herself a total stranger, not only to the country but also to the language. With her she had brought a younger sister, so it was for her to look out for both herself and her sister. Upon their arrival in New York both sisters decided to stay there and try to find something to do to earn a living. In a short time their plans were blasted—a message from Blackhawk informed them that their brother had suffered an eye injury in the mines, and they had better come and help him. Packing up again, Mrs. Dillon and her sister left for the "West," for Colorado. This was in 1881, the year when they came to Colorado.

For the next year Mrs. Dillon lived at Blackhawk and at Central City. When the brother had to go to Denver for medical aid, they went with him. In Denver she met Mr. and Mrs. Joe Goodrich, of Pueblo. So the thirteenth of April saw her in Pueblo. She had been offered a job in a hotel that belonged to Mr. Goodrich. At this time the smelters of Pueblo were running at top speed, and the hotels in the vicinity made small fortunes caring for the men who worked. The hotel Mrs. Dillon went to was called the Smelter Hotel, where over 140 men boarded. Some of the rooms that the men used were cottages off to the side of the main hotel, but many of the men had rooms in the hotel.

A Mr. Lyle and Mr. Goodrich first had the hotel, but Lyle sold out to Goodrich. Then, there were few houses near the smelter of any size, the cottages rented by the hotel, another rooming house, and a saloon was about all that one could find other than the smelter itself.[56] The smelter was running all of the time; the men knew nothing of short-hour regulations and worked whenever they could get a chance.

In the hotel there were three other girls, and about six cooks hired to care for the men who boarded at the place. I thought that I was making a grand salary—considering my little knowledge of English. I made twenty dollars a month and had my room and board furnished. My work consisted, for the most part, in waiting on tables, and going for beer for the thirsty boarders.

On September 6, 1883, I married Pat Dillon and left the hotel, moving over to what was known as East Pueblo. Our home was across the river, and the Fourth Street Bridge, as it is known today, was located up at Fifth Street. In the spring of '84 the Fountain River flooded, and took with it the Fifth Street Bridge. At this time the Fifth Street Bridge was the only one across the river, and when the flood took the bridge traffic was tied up. A makeshift bridge was hurriedly constructed, and for months this rude arrangement served those desiring to cross to the other side of the river. Mr. Dillon, with the police force, had a hard time getting home nights as the bridge was none too safe, so in '85 we again moved this time to Fourth Street. We were in the 200 block, and our home was a one-story adobe house. Right up from our house was located the city jail, and many things happened in this building. Mr. Dillon was with the police force and knew all that went on in the jail. He had several narrow escapes while working at the jail. On more than one occasion he risked his life to capture a prisoner that was trying to make his getaway. This jail was an adobe building.

The night that the towns of South Pueblo, Central Pueblo, and Bessemer were consolidated was one of the wildest nights that I have ever seen.[57] Bonfires were started and fairly lined the streets. Some of the fires were large, others small, but the town was literally a mass of flames. These fires were kept going for the better part of the night, and the sky was a bright red glare. Everyone turned out for the affair, and with them they brought every sort of noisemaker that they could find. Speeches were in order; one could find an ardent speechmaker on almost every corner that night.

With this consolidation of the towns, and the incorporation of the city of Pueblo, the jail was moved from the adobe structure on Fourth Street to a better building on C Street. When the jail was moved, the old building that was left was converted into the city dog pound. Living near to the dog pound had its disadvantages. Mr. Dillon sometimes helped to put the dogs into the pound, and more than once succeeded in catching a dog to put into the pound. In those days there was a bounty paid on all dogs turned in to the pound; there was no licensed dogcatcher, so everyone in Pueblo assumed the role of dogcatcher. When one brought a dog to the pound, he was paid the bounty, and Mr. Dillon made quite a little bit of money catching dogs. However, as I said, living near the pound was not so pleasant. Often at night the dogs that had been caught during the day would serenade us all night long, but we soon put a stop to this procedure. A Mrs. Pinkney had charge of the pound, and her house was right next to ours. In the course of time both the Pinkneys and Mr. Dillon learned how to open the door to the pound. At night when the animals raised too much noise, either Mrs. Pinkney or Mr. Dillon would unfasten the door and let the dogs loose. The next morning would find the pound empty and the dogs roaming at their own will. Of course, that made the dog-catching business better, as one could catch the dogs again and claim the bounty.

My husband served in the police force for a period of twenty-seven years at one time. He had been with the force longer than this, but twenty-seven years represent continuous service. In the early days the firemen and the policemen were both under political party control, and not under civil service as they are today. As a result of this system, Mr. Dillon was out for the time covering the term of office held by a Dr. King, a Democrat. When B. B. Brown came to office two years later, Mr. Dillon was again put on the force.[58] When Mr. Dillon first served there were not more than a dozen men on the force, but today that number has greatly increased. During the time that Mr. Dillon was on the force he held many positions; for a long time he was night captain, and at the time of his death, held the position of turnkey at the county jail.

Pueblo was rather notorious in the early days for its sensational hangings, murders, gambling dens, variety shows, and saloons. Mr. Dillon was often called out on a murder case, and many terrible things happened that he could tell about. One day Mr. Dillon and I were out walking, and as we neared the place where the Santa Fe depot is now we heard a woman scream. We looked up just in time to see her jump from the window of the rooming house. She fell almost at our feet, and there she lay bleeding, for her throat had been cut. Mr. Dillon rushed up the stairs, and there found the man who had cut the woman's throat. The police were called in on the case, but the man had also cut his own throat, and died before he could be taken to the hospital.

I shall never forget a sight that to this day is most vivid in my mind. I went to spend the night with a friend who lived near Lannon's Foundry on Santa Fe Avenue. I got up early the next morning and started for home, but I had barely opened the front door when my eyes fell upon a body of a man who was swinging from the limbs of the cottonwood tree that stood in front of the house. I was very much frightened, and went out another door. It was so early in the morning that I was afraid. I took all of the backstreets home. Later in the day I heard that two other men that night had also been hung on the "big tree." All of the men hung were cattle rustlers. The bark on the limbs of the "big tree" was almost always skinned off—due to the fact so many hangings took place here.

Some of the more notorious places that Mr. Dillon often spoke of were: Tammany Hall—located near Holmes Hardware Company. Here were held "variety shows." Green Light, the Turf—in addition to being saloons, these places had gambling dens upstairs. Here many brawls took place, and it took the police to quiet the place. The flood of 1921 took the building that had housed the Green Light, and the only thing left in its place was a single green sprout from a cottonwood tree.[59] Bucket of Blood—many prominent Pueblo men were mixed up in this place. It has a terrible history, and many unsolved murders took place here.

In the early days about the only place one could go and find amusement was a place called the Santa Fe Park. This park, torn up when the Missouri Pacific Railroad put in their tracks, was located down in the "Grove" district and near the river.[60] Here one found a few scattered cottonwood trees and a wooden platform. On certain days a man with a dancing bear held his show on the platform. There were no other parks in the town, such as there are today.

The Opera House in the Triangle Block (across from the Vail Hotel today) was the scene of many fairs, held for the benefit of the St. Mary's Hospital. A great deal of money was raised for the hospital from these affairs. Sometimes the amount would be as high as seven or eight thousand dollars. The men working at the Steel Works contributed large amounts, for they were working steady. Oftentimes prizes were offered as an added inducement. Upon one occasion two girls ran for a ring. The prize was to be given to the one bringing in the most donations. People either backed one or the other side, and in the end the girl who won had more than sixteen hundred dollars ahead of her opponent's score. Excitement ran high at these contests. In this particular race the boys working at the Steel Works borrowed an immense amount of money from a saloonkeeper so that their girl could win. Many of them were months paying back the amount they had borrowed. Wages at the Steel Works were good, but Mr. Dillon never made more than eighty dollars a month.

Before leaving Germany, I had had a course in nurses training, and whenever Mr. Dillon was unable to work, or politics kept him from working, I did work for the doctors in town.

I have been closely connected with the growth of the Sacred Heart Orphanage here in Pueblo. Colonel Lambert, when he died, willed an immense amount of money to the sisters to found a home for orphan children.[61] He also gave ten acres of land. The home was built under the direction of Dan Mahoney, the contractor. Lambert also gave his family home to the sisters; the rest of the estate went to members of the family and Loretta Academy. The first Ladies' Aid of the Orphanage met at the home of Mrs. Frankenburg, and Mrs. T. G. McCarthy was elected president. The Aid met monthly and sewed for the orphans. At first grocers, merchants, and businessmen were solicited for help, and the sister in charge, Sister Martini, used to go out with a horse and wagon, collecting whatever she could in the line of food. Later, money was donated for the upkeep of the home, and assessments were made amounting to three dollars a year for the members of the Aid. Every St. Patrick's Day the orphanage used to hold a campaign and sell green bows. This method of raising money was forbid when the system of allotting the donations through the Community Chest was installed.

Mary Cox, Pueblo County [344-57]. March 26, 1934.

Interviewer: Elizabeth Cairns

Interviewer's note: Mrs. Rosalie Warden and Mrs. Mary Cox are sisters and at the present time are living at 722 Veta Avenue. Mrs. Mary Cox is a trained nurse and has been a resident of Pueblo since November 10, 1886. Her sister has been here since January 1887. Mrs. Cox gave the following account of their coming to Colorado.

Our old home was located in the state of Kentucky, but when my sister Rosalie and I were just girls we left this place and went to Cincinnati, Ohio, to live. When Kansas was opened up as a country where homesteads were bountiful, my brother got the "land craze" and decided to leave Kentucky in preference of Kansas. He persuaded the rest of the family to accompany him on his journey to the "West." The whole family, Rosalie and myself included, came to Kansas to homestead land. Kansas, we found, was the most barren, forsaken country that we had ever seen. In Kentucky and in Ohio we had been used to dense forest, underbrush, berry bushes, and fertile ground. All of our lives we had spent in a country where the wild berries, fruits, and nuts were plentiful. Kansas, to us, was a direct contrast to what we had been used to having and seeing. Sand, sparse vegetation, dry climate, and uninhabited plains were the things that we found made up the state of Kansas.

We homesteaded in Kansas just about thirty miles from Garden City. My first position as a nurse was in Garden City, and it was here that my hatred for the country grew. Often I wished that I had never left Cincinnati. The task of homesteading proved too hard for my father; he died shortly after we came to Kansas. Mother was hurt in an accident, so we decided to give up the homesteading idea for the time being.

I decided to come to Pueblo, knowing friends here, so came in November of '86. I got work and after a time sent for my sister Rosalie. We worked and in time managed to get the whole family to come to Pueblo. I liked Pueblo from the first, but must admit that it is much different from Cincinnati. Many times I was fooled by friends who liked to take advantage of my being a "tenderfoot." It was hard for me to get used to the sudden changes in the weather; one day it would rain, the next snow, and the third the ground would be clear and the day as bright and sunshiny as one could imagine. The East offered no such diversions of climate; a snow stayed on the ground for weeks.

One of the earliest Sunday diversions that I can remember was that of going for water. We found the water in Pueblo very poor, so hauled all of our water from the artesian wells located on what is now West Abriendo.[62] We lived on the east side of the river, so we had to cross in order to get water. Early Sunday morning we would load the buggy with jugs and start out for water; the water we got lasted us for that current week, and the same process would be repeated the next Sunday. The place where we got the water was called Dr. Worrall's. Sometimes we would go to Clark's Mineral Well for water but we really liked the artesian water the best.

The building of the Grand Hotel was a momentous occasion in the history of Pueblo.[63] When the hotel was finished it was opened for public inspection, and I know that we had quite a thrill when we got to go through the "big, new hotel." The hotel was quite large and was really a building that Pueblo could well be proud of.

City Park was a much-talked-of concern in the early days. Mr. Carlile and Mr. Dittmer held the land that the city park is now located on. Their original idea was to make this a suburban home district that would be surrounded by the park. They also hoped to sell the land to the city as a site for a city park. The foundations for several houses were laid, but never completed. Mr. Dittmer, who was German and Swede, spent a great deal of money and time in improving the park district. He made several trips to foreign countries especially to purchase trees that were to be planted in the park. The assortment of trees that are to be found in City Park today cannot be equaled in this part of the state.

Today the park is owned by the city, and although it does not quite cover the area that Carlile and Dittmer intended that it should, it is Pueblo's largest park.

Chapter 4: The Northeast

Weld, Morgan, and Logan Counties

In 1885 I had the western fever more than ever. I was anxious now to get some land in Colorado and start a fortune for myself as I had such wonderful pictures in my mind of what this country would look like and be like in the near future.

Lizzie Gordon Buchanan

One of the inducements for European American settlement in eastern Colorado was the Federal Homestead Act of 1862, which enabled a homesteader to acquire 160 acres of "unoccupied" land by preempting (that is, by living on it or "squatting" in a sense) for five years and making improvements (such as building a house, digging a well, cultivating or plowing at least ten acres, and fencing a portion). The Homestead Act was especially noteworthy in that it made no distinction based on sex. By this act, a woman head of household had just as much legal right as a man to settle on and own land, and as some of the following narratives suggest, many women were ready to take full advantage of their right. An 1873 revision of the law allowed one to purchase the land for $1.25 an acre after living on it for six months. By the Timber Culture Act (1873) a settler could claim an additional 160 acres by planting one-quarter of it in trees. This act enabled pioneers like Lizzie Buchanan to claim up to 160 acres, plant one-quarter in

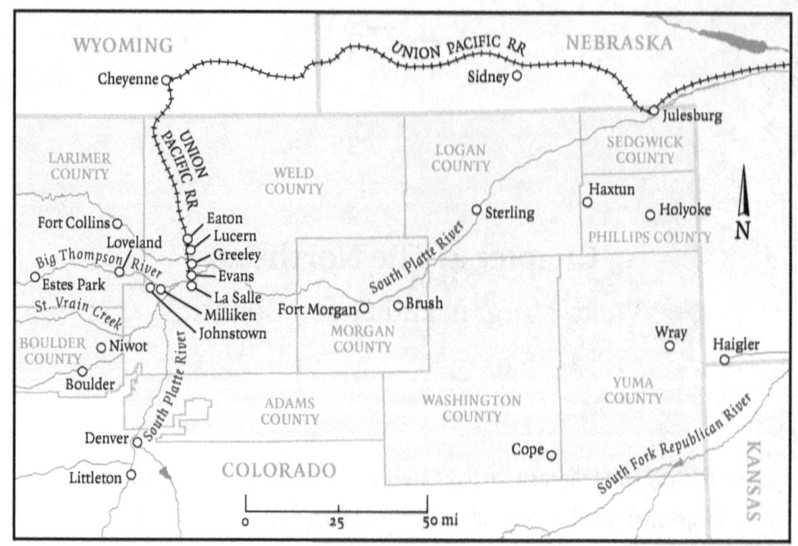

6. The northeast

trees, and after making proof, buy the land at $1.25 an acre. To make proof, a person needed merely to demonstrate that one had in good faith complied with the provisions of the law, give evidence that one was a bona fide resident of the state or territory, and advertise in the closest newspaper one's intentions of buying the claim.[1]

Another enticement for settlers was the Union Colony in Weld County, which Nathan Meeker (who in 1878 would become Indian agent at the White River Agency) established in 1869.[2] After his first visit to Colorado, he returned to New York and immediately proposed a settlement colony to Horace Greeley, his boss at the *New York Tribune*. With the entrepreneur's approval and backing, Meeker planned the Union Colony, and by the spring of 1870 settlement began. Settlers were lured by newspaper advertisements such as the following:

> The scenery is grand beyond description, and the land in the immediate vicinity is unsurpassed for agricultural purposes. To the south and east, as far as the eye can reach, the magnificent landscape seems to rise and fall like the waves of the sea. From the base of the mountains the plain gradually slopes to the eastward, which accounts in part for the mild winters of this region. Thousands of feet above this garden spot the sky is filled with rocky cliffs and snowy peaks, yet the prairie itself is three thousand feet above the level of the sea. The climate is said to be peculiarly favorable for persons troubled with weak lungs.[3]

Union Colony is one of the few such communal enterprises that actually thrived. But despite its success, the colony was essentially absorbed into the city when the township of Greeley was incorporated in 1871.

A characteristic of pioneering in Colorado that becomes especially evident as one reads these narratives is that the women who came from the East brought with them the attitudes toward nature that are at least as old as the Puritan pilgrims' visions of the empty and howling wilderness that was to become Massachusetts. As has been typical of Western civilization in general, the land that supports and brings forth life and which provides one's livelihood has simultaneously been regarded as uncooperative and as an impediment to easy transportation or settlement. Even on apparently trivial matters, readers of these narratives can see how the settlers abused the land and animals through either ignorance or indifference. According to William Wyckoff, "Concomitant with . . . the era's economic expansion was the parallel story of both a vibrant and destructive American imperialism that transformed the geographies of all western North America." Patricia Nelson Limerick argues that the colonists had expectations of what the land owed them as they ranged cattle and plowed for farms or sought drinking water: "They had trusted nature, and when nature behaved according to its own rules and not theirs, they felt betrayed." As Brigitte Georgi-Findlay suggests, pioneer women often appeared to share with their male counterparts chauvinistic attitudes toward the land and nonhuman animals.[4]

Many of the settlers from the East did not have a particularly full understanding of the land they were to settle and make a living on. Mrs. Pitt Smith, for example, confesses that her husband "knew very little of farming" but was enticed by thoughts of freedom and hope of making a fortune. Mrs. Smith's very first experience in the West was to step on a cactus plant. Sallie Cheairs remembers building her house over a rattlesnake den, not having been able beforehand to see the snake or snakes in the thick grass. Unfamiliarity with the new landscape accounts for some of the misadventures, but malice or human arrogance accounts for other interactions with their new environment. Katherine McElroy, for example, had as a "chief amusement" the drowning out of prairie dogs. Understandably, skunks and grasshoppers were ubiquitous and therefore very disruptive. They were declared enemies. Jennie Lucas tells the story of her mother's attempt to shoot an antelope, declaring only after she had accidentally "shot away up into the air" and nearly knocked herself over that it would be a pity to kill "such pretty things anyway."

Because of the somewhat and sometimes inhospitable land and the misfortunes of grasshopper invasions, drought, and severe winters, these women often found establishing a home on the Colorado prairie, as Sallie Cheairs recalls, "hard in many ways." Lizzie Buchanan admits that "anticipations were sweeter than realities." As a girl, Jennie Craig (Lucas) witnessed her mother's disappointment in the entire pioneering enterprise: "Many times I have seen her walking up and down the riverbank crying as though her heart would break." In these glimpses, then, the narratives tell us about the women's hopes and expectations as well as about their alternating peaceful and hostile interactions with the land, about the women's interactions with and attitudes toward the physical geography, toward the very land on which and from which they were attempting to make their livings. They tell us not only about their moments of doubt but also about how, through all this, they persevered.

The field-workers for these counties were W. G. Benneweiss (Weld), M. Amour (Logan), and M. B. Gill (Morgan).

Ada Fleming Sanford, Weld County [343-14]. Greeley.

Interviewer: W. G. Benneweiss

Interviewer's note: Ada Fleming was born at Galena, Illinois, in 1858, and her parents came to Colorado in 1860. They settled on the St. Vrain in what is now Weld County.

My father and mother drove overland to Colorado from Galena, Illinois, in 1860, coming by way of St. Joseph, Missouri, and Leavenworth, Kansas.

From Leavenworth he brought a brick burner, and we stayed in a cabin until he had burned enough bricks to build our house. So far as I know, this was the first brick house to be built in Colorado. The clay was taken from the bank of the creek on the spot where the house stood. This house stood until 1886 when a flood, caused by a break in a reservoir near the mountains, undermined it and it fell into the creek.

My mother brought many garden and flower seeds with her, and one of the first things we did was to plant a garden. We sold vegetables and chickens to the neighbors and made quite a bit of extra money that way. My father also made bricks for the neighbors, and many of the houses along the St. Vrain are built of those native clay bricks.

The Indians used to come to our house and talk about those bricks. They had never seen anything like them. They would rub their hands along the sides of the house and brush against it while they were talking.

Hay was one of the principal crops in those days. My father had a fine meadow and used to cut lots of hay for market. He hauled it to Central City for as much as one hundred dollars per ton. Most of it had to be cut by hand and bailed in a hand press.

I recall that one time about seven hundred Indians camped on our meadow. Each of them had two or three ponies, and they would soon have ruined the hay. My father decided the next morning that he would ask them to move off. Mother objected, fearing that it would anger them and we might all be killed. But Father decided to go, so packing up some meat and other things to eat, he went over to talk to them. He came back in a little while, and the Indians pulled up their tepees and moved about a mile up the creek. After that they often came to our house and Father treated them well. He said that no matter what happened he would not be afraid to go to the chief, Left Hand, and ask his protection.[5]

One day, Left Hand brought his squaw and papooses to our house. We played with them, and when they went they took some of our dresses and skirts with them. The next day they came back dressed in our clothes. One would have on an apron, another a skirt, and another a dress. They laughed and pointed to them, trying to tell us something in Indian.

One time word was passed around that the Indians were on the warpath. All the settlers gathered at the home of Bob Howk, but nothing happened and they came to our house. The neighbors stayed with us a long time fearing to go home.

Rollins, of Rollinsville, had brought with him from Kentucky a fine herd of Durham cattle from the Bates herd in Kentucky.[6] My father bought seven head from him and started our herd of Durham stock. These were very fine cattle, but they did not stand the rough, open winters.

Sometimes food was hard to get. I remember that my father once offered one hundred dollars in gold for a hundred pounds of flour and was refused. Gold dust was in common use. Every man carried a leather pouch for gold dust and a scales for weighing it. He often carried a microscope also, in order to be sure that he got gold and not something else.

When my father came to Colorado, he brought with him for medicine two cases of whiskey and twenty pounds of salts. That was all the medicine there was in the country. And you may be sure that many neighbors needed medicine.

My father built the first ditch for irrigation in that part of the country. It was called the Rural Ditch. Later he built one called the Last Chance. These have both been filled up and discontinued. They took the water directly out of the St. Vrain.

My father also kept a post office at our house. It was called Flemings Ranch. The mail was carried from La Porte by pony or on foot.[7] We lived six miles above the fort.

Grace Brush Mayne, Weld County [343-15]. Millikin, January 30, 1934.

Interviewer: W. G. Benneweiss

Interviewer's note: Grace is the daughter of William Brush, who was killed by Indians in 1868 at the mouth of Crow Creek.

I was but five and one-half months old when my father was killed by the Indians. Our home was near Hillsboro, northwest of Johnstown.[8] After my father's death, Mother went to live with her parents at Niwot.[9] This was in 1868.

The Brush brothers had about fifteen hundred acres of land.[10] This was divided when Mother went to Niwot, and I still have my share. I now live on land owned by my father.

The post office, Hillsboro, has moved about a great deal. At first it was kept by George Keys, five or six miles northeast of there, near the Welcome Hill School. Then John Whole had it. He lived two miles west of Johnstown.[11] Next, John Tilley was postmaster, one and one-half miles north of Millikin on the bank of the Big Thompson. Tilley later moved to the present Hillsboro, which is a half mile west of Millikin. Then, John Brewer was made postmaster and kept the office until it was discontinued when Millikin started.

Etta L. Matteson Kettley, Weld County [343-5]. Greeley, January 4, 1934.

Interviewer: M. G. Benneweiss

Interviewer's note: Etta Matteson was born at Mexico, Oswego County, New York, on December 15, 1861. In 1865 her parents moved to Galva, Illinois.

My father, C. W. Matteson, and family came to Greeley, May 8, 1870, from Galva, Illinois. He was with the first group of colonists that came to Greeley. We came by train to Greeley from Cheyenne, Wyoming.[12] I remember that the racks above our heads as we rode in the coaches were full of rifles. The train had to stop twice to let the buffalo herds go by.

The first night we were in Greeley we slept in a boxcar on a siding. There was only a pile of ties on which to land at the depot. The next day my father put up a tent down by the river bridge, and we stayed in that until our house was built. It was at the corner of Fifth Avenue and Ninth Street. There were plenty of trees along the river, and we had lots of cottonwood to burn. Also there was a coal mine somewheres up toward Eaton, and my father hauled coal for us.[13] My father was a farmer and chose his land about eight miles north of town under the No. 2 Ditch. This ditch had been started a few months before we came by Meeker, Cameron, Paber, and others.[14]

In July 1871 nearly the whole colony went up to Estes Park for a picnic. There were thirty-five teams, and the trip took three days. We went by way of Loveland, over Bald Mountain, and down Pole Hill. There was only a dim trail to follow. We had to keep a fire burning all night to keep the animals away.

There was lots of typhoid fever in the fall of 1871 and every fall after that until the water came. People had only surface wells and river water to use at first. The flies also were very numerous.

A Mr. Gurley and a Mr. Garver were the first teachers. The school was in a building opposite the Hotel de Comfort. Later this hotel was made over into a school, and Mr. Shattock had charge.

I was at the depot when the captives from the Meeker Massacre came home. There was a large crowd out to see them. Alva Adams had negotiated with the Indians for their release. They were taken immediately to the Meeker home. This was in 1879.[15]

The grasshoppers came in 1872–3. They ate everything green. We had planted some strawberries in the garden and put tin cans over them to shield them from the hot sun. The hoppers dug under these tins and ate the plants.

Katherine S. McElroy, Weld County [343-18]. Greeley, February 6, 1934.

Interviewer: W. G. Benneweiss

My father, William S. McElroy, came to Greeley from Pittsburgh, Pennsylvania, in December 1870. He was one of the colonists. A house was built on Fifth Avenue and Tenth Street, and in April 1871 my mother and I came out.

The place where we now live was bought by my father in 1871. It had been owned about three months by someone who got sick of his bargain and wanted to go back East. The present house was built in 1872. We moved in April, and I have lived here ever since. I have reason to believe that this was once an old Indian campground. We have found many arrowheads and beads here, and in the field next to the river are spots about ten feet in diameter where the grain grows much taller than elsewhere. There are many of these spots irregularly placed along the river and on the hills above.

We stopped in Missouri on our way out here to visit my grandfather McCague. He gave me two little pigs which I brought to Greeley. They were the first pigs in town. My father had been a pattern maker for the Knapp Fort Pitt Foundry in Pittsburgh, and after he came here he worked as a carpenter and bridge builder for many years. He built most of the bridges near here across the Poudre and Platte. He also built many of the homes in Greeley.

The old road to Cheyenne went through our land close to the house, and we always were very much interested in the travelers who went by. Sometimes there would be large herds of cattle and at other times movers in covered wagons.

We went to school in Greeley, having to cross the river on a foot-bridge built by my father. Sometimes when the river was high it was impossible to cross. The river rose every spring before the ditches and reservoirs were built. Sometimes it reached from bluff to bluff, and horses had to swim across.

One of our chief amusements in the spring was to drown out the little prairie dogs in the "dog town" near here. They made fine pets for the summer, but by the time they were grown they became vicious and we had to let them go. A prairie dog has no sense of distance or perspective. He will climb up a stairs all right but in coming down he just drops from one floor to the other. We also had a pet antelope. He was just like a pet sheep or goat and would follow us wherever we went.

Our reading consisted of such papers and magazines as *Harper's Weekly*, the *Century*, *Scribner's*, *Godey's Lady Book*, and the *New York Tribune*. Our kitchen was papered with pictures from *Harper's Weekly*, and we used to discuss them every day as we ate.

Being so close to the river, we were bothered a great deal by skunks who tried to get our chickens. One time one got in the cellar and we had a time getting it out. Finally, one of the men suggested that it would follow a light and could be led out. So this was tried. The skunk followed the light until it got to the steps, but there it had a hole under the foundation and went in. It was necessary to pull out a part of this before we got it out.

Mrs. Pitt Smith, Weld County [343-13]. Greeley, January 6, 1934.

Interviewer: W. G. Benneweiss

Interviewer's note: Almira Smith was born in Foster, Rhode Island, in 1843, and she came to Greeley in May 1871.

My husband and father-in-law joined the Greeley colony because they had read in the *New York Tribune* of the opportunities in Colorado and especially in the Union Colony. My husband had been a shop worker in Rhode Island and knew very little of farming, especially of irrigation. But we wanted the freedom and independence that comes with the development of a new country and also the chance to make our fortunes.

My husband and his father came to Greeley early in the spring of 1871 in order to build a house and get things ready for us. We came in May. The house was only partly finished. It had no doors nor windows, but was plastered. My first experience when I got off the train was to step on a cactus. I had never seen one before, and it left a lasting impression. We went immediately to the house for dinner. The men had only a lot of beans cooked. We had a lot of lunch that we had brought on the train. This looked so good to the men that we let them eat our lunch and we ate their beans.

Mr. Smith had not joined the colony soon enough to get in on the drawing of lots for land so bought a relinquishment on a farm a few miles north of town.[16] We soon moved out there and started to farming. As we were but two and one-half miles from town, we thought it would be a good thing to start a dairy. So Mr. Smith bought sixty head of milk cows and we expected to supply Greeley with milk. However, the winter of 1872 was a hard one. There was lots of snow, and the cattle had to range out all the year. Ours had to range outside the colony fence, and we lost all but one.

To make matters worse, the grasshoppers came in the summer of that same year, 1872. They came in the afternoon about four o'clock and darkened the sky like a cloud. It is hard to believe, but the chickens went to roost thinking it was night. They ate everything green, and even ate the cloth screens from our windows. Even the wood on the side of the house was pitted. They were here only a short time and disappeared almost as soon as they came. They left their eggs, however, and the next spring when the wheat Mr. Smith had planted was about three inches high the young ones appeared. They cleared the field.

Mr. Smith now had to go to work in the sawmills. There were two sawmills in Greeley making lumber for the houses that were being built. Logs were floated down from the mountains and made up into lumber and posts. Mr. Smith worked in the sawmill for three years.

The water we had was very insipid. It had to be hauled from the river or from wells some distance away. I had never drunk either tea of coffee, but put some in the water so it would be better to drink. In this way I learned to use both.

It was practically impossible to get fruit of any kind in the early days. My mother-in-law and I had dried a half barrel of apples in Rhode Island and brought them with us. They were a very welcome addition to our food supply. Our meat consisted almost entirely of dried buffalo meat. Mr. Smith would go down the Platte and shoot a buffalo or two, or some antelope. We would rub salt into the quarters and hang them up to dry. They would cure in the dry air and last a long time. I remember that some antelope meat got so hard that it had to be shaved off with a plane. Nevertheless, it was good that way. I sold butter for as much as sixty-five cents per pound.

There were lots of rattlesnakes on our farm, and I used to dread to go out of doors. One day my father-in-law killed one with the spade and stooped down to examine the head and a piece of the body about four inches long. It made a jump at him and struck hard enough to pierce his leather boot.

We had no money after our losses, and my husband often wished we were back in Rhode Island where he could get his weekly pay. However, nearly everyone was in the same plight. We had to run bills from one season to the next, hoping that crops would be good so that we could pay them then.

On Sunday we drove to church in a lumber wagon hitched to a team of mules. Everyone did the same, so we thought nothing of it. There was a long row of hitching posts near the church, and on Sunday it would be full of horses and mules that had brought people to church in lumber wagons or high-seated buggies.

For fuel we had to burn a poor grade of coal from a mine up near Eaton. Wood was scarce because there were but few trees along the river, and slabs from the sawmills were our only supply.

Those early pioneering days were strenuous but we developed strength and courage, and now I am over ninety and still feeling fine.

Jennie [Craig] Lucas, Weld County [343-26]. Greeley, February 19, 1934.

Interviewer: W. G. Benneweiss.

Interviewer's note: Jennie Lucas was born in about 1862 in Thompsonville, Connecticut. When she was fifty-six, after having lived in Colorado for forty-six years, she took up and lived on her own claim in Wyoming long enough to prove up. She then returned to Colorado.

My father, Alexander Craig, came to America from Scotland in 1848. He had been a silk weaver there and brought many silk pieces with him to this country. He settled in Thompsonville, Connecticut. There he read of the founding of the Union Colony in 1870, and resolved to come west with it. He could not leave his business that year, but sent my brother in his stead. He came out the next year. My mother and three daughters came in March 1872. I was ten years old.

My brother had written from Greeley that he doubted our ability to make a living on the small tract of five acres and a lot in town that my father had bargained for as his share of the Union Colony project, so Father wrote him to file on some land farther out along the river. This he did, filing on a farm south of the river near the Ennes and Hoffsmith places. My father came out the same year, and they both lived in a little shack on the land.

My mother and I and two younger sisters came out in March 1872. We were just one week on the train. As we got off the train at Evans, my father and brother were there to meet us with a big lumber wagon. Mother was surprised and said, "Didn't you have anything else to come after us in?" She was very tired from the long trip, and a jolt over the prairies for several miles in a big wagon didn't appeal to her.

They did not have a house built for us, so we stayed a day or so in the shack, and then father rented a sod house from Jim Bailey for two dollars per month until he and Brother could get the adobe house up. Mother did not like it here at first. She was born in Scotland of somewhat genteel parents and did not like a pioneering life. Many times I have seen her walking up and down the riverbank crying as though her heart would break. She disliked the monotony and the hardships. She became reconciled in a year or so, however, and never complained.

I remember that one time Mother even tried to shoot an antelope. Father had gone to town, and about the middle of the forenoon a big herd of antelope came running over a small hill near the house. They were going to the river to get a drink. Mother shouted, "Where's the gun?" and running into the house brought out Father's shotgun. She rested it across the wagon and fired. It shot away up into the air and nearly knocked her over. The antelope ran away unharmed. Nearly crying, she remarked that it was too bad to shoot such pretty things anyway.

Shortly after we came to Colorado, Father went down the Platte on a buffalo hunt. He was gone three or four days and brought back a load of buffalo, hung it on the north side of the house. It dried and was the best meat one ever tasted. We had wild meat all the time for many years.

In the summer that we came, the grasshoppers ate everything green. They came one afternoon like a great cloud, settled down on the ground, and started eating. The ground was covered with them. Mother had a few cabbages out in the garden. She ran out and put them under some bunches of hay, but the hoppers found them and did not leave a piece. In a few days they were gone as suddenly as they came. But they had left their eggs and the next year, and every year since there has been lots of grasshoppers.

I went to school in a sod schoolhouse near Latham.[17] It had a rough board floor and a dirt roof. There was a window on each side, and there was always a broken windowpane. The walls were about two feet thick, and we used to pile our wraps in the windows for there was no place to hang them. Sometimes a button would strike against a pane and break it, or the boys would throw a ball through. Whenever it rained the roof would leak for an hour or so afterwards. There were about twelve pupils. We sat in high straight benches that a carpenter had made. They were much too high, and our feet seldom touched the floor. At class time we recited from a long bench up near the teacher's desk.

We lived a mile from the school, and at times the storms were bad. We had to walk all the way. Sometimes the wind would nearly blow us off our feet. I think we had much harder windstorms then. There were no trees to break it, and it swept across the prairies unhindered.

Our only amusements were dances. We used to go to Evans once in a while for a dance. And sometimes the neighbors would clear the floor and have a dance. Everybody went, young and old, married and single. People always were friendly, everybody knew everybody else, and all had a good time. On holidays we came to Greeley for picnics and speeches. The people in Greeley were more stiff and reserved. They had few dances, but many Sunday schools.

The dances lasted nearly all night. The music consisted of a fiddle and bass viol. On special occasions we had two fiddles. The dances were called by someone who knew the changes. They were called square dances. Round dances, such as are common now, were seldom danced. Sets of four couples would form in the shape of a square, then the caller would shout the changes and each couple would go through the movements. A good caller could call all night and never call the same change twice.

The year I was sixteen a party of us went up the Thompson Cañon for a picnic. It took two days. The roads were very rough, and sometimes we had to get off the wagon and walk down a hill. I remember that a hillside was red with raspberries. Some of us gathered a panful and tried to take them home, but the rough roads shook them so that they were all juice before we got home.

There were few amusements those early days, but we appreciated them more than we do now. In 1918, I went up into Wyoming and took up a claim. I lived on it until I proved up, and enjoyed every minute of it. It brought back my early days in Greeley.

Sallie J. Cheairs, Logan County [341-10]. Sterling, December 20, 1933.

Interviewer: M. Amour.

I, Mrs. Sallie J. Cheairs, wife of the late J. J. Cheairs and daughter of the late Mrs. Sarah Ann (Mrs. Calvin) Cheairs, was born August 18, 1852, in Marshall County, Mississippi, the town now being known as Michigan City.

My youth and education was received in the South. I attended and graduated from the girls college at LaGrange, Tennessee, in the year 1868. Several years after coming to Colorado I burned my "sheepskin," feeling that I knew so little that I did not care for anyone to see it, and realizing that the colleges in those days were much inferior to the present-day colleges.

I was married to J. J. Cheairs on January 17, 1869, in northern Mississippi, near my birthplace, and resided there for about seven years. My four oldest children were born in the South: Minnie L., Maggie, Joe, and Andrew—the last mentioned having passed away when about one year old.

Some of my relatives having already moved to Colorado and my husband's health not being good, he decided to come out, which he did in 1877. He looked the country over and thought the climate might benefit him; spent four months, part of the time with relatives and rest of the time in Colorado Springs and Manitou. He then returned to the South, settled up his business, and we moved to Colorado in June 1878. Coming with us were my husband's parents, Calvin and

Sarah Ann Cheairs; my grandparents Mr. and Mrs. Hugh Davis; my aunt Amma Davis; and of course my four children.

The nearest railroad point to the settlement here then was at Sidney, Nebraska, and our relatives who were here came to Sidney in wagons to meet us.[18] We arrived here about June 5th, 1878. When we were met at Sidney, our folks camped out the night before near the town, and the next morning just before they were ready to leave for the settlement, they prepared breakfast for us and themselves at this camp on the lone prairie, and then came to the hotel in Sidney to get us and take us to the camp to eat breakfast with them. After driving to this camp and getting out, I remember that they had a huge coffeepot sitting on the fire where prairie chips had been piled to the top of it to make the coffee boil. When they picked up the coffeepot and poured it in tin cups to pass around to those who were standing, there being nothing to sit on, when they came to me, I thanked them and told them that "I didn't care for coffee this morning." When we got to the settlement they told the family that I refused to drink coffee because the prairie chips were used in the boiling of it. It created quite a little amusement, and some of the old settlers teased me about it as long as they lived. Many of the families used these chips for cooking and heating purposes in those days.

On the way over from Sidney there was nothing in sight but great herds of cattle, and it was certainly a desolate-looking country.

We stayed a few days with relatives here who had preceded us, waiting for lumber to be hauled from Sidney and Greeley to build a temporary shanty in which we lived until our home was built. The lumber for this home was all hauled from Greeley in wagons, and it took almost a week to make a trip.

Incidentally, we built this shanty over a rattlesnake's nest; there was no floor, nothing but the native grass, and of course we could not see the nest. Evidently the mother snake had become frightened and left. The young ones, about six or seven inches long, began to crawl out, one by one, for several days, until they were all hatched out, there being seven or eight of them. They looked as if they were frightened and hungry, and did not attempt to bite, but when we think of it now, it makes us shudder.

It had been told to us that it was a very dry country, and while we still were in our shanty waiting for our house to be built, we had a hard rain which was very unusual at that time, and as the shanty was not built rain-proof, our bedding and clothes were almost ruined by the rain. The roof was nothing but boards with dirt thrown on them, and the rain poured through. My mother and I would try to hold quilts up to keep the rain from getting on our clothes, but of no avail.

There was a partition in the shanty, making two rooms, and there were eight of us in it. Had boards for temporary beds. All provisions were hauled from Greeley or Sidney. The first settlers ate a great deal of buffalo meat as they were quite numerous on the prairie then, but there were none after our coming here. We would exchange chickens and eggs for eatables, such as sugar, coffee, and flour, and for what few dry goods that we needed. The main cloth used in those days was calico, five cents a yard, and we made and wore these dresses to church and Sunday school in the little sod schoolhouse.

In September this same year, 1878, our house was ready for us to move in. It was built by my husband and father-in-law and assisted by a man who was somewhat of a carpenter. This house was lined inside with adobe-mud brick for warmth. It was a story and a half, consisting of two rooms upstairs and two bedrooms downstairs, dining and kitchen. Some of the settlers had sod houses and some lived in dugouts. Our furniture was bought in Greeley, and when we got moved and settled we felt as though we were almost living in a palace in comparison to the shanty from whence we moved.

Soon after in the same month, the cowboys put out a report that a band of Indians were going to cross the river near the settlement of Sterling. It frightened the men so that they had the women, children, and old men put in wagons and taken to Sidney, Nebraska, for safety, where we remained for two weeks. The men would all gather at one house at night with their guns, prepared to fight the Indians if they should come to the settlement. But they did not cross the river very near to the settlement. Our husbands came to Sidney and brought us all home, after which there were no more Indian scares. We lived quietly and peacefully and were not molested in any way.

The long-looked-for Union Pacific Railroad train gladdened our hearts in 1881.[19]

While living on the ranch in the year 1882, I was preparing to get supper one Sunday evening and had built the fire in the kitchen range; a storm came up and a ball of lightning came down the stovepipe near where I was standing and rolled into a little room, called the pantry; the door being opened. This ball of fire exploded there, filling the room with smoke as though a gun had been fired in the room. No other damage was done other than the hole in the stovepipe.

Our home was built on the land taken as a homestead by my husband, and he and the late R. C. Perkins had a good many cattle. These cattle were kept on the range and rounded up twice a year. Once during a roundup, my husband's horse fell and broke his leg; there were no doctors here at that time, so his father set the leg, and I think set it as good as any doctor could. That winter was a hard one and they lost a good many of the cattle, and my husband was indoors all winter with his broken leg. At one time his foot was so badly swollen and had turned quite dark, so we had a doctor from Sidney to come over and look at it and prescribe for him. The doctor thought he was going to lose his foot, but he came out all right and did not even limp afterwards.

We lived on this ranch for ten years, and four more of our children were born: Sam, Oscar, Dave, and Calvin. Dave lived only five years. We then moved to the town of Sterling.

In 1882 Father and Mother bought four acres of land, which is now the townsite of Sterling, and built the first house in Sterling from the first lumber that came in on the new railroad. This house was built on the ground where my present home now stands, 1012 South Division Avenue.

In 1888 we built a two-story frame house, consisting of ten rooms, where the Columbia Park is now located. Two more children were born here, Ralph Grady and Marcia. We lived at this home for twenty-two years and then sold it to the town for a park.[20] In the meantime my husband passed away April 1, 1907, with heart trouble; he was president of the Logan County National Bank here at the time of his death, and had been for four previous years. My son Sam died of Spanish influenza in November 1918, and my mother died one month later at the age of eighty-five years, at my home.

In 1906, while living in the above-mentioned home, my husband, myself, and two daughters, Minnie and Marcia, spent the summer in Los Angeles. My mother was alone in the house. A storm came up and the lightning struck a tree outside and followed the telephone wire into the house, injuring the phone and causing the lace curtain hanging near to become perfectly black, but no fire resulted from it, for which we were all thankful.

I am the only one living of the old settlers who were at that time the head of families, excepting Mrs. H. L. Spencer, who now resides at Huntington Park, California, and is about eighty-eight years of age.

On account of poor eyesight and being quite hard of hearing, I am confined to my home all the time, and feel that I am denied much pleasure in not being able to attend Sunday school and church. For several years I was teacher of the Golden Rule Sunday School Class of the Presbyterian Church; this class was made up of ladies of my own age and some who were younger. I have been a member of the church since I was sixteen years old.

I belong to the First Chapter of War Mothers in Sterling; having had two sons, Grady and Calvin, in the world war.

While the pioneer life was a hard one in many ways, the settlers were like one family and had many things together in common. Most all of them attended church in the sod schoolhouse; literary societies and other meetings were held there too. Occasionally we had a picnic.

While it was not all hard, it is a pleasure to recall those days and think of the dear ones who have passed on, and I hope none of the present generation will have to go through the hardships that some of us did.

We have a thriving little city now, for which I am very proud, and am very glad that we were able to add our little to the building of it. I am now eighty-one years old, and my oldest daughter, Minnie, and youngest son, Grady, live with me.

Lizzie Gordon Buchanan, Logan County [341-18].

Interviewer: M. Amour.

Interviewer's note: Lizzie Gordon Buchanan was born on January 9, 1857, in Green County, Pennsylvania, about eighty miles south of Pittsburgh. Mrs. Buchanan was married to Kossuth Buchanan on June 21, 1899; before her marriage Miss Gordon was a teacher in the Sterling High Schools for five years, 1893–98. Mrs. Buchanan celebrated her seventy-seventh birthday on January 9, 1934.

I came west in September 1883 with two brothers-in-law, W. H. Moore and B. F. Moore, and their families. Our destination was Wahoo, Nebraska, owing to glowing reports we had from friends who had gone from our locality to this place.

There was a vacancy in the grade schools in Wahoo, and I was fortunate enough to get the place. I well remember I was paid in gold—forty dollars per month—the first month. I do not remember how long this continued.

In 1885 I had the western fever more than ever. I was anxious now to get some land in Colorado and start a fortune for myself, as I had such wonderful pictures in my mind what this country would look like and be like in the near future. I remember, when probably ten years old, of seeing a young lady and her brother who had been to Denver and hearing them tell of Colorado. Oh! how it charmed me, especially the name "Colorado," and it is dearer to me today than ever.

In September 1885 I came to Colorado and filed on a timber claim south of Haxtun.[21] At that time you were not required to live on a timber claim, but were required to plant ten acres to trees. I did not feel brave enough yet to try to live on a claim, but later on, listening to the experiences of others, I felt equal to the undertaking.

In 1886 I came back and preempted 160 acres on which a person was required to live at least six months and make certain improvements and pay $1.25 per acre. An eight-by-ten plank house was erected with one door and one window, and all of the "built-in" features—a cracker box over the head of my bed for books and one over the table for dishes. The table and bed were stationary, made of up-to-date planks. A trunk, small stove, and two chairs were the furnishings of one of the first domiciles where Holyoke is now situated.[22] It was Logan County when I filed and made proof on this land.

The nearest land office at this time was in Denver, where I made proof. An agent of the Lincoln Land Company made it a point to be in Denver when I made proof, as my claim was one of the quarter sections that the Burlington and Missouri Railroad Company wanted for a townsite. In a short time I sold the land to this land company, the first eighty acres in July 1887 for one thousand dollars, and in September 1887, the other eighty acres for five thousand dollars.

The first bank in Holyoke was built by George E. Clark on the southeast corner of this claim. Holyoke had three banks in a very short time. To give you an idea how the lots sold, Mr. Clark paid fourteen hundred dollars for his lot.

When I sold my land I agreed to put up a building, which I did. The building was a two-story hotel, known as the Gordon House. W. H.

Moore was the first proprietor. Many living today remember this hotel as a place where they enjoyed the eats, tidiness, good accommodations, and the genial host and hostess, Mr. and Mrs. W. H. Moore. While Holyoke had nine saloons at this time, no liquors were served at this hotel, and only the better class were taken care of here.

I realized before I was through seeking this fortune that "anticipations were sweeter than realities," for a panic and drought soon followed—1891 to '94—and Holyoke soon looked like it would never recover.

I will tell something of my life on this claim: I was so hopeful of the outcome of my undertaking that time did not drag. The most of the home seekers were good citizens—people you could trust. You could lie down at night and sleep, as it was not likely any undesirable characters would be in this section of the country, as at that time there were no automobiles and no railroad.

Of course my relatives had thought I should have a gun and know how to use it. I was prepared to defend myself, but never had an occasion to use the revolver. I never risked a light in the house at night; I ventilated by taking the two lids off of my stove. I had no trouble to sleep. If not a native of Colorado, you no doubt remember your experience about "sleep" and "eats" when you first came to Colorado.

One night, shortly after retiring, I heard someone walking towards the house. I was frightened. I knew by the noise—the boots striking together—that it was not one of my people, but a stranger. He knocked on my door and asked to be directed to a nearby place. I sent him to my brother-in-law, B. F. Moore. This stranger told my folks he guessed there was a woman alone in the shanty northeast of there, for her voice sounded like she was scared to death. I thought I had done wonderfully well and had not given away that I was frightened. My door was locked, and a very large trunk, a "Saratoga," was wedged in between the foot of the bed and door.

Another time I felt alarmed, I saw a large herd of cattle approaching, looked as though there were thousands, and I guess there were. A cowboy came galloping up to my door—my heart was in my mouth—I wonder when I think of it that I did not expire from what I had read and heard about cowboys. My fright was for nothing. He inquired something about the cattle that had passed, very courteously, and away he went.

One more fright during these months on the claim: this was my first and last experience in a lonely shack alone through one of the worst blizzards I ever saw. It was in February 1887. The day before was a beautiful day and I was having breaking done on my claim, getting ready to make proof.[23] There was no warning whatever the evening before the storm, what we might expect. I had only enough coal in the house for one fire, and it was not safe to try to get out or go anyplace or for anyone to get to me. I soon found out too that it was not safe to have a fire. I realized the only thing to do with any safety was to go back to bed and stay there until the storm was over. My house was well anchored, and banked up with sod. I was well and comfortable physically, but not mentally. I knew a brother and brother-in-law and some friends had only a tent to shelter in through this storm. They had gone the beautiful day before to be located about twelve miles southwest of our settlement. All survived. The second morning the sun came out and "We looked upon a world unknown, / On nothing we could call our own." Neighbors came bright and early to see if Elizabeth Gordon and her shack could be found. The snow was piled to the eaves, but they soon dug me out and were on their way, rejoicing to see what they could do for others that might be suffering. I memorized, during this storm, "Rock Me to Sleep, Mother," but I could not be rocked or put to sleep.[24] There was no sleep.

When in Denver, after making proof on my preemption, I decided to file on a homestead on a vacant 160 about two miles southwest of Holyoke. At this time you were not required to live on the homestead five years, but could commute after six months' residence by paying $1.25 per acre. At this same time when I was in Denver, a young man heard I was going to file on this claim and he rushed up a shack on this land, hoping to beat me out of the claim by right of possession. I lived on the west part, and he lived near the east line. He contested my right, but I won the case. I complied with the law and proved up on this place.

Holyoke was a flourishing town at this time, with her three banks, nine saloons, and a railroad, and I did not have the assurance of safety that I did on my preemption. My dwelling was near the public road going west from Holyoke. One beautiful moonlit night I heard a racket that I could not understand—looked out my east window and could see a lot of men around this shanty on my claim. I supposed they were drunks and pilferers and would soon be at my place, so got off to a neighbor's as fast as I could run. This is another time "I crossed the bridge before I got there." A lot of the good men of the neighborhood decided this young man was only pretending to live on his claim, and to prove it they turned his shack over. As there was no floor in the house, the furnishings were exposed outside the next morning—just a bed. He was living with his parents on an adjoining claim.

As to social affairs in our community when preempting, we had a literary society and a Bible school and occasionally just a social gathering where we laughed and chattered over nothing and feasted on "canned peaches" with cream—sometimes cake.

Some of the early settlers in this and adjoining communities were Stewart Beggs; W. F. ByBee and wife; Charles B. Timberlake and wife; J. C. Aiken and wife; and many others of this type that I could name. I mention a few who are well known in eastern Colorado because some refer to the first settlers as "undesirable citizens."

Were we happy under these conditions? I would say yes. It was sweet hope that kept our spirits buoyed up and gave us happiness.

It's wanting keeps us young and fit,
It's wanting something just ahead,
And striving hard to come to it,
That brightens every road we tread.[25]

Mrs. W. H. Clatworthy, Morgan County [351-106].

Interviewer: M. B. Gill.

At the close of the Civil War, among those who went from Baraboo, Wisconsin, to Greeley, Colorado, were the Clark and Baker families. These each were families of six. In 1870 the Clarks arrived in Greeley [along with] Max Clark's brother-in-law, A. S. Baker (Abner).

The last move the Baker family made westward was to Fort Morgan in 1884, when Abner, Lyman, Frank, and my husband, W. H. Clatworthy, and myself arrived with my family and forded the river Platte in a buckboard. By April 1st, when the rest of the Bakers came, the river had risen so high that it was necessary to use a lumber wagon to cross.

Among my memories of that first summer were first, the naming of the town Fort Morgan by Postmaster General Gresham.[26] Second, although an occasional preacher came through that first summer, the main support of our services came through two staunch Scotch-Irish Presbyterians who had taken up claims near here, Father Glassey and John Anderson; Father Glassey proved up on his claim at the age of ninety-four. Third, in our first home, the claim shanty, we hung the chairs up on the wall when we let the bed down at night. The shanty was twelve by twelve and contained our bedroom suite, oil stove, and also the George F. Prince Melodeon, which later furnished music for the Presbyterian Church for years. Antelope—curious creatures that they are—often came close to the cabin to watch the clothes blowing on the line. Our daughter Nina's first birthday was celebrated in this shanty, and her uncle Max Clark threw a beautiful bisque doll to her from the train, on his way to Brush. One wash day, while hanging clothes on the line I heard a slight noise and going around the house found my baby, head-first in the tub of rinse water where she had toppled over the board, placed in the door for safety. She was rescued unharmed but badly frightened.

Fourth, after living in the shanty about nine weeks we moved into the rear of the new Abner Baker store building. That summer I cooked for eleven section men besides baking bread and making yeast to sell.

Our present home was first built in 1885 on five acres, purchased from Lyman Baker. Our two younger children were born in this home, and we have here resided for the last forty-eight years.

I was graduated in 1875 in the class in which Belle Case La Follette was valedictorian in Baraboo, Wisconsin.[27] I taught that first winter in Wisconsin at twenty dollars a month. Hearing that wages were better in the West, I went then to Iowa and taught there the following summer. Then my brother Abner, who had been in Colorado six years, told me that I could get forty dollars in Colorado, so from there I came to Greeley in the fall of 1876. My brother Lyman came to Greeley in 1870 to work for the *Greeley Tribune*.[28] He was a printer and had learned his trade from Ansel Kellogg in Wisconsin, who afterward made an enormous fortune with a newspaper patent.[29] I taught in Greeley a year and a half and then was called to Wisconsin because of Father's illness. The chief industry from '73 to '76 in Greeley was the tanning of buffalo hides. The year 1876 is memorable to me because of the grasshopper plague. Max Clark, my brother-in-law, had a little patch of lawn, and morning glories hung in festoons of grasshoppers.

In 1882 I was married to Mr. Clatworthy in Baraboo and went from there to Edgerton, Wisconsin, where Mr. Clatworthy was a foreman of a tobacco warehouse in the winter and in the summer he painted. The Greeley colony, because it was founded on temperance, it being written in the city's ordinance that no liquor should be ever sold within its jurisdiction, it attracted people from many places, and the Earl of Airlie so arrived from Scotland. He established a large ranch on Crow Creek for his son Lyluph.[30] It was while building the Brush canals in 1883, financed by the Earl of Airlie, that Abner thought of establishing a settlement up the river. However, Max Clark said "there never will be any water taken from the Platte River because of the sand."

When Abner wrote that there was still government land here, I was unwilling to proceed to Colorado until Mr. Clatworthy saw the land because of my grasshopper experience. One Monday morning Mr. Clatworthy came home, said he had, and said he had been laid off work for a week or ten days and we decided that he should come out and look at the land. My mother accompanied him home from Greeley at the end of the next week. As a result we came to Colorado about November 1883. My mother, Lizzie Kitel, and my baby and myself arriving in Greeley about Thanksgiving time. Mr. Clatworthy followed me the following January. My first months were spent with my brother Ed, a well-known engineer. On March 29, 1884, we came to Fort Morgan in a storm which started with blowing off the roundhouse roof in Sterling, lasting four days and ending with nine-foot snowdrifts. We forded the river below the Narrows following the old Indian trail, to reach the horse camp, established for the ditch men by my brother Abner.

Mr. Clatworthy had taken up a tree claim and had moved a shanty onto it west of the town of Fort Morgan. When he took up this tree claim, he thought it was going to be under the Morgan ditch.

In three days there were a dozen families at the horse camp, mostly Bakers and their relatives, so we moved into our claim shanty.

The only building I could see when we arrived was the framework to my brother's store, on the corner of Railroad Avenue and Main Street. The post office was established in this store in August of the same year.[31] Postmaster General Gersham appointed Mr. Clatworthy as postmaster at this time. He also was in charge of this store. We lived in the rear of the store, and Mr. G. W. Warner, brother Abner's secretary, had an adjoining room as his office.

In order to get the Burlington Railroad to move its station from Ensign, Abner gave them half the lots.[32] The first land platted here was on eighty acres belonging to Ella Courtney and eighty acres on my father's land.

The first school was built by J. H. Farnsworth who sold the building to the district for four hundred dollars. He also built the first hotel. Mr. Sidney Prince was the first school teacher. I was president of the school board when the first graduates were presented with diplomas.

Lyman Baker's house was the first in Fort Morgan. It was located on the corner of Main and Platte Avenue. My father's claim shanty was located where the first *Fort Morgan Times* building was built. In August 1884 the first issue of the paper was published by George Warner.[33]

Weld County was 110 miles long and 55 miles wide. School district number 3 was 19 miles long. The school was built close to the railroad, as the railroad was supposed to pay big taxes.

The Ladies' Library Association was formed during the time Mrs. Anna R. White was county superintendent. The Carnegie Library foundation was established.

In 1889 the town bought trees in Otis, Colorado, and outlined the streets.[34] The town was incorporated in 1888.[35]

Our start came from the post office and from the sheep business. Our hardware store or general store was established in 1884 and continues to this day.

I sold yeast cakes made by myself and cooked for eleven section men besides caring for my baby, doing my own washing and the rest of housekeeping that goes with it.

The Relief Corps was one of the first organizations.

The dining room of the present residence is the original home built in 1885.

Chapter 5: The Eastern Prairie

Kit Carson and Prowers Counties

Many a time I have walked one and one-half miles to town to get a drink of fresh well water and bring home a pailful for the children.
Cynthia E. Pierce Boyles

Before much of it was turned to farmland and rangeland, the eastern third of Colorado was short-grass prairie with an average rainfall of below twenty inches a year. A concern mentioned by nearly every narrator in Kit Carson County, therefore, was the scarcity of water. The drying effect of hard winds can cause drought, severe lightning storms, and tornadoes in summer and intense cold, blizzards, and deep snow in winter.[1] By the time these women settled on the eastern prairie, the Plains Indian tribes—the Arapahos, Comanches, and Pawnees, for instance—no longer traversed this area in large numbers. Even before the extermination of the buffalo during the 1870s, mentioned by several narrators, Native Americans had been essentially forced off the land, especially following the Sand Creek Massacre (1864) and its aftermath, when even the peaceful Indians were not safe.

The area that became Kit Carson County was known to the rest of the United States as early as 1843 when the explorer John Frémont—looking for a way through the mountains—followed the South Fork of the Republican River toward its source before he turned north.[2] In

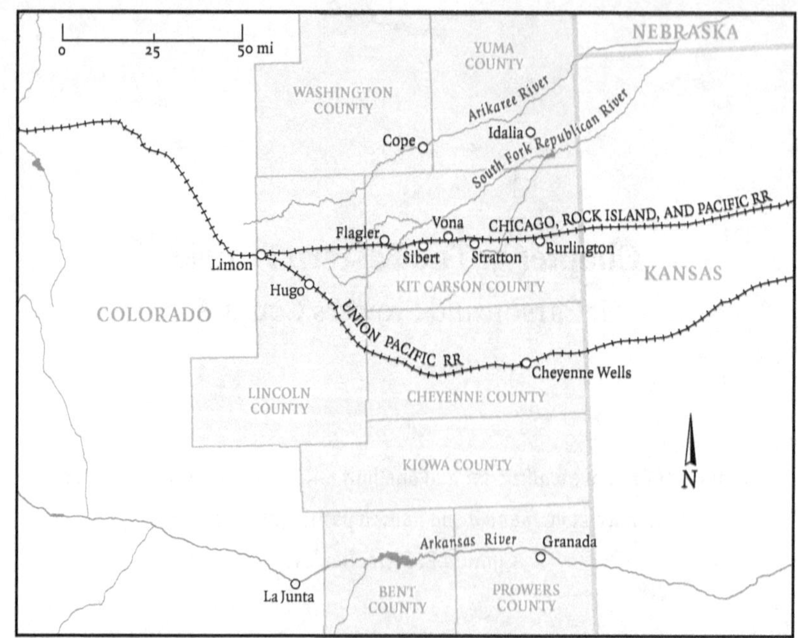

7. The eastern prairie

1858 the same route was surveyed for the Pikes Peak and Leavenworth Highway, which was used for a year until it was abandoned in 1860.

The rush of European American settlers into what became Kit Carson County coincided with the completion of a railway through Burlington and Limon on its way to Colorado Springs in 1887 and 1888. The Rock Island Railway follows an almost due west route through what remain the only communities in the county: Burlington, Stratton (formerly Claremont), Vona, and Seibert, for instance. The first trains ran the route in the fall of 1888. In response to the influx of settlers that the railroad brought, Kit Carson County was organized in 1889, taken from the eastern section of Elbert County, which had been carved from the original Douglas County in 1874.

As in the northeastern part of the state, many of the settlers here took lands under the Homestead and the Timber Culture Acts, which allowed a settler to claim up to two 160-acre plots by living on that acreage and improving it by building and farming or, in the case of the latter act, planting ten acres in trees. Although initially a settler had to remain on the land for five years, by the time of the Timber Culture Act in 1873, six months sufficed. After the specific time period, if a settler could prove up, that is, show that the requirements had been met, he or she could buy the land at $1.25 an acre.

A severe drought in 1893 and 1894 ruined many of the would-be ranchers, but as is evident from the following accounts, many settlers did remain on the land. The railroad provided a livelihood, as did cattle ranging, and, with irrigation, farming became possible. Wheat and cane or sorghum (for both cereal and for livestock feed) were important early crops in eastern Colorado, and their production provided valid reasons for settlement. As mentioned by these narrators, there were continual conflicts between the farmers and cattlemen.

Although, as several of the following narratives suggest, procuring a minister was not often easy, the Methodist Episcopal Church South was popular among the early settlers. This church had come into existence in 1844. When faced with the moral and political issue of slavery, the Methodist Church divided, and the new church counted among its communicants many African Americans.

Most of the narrators here admit that their first several years were very difficult. They had to face and overcome scarcity of water, severe weather, poor housing, lack of knowledge of farming, and sometimes even the early deaths of their husbands. But these women confidently overcame such setbacks, adapting quickly and competently to the demands the environment made on them. For example, Clementina Morrison-Guthrie, who had come from Scotland with her husband, settled in Colorado in 1889. She acknowledges that she was "rather timid at first" but soon became a good farmer who could, for example, "make butter as well as any old-timer." Sarah Blakeman was at first so afraid of coyotes, centipedes, and cowboys that she would not step outside at night. Despite their early fears, these women quickly adapted and became competent farmers, teachers, or nurses, for example. Anna Homm recalls that her daughters all helped their father in the fields and with the cattle and the irrigating. Her husband did not live long after settling, so she took care of the farm, raised her children, and invested in real estate to supplement her income. When only twelve years old, Jennie Jones (Davis) recalls that she had the responsibility of rounding up the cattle on her own.

Like their neighbors to the north in Weld, Morgan, and Logan Counties, these women saw wolves, coyotes, and snakes as vermin and recorded satisfaction with their extermination. Elizabeth Richards recounts that wolves killed two colts and many calves and that coyotes killed the chickens. The wolves were killed off in a few years, she says, but coyotes seemed to endure. Luella Bell McKenzie remembers that there were "plenty of rattlesnakes" and that she killed every one she saw.

Despite all the difficulties of farming on land almost too dry and severe for such use, most of these women record that they were proud of their accomplishments, and they insist that they are happy to have been part of the pioneering of the state. Not all were so fortunate as the women here interviewed, however. McKenzie suggests, for instance, that on rides across the prairie she saw plenty of signs of discouragement and failure: "Many times we could see an old stove here and there on the prairie, and we knew that the shack had blown away, and left the stove sitting on the dirt floor. Perhaps just another instance of blasted hopes."

The field-worker for Kit Carson County was B. B. Guthrie; Margaret Merrill reported from Prowers County.

Nellie Buchanan [350-4]. Seibert, January 18, 1934.

Interviewer: B. B. Guthrie.

I was born in Indianapolis, Indiana, in 1857 and grew to womanhood there. I married while quite young, and in our early twenties my husband and I got the western fever, so we sold our little home, crated our furniture, and took the train for the West. We did not plan where we were going to stop, nor just how far we would go. When we reached Kansas City, the weather was getting colder, and it was snowing very hard, and we soon had the experience of a real blizzard. A few hours out of Kansas City our train got stuck in a snowdrift; it took them twenty-four hours to get the train moving again. We traveled very slow, and the car windows were covered with snow and ice so we could not see out. We were rather tired of such a tedious trip. It took us all day, all night, and until eleven o'clock the next night to get to Atchison, Kansas. We decided to rest a bit, so my husband and two babies and myself got a room in a hotel there, got a good hot bath, and went to bed and slept until eleven o'clock the next day. Then we got a good breakfast and at noon took the train for farther west. The train traveled so slow, and as the windows were covered with ice we could not see the country, so we at last reached a little town by the name of Gaylord,

Kansas, and we decided to stop and rest until the weather got better.

The next morning when I went out on the hotel porch, I was just thrilled, for the great prairie was one big blanket of pure white snow with here and there a little home like a dot on the whiteness; nothing in sight but the beautiful snow and the sky. Right there I knew I would never be contented until I had a home of our own in the wonderful West, so I urged my husband to take a homestead and build a sod house and settle down. I had never seen a sod house, but had learned that they were warm in winter and cool in summer, so I felt that was all that was necessary. My husband looked at me, and smiling said, "Nellie, you don't know what you are talking about." But a woman's job is to talk, so I finally induced him to buy a team of horses, a covered wagon, six cows, and two dozen chickens, and we started west. The sun was shining bright, and the snow was melting fast; we traveled two days and two nights, and the evening of the second day we saw a sod house on the prairie. We drove up to it, and a man and woman came out. They asked us where we were from and where we were going. My husband told them we came from Indianapolis and were going west to take a homestead. The man said, "Man alive, go back to where you came from; go back now while you can, for in a year from now you won't have anything to go back with. Go back before you have to starve." My husband replied that any man in America that would work did not need to starve, so we bid them good-bye and drove on to the next water hole, where we made camp, about two and one-half miles from the sod house and the discouraged man. The next day we filled our kegs with water and drove for miles and miles with not a thing in sight but land and sky, and camping at night on the open prairie.

On the evening of the third day we saw an object on the prairie; we thought it another home, but when we drove up to it we found it was a schoolhouse. We made our camp there and just got through eating our supper when the wind began to blow the hardest I had ever known; then the rain came down in torrents, so we made our beds in the schoolhouse.

About three o'clock in the morning a bunch of coyotes came howling about the schoolhouse, and my husband got up and shot at them two or three times out of the windows. They went away and we went back to sleep, and did not wake until sunrise. Then we got up, ate our breakfast, and started on another day's travel into the enchanted West.

We drove for two days, and about noon of the third day we saw another object on the far prairie, and when we got close to it we discovered it was a big covered wagon with big letters RESTAURANT written on the side. There we ate our lunch and learned that this was the first restaurant on the ground where Colby, Kansas, is now located.

After driving for some days we came to two little towns built close together; one was called Voltaire, the other Sherman Center. Each town was striving for the county seat. Goodland was then platted as a townsite, and when the Rock Island Railroad was laid through this part of Kansas, Goodland was chosen as the railroad center, and the next election won it the place for the county seat.

All the excitement made it so interesting to us that we decided to file a homestead south of Goodland. So we got a claim, built a sod house, and I settled down to be a "homesteader" in every sense of the word. My husband worked at the Rock Island shops in Goodland, and my two babies and I stayed on the ranch fifteen miles south of Goodland. We put barrels in our wagon, and I hauled water from the Smoky River ten miles south of us. I took care of the cattle—our six cows—and learned to hitch and unhitch a team in record time. There was not a soul near us, and not a house in sight. Nothing but the great broad prairies, the wide expanse of the blue sky, and the howling of the coyotes for music. I lived on this ranch for two years.

I remember the first Fourth of July celebration in Goodland; the big excitement of the day was a chance to ride over the new rails that had just been laid. A car had been brought in from further down the line, and everyone that wanted to could get a free ride over the new railroad. My, that was so exciting.

My husband was a lineman, and helped line the new railroad from Chicago to Colorado Springs, and there were times when I would not see him for three to six months at a time.

The railroad went on west, so they moved my husband to Burlington, the county seat of Kit Carson County, Colorado.[3] Most of our western towns grow overnight, and the excitement is the biggest part of them for a number of years. Burlington had a hard struggle for some years, but it is a quite nice little city now, and one of which we are all proud.

Later my husband was moved to Seibert, Colorado. Seibert was not on the map until after the railroad was built. So my husband wrote to me, and told me to sell the ranch and come to Seibert to live. Although I was as much a homesteader as ever, I decided it was best for myself and my two children to get nearer civilization, so we sold our ranch and moved to Seibert. But I certainly did not think much of the town; it was such a dry, shabby little place. There was no water there; all water was hauled from the river four miles north of us, or from the well in the old town of Hoyt. Later the railroad built a section house, and dug a well, and then locked the pump on the well and gave instructions that no one but the railroad employees was to get water from the well. However, the instructions were given to my husband, and not to me. So when a poor settler or one of his family came asking for drinking water or enough to make a cup of coffee, believe me, I did not turn them down. If the railroad was helping to build the country, what about the settlers who were brave enough to withstand the hardships of thirst, of starvation, of lonesomeness; I felt they had as much right to that good water as any of the railroad employees did. So I used to give away a pailful now and then, and then one day I learned that I had been reported. Not through malice, but by someone grateful for the kindness I had shown them, and they were merely relating this kindness. But the outcome was that the supervisor came to my husband and told him that the key would be taken away after the pump was locked and we would have to use the hauled water. My husband regretted the affair, but told him to notify me too, as I used the key. When this man came to my home and told me what he was intending to do, I remember I told him that if he was leaving orders with that key to take it with him, for as long as there was water there and people needed it I would give it to them. That I would be glad to haul water and share it with those around me just as they would do if I needed water. When I got through talking, the supervisor did not say anything, but he bid me good-bye and left the key with me. I really believe he saw what it meant to the people of that community to have a drink of good clear water once in a while; a drink of water that had not stood in a barrel in the hot sun. We had no more trouble after that. Of course, I was careful with the water, but the well never ran dry in spite of all the drinks I gave away.

Everyone was poor, some poorer than others. My husband had a good job with the railroad, so we were more fortunate than a great many others, who had to depend on their cattle and farms for a livelihood. I remember one poor family who had had a great deal of sickness, and on the day that the eldest little child died, another baby was born, and the poor mother had no clothes for the new baby and nothing decent to bury the other little child. So a few of the neighbors got together, and we sewed for the new baby and the mother, and I made a pretty little white dress for a burial dress for the little child. A neighbor man made the little casket, and we lined it nicely with soft white goods and trimmed it with a bit of lace and some white ribbon. I remember after we had the wee one all laid out it looked like a sweet doll, so we took it into the bedroom so the poor mother could see it, and I shall never forget how very grateful she was that her darling was to be given a decent burial. It was just such instances as this that made the neighborhood one big family, all ready to share each other's joys or sorrows.

We lived in cars on the siding until the section house was built, then we lived in Seibert for a number of years, getting acquainted with a number of the pioneer settlers of that town, an acquaintance that has ripened into a lifelong friendship. We again were transferred to Seibert, and we decided to get a ranch and go into the cattle business. The children and I took care of the ranch while my husband did his work on the railroad. We lived here for some years, then my husband died, and my children got married, so I moved to town and am now making my home with my daughter, Mrs. Zella Hutchens, the present postmistress.

I am happy and contented, and enjoy recounting my experiences of the early days in this new country. I am glad that I was one of the pioneers that helped to develop the country, that I was privileged to do my bit towards making a bit brighter the lives of those around me.

Elizabeth Gutting Lengel [350-3]. Burlington, January 10, 1934.

Interviewer: B. B. Guthrie.

I was born in Patterson, New Jersey, on January 31st, 1866, and went to Omaha, Nebraska, with my parents when five years old. In the spring of 1886 my father, Chris Gutting, came to Colorado and built a little frame house and dug a well. I went to Haigler, Nebraska, from Omaha, then traveled by wagon to Lansing (formerly Kingston), and then hired a team and wagon to bring me across with the few supplies I had brought with me.

The country was so strange to me, so very few settlers and homes to be seen, although the rolling hills and nearness to the river made this part of the new country much more attractive than that south of the river.

I took a preemption and a timber claim in what was then Arapahoe County, and my father and I planted the trees together.[4] That clump of trees you see yonder is my timber claim, which I still own.

I never saw any buffalo, but there were plenty of antelope, and there were gray wolves in the vicinity, although I never saw any of them. How lonesome it was at nights when the cold winds blew and the coyotes howled so mournfully. But as time went on, I learned to keep myself busy with sewing or reading and forgot the lonesomeness in the plains and work of my prairie home. I kept house eight years for my father. We had homemade bedsteads, table, and cupboard, but bought our chairs and stove in Haigler and brought them overland. I had no clothesline, and I would hang my washed clothes on the buffalo grass or on the tips of the soapweed—or yucca—plant, which grows so plentifully here.

Mail was brought from Jaqua, Kansas, and from Cheyenne Wells, Colorado, to the Landsman post office, and we got our mail there.[5]

I was well acquainted with Munsinger, a man who today would be classed as a "gangster."[6] He kept our community fearful of just what he would do and who would be the next victim, for one never knew what would be said or done to get into his bad grace. I knew Mr. Allen, the foreman of the Bar-T Ranch whom Munsinger shot; I spoke to Mr. Allen that morning when he was on his way out to fix fence and he had no firearms with him then, but at the trial which followed the murder it was claimed a gun was found beside the murdered man, thus helping to establish the plea of self-defense on which Munsinger was freed. My father and I were questioned about the visit with Mr. Allen and as to whether or not he carried a gun, and our replies being in favor of the man aroused the ire and enmity of Munsinger, and he had our little home burned to the ground in revenge. We lost all we had, including the keepsakes of my deceased mother. Then Father and I built a sod house and started all over again. It may sound rather heartless, but the community was really relieved when we heard of Munsinger's death. He and Mace, Old Bill, kept the community in fear as to where they were, what they were doing, and who would be the next victim of their revenge.

After living with my father for eight years, I married J. L. Lengel, and filed homestead papers on the land on which we are still living. We raised a family of seven children and gave them all a good education.

I boarded the men who built the Emerson Ditch, a project headed by a company in Boston and managed by a man in Kansas. The plan was to use this ditch for irrigation purposes, taking the water from the Republican River and using it on the farms of eastern Colorado and western Kansas. But it never got further than the Kansas line.[7] This ditch is just a short distance north of our home.

It took us two days to make the trip to the nearest railroad to market our wheat and hogs; we had nothing but the wagon to travel in, and the trip was so long and so lonesome. Just think of our going to Burlington in less than an hour now. We live twenty-two miles from Burlington.

We have endured the hardships of pioneering in this new country, have withstood the severe storms in summers and the terribly cold winters, have taken our losses of livestock and crops with the rest of the settlers; and it all went towards the development of a state of which we are proud. We are living alone now in the big home we built when our family was small and growing. But I feel the sacrifices made, the hardships endured, and the loneliness of my early days on the plains has given me an appreciation of my home and the land which only a pioneer can enjoy.

Cynthia E. [Pierce] Boyles [350-55]. Burlington, February 1, 1934.

Interviewer: B. B. Guthrie.

I was born in Scotland County, Missouri, on May 4th, 1856. I spent my youth and girlhood days with my parents in Missouri, and on September 18th, 1878, I was married to William Boyles. We moved to Kansas and lived there for about three years, then my husband came to Colorado in 1885 and located a homestead south of what was then Old Burlington.[8]

We traveled in two covered wagons, my husband, my three children and myself, and my husband's father, who came with us to help us get located and moved. We arrived at my husband's located claim on the fifteenth day of September 1886.

We took the top boxes off the wagons and placed them on the ground, and used them for bedrooms, and did our cooking and eating out in the open over a campfire. In a few weeks we had our two-room sod house built, plastered it with native lime, but could not put in a floor as we had brought no lumber with us and there was none to be had nearer than Cheyenne Wells or Haigler, Nebraska; so we used the dirt floor, and by spreading rag carpet over it, we managed to enjoy a comfortable and warm home to live in.

Our water was hauled from the Beaver Creek Spring, about seven miles west of us.[9] Many a time I have walked one and one-half miles to town to get a drink of fresh well water and bring home a pailful for the children. There were just three in the community then, and they supplied the settlers for miles around. Some months later my brother Carman, who lived near us, dug a well and got a good depth of water, so we got the water from his place, and then had all the water we needed.

We went to church and Sunday school in a little sod schoolhouse on Beaver Creek, about seven miles west and south of us. In the winter we would load into a bobsled, wrap up good in comforters and mufflers, and enjoy the ride over the prairies on the snow. We have traveled many a mile this way and always enjoyed it immensely. Elder Thomas was the preacher here then, and later he helped to organize the first Methodist Episcopal church in Burlington.

The first winter after we came to Colorado, my husband and his father returned to Kansas for supplies, and the children and I stayed alone on the homestead. I never felt frightened, although this country was very unlike what I had been used to. We had plenty to eat and were comfortable and got along nicely. We had difficulty in getting fuel; there was no wood here, and it was necessary to haul the coal from

Cheyenne Wells, so we would gather bits of timber or wood from old trees, buffalo chips, and anything else we could get to burn, and by doing this it made our coal last longer and kept the "home fires burning." My brother hauled our supplies for us from Cheyenne Wells.[10]

In the spring my husband returned from Kansas bringing out food supplies and forty head of cattle, a team of horses and two yoke of oxen, and a plow and harrow. The oxen were used in the fields and in breaking sod and plowing the timber claims. We then built another room on our soddy, dug a well, and built a frame barn, and settled down to homestead life in earnest.

The second winter we were here we had a terrible blizzard and snowstorm; our cattle and oxen drifted down to the Beaver Creek, and when we found them they were embedded in snow up to their horns and we had to dig them out. One of our neighbors lost a good team of horses by being buried in the deep snow and were unable to get out.

When we landed in Burlington we found it was more of a name than anything else; there were just a few shacks, and the townsite of what is now New Burlington was not even platted. There was no railroad and no other buildings but what was grouped around the well in Old Burlington. There was no store here, and I think the first store was brought here by Charles Lamb, and he moved it from Cheyenne Wells. Later a man by the name of Hendricks started a small store, and then later everything was moved from the old townsite to the new one further west, where the depot had been built after the railroad was laid.

I still remember what excitement there was in the community when the railroad crew got to Burlington and the first freight train came over the new track. Everyone came to town to see the train, which was hauling the material for the railroad going west.

Until the railroad went through this county and the post office established, we had to get our mail at Cheyenne Wells. It was usually brought to us by anyone going over for provisions; a neighbor would bring the mail for several families, as well as any supplies they needed.

We got our mail about once a month; in stormy weather it would be much longer than that.

The first school was held in a little vacated building in the town, and the first teacher was a Miss Mary (Molly) Davis, who taught the few scholars that attended. Miss Davis had located her homestead right close to the townsite, so she did not have far to walk to school.

We lived on this farm for some years, then finally sold out and moved to Burlington, where my husband operated a livery barn for a number of years. After our children had grown up and moved away to homes of their own, my husband and I bought a home in east Burlington. We celebrated our golden wedding in 1928, and my husband died a few years later. I am living in my little home in Burlington with my stepson, and enjoy my church work and my neighborhood visits as much as I ever did. I think we had such good times in the early days; we were all contented with the little we had, and got along very well. We always had plenty of good plain food and never went hungry; and that is more than one can say of a great many people today.

Flora Linford Ferris [350-64]. Vona, January 24, 1934.

Interviewer: B. B. Guthrie.

I was born in Tecumseh, Nebraska, on November 11th, 1878, and came to Colorado with my parents in May 1887. We came by wagon train with the S. L. Howell and the DeWitt Walton families.

Father took a homestead nine miles north of where Vona now stands, and then got a tree claim right east of and joining the homestead. He built a sod house for us to live in, and we furnished it with the little furniture we had brought with us. We got our water from a spring in the Republican River and from the well that was used in that community; it was 249 feet deep and furnished us with a bountiful supply of water for some years. The water was hauled up by a windlass pulled by horses; later we put up a windmill, and our water troubles were over.

I helped to plant the trees in my father's timber claim; he would plow up the ground, and I would walk behind and stick the young trees into the soft earth. In the first two or three years we had enough rain that the trees grew very well.

There was no railroad in the country at that time, and we did not know that there was any contemplation of putting a railroad through, so when we saw the smoke of the grading and building outfit, we drove over to find out what it was all about, and there we saw the supply train.[11] We were surely surprised and thrilled too.

We got our mail at Lansing, and most of our supplies came from Haigler, Nebraska.[12] Whenever a family in the community would go for supplies, he would bring back the mail for everyone in the community in a grain sack, and when it was to be distributed the mail was dumped out and each man got his own mail.

When we first came to this country, we lived in Arapahoe County with Denver as the county seat; then it was changed to Elbert County with Kiowa as the county seat, and later it was changed to Kit Carson County with Burlington as the county seat.[13]

I went to school in a bachelor's home on his homestead, and he was the teacher. His name was Daniel Corral. Our second teacher was a man by the name of J. L. Gilmore. We used homemade desks, and our books were those brought out by the settlers. The second year we used a set of books furnished by the teacher, and then soon we were following the prescribed course of study recommended by the state, and we got our textbooks from the district.

We organized a Sunday school, and our superintendent was a Mrs. O. P. Gardner, who had a very beautiful voice, so it was not long until she had organized a singing class and a choir, and many a happy time we had at her home. We had no musical instruments except my father's violin. Some time later I remember a family moved in six miles north of us, and brought an organ with them. The man was a good singer too, so oftentimes we would drive the six miles in our wagon and enjoy an evening of music and singing. I wonder how many young people would be content with such entertainment now? I fear it would not be exciting enough for them. We had such good neighbors, such good wholesome times, and would enjoy real visits. Nowadays people do not enjoy the simple things of life—the real things that bring people together.

The first winter we were out here we had enough flour to last us during the entire winter, but owing to the heavy snows we could not get out for supplies, and towards spring our flour supply got low, and so we younger folk had to eat corn bread three times a day and leave the white flour for the older people and the grandparents. Fortunately we had a few squash which we had raised the summer before, but we got so tired eating squash and corn bread, for it was some time before our people could get over to Haigler for supplies. For a long time I could hardly eat corn bread or squash; I got enough to last for some time when we were on the homestead.

We had no reading matter of any kind, and I don't know how many times we exchanged books and read and reread them. I think that is one reason why we enjoyed the singing so much; it gave us something to do and was a pleasure to all.

I remember that J. D. Cope, the founder of Cope, Colorado, invited our little Sunday school to a meeting they were to hold at Cope, so Father and my sister and I drove the twenty miles in a buggy with one horse, and enjoyed the meeting, which was held in a little outdoor room protected by a canvas cover and side. We had such a nice time, and drove back that night to our home.

My father had a blacksmith shop at Lansing for two summers, and Mother and we children stayed on the ranch and took care of the stock. My grandfather lived south of us about one-quarter mile, so he helped us in the work. These prairies used to be the grazing ground for great herds of Texas cattle, and the cattlemen resented the intrusion of the settlers on the grazing ground, and they would drive their herds of cattle over our new fields and trample down the grain. We had no fences nor any protection for our fields, and the cowboys knew this.

When we first came to Vona it had but one little store, and that soon went out of business, so we had to get our supplies from Stratton, Seibert, or Denver. I was married to Archie Ferris, and he took a homestead and built a frame house in which I went to housekeeping. Father Ferris came to Vona in 1887 and took a homestead northeast of Stratton about twenty miles; then the mother and children came out in 1888. They lived on this claim until 1890 and then came to Vona, where Mr. Ferris was employed on the railroad. At one time the Ferris family were the only residents of Vona. He finally became section foreman of this division, and worked in this capacity for a number of years.

Mary Belle Kiser Haynes [350-63]. Vona, January 24, 1934.

Interviewer: B. B. Guthrie.

I was born in Clay County, Kansas, on September 21st, 1864. I spent my youth in Kansas with my parents, then was married to Elmer H. Haynes in 1884, and came to Colorado with my husband and baby son in 1887. My husband had come out eight months before and taken the homestead on which we are still living, and is part of Haynes's addition to the town of Vona, Colorado.

On this homestead site he built a dugout and we lived there for a few weeks, then we bought a frame building which was originally a saloon, and moved it to our location, and lived there for seven years until we proved up.

My husband was a contractor, and helped to build three miles of the railroad. His business was what caused us to come to Colorado. He followed this work for about fifteen years, and we lived in different places during that time, but always keeping our homestead. Finally we returned to Vona, and built this frame house in which we are living.

When we first came west the little station at Vona had just been built and the place named "Vona" after a daughter of one of our pioneer printers, Fred King, living at Burlington. The railroad had dug a well here, and this was where we got our water; water was hauled from this well by people who were living on homesteads ten or fifteen miles away.

Our very first school was held in a little frame building, and my husband taught the first term. We had no church or Sunday school then, and how I did miss it. People interested in Sunday school were too few and far between to organize, and it seemed as though the traveling preachers did not get up our way. Our mail was brought direct to the station, and all the food supplies were shipped in by train for the railroad crew. What little bit of furniture we had, we shipped from Kansas to Vona.

I shall always remember how very frightened I was in this new place. So many strangers around, and so many tramps going across country and following the railroad. My husband was away so much of the time, and he gave me a revolver with the caution to always keep it handy, and never open the door at night. One night a knock came to my door, and I did not open it, but called out "Who is there?" A gruff voice answered, "Open the door, I'm about friz." I did not open the door, but told the man to go on down to the section house where he would find shelter. Next day I learned it was just another tramp. While returning to Vona from Burlington one day, the conductor on the freight train told me that the day before they had seen a woman running towards the train and waving to the crew, and a man was running after her. This was on the prairie between Stratton and Vona. So the conductor stopped the train, and when the woman came up they learned that the man was a tramp who had broken into her home, and she had gotten away from him, and seeing the train, ran to the train crew for protection. The crew chased the tramp over the prairie for some distance, and he ran towards Burlington and got away, but had the train crew gotten him they would have given him something to think about for a while.

The first settlers that came out seemed to be a nice class of people, but later others began coming in who would steal everything they could get their hands on. Someone stole our chicken house; we had it bolted onto posts put into the ground, and they simply sawed it off the posts and took it away. We had made it from some lumber and from packing boxes in which our goods was shipped. One day a neighbor lady and I were invited into the country for dinner, and what was my surprise to see our chicken house in the yard. Evidently, the lady did not know where it had come from, so I said nothing to her about it.

My brother was building a lean-to kitchen on his house, and did not have it fastened to the house, and the next morning when he went to his work the kitchen had been moved away.

I remember hearing about a man who was in his home when a group of men came to look at the house preparatory to moving it away that night. He did not let himself be seen, so that evening the men came and moved the house to the place on which it was to stand. Then the owner came to the door and said, "Now gentlemen, you can move me back again to where I live." This they did and were glad to make a quick getaway afterwards. For a while one could not leave a thing out of doors and expect to find it again, for it seemed as though someone was always around picking up what belonged to others. I am glad we do not need to live in a community like that now.

Our nearest doctor at that time was Dr. P. B. Godsman at Burlington, twenty-eight miles away. Many a time he has answered a call to a patient at Vona, and at all of the towns along this line.

After returning to Vona and building our house, we lived here a year, and then my husband was elected county judge of Kit Carson County. We then moved to Burlington and lived there for eight years; then returned to our old homestead and have lived here ever since. My husband and I live here alone now; our five sons and one daughter have grown up, married, and moved away.

I enjoy recounting the experiences of the early days in this country; I shall always appreciate the friendships made and the neighborly folks who were always willing to share in our joys and sorrows. We have seen the town of Vona grow from a railroad well and section house to the substantial little place it is today, and we rejoice to know that we did our bit towards the development of this new country.

Angelina Fuller [350-38]. December 28, 1933.

Interviewer: B. B. Guthrie.

Interviewer's note: Born in 1855 in Warren County, Illinois. Spent youth in Illinois, and came to Colorado in April 1888 with husband and two children in a covered wagon.

We were ordered west on account of my husband's health, so we shipped our goods to Haigler, Nebraska, and later had them freighted across to our homestead.

We lived in our wagon until our sod house was built, which was in June. We were located in what was known as Old Columbia and there wasn't a thing in sight then, nothing but stretches of these great prairies. Old Columbia was situated about four miles east of where the town of Stratton now stands.[14] We dug a hole in the ground, cut a piece of stovepipe in half, laid it over the top of the hole, and built our fire there. We slept in the wagon box on a straw mattress and used no pillows or sheets. Can you imagine how thrilled I was when we had our house built and got our furniture to use again. I remember that after I had my bed all made up, clean sheets, feather pillows and bed, and clean comforts, I felt rather queer going into it. We had slept in our clothes for so long that it seemed rather strange to undress and go to bed. And how much we did appreciate eating on a table and having our cupboard for our dishes instead of putting things away in a box.

We brought cornmeal and beans with us, and that is what we lived on for months. We would have fried mush for morning and evening, and bean soup for dinner. When we got some flour, I made biscuits and baked them on top of the "stove" we had, getting them brown on one side, then turning them over to brown on the other side. And we surely would enjoy them too. We could get no milk, eggs, meat, butter, or potatoes, so had to be contented with fried mush and bean soup.

I remember the first Sunday after we had our house all fixed up that my husband jokingly said we would invite the Camps over for dinner. The Camps were people who lived in Iowa. But as he could not invite them, he brought home two lady schoolteachers and the Methodist minister, Elder Thomas, and we had bean soup and bread for dinner, and had a very happy time.

When we first located on our homestead the greatest problem was to get water. There was a well about four miles east of us, and we hauled water from there, but so many others hauled it too that my husband had to get up at two o'clock in the morning and get in line so he would get home before night. When this well got out of order, we had to haul water from a water hole about three miles west of here. Oftentimes we would find pollywogs and other things in the water, but we strained it through cloth two or three times, then would boil it, and in that way make it fit for use. Later we got water at the railroad well dug in this vicinity. On September 8th our own well was finished, and we hauled water up with a windlass. My, we felt we were the richest and happiest people in the whole community. We were never sick, and my husband was gaining in health every day.

My husband built a blacksmith shop, and operated that for three years; then he sold that and went into the general store and grocery business, and operated that for a number of years. We built a two-story frame building and we lived upstairs and had the store downstairs. One evening my husband went down to the store to get some papers, and fainted, for I heard two thuds, as it were, and I ran downstairs, and found the store in flames and my husband lying face down on the floor. I quickly pulled him outside and called to a neighbor living close, and he came running over and helped me get my husband out of the way of the fire. But we lost everything, for the building was burned to the ground.

As I told you, we came direct to Old Columbia, and it was not known then where the depot of the new railroad would be built, but when the railroad was put through and the depot built four miles west of where we were, the name was changed to Claremont. Later the name was again changed to Stratton. When the townsite was changed, everyone then moved to the new town, and that is where we started our store business. In the fall of 1888 my husband went back to Iowa to help harvest a corn crop, and when he returned to Colorado he came through on the first passenger train that went over the new railroad right into Denver. Prior to this time the trains had come as far as Goodland, Kansas, but this was the first time a passenger train had gone straight through into Denver.[15]

When we first arrived, I asked at once whether or not there would be a school for the children of the community. I was assured that a school would be started just as soon as possible, so the following May a school was started in a little frame shack that had been built for a butcher shop and then vacated. Charley Dickinson was our first teacher, later a state representative, and I think there were seven scholars enrolled.

Our first Sunday school and church was held in a grocery store. We had no building, and wanted church services, and the grocery man kindly offered the use of his store. We would hold the service, then whenever church was over, the grocery man began selling his wares to whoever wanted to buy. Later we held church in the schoolhouse, and when that privilege was denied us we met at the gate of the building and held meetings there until the weather got too cold to stay outside. The man who had the grocery store was a Mr. Dyer; Reverend Meade, our first minister, was a Congregationalist. Later Elder Thomas, a Methodist minister, preached for us. Later our first little church was built.

A man by the name of Rogers started a little newspaper, and that was all the reading material we had.[16] But everyone was so friendly, and we had literary society and school plays and parties that got the folks together and kept us from being too lonesome.

I well remember the first baby that was born in the community and how the people gathered round the mother to get a glimpse of the baby the first time it was brought to church. The family's name was Fletcher, and it was the eldest little girl in this family who invited us all to our first Thanksgiving dinner, and when folks came from miles around and came empty-handed, the mother could not help but wonder just what it was all about. Suddenly it dawned on her that this was an "invitation" affair, so she asked the little girl if she had invited the people there for dinner. "Yes," said the child, "I was lonesome"; she thought it would be nice to have a party. So the women got busy and helped the mother do up the work and prepare dinner, and we had dinner, but certainly not anything like a Thanksgiving dinner.

One day my husband and I went to the west well to get water, and while we were away the two children noticed a group of men coming across the prairie. Of course, they thought it was Indians, and they ran to a neighbor's home. The neighbor too thought the Indians were out again, and they hitched up their team and were ready to go to the nearest town and give the alarm. Later we found out it was a group of Italian workers who had been looking for work on the railroad and were returning to Cheyenne Wells afoot.

Anna Quinn [350-10]. Stratton, January 3, 1934.
Interviewer: B. B. Guthrie.

I was born in Ohio on September 7th, 1858, and came to Iowa with my parents when six years of age. I lived in Iowa twenty-two years, then came to Kansas in 1885.

On March 28th, 1888, we arrived in Kit Carson County and made camp at the place where Flagler is now located. We had come west with the P. J. Murphy grading outfit to build the grade for the Rock Island Railroad from Goodland, Kansas, to Colorado Springs. We came out on the U.P. [Union Pacific] Railroad to Kit Carson, Colorado, and unloaded the mules, horses, and grading outfit; then it was taken overland to our location.

There was no town then, not even the beginning of one. Nothing before us on the stretch of lonesome prairie but one home where lived Grandma Doughty, with her son Ben and his children. Two of these Doughty girls later taught school after the settlement started, and taught for some years throughout the county.

We had no idea of the hardships we would meet, so we were unprepared for blizzards or storms, and had but one ton of coal. The men pitched camp, setting up the tents, the feed racks, et cetera. I had five small children, and there were two other women with small children, and over one hundred men. My husband, Mike Quinn, was walking boss, so we stayed in camp until our contract was finished.[17]

My husband was then appointed section foreman with headquarters at Flagler, so we then located on a claim two miles north of where the town of Flagler now stands. We built a one-room sod house, and as the walls were unplastered we were bothered terribly with the prairie fleas; they were so plentiful here in the early days. My five children and I lived on the claim while my husband bached in town. On Saturday nights he would walk out the two miles to our claim, carrying the week's provisions on his shoulder. We had no horse or vehicle at that time, and had but two milk cows. These were lariated out on the prairie, and oftentimes they would break loose, and I would need to walk miles over the prairie looking for them, and leaving the children alone in the sod shack.

The town of Flagler began to be built by this time, a few shacks, a sod schoolhouse, and a tent grocery store.[18] My two older girls, then being of school age, walked to town to school. Many a day of worry

I put in, for the terrible blizzards would come up so suddenly, and I would fear the girls would get confused in directions and become lost on the prairies. So I would leave the three small children in the shack alone, and go out to meet the girls. I never stopped to think that I too could easily become confused and lost as well as the girls.

I carried water one-quarter of a mile from a well on the creek, always using buckets, as we had no other means of hauling it. When wash day came, I would take my washing and wash boiler to the well, dig a hole in the ground, and fire with buffalo chips, set the wash boiler over the fire, and do my washing, drying the clothes on the grass on the prairies. Oftentimes I have taken my baby along and set the little fellow on a quilt on the prairie while I did my washing. Of course, I had to keep a sharp lookout for snakes, for there were many of them on the prairies. And there were thousands of wild range cattle that would flock around our little sod shack at night, and dig their horns into the walls and bellow. Then we would open the door and yell at them, and when they were running away the noise of their hoofs sounded like thunder. Hundreds of antelope furnished meat for the settlers who were then coming in. And there were plenty of coyotes too.

After proving up on this claim we took a preemption one-quarter of a mile south of Flagler and nearer town, so my husband lived at home with us and helped more with the work, still doing his work as section foreman on the railroad. We went into the cattle business, the older children and I running the ranch until my eldest son got old enough to help. Oftentimes we would hear the wind blowing ahead of a blizzard, and we would go out at night and get our cattle rounded up and home before the blizzard struck us and the cattle started to drift.

I remember one time an awful blizzard came and snowed us in in our dugout south of town. My husband shoveled the snow back into the house and burrowed his way out. When the snow melted there was about a foot of water on the floor, and the children had to stay on the bed and on chairs until we got the floor dried up.

As time went on we were able to improve our place, and when the children got older we moved into town and lived there for some years. After my husband's death I stayed with my children for a while, but I enjoy my own little apartment now, and still get a lot out of life.

Clementina E. Morrison-Guthrie [350-65]. Burlington, January 23, 1934.

Interviewer: B. B. Guthrie.

I was born in Greenock, Scotland, on May 24th, 1860, and spent my girlhood days with my mother and sisters and grandmother in the old family home in which the fifth generation is now living.

I was married to Peter Guthrie on November 1st, 1883, and after living three years in Greenock we moved to the United States, going to live in Philadelphia, where my husband's brother Alexander was then living. This was in April 1886, and the two brothers then worked at the contracting and carpenter trade, building ninety houses and stores in the two years we lived there.

In 1888 I returned to Scotland on a business and pleasure trip combined, and while I was away my husband received word from a lawyer in Burlington, Colorado, that a brother, James Guthrie, who had taken a homestead in 1887, had been found dead in his claim shack under suspicious circumstances that looked like murder. My husband left at once for Colorado, coming west on the Union Pacific Railroad to Hugo, Colorado, and then traveling by stagecoach across plains to Burlington.[19] The body had been buried on a corner of the homestead—and was exhumed for inspection, and fully convinced my husband that the findings of the coroner and Dr. Bishop were true: that the man had come to his death by being struck with a blunt instrument on the back of the head. Two men were suspected, but nothing could be proved at that time, so my husband returned to Philadelphia, leaving the affairs in the hands of a lawyer, Mr. S. K. King. James Guthrie was a very quiet, reserved man, very reticent in his manner, and had no bad habits, so no reason could be given for the deed except that this claim was close to town and right by the new railroad line, and was envied by others in Burlington.

After returning to Philadelphia from my trip abroad, I had a very severe sickness and was ordered by the doctor to return to Scotland, or go further west. My husband was so thrilled with the new western country that he was eager to go to Colorado, so we packed our furniture and bedding in a freight car and came to Burlington on the new Rock Island Railroad, arriving here in April 1889, and getting to Burlington at night and in a cold drizzly rain. We went to the little hotel, a two-story cracker-box-like structure, and tried to rest, but the western atmosphere rather frightened me. In the morning I looked out on open prairie on one side and a few dingy shacks on the other, and felt rather disconsolate over the prospects of a home in such a place, but decided that we would have to make the best of it. We bought a home in town and lived there for a short time, getting acquainted with western ways and the new land. Then my husband took a homestead, or rather, bought a relinquishment from an old man named Peter McGinnis, and we moved into a dugout—my husband, myself, and eight children—to hold our claim until our house was built. We had no well, so had to haul water from a farmhouse south of us which my husband owned and on which we had lived a short time. It was while we were living in this dugout that my husband took very ill with pneumonia, and what an anxious time I had nursing my husband and trying to run a farm I knew nothing about. But my husband got well, and our new sod house was soon finished and we moved into it; and my, how we did expand. I had so much to learn and had to work so hard, but thank God, I had gained in health and was able to do my work for my family. Then we put down a well, and got a large water tank, and built barns and sheds and started farm life in earnest. I was rather timid at first, but soon got used to the farm animals, and got so I could raise chickens and ducks and make butter as well as any old-timer.

Our first buying venture in cattle was seventeen milk cows, sold to us as thoroughbred stock. The first year we lost the calves through blackleg.[20] We had bought two fine mares, and six weeks after, one of them died. We were rather discouraged, but kept hoping for better luck ahead. So we bought another team and some farming implements, and put in the crops. Owing to the severe drought, we lost our crops for several years in succession. But although I was pretty discouraged by this time, my good husband was no quitter, and he never once lost faith in this country.

We had our gains and losses, our many ups and downs, but we never gave up; we always managed to have enough to eat, good plain food that helped to build the sturdy bodies on our twelve boys and girls. I was the mother of the first pair of twins born in Kit Carson County—Sara M. and Clyde Guthrie—and three years later gave birth to my second pair of twins, Laura K. and Tobin H. Guthrie.

We managed to clothe our children respectably—they did not need as much as boys and girls do now—and we attended the little M. E. [Methodist Episcopal] church and Sunday school in Burlington, for our ranch was just one and one-half miles east and north of Burlington. The wagon and team was our conveyance wherever we went, and we felt quite rich when we acquired a two-wheeled cart and then later a buggy.

My children attended the first schoolhouse built in Burlington, the bricks used in this building being made from clay dug at Beaver Creek south of town. This little schoolhouse is now replaced by a beautiful building about four times as large. I remember when the first schoolhouse was built, it was considered very large, as it had four rooms in it, and the community doubted very much if there would ever be enough children to require the use of the four rooms; today the school has fifteen teachers, and the great building is crowded.

Our fuel was buffalo chips, which was gathered from the prairies and put in large piles for future use. These made good heat, but were not lasting.

We lost quite a number of our cattle on the railroad. There were no fences then, and they would wander down on the right-of-way looking for the new grass, and then, becoming frightened when the train came, would get run down on the track. We also lost thirteen of our milk cows in a cane field one night; this meant a lot to us, for we were then making our living by selling milk and cream.[21] But we were fortunate in having very little sickness in our family, and in some way or other we always managed to get along and live respectably.

The increasing family called for more room, so my husband built a nine-room cement-block house with a large frame kitchen attached, and a roomy attic. This house still stands on the old homestead which has recently come into my possession. After my husband's death in May 1916, I lived on the ranch for two years longer, then moved to Burlington, where I had bought a home, and where I am now living with my oldest son and daughter and three small grandchildren whose mother, my daughter Sara, passed away in 1928.

After my family grew up and were able to take care of themselves, I began to do a bit of practical nursing, and was often called out to wait on some expectant mother. I was out in all kinds of weather, and traveled in all sorts of conveyances to my destination. I remember that one time an old-fashioned auto came for me, and when we came to a hill I had to get out and help push, and the driver sat at the wheel and coaxed the motor to go ahead. Then the engine got hot, and the driver discovered that it needed water, so he left me sitting on the prairie while he walked a half mile for a bucket of water. We finally reached our destination, but what a sight I was with mud, for it had snowed the night before, and my having to push the car did not help my appearance any. I have traveled miles in a topless buggy with the rain coming down in torrents; sometimes in a blizzard we would lose our way, and wander around on the prairie until some landmark was found that would give us our bearings and put us in the right direction for our destination; other times the horses would find their way home, thus relieving us of the worry of looking for a road.

But like all other adventures, these too came to an end, and many a little lad and lassie I have welcomed into the world and given a start towards good citizenship by giving them their first bath. A number of these boys and girls have now graduated from high school, and some of them are in college, and I am proud to say that none of them that I know of have ever been in serious trouble or brought disgrace on their parents or friends. May God bless and keep every one of them.

One of our early day annoyances was the fleas; sand fleas, they called them, but they did not stay in the sand; they got on our clothes and made us most miserable by their savage biting. When we walked over the prairie to our way to church, the preacher did not need to impress us with the story of a place of torment, for when these little insects got busy on our bodies we were assured we were already in torment. When church was over, we hurried home to be the first undressed and get outdoors so we could shake our clothes and thus remove these intruders. It is rather amusing to think about it now, but it was a very serious matter in those days.

I could never be contented to live anywhere else than in Burlington, where my husband I went through our trials together; here my children were born, and those loved ones who have gone on are at rest in our little cemetery here. I have watched with pride the growth of Burlington from the few shacks I first saw to the nicest little town between Denver and Kansas City.

Elizabeth Richards [350-26]. Burlington, December 18, 1933.

Interviewer: B. B. Guthrie.

Interviewer's note: Born April 26, 1862, in Wales. Husband born August 28, 1851, in Wales. After her husband died, Mrs. Richards moved to Burlington and purchased a modest and comfortable little home where she now lives. She enjoys her church work and is a very interesting person to listen to.

Mr. Richards came to Colorado in February 1886 and filed on a homestead in Arapahoe County, now Yuma County, where he lived until his death in October 1923.[22] He was one of the very first settlers in this vicinity.

I came to Colorado on March 4th, 1889. My husband had built a little sod house twelve by fourteen feet, and a little lean-to at the back which was dug partly in the ground. Our nearest neighbor lived two miles north of us, and east, south, and west of us were miles and miles of open prairie land, not even fences to break the monotony of it all.

Our mail came from Wray, Colorado, forty miles away, and was brought to us only when some of the farmers went north to Wray to bring supplies.[23] Two or three of the twelve families of farmers living along the road would make the trip together and bring supplies for all along with the mail. Sometimes it would take over a week to deliver the mail that was brought in. And, if the weather was stormy, it would take longer than that. The trip to Wray always took two days, and the farmers felt safer when two or three went together. Oftentimes a storm would come up after these men had gone, and what an anxious time those at home put in until the men arrived home safely.

My husband saw some buffalo when he first came to the country, but I did not see any. But I did see plenty of antelope and wild horses, or wild ponies, as they were then called. I remember that there was a herd of about one hundred antelope that grazed about one-half mile from our claim. There were plenty of coyotes that used to kill our chickens, and there were a few gray wolves too.

I shall always remember an experience we had with them. One night I was awakened by the shrill whinny and screaming of our horses that were ranging about one-quarter of a mile from the house. Waking my husband, we hurriedly dressed and went to where the horses were, and just before we reached them we saw two big gray wolves running away from the herd. We found that the wolves had attacked two little colts that were with their mothers, and had hurt them terrible, as one of the colts had its hind leg and shoulder eaten off, and other had the hind leg torn badly. We put them on a sled and took them to the house. The first little colt died in about an hour, and the other lived for about six months. The poor mothers and two working horses were white with sweat with fighting these wolves. Later my brother-in-law saw the wolves coming back and shot at them. We lost many calves during the early years by this band of wolves. Later the Bar-T Ranch outfit killed them off, or at least they disappeared in about four years.[24]

We kept just a few cattle and horses for farm use. We hauled water from the Republican River four miles away with a team of mules and a wagon with four barrels in it. We had no drinking water, and I could not bear to drink the water from the river when I knew that the range cattle and horses were standing in it. So one day we set out to find some clean water, and after wandering around for some time, to our delight we found a little spring and a tiny steam of water running from it. It took about two hours to fill the two buckets we had with us, and for once we had all the water we wanted to drink, for we were so thirsty and drank so much at the little spring. We carefully carried the water home, and the next morning when we took a drink of it we found it was bitter as could be, and unfit for drinking.

How disappointed we were. We discovered that the water turned bitter when it was kept for any length of time, so every Sunday we would drive the three miles to the spring and fill a bucket with water so we could have enough to drink for a few hours. When the snow came, we could melt the snow and drink the snow-water. We got our water from the Republican River and from the little spring for about three years. Then later in the spring we had a well bored about 190 feet deep, and the water was brought up by a chain and a long bucket, pulled up by a mule. It was not long until the neighbors heard that we had a well, and they came from miles around to get water, hungry for a taste of good clean well water. In another year we put up a windmill, and how happy we were, and just about the richest people in the community, for we had a windmill and plenty of water. It was not long after that until several of our neighbors had wells bored, and the search for good water was at an end.

The first wells in the country were hand dug; these were very expensive and not always successful, for one did not know how deep they had to go for water. Later a man brought in a well-boring outfit; this was a huge auger that bored its way into the earth, and was turned by one or two horses that walked round and round as the auger went deeper into the earth. Now we have the well-drilling outfits, which are much quicker.

Having plenty of water now for all purposes, we bought ten head of milk cows, and I made butter for sale. We drove ten miles to Friend, a Quaker colony near the Nebraska line, and there I sold my butter for six cents a pound, and got five cents a dozen for eggs.[25] That year we had a fairly good crop of corn, wheat, and rye. The next two years we raised very little, and managed along on what we could get from our butter and eggs and chickens.

For many years we would have prospects of such good crops, and then the hail and terrific wind would come and destroy our crops, oftentimes leaving us very scarce of feed for our stock. I remember one year we had a splendid crop of wheat, 150 acres that looked as though it would bring from forty-five to fifty bushels per acre. My husband went to town and bought a new binder, and upon reaching home he discovered that one of the parts was missing. The following day he went to town and got the missing part, and on Saturday afternoon started in to cut the wheat. About three o'clock on Sunday afternoon a terrific hailstorm came up and destroyed the wheat, ruined our corn and other crops. We sowed cane in one of the fields, and that gave us feed for our stock that year. Another year I remember we had a pretty good crop of oats, wheat, barley, and rye, and then it turned so dry that we could not cut our corn fodder during the day, but had to wait until night dews were on, then cut the fifty acres of corn with the knives and by moonlight. But we saved our feed for the cattle.

And I shall not soon forget the storm we had on April 10th; then we had a three-day blizzard, one of the worst that has ever been experienced, and is remembered by the cattlemen especially. The snow was so fine that it would easily smother anyone or any animal that tried to face it. Thousands of cattle and horses perished that year, and hundreds drifted away and were never found by their owners. I remember we turned out fifteen head of cattle that morning, and when we realized that a blizzard was coming we tried to get the cattle headed back towards home, but the wind was so strong we could do nothing with them, and we had to leave them and get home before the storm started. We turned our eight head of horses loose in the shed and in the barn. There was plenty of feed but no water near them, but they did not suffer for that, as they ate snow. The fine snow drifted into the shed and barn, and as it kept filling up it pushed the horses up with it. Finally the snow pushed the roofs off the barn, and when we looked out of the window we discovered that the eight head of horses were on top of the barn, and so covered with snow that one could hardly tell what they were. The snow had drifted up even with the barn, but we had quite a time getting the horses off the roof and down on the ground. The poor things were so cold. In trying to get to the barn during the storm my husband tied ropes from the house to the other buildings, but the snow would choke him so he could not go on, and he had to wait until the storm abated before he could venture out. We found all of our cattle excepting two about four days later. I think we were very fortunate, for some of our neighbors lost all their cattle. We found cattle that had drifted down one hundred miles from the north, and then perished in the great snowdrifts.

We have blizzards now, but nothing like that one. And too, the farmers now have better barns and sheds in which to shelter their livestock.

We had to work very hard to get ahead; we met many disappointments and discouragements, but we had good kind neighbors, friendly visits, and social gatherings that were always enjoyed.

Martha Gilmore Lundy [350-13]. Burlington, January 2, 1934.
Interviewer: B. B. Guthrie.

I was born in Putnam County, Indiana, in July 1856 and spent my girlhood and young womanhood in that state; then after my marriage to Charles L. Lundy, we came west with our two small children to visit my mother and sister, who were then living in Beaver City, Nebraska. That was on May 20th, 1888, that we arrived at Beaver City. My husband had been ordered west for his health, and he came on out to Colorado, and liking the looks and prospects of the country, he drove to Denver and filed the papers on his homestead. He then returned to Beaver City, and in March 1889 we came out and settled on our homestead. We built a sod house, and our goods were shipped to Denver and then down to Burlington.

Water was hauled from Carlisle, the place now known as Peconic Siding.[26] The railroad had dug a well there, and people of the surrounding country would go there for water. It was six miles from where we lived, and we hauled with a team and wagon and barrels. Later we had a well drilled, and had the water hauled up by a windlass.

A short time after we were settled, a sod schoolhouse was built, and our children were sent to school. At first school was held just three months in the year, as we were always so worried about our children getting lost in the storms that would come up so suddenly; in the early fall and spring we would have the terrible dust storms, and in the winter the blizzards. My children had to go so far that I was glad they concluded to have school in good weather only.

There was no church or Sunday school; this was a missionary field of the Methodist Church, so my brother-in-law, Reverend Frank Thomas, was sent here as the first minister. He preached in schoolhouses and little churches all over this county and helped to organize many a

Sunday school in the little communities scattered over these broad prairies. When the visiting preachers would come to the community, I was the one who always entertained them, and kept them overnight, and we would enjoy their visit, for we got glimpses of the old home and news of the outside world from which we would often feel so far removed. Although I was a Presbyterian, I acted as Sunday school superintendent of the M. E. [Methodist Episcopal] Sunday school for some years; our preacher was Methodist, and one of the teachers was of the Christian faith. We used to have some good-natured arguments, but we all did what we could for the furtherance of the good work in this new field. My brother, James T. Gilmore, was one of the pioneer teachers in this county. Reverend Frank Thomas organized the first Methodist Episcopal church in Burlington.

Our supplies were either freighted in from Haigler, Nebraska, or gotten at the small store at Lamborn, Kansas, now Kanorado.[27] We could not always get what we wanted, so just had to be content with what we could get. My husband worked in Denver for a while, then went east to work for the Foster Lumber Company, and while he was away I stayed on the homestead with my children. His wages were the means of getting what supplies we needed, so we did not suffer the hardships of a great many other pioneers who could not get work and had not the money to get the needed supplies for themselves or their children.

We would have such terrible storms during the winter, and it was always a worry when our husbands or children were out on the prairies for fear of a storm coming up suddenly and causing them to lose their way home. It was so easy to get lost, for there were no fences to follow, no trails, no landmarks of any kind. It has always been a wonder to me that more people were not frozen to death on the prairies.

I remember that my brother-in-law, Reverend Thomas, told of his first meeting in the new town of Burlington being in or very near a saloon building, and when some of the converts became happy over their religion, and some of those in the saloon became loud from too much tippling, there was quite a babble of voices. But it was not long until the little frame building was put up, and the first M. E. church held meetings there.

I did not see any buffalo, but my boys picked up a hunter's knife and steel on the prairie, and we always thought that some hunter had been skinning a buffalo and happened to leave the knife lying beside the carcass, as there was quite a pile of bones at the place where the knife was found. And it was no unusual thing to pick up Indian arrowheads on the prairies.

My husband returned to Colorado and helped transcribe the county records after Kit Carson County was organized. He worked in the Office of the County Clerk for some years, and finally served one term as county clerk and recorder.

When we first came to Colorado there was no cemetery anywhere near us, and the dead were laid to rest in a corner of the homestead. Finally someone donated an acre of ground, and a neighbor lady and myself went round the community and into Burlington and solicited funds enough to put up a woven wire fence round the plot so our dead would not be molested by coyotes or badgers that always dug holes into the soft earth that was on the graves.

Luella Bell McKenzie [350-1]. Seibert, January 9, 1934.

Interviewer: B. B. Guthrie.

I was born in Fulton County near Bushnell, Illinois, on November 16th, 1876. My father came to Colorado in the spring of 1889 and built a sod house with a wooden floor and a roof made of wide boards, then covered with tar paper that ripped off whenever the wind blew hard, and that was quite often. Then Mother and I came out in the fall and settled down on a homestead to make our fortunes and help to develop the new land for those coming after us.

I went to school in a sod schoolhouse at Cope.[28] We had the regulation desks, do not know where the school board got them then, and our first teacher was May Haynes, the daughter of the man who owned the general store and post office at Cope. When there were enough scholars to have a school, the community at once voted a district. This was in Arapahoe County, and before the organization of Kit Carson County. Denver was the county seat at that time. Soon another school was organized nearer to my home, so a group of us went to this school. It was held in a vacated sod house and we used the old cookstove for a heater, and as there were no desks we sat around the heater on chairs and would have our books by our side on the dirt floor. Later the teacher had his bedroom in the same building. There were no blackboards, we used paper and charcoal. The teacher's name was Charley Laybourn.

I remember one term we had a young high school student for a teacher; his father had really been hired as teacher, but had sent his son to act as substitute. The young man was quite inexperienced, of course, and could not always get along with the pupils, so when a disagreement arose that he could not at once settle, he just expelled the pupil, and it soon got that there were just two or three pupils left in the school. Then the father came down and took the position, and after that all got along much better.

We hauled water about one and one-half miles from a well for one winter; then the next summer we got a well dug which was 160 feet deep. We lived six and one-half miles southeast of Cope; the mail was then carried from Seibert to Cope, and we would go there and get our mail.

I never saw any buffalo, but there were plenty of antelope. I found a baby antelope on the prairie, and we kept him as a pet for a year. I herded the cattle we had, and later when we got a windmill it was my delight to sit up on the high windmill tower and read while I kept watch of where the cattle were grazing. I was warned time and again that I would get blown off, but no harm came to me. We had plenty of rattlesnakes too, and I killed every one I saw.

We had some very severe winters, and I remember that one time the wind and blizzard blew the tar paper off our roof and in the morning there was an inch of snow on my bed. In the summer we had such terrible electric storms and hot winds that would dry up a big field of good green corn in two days.

The big cattle ranches were south of us, so we did not have so many near us, but I remember when we came to Colorado we were told of the narrow escape one of our neighbors, a Mr. Swisher, had from being attacked by one of the longhorn Texas steers. He was walking on the prairie when this steer started after him, and he ran at once to his sod home, which, fortunately, was built with walls about three feet thick. He ran into the house and closed the door, and this steer dug his long horns into the sod, and pawed and bellowed in his rage. He kept Mr. Swisher a prisoner for one-half day in the house, and Mr. Swisher always thought it was owing to the thickness of the walls that the house withstood the savage attacks of this steer.

Seibert was just the beginning of a town when we got here, and my father and brother helped to haul water from the old town of Hoyt to the new town of Seibert.[29] At that time they had to haul all the water for the cattle and horses shipped in by railroad or driven overland. Dr. P. B. Goodsman owned the lumberyard in Seibert, and later my father, Stephen Bell, bought this lumberyard from him.

I have driven to Seibert many a time in a two-wheeled cart, and the old horse I drove was never as enthused about the trip as I was, and he would limp badly all the way to town, thus prohibiting my driving him very fast. I usually stayed overnight and would go home the next day, and whenever our faces were turned homeward the old horse forgot his limp and would go along with his head up and happily trotting home. Our claim was twenty-five miles from Seibert, so you may know it took us a while to drive that distance. And we always wore our sunbonnets on the road, and kept our hats to wear in town.

Many times we could see an old stove here and there on the prairie, and we knew that the shack had blown away, and left the stove sitting on the dirt floor. Perhaps just another instance of blasted hopes. And there were numbers of old sod ruins where once had been someone's claim shack and home. The old Santa Fe Trail passed our old ranch, and there was an old fort close to the trail. It was told that there was a fight there between some emigrants and the Indians, and the whites had built this old fort. We never knew the name of the fort, nor the time it was built, but I have seen the ruins many times, and my brother found an Indian hatchet there, and we picked up many arrowheads. This old ruin was north and east of where Seibert now is.[30]

We were always on the watch for prairie fires which would start from lightning, ashes, matches, or a careless camper. I remember that one time I fought fire all night, and Mother got anxious and sent a neighbor boy to find me and bring me home. I did not realize that I had followed the fire so far, but found I was a number of miles from home.

We had nothing to play with but tumbleweeds, which we would harness and then let them pull us over the prairie. Reading matter was so scarce, and I was so glad to get books to read that I often read what Mother thought was too old for me, but I was glad to get anything. I began teaching in Seibert when I was eighteen years old, and that has been my profession ever since.

I was well acquainted with Jonathan Calvin Cope, the founder and owner of the famous "Cope Grove" where the Old Settlers Reunions used to be held. Mr. Cope came to Colorado in the spring of 1887 and took up a preemption and timber claim, thus taking in the one-half section. He built a sod house and put down a well, then carefully surveyed and plotted the grounds for the grove and planted the little seedlings in the place prepared for them.[31] Soon a general store was started, then the post office was made a part of the store, and a livery barn was built and managed by James Wilson and his son, and a feed store was owned by John Brandt. We had a newspaper too, the *Diamond Telescope*, but I do not remember who was the publisher.[32] When I went to school in Cope I stayed with the Cope family, and I remember the big sod house was partitioned off with sheets. This was a very kind, nice family. Water was easy to get, and Mr. Cope soon had irrigation ditches on his place, helping the little seedlings to grow into the famous grove in which the celebrations were held. A son, William D. Cope, lives in Seibert.

Anna Homm [350-2]. Burlington, January 10, 1934.
Interviewer: B. B. Guthrie.

I was born in Warsaw, Illinois, on September 29th, 1858, and spent my girlhood days with my parents there, then came to Kansas and lived there for nine years. I came to Colorado on July 19th, 1892, traveling by railroad to Burlington, and hiring a wagon and team, went to a rented farm then owned by a Sam Shepard of Denver, Colorado.

We built our sod house, plastering the walls with native lime, and covering the roof with tar paper and sod, and putting in a wooden floor. We had no furniture, so we made our cupboard out of packing boxes, and getting a little lumber, built a table, a bedstead, and a bench or two. Then we bought some chairs and two other bedsteads and our stove. Our supplies were brought from St. Francis, Kansas, from Wray, from Burlington, and shipped in from Kansas City.

I had six daughters before my sons were born, so the girls had to help my husband in the fields, with the cattle, and with the irrigation. We were then located on the Republican River bottom and could always raise something by irrigation.

Mail was brought every other day to Newton, Colorado, a post office about one and one-half miles from us. A Miss Linnie Jones was the mail carrier.[33]

My children went to school at Newton. Miss Annie Attis was the first teacher, and Sam Nelson was the second teacher. The children always walked, and when it got real cold weather, they used to wrap their feet in gunnysacks to keep them warm.

We kept a herd of 250 cattle, and it was up to the girls to help care for them. I remember one very severe winter when we had to feed the cattle all winter long, and then in the spring we lost forty-five head from a disease called blackleg.[34] We lost many cattle, but that goes with the life of a pioneer farmer.

My husband did not live long after we settled here, and I then had to raise my family alone. But we managed to keep going, and when land was not selling at "boom" prices I bought 305 acres right down on the river bottom for which I paid $1,050. Later I sold this same piece of land for $10,000.

In the early days we did not buy anything but what we really needed. I bought calico and made my girls their dresses, and when a bit of lace was added, that became the "best" or "Sunday" dress. And they were just as contented as could be. I made my own yeast cakes and all my own soap. I saved everything I could, and we always had enough to eat, and although we worked hard, we had good times too, for we had a number of kind neighbors around us.

We were well acquainted with the man Munsinger, whom we always classed as a sort of desperado, and who kept the neighborhood in fear by his actions. He killed one man—a Mr. Allen—shot at others, and burned the home of a neighbor, and was finally shot down by one of his neighbors in our backyard. He always carried a pistol, and this night he had come to our home to ask for some cough syrup for one of his children. We noted then that he had a revolver with him. He went out, presumably to go home, but met two of the neighbor men coming into our yard. One of these men accused him of stealing a pig. There were some words, and then we heard a shot, and discovered that Munsinger was lying dead by our cellar door. None of us saw the shooting or heard the quarrel, but the man claimed he shot in self-defense, as Munsinger tried to get his gun first. The body lay there all night; there was no coroner near, and the two neighbor men left at once to go to Logan, Kansas, and surrender and send the coroner out. The postmortem and trial was held in our home. It had snowed during the night, and it seemed rather cruel to leave the body lying out in the snow, but we did not dare to touch it until the coroner came.

It was a sad affair, but the neighborhood really felt safer when we knew that this man was gone, for one never knew where he would strike next. He had a very dear wife and three nice children. We felt so sorry for them. We did what we could for the poor mother and her babies, but they finally moved away. Munsinger hated the cattlemen; he made it as miserable as possible for that person. He and a man by the name of Mace kept us guessing for some time, for we never knew what either one of them were up to.

Miss Lizzie Gutting, now Mrs. John Lengel, was one of the early settlers here, and she too could tell you all about Munsinger, for it was her home he had burned.[35]

I have my own little home here on the land I have lived on for so many years, and I am contented and happy. Although we suffered much during the early days, we were very fortunate compared to some of the settlers who staked their claims on the dry prairies far from water, and no chance for irrigation. I would much rather live here than in any town home.

Sarah Blakeman [350-37]. Stratton.

Interviewer: B. B. Guthrie.

Interviewer's note: Born February 26, 1858, in Delaware County, Indiana. Moved to Iowa with parents, then came to Colorado with family in 1892. Husband came to Colorado and located a homestead at Claremont (now Stratton) and then wife and children came out on train, bringing their household goods with them, and also meat and lard from three hogs butchered prior to moving. Mr. Blakeman (now deceased) had work as section foreman with the railroad company, and had a frame house built for the family about three-quarters of a mile east of Stratton.

Mrs. Blakeman lives alone in her little home in Stratton, Colorado.

I cannot tell you just how I felt when I got off the train in Claremont and looked over the great stretch of prairie. There were about one-half dozen houses in the town, and all the rest was prairie. I said to my husband, "Where have you brought us to," and he replied, "To Colorado, woman, a wonderful land." What was there about it that was so fascinating? For it was not long until I too liked the place. I was so afraid of the coyotes, and would not step out at night for fear of stepping on a centipede, for I had been told the grass was full of them. Later I found out there was nothing to this tale. And I remember I was afraid of cowboys until I got acquainted.

There was a town well from which we got our water, hauling it in barrels in a wagon to our farm. When the town well got out of order, we hauled water from the railroad well three miles west of us.

We saw plenty of antelope, and enjoyed antelope steaks quite often. There were lots of wild horses, and three of our horses were lured away by the wild horses, and we never found them again.

In about a year we had a well drilled and hauled the water up by a windlass, using a long "double deck" bucket. Then my husband sent to Kansas and bought twelve head of cattle, and we had to haul water for them, and I used to wonder why they were always so thirsty and could drink so much.

We had no building that could be used as a meeting place, and could have no Sunday school, so a man who had a small grocery store allowed us to meet in the store building and have our Sunday school. Folks came from miles around to attend. Later we had a sod schoolhouse and held our meetings and church there.

When we shipped out our furniture I included the organ and my guitar, and how glad I was that we had brought them along, for oftentimes we would load the organ in the wagon, and go miles to attend a dance, and I would play almost all night while the rest of the folks danced. Again I would accompany the fiddler on my guitar. We had such good times. Neighbors lived miles apart, but we had dances and parties and folks were so congenial and always so glad to see each other. I believe we were happier then than folks are today, for we didn't need so much to make us contented and happy.

I remember my husband writing me before we left for Colorado, and telling me that meat was selling at six cents a pound in Claremont, and that I should sell the pork and lard we had prepared to bring with us. I could not make up my mind to do this, and decided to bring it along. How glad my husband was when he found I had done this, for when I got here there was no meat to be had anywhere. And I can assure you, we had plenty of company as long as the meat lasted, for people were hungry for meat and visited us often to get a meal.

Jennie E. [Jones] Davis [350-9]. Stratton, January 3, 1934.

Interviewer: B. B. Guthrie.

I was born in Shelton, Nebraska, on February 1st, 1883, and came to Colorado with my parents in April 1892. We arrived at Limon by train, and at that time Limon was composed of a hotel, the section house, a small store and post office, and one or two houses.[36] Father took a homestead sixteen miles north of Limon, and we built our sod house and settled down to life on the prairies. Hugo, forty miles away, was our nearest town and doctor, so we did not dare to get sick. We could buy no furniture, so Father made what we needed from packing boxes. Whenever we got newspapers, we would put them on the walls, thus saving all reading matter, and keeping our house warm.

We got our water from a well and from springs close by. We always enjoyed living water, and never had to drink from water holes like many another pioneer in this county.

I remember of Mother selling eggs for three cents per dozen and butter for three cents per pound. We could not get any more for it, and perhaps if it had been higher people could not have bought, for there was very little money in the country then.

When we first came to Limon the "trail herds" used to pass our place about a mile east of us, great herds of from five to eight thousand head of longhorn Texas cattle on their way north to Montana to grass and pasture for the summer. There was plenty of water near us, and the crew always camped there overnight. There were usually about eighteen cowboys, and a chuck wagon, and the supply wagon. My brother-in-law worked with this outfit for three summers, and we always felt interested in the trail herds. We have seen a steady line of cattle moving north from daylight to dark; I often think of the great herds that used to pass over the prairies where now there are fields or fenced pastures.

As you know, there were no trails or roads or fences in those days, and it was so easy to become confused as to directions and lose your way on the prairie. I was a little girl about twelve years old, and as my brother was working in the field, I was sent to bring home the cows. I was riding horseback, and started out in plenty of time to get the cows home before supper time. They had wandered rather far that day, and it was hard to get them turned homeward until sunset, and it got too dark for them to eat. By this time I did not know where I was and drove the cattle in the opposite direction from home. It got cold and soon began to rain, so I got off my horse and put the saddle blanket around me. I had bare feet, as it was warm when I had left home, and we always had to go barefooted as soon as weather permitted and save our shoes. I got so cold and frightened and did not know what to do. About ten o'clock that night my folks and some of the neighbors began hunting for me, and they built a big bonfire on top of one of the hills and then took lanterns and followed the gullies or draws, calling me all the while. When I saw the bonfire, I rounded up the cattle and started towards it, but soon came up to where my brother was, and oh, how glad I was to see him. I know the night was no darker than many another night, but to me it seemed so dark and the prairies so big and lonesome. I was very fortunate in that a severe storm did not come instead of a gentle drizzling rain.

Through much planning, saving, and hard study, I managed to get an education and became a teacher. I was teaching in the Tuttle District when I met my husband.[37]

Zelma Ackelson Davis [May] [350-47]. Burlington, February 8, 1934.

Interviewer: B. B. Guthrie.

I was born on September 30th, 1881, at Winterset, Iowa, and moved with my parents to Nebraska, where we lived for two years.

In the spring of 1893 my father, William Ackelson, came to Colorado and filed on a relinquishment situated on the "divide" between the Republican and Arikaree Rivers.[38] He had to drive to Akron to file his papers on this land. He bought the buildings, mostly of frame, from the former homesteader, and fixed up the place a bit before he returned to Arapahoe, Nebraska, where we were then living, and we all came out to our new home. We went to Haigler, Nebraska, then across country in covered wagons, and I remember that we were not bothered a bit by traffic or crowds of people. We brought our own milk cows, horses, chickens, and household goods, as well as a supply of food. We had a good well on the farm, so did not need to haul water like so many of the new homesteaders did.

We were fortunate in having two schoolhouses close to us, each about one and one-half miles away, so we could go to whichever school we wished. We had the regular desks and bought our own books; some of the pupils used the books they had brought with them. Both of these little schoolhouses were of sod, and no doubt they have both been replaced by modern frame buildings.

We had Sunday school at the schoolhouse; that was about the first place we went to after we arrived in Colorado. We very rarely, if ever, had preaching services; we were so far away from a town where a preacher might be.

Amusements were very limited—once in a while we would have dances at some home, and Dave Manley, a fiddler living near Kirk, Colorado, used to be the standby for music—but we always had a good time when we did go anywhere.

We tried farming, but Father did not raise anything, so the next year my two older brothers left for the Arkansas Valley and there found work, then wrote home advising that we had better bring our stock to the valley and winter there. So we loaded our wagons with supplies for camping and with barrels of water, and started south. We traveled for days and would not see a building or a human being. There were plenty of antelope on the prairie and lots of coyotes. I remember when we got to the place called Big Springs.[39] I thought we would find plenty of water, but imagine our surprise when some of the cowboys who were then working in a roundup outfit came to us and asked for water. We gave them as much drinking water as we dared to, for we did not know where we would be able to get good water again. We kept water in the barrel for our own use and for the horses that were pulling the wagons; the other stock had to do without until we got to the water holes or some ranch where we were allowed to water them.

In the spring following, we trekked back across the prairie to our own homestead, and as a number of families had left in this caravan, there was quite a number of wagons and families, all eager to get back to their own homesteads. On our last night out we camped down south of Old Claremont, now Stratton, and had one big meal together. My mother made biscuits for the crowd, and they were nicely baked on our little sheet-iron camp stoves. And what was our surprise on returning to our ranch to find the cattle we had left behind in much better shape than those we had "wintered" in the Arkansas valley. But we enjoyed the experience of camping and traveling, following an old trail across the prairies to our destination.

Malinda Jones Brammeier [350-42]. Denver, February 14, 1934.

Interviewer: B. B. Guthrie.

I was born in Ulysses, Nebraska, in July 1872. My father, Sidney L. Jones, and my mother and eldest brother went from Illinois to Nebraska, settling in Seward County in 1871. Father and my grandfather came out first, taking adjoining homesteads and building a frame house on the line between the two homesteads. They drove forty miles to Lincoln, Nebraska, for their lumber and supplies for the buildings. They built a sod dugout on the side of a hill and covered it with lumber and sod, and used it for a barn. One night a terrible blizzard came up and covered this little dugout, and when they got it uncovered they discovered that their only team of horses had been smothered to death.

In the early spring of 1892 Father came out to Colorado and located on a homestead thirteen miles straight north of Burlington. He stayed at the home of my uncle J. T. Jones, who had come out at an earlier date, and who helped Father build the frame house and get the various dwellings in readiness for the family. Then in the summer of 1892 Mother and my three brothers came to Colorado. They came out on the Rock Island and shipped their household goods and livestock out on the railroad. I stayed for two years longer in Venango, Nebraska, then came out to Burlington to live.

Father hauled water for a few months after the family came out from my uncle's place; then he got a well drilled on his own farm. Uncle's place was just two miles away, so we never had to go far for water.

The lumber and building supplies were purchased at Burlington from David Carnahan, who then owned the lumberyard.

We had no schoolhouse near us; there were no children in the neighborhood or in the district of school age, so the schoolhouses were a few miles east and west of our home. There was no church or Sunday school; the neighbors lived so far apart that no Sunday school was organized, and when we wanted to attend preaching services we drove to Burlington. This was not done often, for thirteen miles was quite a distance with a team and wagon.

There were very few amusements for the young people; once in a while we would have a party at some neighbor's home; maybe once in a while a dance, but not often. Sometimes we would drive to Burlington to attend a dance.

Our mail was delivered at Burlington, then bought out on the route to Hale post office. My brother was a mail carrier for some years, and when he was unable to go I drove the route for him with his horse and buggy.[40]

We did not suffer the hardships of many other pioneers who came out earlier than we did; the railroad was built and Burlington established, so we were near a trading center, and could enjoy the privileges of church, meetings, and amusements which could not be had by those further away from town.

I am now living in Denver. We sold the homestead after my father's death, and all moved to homes of our own. I like to visit Burlington; I still have an interest in it, for I saw it grow from a few poor little houses to the attractive town it is today.

Louise A. Merrill [355-52], Prowers County. Granada, January 14, 1934.

Interviewer: Margaret Merrill.

Interviewer's note: Miss Louise A. Merrill came to Granada in August 1887 with her parents, Mr. and Mrs. Joseph Chandler Merrill, from Catlettsburg, Kentucky.

My bedroom was next to the garden, in which I took great pride. One morning I awoke and heard a peculiar noise in the garden. I ran to the window and saw something strange was going on. When I got outside I saw that every row of vegetables was covered with queer bugs with terrible jaws and voracious appetites. They were there by the thousands. I went to Mr. Jones for help and we got pans and brushes. We put oil and water in the pans and went down the rows brushing all the bugs into the pans. Afterward we burned them, but there was not much left of the garden after that. These bugs were over an inch long and were gray with red underwings.[41]

During my first week there at the Wolf Creek school, in the early part of April a terrific sandstorm began about ten o'clock in the morning. The shanty yielded so to the blasts of wind that it seemed unsafe to stay in it, so untying a long sash on my dress I made all the children take hold of it, and we went out together, taking turns getting down on the ground to find the path, which was a cow trail. After two hours we succeeded in reaching a farmhouse with faces badly cut by the sand. Much to our surprise, we found the claim shanty still standing the next day.

The trips to and from school were given a touch of moving-picture excitement because of the Texas longhorns pastured on the range. They just naturally didn't like schoolteachers. I often put them to flight by waving my lunch basket, but on one occasion when there were calves with them, they drew up in battle array and I was the one put to flight and wild speed was all that saved me.

Gray wolves howled at night, and twice calves were attacked by them in the barn lot.

So sparsely populated was the Wolf Creek region at that time that it produced real excitement for a wagon to be seen on the road half a mile away.[42]

I taught there two terms then came into a little two-room school in Granada.[43]

One of the most exciting episodes in our life in Granada was the cyclone that descended upon us suddenly one summer day. After chasing through the south side of town and doing no harm worse than snatching glasses off people's noses and picking up every stray article that was loose, it crossed the tracks and struck the little white church with fearful fury, tearing it to bits of wood not much larger than matches. It ripped the two organs to pieces and left the big old Bible literally in separate leaves. This was a great grief to the people of the town, for the little church had long been the principal center of social interest as well as the only religious institution for many miles.

An amusing and interesting experience our family had during the first year in Granada was the episode of the rug. Not understanding the climate in the least when we furnished the little house, Mother placed an attractive new square of Brussels carpet at the front door, thinking to add a touch of pleasant welcome to guests. It was but a short time until a high wind came up in the night and carried the rug far away. Much grieved at the loss, I ranged the hills south of Granada hunting for this little treasure. Every sagebrush and tumbleweed was investigated. It became the fashion for a time in the family when out walking to hunt for the rug. After so long a time it was forgotten. Then Father put a barbed-wire fence around the lot because we were planting trees and were determined to have shade and fruit if possible. One morning over a year after we had settled in the new home there was a very windy night. We were astonished in the morning to find the little rug not much worse for wear hanging on the wire fence south of the house. Knowing more about the climate then, Mother tacked the rug securely to the porch floor.

The settlers in Granada at that time were a very fine class of people. They were mostly young married couples and had a good deal of style and culture.

The most interesting association perhaps that we had in Granada was the delightful friendship with Mr. and Mrs. W. W. Jones. He was one of the earliest pioneers in Colorado, having herded cattle on the Denver townsite and freighted from Nebraska to Denver for the government before the Civil War. He it was who, noticing the great boulders in Boulder Creek, suggested that name for the canyon and creek.[44] He was a unique and most interesting person with a fine mind, a marvelous memory, and possessed of a vocabulary that would have staggered a college president. One of the most amusing things I remember about him was his description of the stupidity of the Indians. He said you couldn't make them understand anything, that they had no knowledge of the meaning of words. For example, he said he was trying to explain to an Indian why he was called Jones. The Indian couldn't see the reason. Mr. Jones said he told him that Jones was "just an appellation used to designate an individual, but," he said, "the darned Indian couldn't see through it!"

He was a horticulturist of exceptional ability. The vegetables and fruits which he raised on a little piece of ground in Granada were the finest of their kind. He knew how to make a little peach tree produce the kind of show peaches you see in California exhibits. He raised the finest of grapes, and by sacking them, cutting and sealing the stems, and keeping them in a dry fruit cellar was able to send them to friends as a Christmas present in perfect condition. He did the same thing with watermelons, which he grew in great quantity.

He had had in the early eighties great herds of fine-blooded stock on a ranch south of Granada. Almost his entire herd was destroyed during a most devastating blizzard in the eighties. Too discouraged with the business to attempt to go on, he gathered together his means and settled in a comfortable little house in east Granada where he spent the rest of his life experimenting with the growing of all sorts of things, including fish, which he raised in a small pond in front of his house.

His wife, a woman of education and great charm, had borne the hardships of pioneering cheerfully because she owed her life to the healthful climate in that section. She often told me of the first eleven months that she spent on the ranch without seeing one white woman and only a very few squaws.

Among the many thrilling stories that she told of her experiences during Indian raids and cattle-thieving exploits was the event that almost wrecked her life and left her with a nervous trouble from which she never fully recovered. Mr. Jones having been called to Las Animas on a matter of grave importance, she was unavoidably left alone at the ranch. Near sunset she was disturbed to see a group of Mexicans riding up to the hill above the ranch. After a short colloquy two of them rode down to her gate. They asked for her husband. She told them he was on the range and would be in any moment. They asked to borrow an ax lying in the yard, which she allowed them to have. They made camp on the hill. Very much disturbed, she barricaded the house as best she could, and with rifle close at hand, for she was a noted shot, she kept watch through the long hours of the night. With the early rays of morning sun, they broke camp, and she saw that the bold-faced leader ordered the rest of the group to ride on. He watched until they were over the hill, then with a cool and brazen swagger he mounted his horse and approached her gate. She was ready for him. With her gun in hand she spoke in a ringing voice through the half open door: "Throw down that ax and put up your hands." Startled greatly, he obeyed. "Now," she said, "with your hands up, ride over that hill and if you make one false move it will be your last for I am a dead shot." She related that he stared at her for some time in amazement. "I see you're no tenderfoot," he said, and then obeyed her command. After he rode over the hill and disappeared from view, she locked and barred the door and then fell in a faint from which she had not recovered when her husband returned some time later.

Among the many interesting people in that early settlement of the town was Mr. Hamer Norris and his mother. Mrs. Norris was the foster sister of Mrs. Abraham Lincoln. Her aunt was Mrs. Lincoln's stepmother, and many years of her girlhood were spent in the home of the Todds.[45] She was a fascinating talker and had seen the most interesting phases of pioneer life in this country, having lived in central Kentucky and Illinois and afterward married a judge of the Supreme Court in Ohio.[46] After his death the family moved west. Her son was the first editor of the *Granada Exponent*.[47] Mrs. Norris's stories of Mrs. Lincoln's girlhood and her accounts of the courtship were most interesting and revealed that many stories relating to that event were entirely untrue.

Within a year after we came to Granada the boom dropped. Property values faded from sight, and most of the people moved away. My father always had great confidence in the future of the country and could not give up until his fortunes were so depleted that it was difficult to start again. He engaged in the grocery business there until his death in 1903. He had the highest regard for the people living in that section of the country and strove constantly to help the farmers by every means in his power. In spite of his early Massachusetts training, he liked pioneering and had spent his younger years in Kentucky settlements and always found great interest in the development of new country.

Chapter 6: The Southwest

La Plata and Montezuma Counties

Coming out of the canyon, I was driving the lead wagon and there was a big tree sticking out into the trail. I could not stop, the wheel team could not hold the load, and if the leaders stopped we would have been piled up, so I swung the leaders out into the oak brush; the wagon nearly tipped over, but we made it.

Sarah Ann Menefee

Named for the mineral wealth to be found in the area, the county La Plata (Spanish for silver) on the New Mexico line in southwestern Colorado was established in 1874 from the area that had, for the most part, been Guadalupe (Conejos) County originally. Though initially the county seat was Guadalupe (Conejos), Parrott City—named for Tabucio Parrott, a San Francisco banker who helped finance the settlement—was county seat from 1876 to 1881. As such it is often mentioned in the narratives that follow. Durango—with its central location, its connection with the Denver and Rio Grande Western Railroad by July 1881, and its smelter—became the trading and economic center of the county. In 1881 it also became the county seat, and Parrott City was thereafter essentially abandoned.[1] In 1889 La Plata County was divided, and the western portion became Montezuma County. The town of Cortez, established in 1886, was chosen as the county seat. Big Bend,

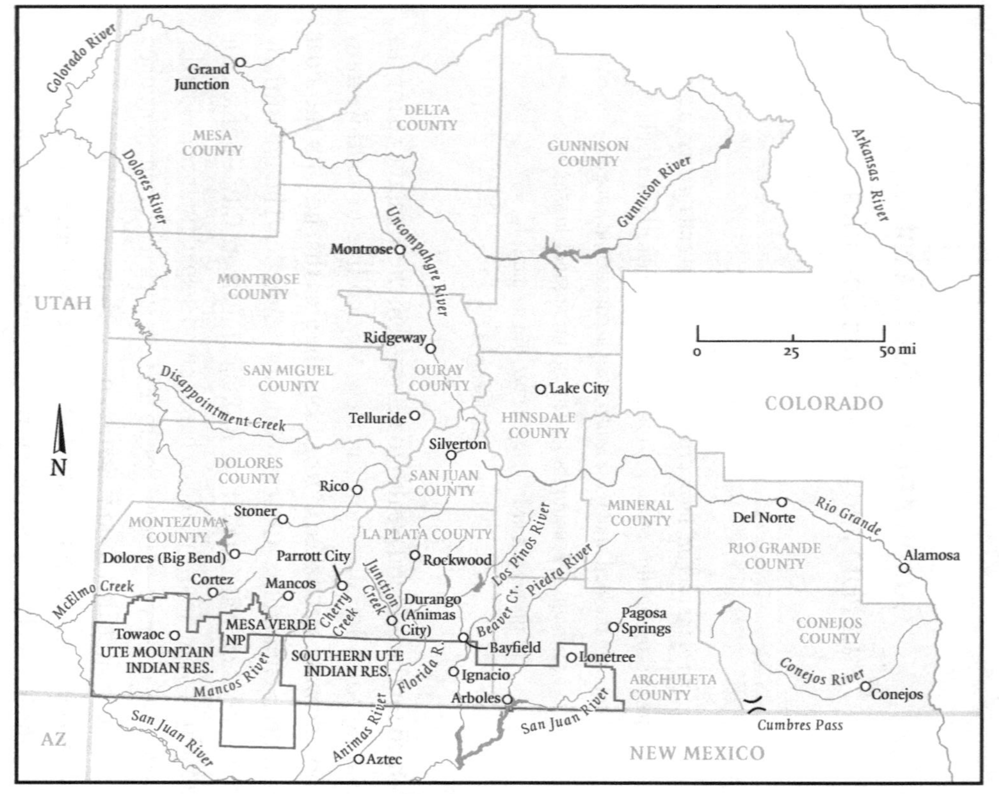

8. The southwest

referred to many times in the narratives, was so named for the bend in the Dolores River at its southernmost point. In 1878 Big Bend was essentially replaced by the town of Dolores, named after the Spanish for the river, Rio de Nuestra Senora de los Dolores (River of Our Lady of Sorrows), two miles upstream from Big Bend.[2]

In addition to mining, ranching and farming were inspirations for settlement in the area, and many of the narratives give pictures of daily life on the farms or ranches. There is one delightful moment, for example, when a narrator recalls that one farmer was discovered using his rifle as a plow. There are also many narratives of details that have come to represent the West: these narrators describe difficulties of overland travel, hangings by vigilantes, gunfights in the streets, the rustling of cattle, and attacks on and by American Indians. Although the American frontier is commonly thought of as a general westward movement from the eastern United States, these narratives demonstrate that settlement of "the West" came from many different directions. Although many are from the East, several settlers also arrived from Europe, Canada, and places within the United States such as Oregon, Utah, and Texas.

Given their proximity to the Southern Ute Reservation, these women frequently encountered Indians, especially Utes and Navajos, and not all encounters were peaceful. As several narrators note, however, white settlers rather than the Indians usually initiated the troubles. Mary Hansen asserts, for example, that "the only Indian uprisings seem to have been when white people did them wrong." Kate Smith Myers states that "white settlers who did not bother the Indians or the Mexicans were not molested." Along with the acknowledgment of blame, however, these narrators often reveal an implicit bias against their American Indian neighbors. In describing a battle in the Sierra La Salle Mountains, for example, Ormiston distinguishes between "men" and "Indians," declaring that "about ten men were killed, but so far as can be learned there were no Indians killed." Mella Bohlick even recounts that she had essentially been raised by a Paiute woman who had been "given" to her mother. This "personal servant," as Bohlick calls her, spent her life in the Bohlick household, earning her keep and finally her epitaph: "faithful."

Notwithstanding such bloody encounters, living close by Utes and Navajos often also provided the white settlers opportunities to become better acquainted and sometimes even friendly with their American Indian neighbors. Mary Hansen, for example, seems on the one hand to accept the prevalent stereotype of the stoic Indian, but on the other hand she acknowledges that her experience with the death of a young woman does not support such a stereotype: "Indians are supposed to have little feeling, but old Washington and his son suffered pitifully and tried so hard to do what they could for the pretty young girl." Sarah Ann Menefee gives an account of her day-to-day encounters with American Indians. According to her narrative, she was firm and straightforward and thus got along well. She sums up her relationship this way: "Most of the Indians were good people. They often tried to scare me, just running a bluff, and laughed when I would not be scared. They did not cause trouble if they were not bothered. Most of the early trouble was caused by the whites who tried to steal from the Indians or shot at the Indians or their children."

Unfortunately, the counties' archival records contain no accounts by Native American women themselves. Nevertheless, these narratives do complicate the history of interaction between Indians and non-Indians by providing descriptions of several different levels of communication between the white pioneer women and their Indian neighbors. Firsthand accounts of these interactions suggest ways in which non-Indian women in the West participated in and ultimately benefited from the subjugation of Native Americans.

These narratives, like those throughout the state in general, are told by survivors of migration and settlement, and in this sense they are success stories. Several women describe how they managed—by farming, by becoming practical nurses or teachers, by hard work in general, and by a general community effort. As Mary Lee Lamb says, "In this country, we have had to be pretty independent and learn to do many things." Despite the ultimate survival of these pioneers, however, several of the narrators are forthright about difficulties and disappointments. In addition to the specific external troubles like the deaths of children and skirmishes with American Indians, there were the internal or mental barriers to overcome. Eva Adams House tells of her early days that she was "very homesick. I would go down and sit on the riverbank and watch the water and cry. But I wouldn't give up and go home, because everyone would think I was acting like a baby."

The field-worker for La Plata County was A. L. Soens; for Montezuma County, Anna Florence Robison.

Dora Provis Pedersen, Montezuma County [360-52]. March 28, 1934.

Interviewer: Anna Florence Robison.

Interviewer's note: Mrs. Pedersen, herself an old-timer, wrote this paper to be read at a meeting of her woman's club and kindly permitted me to make a copy of it.

EARLY HISTORY OF MONTEZUMA COUNTY

Inasmuch as Montezuma County was for many years a part of La Plata County, I shall begin this history by speaking briefly of the history of La Plata County.

Prospectors and trappers following the streams found their way into the La Plata Mountains, where, followed by other pioneer types, they founded a settlement known as Parrott City. With this little town as a base, small parties of men followed the headwaters of the Mancos and the Dolores Rivers. They explored and eventually formed the first settlements in what is now Montezuma County in these river valleys. In 1874 a small party of men located in the Mancos River Valley, one of whom, John Merritt, erected the first house, a log cabin, ever built in Montezuma County. This house is interesting as having served as the headquarters of the Moss Expedition, which, accompanied by a reporter from an eastern newspaper, was among the first to explore and bring before the public the now world-famous Mesa Verde ruins.[3] This same year, a post office was established in the home of another of these settlers and known by his name: McIntyre.[4] At this time, the nearest railroad station was at Alamosa, the mail being taken from there to Parrott City by stagecoach and from Parrott City to McIntyre on horseback in the summer and on snowshoes in the winter.[5] This was a long, hazardous trip at that time. A few years after the establishment of the McIntyre post office, a mail carrier froze to death in Thompson Park.[6] True to the very last to the trust reposed in him, his sack of mail was found hanging high in a tree.

The first permanent settlement on the Dolores River was made in 1877 by William, Dick, and George May. Locations had been made previous to this date but abandoned. In 1880 a post office was established on the May ranch with Billy May as postmaster. By this date a number of settlers were already located on the Dolores, and others were rapidly following them. I shall only mention the name of one, Charles Johnson, familiarly known as Grandpa Johnson to everyone for years. He located at the present site of McPhee in 1881.[7] Mr. Johnson specialized in raising fine saddle horses. Jim Douglas, racing champion of this time, was bred and raised here.

This same year, 1881, the railroad was expanded to Durango, from whence George Bauer packed a few staples in the way of groceries on burros to the present site of Mancos, establishing the first store in Montezuma County. And three years later, in 1884, he established the first bank in the same building. The first school: a three-months' term was taught at Mancos by Miss Lizzie Allen, a girl of sixteen from Parrott City.

This school was taught in a log cabin heated by a large box stove. Pupils, whose ages ranged from tots of four and five to young men and women nearly twenty, furnished their own seats and desks, homemade, of course, and their own textbooks consisting of any textbooks they were fortunate enough to secure.

The first birth, death, and wedding occurred in the Mancos neighborhood.

Passing on to the Dolores section, we find that the first store, put in during 1884 at a point a few miles below the present town of Dolores and known as Big Bend, was established. A little town grew up there, but in the year 1892 the railroad reached the present site of Dolores and the people of Big Bend and most of their houses also moved and located there.

I shall mention a couple of other outstanding events in the early history of Montezuma County and then pass on to the history of, to us, the most interesting part of the county, our home, the Montezuma Valley. In the fall of 1881 Ed Caldwell and Clark Brittain owned and operated a horse-power threshing machine within the present limits of our county. And in 1882, Mr. H. F. Morgan established a sawmill on Lost Cañon.

Montezuma Valley: About the year 1884 or 1885 Mr. Simon located a ranch in the Lakeview neighborhood, thereby establishing the first permanent home in the valley. An amusing story is told about the erection of this dwelling. According to pioneer custom, Mr. Simon assembled his building material, then invited all who could to come to a picnic dinner and help lay up the house. The guests consisted mainly of young men, mostly cowboys. One of the young waitresses, being quite enamored with one of the cowboys, served him so frequently and generously with a particularly tempting delicacy that the supply ran out long before it could go around. The other young men, offended at this show of rank favoritism, got up and left, and the house-building was indefinitely postponed.

The first town in Montezuma Valley was situated about two miles south of Cortez, across McElmo, and known as Toltec. But this little town was soon abandoned for Cortez, which was properly surveyed and laid out as a townsite in 1886, Mr. William Blake, now living at Cortez, acting as assistant surveyor.[8]

Very early in the history of the valley, in about the year 1876, cattlemen, attracted by the then luxuriant grass and the timber for shelter, drove vast herds of cattle into the valley. It is said that one of these pioneer cattlemen, Pat O'Donnell, purchased the foundation stock for his herd in the Blue Mountains at the rate of one dollar a head, thereby laying the foundation for the extensive cattle business which made him a wealthy man.

After two unsuccessful attempts to get water into the valley, a successful survey was made which resulted in 1888 in water's being poured into this valley through the tunnel and the Big Cut. Mr. William Blake became our fist ditch superintendent, serving in this capacity until the year 1910 when he resigned to enter the government service. Settlers thronged into the country. The herds of cattle were driven out to other ranges, many of them westward into the region we now designate as the Dry Lands. The country had now become so thickly settled that this year, 1888, the present county of Montezuma was formed with Cortez as the county seat. Schools were established and churches built. The day of the real pioneer was over.

The pioneers themselves: It seems particularly fitting that in these depression days of hardship and doing without, we should pause and remember the hardships endured by those who first led the way. The little stores with limited capital and obliged to bring in all their supplies in freight wagons over primitive roads were frequently without what we term necessities, especially in winter. Coal oil, tea, sugar, salt, etc., were sometimes hard to get. And, worst of all, they sometimes ran out of tobacco. Well-known drugs and a few patent medicines were carried by the stores. But when sickness came, the demand far exceeded the supply. The nearest competent physician was in Durango and of course could only be summoned in dire extremity.

An uncle of mine made the trip from about four miles east of Cortez to Durango in December 1889 through snow and mud and succeeded in returning with a doctor in twenty-four hours, thereby saving the life of the young mother for whose benefit the trip was made. This was considered quite a notable achievement at that time.[9]

The pioneers, however, made good use of all natural resources. Most homes were equipped with a fireplace which served as a source of light as well as heat. Many old-timers still believe sagebrush tea to be a panacea for all ills. We are all familiar with the picket fence still standing in Mildred west of the schoolhouse, a testimonial to the patience and energy of one of our pioneers.[10]

Several Indian massacres occurred in the early history of this country so that the fear of Indians always hung like a pall over the settlers. The last trouble with the Indians occurred in 1886.[11]

A band of cowboys on Beaver Creek, having tried in vain to stop the Indians from wantonly slaughtering their cattle, fell on a band of Indians and lawlessly murdered them. In retaliation a band of young bucks rode into the Lakeview neighborhood to the home of a family named Gentner, called him to the door, and shot him. Mrs. Gentner, with a child in her arms and one clinging to her hand, was ordered by one of the leaders whom she had befriended to "Run, Squaw run!" while he held back the mob to the best of his ability. She escaped, though slightly wounded. The Indians burned the house to the ground.

Let us honor the pioneers. Many of them have gone West over the Great Divide. May we follow the trail they so heroically blazed and like them "look the whole world in the face straight forward and unafraid."[12]

Kate Smith Myers, La Plata County [362-8]. February 2, 1934.
Interviewer: A. L. Soens.

I was born in Leavenworth, Kansas, July 30, 1861. The family came to Pueblo about the time I was one year old; we lived on a ranch near the present site of Pueblo. Father came down here in '77. He located about five miles north of Aztec.[13] He built a cabin out of cottonwood logs. We camped out while the cabin was building; we had no stove and baked in a Dutch oven. There was nothing at Aztec then, and we had to get our supplies from Alamosa.

We left the Arkansas River April 1st, '77, and came to Del Norte by way of Alamosa. We came through the Wet Mountain Valley. Between Conejos and Del Norte the sand was very bad, and we had an awful time getting through. We had two wagons and two teams, one of mules and one of oxen. We made road as we went along and could not go very fast. At times we were in camp two weeks before we moved a wagon. It took about six weeks to get over the hill.

While we were camped on the pass, Summers and Wolf came past and camped about a half mile below us; they had three wagons and about two hundred head of cattle. They left two wagons loaded with supplies at our camp. Summers and Wolf had a quarrel and split up; Summers wanted to take a couple of Wolf's oxen to haul a wagon from our camp; Wolf objected and told Summers to use his own stock and in that way he would not have to return them from Nim Hammonds where he was going to leave his wagon. This was on the west side of the mountain. The next morning they quarreled again, and Summers shot Wolf through the head. Wolf was killed, and Henry Nelson made a coffin out of the sideboards of a wagon. Wolf is buried on the hill just above the creek.[14]

We had a hard time coming down the hill, cut down a pine tree and tied it to the wagon to act as a drag and let the wagon down the hill. Shortly after we got down the hill, Cox caught up with us. His was a large outfit; he had his sons and daughters and their families; they had three wagons and about two thousand head of cattle. We traveled together to the Animas River, and they helped build a road so we came along faster. There were berries and chokecherries along the road and plenty of feed for the stock. We struck the San Juan River about two miles below Pagosa Springs; there were no buildings at Pagosa Springs then.[15] We had a Wheeler and Wilson sewing machine, and while we were at Del Norte the Mexican women came over to do their sewing.[16] We had no furniture, but used packing boxes to make our furniture.

I walked most of the way to the Animas River driving two pigs and some lame cattle. We never had trouble with the Indians; the settlers had built a stockade against a possible attack, and my father took us into it once when an uprising was reported. We stayed a couple of days and Father said he was going back to the ranch; he could be killed up there as well as in the stockade. The Indians told him that they would not bother him and he should stay at work. White settlers who did not bother the Indians or the Mexicans were not molested.

Dan and I were married on May 15, '79, and of course he fetched me up in the mountains. Cox and Smithe were the first settlers on the Animas River near Aztec. We got to the river about November '77. McCoy came early the next spring.

Mella McCluer Bohlick, La Plata County [362-41]. March 22, 1934.

Interviewer: A. L. Soens

Interviewer's note: Mella was born in La Plata County, January 1885, on the McCluer homestead; her father and mother came from Huerfano into this country in 1875.

Mother often told me that when she first came into the Florida River valley the Indians used to dance on a hill just east of our house and each time she thought that the Indians would come down and kill them.[17]

One day a mean Indian came down and asked for something to eat. We always fed them when they came, but this Indian poured his cup full of sugar, and dumped the rest of it on the floor. Mama said that if she was going to get killed she might as well get it over with, so she picked up a chair and knocked the Indian down. After that he was one of her best friends among the Indians.

My brother Tim was the first white boy born in what is now La Plata County in February 1876.[18] When he was a baby, a squaw living near us, whose papoose was about the same age as Tim, came to the cabin and wanted to take Tim home with her. Mother said she was afraid to let him go but she was afraid not to, so she let him go, and when she went after him she found him stripped naked and painted up like a warrior. The squaw was very good to Tim, took care of him and nursed him the same as her own papoose.

Mother's family had a large land grant from the Spanish Crown; the town of Trinidad is located on part of this grant.[19]

When mother was married, her family gave her an Indian girl as her personal servant. The girl was a Paiute who had been stolen or carried away from her tribe by other Indians and given to Mother's family. We called her Trudy. She came to the Florida with Mother in 1875, and practically raised all of us children. She was especially fond of Tim and hid him when he had done anything for which Father might punish him. Even after he was fourteen years old, she used to drag him around on her back. She was small, and by that time Tim was as large as she. She married an Indian and was away for a year but came back to the McCluers. When she died about 1908, she was buried in the family plot. Her stone bears the name "Trudy" and underneath the word "faithful." Father said that word completely described her.

The Indians were friendly toward us, and Ignacio often came to see Father when there was trouble brewing for the whites or for the Indians.[20] Ignacio had several children, and all were named after the McCluers: Holbert, Mella, and Tim. Whenever an Indian outbreak threatened, the settlers on the Florida gathered at our place. We never had serious trouble with them.

Pinkerton of Pinkerton Springs told us that when Animas City was first started they were expecting an attack and had gathered at a cabin.[21] Everything was quiet and orders were to keep still. Pinkerton had just received a new gun and went to Schisler's store to get some ammunition. As he was leaving Animas City he tried out the gun. The noise startled the settlers, alarming them as they feared it would precipitate trouble. Bob Dwyer, an officer at the time, came out and got Pinkerton. Pinkerton told Bob that the discharge was accidental, which story Bob allowed to pass.

"Putt" Putnam, a prospector, used to come out and stay at our place for three or four months at a time. Father liked him but we girls did not like to have him stay so long, as it made more work for us. Later Putnam became very wealthy, and he sent for Father to come to Denver and stay with him at the hotel. He paid all expenses of the trip.

Father had the first water right on the Florida River, and when the city of Durango fixed their reservoir they bought the ranch to get the water right.

Father made two trips from Missouri to California with cattle when he was just a kid. He went with his brother and said he slept with his fingers hooked in his brother's clothes. He fought for the South in the Civil War and his brother fought for the North. Father's outfit was captured by his brother's company, and Father was a prisoner in his brother's company.

It was necessary that the early settlers know who was around the neighborhood, and one day John Waters and Father found some wagon tracks that no one knew anything about; they followed the tracks all day to find out who had made them.

One time Mrs. Evans Hampton and Mother were out gathering buffalo berries. They heard some noise in the brush nearby made by a bear. Mama outran Mrs. Hampton, who was very large, and Mrs. Hampton tried to hide under a tub. Another time Mama locked Mrs. Hampton out when they thought they heard a bear while gathering wood, and Mama reached the house first.

Mother's family name was Gallegos. Her grandmother received land from the Spanish king in Taos Valley, New Mexico.[22] Trinidad is named after my mother's cousin.[23] Mother's grandmother's name was Baca.

When the first sheep came into the San Juan (in the seventies), Father and Bill Swire decided to drive the sheep out of the country. After taking a few drinks they began the drive. They finally rode in opposite directions around the sheep and eventually met, and when they met Father began to shoot at Swire. Swire finally made him understand that they were partners in driving out the sheep, and went away together, and the sheep were not driven out.

Sarah Ann Menefee, La Plata County [362-39]. March 23, 1934.

Interviewer: A. L. Soens.

I was born twelve miles southwest of Ottumwa on the Des Moines River, Iowa, in 1850. When I was thirteen years old, the family moved to Walla Walla, Washington. We crossed the plains in wagons; there were sixty wagons in the train and over three hundred people. Father had five wagons and had from one to five yoke of oxen on each wagon. We left Iowa June 1, 1863, and arrived in Washington the latter part of October. There were eleven small cabins in Walla Walla Town; at that time it was smaller than the fort.

On the way out we passed through the valley where the Mountain Meadows Massacre had taken place six years earlier.[24] About a day's travel before we reached Mountain Meadow, we entered what we called Gooseberry Canyon. I was out ahead of the train with some children and picked gooseberries until the train passed. We stayed too long and dropped behind the wagons. The train captain rode back and told us that we had better keep up with the wagons, as there were white men—Mormons—watching from the cliffs and that there might be trouble. He had ordered all of the men to carry their guns close at hand and to push on out of the canyon before night.

We lived in Walla Walla four years; then I was married in 1867 and moved to the north side of the valley on the Touchet River, where we lived for eight years.[25]

The vigilantes were working in Washington then. One night in '65 I stepped to the door and looked out. About a quarter of a mile away stood a large tree; three men were hanging from one limb. They were Ten-Toed Pete, Slim Jim, and a Negro, members of a gang of highwaymen, and had been hung by vigilantes. At another time they came to the house where I lived and searched it, looking for a man whom they believed was hiding there. I was asleep at the time they searched my room and did not know about it till the next morning. Bob McGrew told me that he was attending a Baptist camp meeting on Tumbleum River, and while the preacher was speaking a party of horsemen rode up, took a man from the congregation, carried him a few hundred yards and hung him. Some of the congregation followed and wanted to take the body down after the man was dead but were warned not to touch the body under penalty of similar treatment.

In '67 I was living with the Myers family and went out one morning to get some water; a man wearing a brown suit was passing the cabin. As I was going in I heard a party of five horsemen; they rode past, and when I got into the house, and, as I called Mr. Myers, I heard some shots fired. Before long someone knocked at the door and said that there was a dead man lying in the road. The victim had gotten drunk and boasted that he was one of a gang of stage robbers.

We left Washington in June 1876 and came back to Colorado bringing eighty head of horses averaging in value fifty to one thousand dollars. On the way, near Little Blackfoot, the horses were stolen.[26] The boys followed and brought them back from a corral five miles away.

We arrived in Denver September 1. We stayed there about three weeks and then moved down to Huerfano for the winter. The next spring, '77, we came down to the Mancos Valley.[27] In our party were Andrew and Will Menefee, John White, George May, Joe Morefield and wife, myself and three children, John, Gus, and Edward.

On the way in we stopped at Charles Johnson's place and talked to him. He was located on Pine River at what is known as Middle Bridge, about four miles above Bayfield.[28] He was running a road house and post office. We drove on and camped at some springs between the Pine and Florida Rivers.

The next day, Mr. Menefee, Uncle John White, George May, and Will Menefee started to Animas City. Mr. Menefee was riding a bronco and was thrown, breaking his collarbone and dislocating his shoulder. The boys brought a doctor from Animas City. But he did not help any, and we were held up four weeks when Mr. Bean and his son came over to our camp. Bean had a ranch about four miles below Johnson's. He was so drunk that he could hardly stand, but he told me, "I fixed my boy's shoulder and it is all right and I can fix Mr. Menefee." I asked him what I should do to help, and he had me roll up a ball of cloth that he put in an armpit; then we set the collarbone and pulled the shoulder into joint and tied it up. The next day he was much better.

Uncle John White hired a man at Animas City to drive the team, and we left for the Mancos. That man could not drive four horses and nearly upset us twice. The second time was near Junction Creek close to Bob Dwyer's place. I told Mr. Menefee he would have to discharge that man and I'd drive, which I did. Just this side of Parrott City, crossing the Cottonwood Canyon near the head of Cherry Creek, we had to let the wagon down with ropes. Coming out of the canyon, I was driving the lead wagon and there was a big tree sticking out into the trail. I could not stop, the wheel team could not hold the load, and if the leaders stopped we would have been piled up, so I swung the leaders out into the oak brush; the wagon nearly tipped over, but we made it. The men were mad when I turned out; they could not see what was the matter, and when Uncle John came along with his team he had a hard time getting around too, so they did not think I was so reckless. We camped on Starvation Creek that night.[29] When we were coming down off the divide into the Mancos River, there was a very steep trail. I told Mr. Menefee to take the leaders off and bring them down, so he and Mrs. Morefield walked with the children (three boys) and led the team. I drove down the hill. John White was ahead of me and saw me coming down. I will never forget how he looked. He had taken off his hat and forgot to put it back on. He thought I was going to turn over, but I didn't.

The first Indian we saw was just after crossing the West Mancos. I was driving ahead, and the men were coming along with the horses and cattle; we had eighty head of horses and about forty head of cattle. This Indian, Red Jacket, stood in the trail with a rifle and motioned for us to go back.[30] Mr. Menefee told him we would go out in one moon. He said, "Go now." We talked to him for a while; then he saw the other men coming through the brush and he left. We went on and stopped at Uncle John White's. We stayed there from July 28 to the twelfth of the following March. For some time we stayed in a tent, until a cabin was built. William Munroe Menefee was born September 3, a month after we reached Uncle John White's place, while we were still in the tent. We cooked over his fireplace, and one time almost burned his cabin down.

Just after we moved into the cabin, four Navajo Indians came and one said he was cold. I let him in. He saw Mr. Menefee's hat and said "John's hat" and was going to get it. I took hold of his arm and led him out. Another one started for the cellar, so I gave the baby to Johnnie and got a club. They all got on their horses and rode away laughing because the white squaw got mad.

Mr. Menefee was still disabled as the result of being thrown from the horse, and he stayed with the children while Mrs. Morefield and I went down to pick some wild currants. As we returned we saw sixteen horses near the tent. There were sixteen Indians in the tent, smoking, talking, and grunting. One was lying on the bed: I was furious because I did not want those lousy things on my clean bed. They were all lousy then, and I asked Mr. Menefee why he allowed those dirty Indians in the tent. He said that he was not able to fight them and did not want to start a fight; about that time the one on the bed raised up and said "Ugh." I told him, "I'll make you grunt," and I went out and got a big stick. I came in and started to beat them. They went out in a hurry, anyway, to avoid a beating from a squaw. I followed them out and pointed at one and said, "Shame on you Indian men, going into a white squaw's wickiup." They understood me. One of them grinned and said, "Wano Squaw," and that name stayed with me as long as an Indian came to the valley. The chief of that party was Mariana, and he was always friendly to me from that time forward.[31]

The first Indian scare we had at Mancos was at the time of the Meeker Massacre, and there was a lot of excitement among the Indians in the valley. A Ute named Hardy brought some goats and sheep over to me and asked me to take care of them. He was going over to the agency at Ignacio to keep out of trouble; all of the Indians went back to the agency for fear of the whites.[32] I told Hardy that the Indians might steal his stock, but he said, "No. Indian no steal um Wano Squaw's sheep."

In a few days, four men came and told us that the Indians were on the warpath and Major D. L. Sheets had sent word from Animas City for the settlers to get together to protect themselves against Indian attack. The valley people went into a cabin and stockade just south of town. I told them I did not think the Indians were on the warpath, as several Indians had been there just a short time before and were very friendly. I told them to go to Sheets's cattle camp and see what the boys had to say. They went and two of the boys came and asked me what I thought. I said I did not believe there was anything to it, but if Major sent that word they had better do as he suggested. They did and had everyone in the fort by midnight.

I did not go, and at 2 A.M. they came to the cabin. I was asleep. Mr. Downs asked what was the matter with me that I should sleep when the Indians were coming. I told him there was no danger. He said if the Indians did break out they could not protect me and themselves too. Menefee was in Utah that fall, and he advised me to come along, so I did. As we drew near the stockade we were stopped by two guards. I told them there were no Indians in the wagon and they got mad.

Nothing happened, and I went back to the ranch.

One evening I heard an Indian calling from down by the corral. He called a long "Oooh, Wano Squaw." I went out and found Hardy. He said, "White squaw afraid of Indian?" I said, "No." He had come for his sheep and wasn't sure that it was safe to come to the house.

Mancos Jim and Red Jacket came to our place very often.[33]

Most of the Indians were good people. They often tried to scare me, just running a bluff, and laughed when I would not be scared. They did not cause trouble if they were not bothered. Most of the early trouble was caused by the whites who tried to steal from the Indians or shot at the Indians or their children.

The Mitchell family came to the valley four days ahead of us. They were the only other family in the valley at the time. Later in the fall came the Webber, Bradford, and Willis families. Cal House and Melville, and also Bob McGrew came in the fall of '77. Mitchell and Sheek went into the Montezuma Valley with their families that fall.

When the Mitchells first came in, the men were out getting some wood and some Ute Indians came into their cabin. One of them stood the women in the corners and made motions as though to shoot, saying, “Indian kill um. Boom.” He just about scared the women to death. When the men came back, the Indians outside heard them coming and said, “White man come”; then he left.

In ’78 Doc and Manse Reid, Nick Arney, Downs, and Jasper Butts came in from Huerfano. In the fall of ’78 Doc Reid left for home, taking with him a man he had met on the way. When they were crossing the range, Reid’s companion tried to rob him, and Doc was awakened. His companion shot him and left, but Reid recovered.

Ouray was friendly to the whites, and when there was a powwow in the fall of ’77 down here two of the sub-chiefs went up to Ouray to get him to help exterminate the whites. Ouray refused to help and the chief insulted Ouray, calling him a vile and derogatory name. Ouray ordered him shot. Ouray was poisoned two years later by some of his discontented tribesmen because of his friendship to the white people.[34] He said he had made a treaty with the white people and his word must be kept.

Dick Giles was the first sheriff of La Plata County. This was all part of La Plata County in ’76, and Giles was appointed. Bob Dwyer was elected at the election following. Giles was not a candidate for sheriff. In ’78 we rented the Giles place. Dick Giles had pneumonia, and I took care of him while Mr. Menefee was in Utah after cattle. About a month after Mr. Menefee returned, Giles died, and when his property was sold we bought the ranch from his executor for $775.

In ’78 the first picnic was held in the valley. John White, his sister Elizabeth Menefee, the Willis, Bradford, Webber, Andy Menefee families and a bunch of cowboys went to what was later the Johnson place on the Dolores for a camping and fishing trip. We fished all day and danced all night. We were up there two nights and caught a lot of fish.

In ’76 some Mormons guided by Peter Shurtz settled at Bluff City on the San Juan River.[35] They built a church and brought in an organ.

In '84 the river washed them out and they came up and brought their organ with them to Mancos. It was the first organ in the country. We had some good times at our place. Mr. Brittain brought his fiddle over, and one of the boys played the organ.

Shurtz acted as guide for Mr. Menefee when he went over to Utah in '77 to trade his horses for cattle. They left October 1 and returned January 15. While they were gone, I ground wheat in the coffee mill. The first supplies, flour and groceries, we bought were from Utah. Mr. Menefee left the cattle at Sierra La Salle for the winter and on March 15 he went after them, and arrived here the fifteenth of April. He brought about three hundred head. We had very good horses when we came down here. Part of the cattle which Mr. Menefee had were remnants of short-horn stock that had been taken in the Mountain Meadows Massacre.

Later we bought flour and supplies from Kephart in Durango. Kephart and I sent a man to Alamosa for flour, but he took the load down into New Mexico and sold it, and we didn't get any of it.

Henry Porter came to our place in September '78 and worked for Mr. Menefee till February of '79; he then carried the mail, afterwards replacing the carrier who froze to death in Thompson's Park. He was a government mail carrier, and the post office was at our house. He was killed in Mancos in '81.[36]

The first school was taught by Lizzie Allen, sixteen years old, and was taught for three months. The school was held in a log cabin, south end of what is now the highway leading into Mancos. It had a dirt roof and floor. The seats were blocks of wood sawed from a pine tree. It had no blackboards, and the books were those that had been brought in by the various families.

We did not have much trouble out here; at the dances the boys frequently got on a little buster and shot out the lights, but there was nothing very serious.

Eliza LaCount, La Plata County [362-1].
Durango, February 17, 1934.

Interviewer: A. L. Soens.

I was born in Canada. We moved to Iowa, and I was married in 1874. We came to Colorado in 1878. We lived in the mountains above Alamosa. It took all day to drive to town. Alamosa was the end of the railroad at the time.[37] We lived there until June 1881, then came to Durango. We came on the train to Amargo, the end of the railroad.[38] When we left Amargo, Tom Graden, R. E. Sloan, Mr. LaCount, and myself made up the party. We were to take a buckboard from Amargo, but Mr. Sloan put the team and wagon on a flatcar and we came down to the end of steel on the flatcar. We forded the river near Arboles, and there was a contractor, Mr. Corrigan.[39] He was standing on the riverbank with a loaf of bread under his arm and a piece of meat in his hand, eating his breakfast while directing his drivers in crossing the ford. It took all day to reach the sawmills on the Pine River, where we stopped.

At Durango we stayed at the Grand Central Hotel; it was crowded and very hot. Tom Rockwood was running the hotel. We moved out before our house was completed, before even the chimneys were built.

The first public school in Durango was held in the Episcopal church; Miss Pearl Gaines was the teacher.

Parson Hoge was the minister of our church. He came into the San Juan from Texas in 1876 and held services in Animas City in 1877 in a log cabin. When the railroad came into Durango, it is reported that James Lutterall and Captain Anderson tried to reach an agreement with the town of Animas City; they failed, and the town of Durango was started. Within three years Animas City was practically deserted.[40]

Dr. Bell was induced to offer two lots to the first church denomination ready to build on them. While a wagon was on the way to the

Florida divide to get a load of lumber to erect a building, Parson Hoge went to C. M. Williams, a lumber dealer in town, and got some lumber which he carried up to the lots on his back, and he started work on the Episcopal church on the lot where the telephone building now stands.[41]

Parson Hoge was liked by all elements of the settlement. He had been a gambler at one time, and he knew and sympathized with the troubles of the sporting element. His work among them was effective, and at times he went into the saloon or dance hall, told the proprietor that he would like to talk to the boys, and he was seldom if ever refused. On the wall near the Fargo Bank game in the Clipper Theatre[42] was a box on which was written: "Don't forget Parson Hoge." The players often dropped in chips which the parson cashed for their game value. Brownie Lee, a gambler, took up a collection to help build the church.

The parson was tall, slender, and slightly stooped, of dark complexion, and had a magnetic personality. When the church was first built it had a sawdust floor and plank benches for seats. There was a low platform on which Hoge stood. His congregation was mixed, as the gamblers and sporting element always liked him and gave him their moral support as well as donated money.

Hubertine Pulvermiller, La Plata County [362-23]. January 1934.

Interviewer: A. L. Soens, Durango.

I was born in Cologne, Germany, November 18, 1848, and came to America when I was twelve or fourteen years old. We lived in Quincy, Illinois, for about four years, and then moved to Lawrence, Kansas. The town was still burning as the result of fires set in Quantrill's Raid.[43]

My husband, Conrad Pulvermiller, came to Durango in 1880 with Mr. Melville, who had a contract for carpenter work on the new smelter. In the party were Melville, Mr. Pulvermiller, Joe Steele, Billy Keeney, and George Lintner, and after the work at the smelter was finished they all returned to Kansas except Mr. Pulvermiller.

With them they brought a small Steinway piano for Mrs. Williams; the wagon in which they were hauling it got away on a steep hillside and turned over; they gathered up and mended the piano, and it was a good musical instrument afterward.

I arrived in Durango on the train, May 18, 1882. On the way out I contracted pneumonia and had to be carried to the train at Pueblo. Dr. Bellinger, who was coming to Durango to locate, was on the train, and I was his first patient. I was disappointed in Durango after I was able to get out; I had expected to see a grassy spot covered with trees, instead there was only scrub oak, sage, and serviceberry brush, and only a few trees. In the winter of '83–'84 I played croquet on Christmas Day, and the weather remained fine until the second of February '84, then it began to storm, and when the snow stopped falling it was so deep that we could not look out of the trenches that we shoveled for paths. All trains were blocked for ninety days; there was no coal oil, so we made tallow dips for lights. Coffee was all gone, and stocks of groceries were very low. The last flour was sold on the day before the trains got through. The newspaper was printed on butcher's paper, building paper, and even on some wallpaper.[44] Meat of course was plentiful; I have seen wagonloads of venison hauled into town. We bought a big deer, dressed, for $1.50, and we never paid more than $3.00 for one.

Before I came out in April 1881, my husband was working on the Leland Hotel building located where the Elks Building now stands. The lumber was piled in what is now Ninth Street; my husband was talking to Charles Ambold when the Stockton-Eskridge-Garrett gang of cowboys fired on a bunch of Farmington cowpunchers who were riding along the top of reservoir hill, just east of town. The Farmington men returned the shots, and my husband—who had just said to Ambold, "I had better get out of here, it would be just my luck to get hurt"—was struck in the leg. He afterwards died from the effects of the wound. The Stocktons had stolen some cattle belonging to the settlers on the lower Animas in New Mexico, and they sold the stock and were boasting about their cleverness in the Coliseum. The Farmington men came after them but did not come into town.[45]

In the spring of '84, June 11, we had very high water. Mr. Pulvermiller was working at Fort Lewis, the children were out playing, and I was making dried apple pies, that was our only fruit, when Mr. Kincaid and Mr. Moore, neighbors who were hauling freight to Fort Lewis, came over and told me to get out of the house, or the water would wash me away. I opened the back door and a dead cow almost floated onto the step. The water carried away my washtubs, clothesline, and some lumber we were going to use for building, and before I got out of there the water was up to my waist. Charles Naeglin came up and tied a rope to the house to keep it from washing away.

People had good times; they were generally pretty friendly, but the town was very tough too. I was standing about twenty feet from Henderson and Fulcher when the latter was killed. Henderson had a bunch of ore sacks; he had just come from the smelter, where he was packing ore from the Junction Creek mines and had come down to the corral on Fifteenth Street which Mr. Briggs afterwards owned, and there he met one of the Fulcher boys. They were arguing about something when Fulcher's brother suddenly exclaimed, "Look out, he is going to kill you!" I was watching them and Henderson had not made a move, but Fulcher reached for his gun and Henderson was too fast. He killed Fulcher. He was not punished, as it was obviously self-defense. If the Fulcher boy had kept quiet I do not think there would have been any bad trouble.

After Mr. Pulvermiller died I worked as a midwife, and I went all over the town at all hours of the day or night. I carried a lantern when I went out at night; and while the town was full of toughs—there were about six hundred sporting women in town at one time—I was never molested.

Clara Morris Ormiston, La Plata County [362-34]. Mancos, March 15, 1934.

Interviewer: A. L. Soens.

I was born in Marionville, Lawrence County, Missouri, in 1872.

The family moved to Texas in '74 and in 1880 my father and mother and two sisters came to Colorado in a covered wagon. We had a big team of mules and some saddle horses. We brought some cattle with us which we sold at Alamosa. When we left Alamosa, we hitched two of the saddle horses on as leaders ahead of the mules. We started for Colorado about the first of May and arrived in the Mancos Valley about July 1, 1880.

Father had started to Rico, but upon reaching the valley he decided that Rico was not as good as he had been led to believe so we stopped here.

When we came in, Parrott City was the county seat of La Plata County, which included Montezuma; Animas City was a thriving town, and Durango had not yet been started. The post office was at Menefee's in Mancos Valley.

We had some trouble with the Indians, and one time, in '84, we left our ranch and went down to Bluff City, went down to buy milk cows. That was the time that the government interpreter Wormington was killed near Elk Mountain.[46] The cowboy "Rowdy" was Jim Higgison. I knew him, and he had started down to call us back, but decided that he could not arrive in time and could do more good by going to help chase the Indians near Carlyle's. George Bauer came into that valley in '81. He packed in [a] stock of goods on burros and opened his store. He opened the bank in '83.

We stayed at Dave Willis's place; he was killed by the Indians about '81. The year before we came in, the mail carrier was frozen to death in

Thompson's Park. He was within shouting distance of the Cavines's cabin, and Watson McGeoch brought the mail on over the Mancos.

The first school was held in a cabin on the Root place. Miss Lizzie Allen, who was staying in Parrott City, and who was sixteen years old, was the teacher. The cabin was too small, so everybody went to work to build a new one. The latter part of Miss Allen's term was held in the new building while a stockade of pine trees was being built around it. This log cabin stood in back of what was later the Bauer Mercantile Company's store. It was used for all public gatherings until 1887 when a new high school was built, and the first floor was used thereafter for public meetings and entertainments. One day a couple of Indians went to school. Mr. Rush, who was hauling a load of hay, saw their horses outside, and he took his pitchfork and drove the Indians out of the school. Miss Allen was frightened, and the Indians were angry. They told Mr. Ratliff that a man with a pitchfork was going to stick them.

On the first day of May 1881, John Thurman, Richard May, and Byron Smith were murdered, and the cabins on the Thurman and Willis ranch close to the Colorado line near the Blue Mountains was burned and their stock driven off. Mr. Thurman was in charge of a large heard of fine horses belonging to himself and H. H. Alderson. Willis was in the cattle business, and Mr. May had gone out to the camp to purchase horses and had taken Smith with him. The news of the murder reached Mancos on the second, and on the third a party among whom were H. C. Goodman, C. A. Frink, W. W. Puett, M. W. Reid, George and Will May, brothers of the dead man, George Phelps, Mike O'Donnell, Ben Quick, and others went out and buried Thurman and May but could not find the body of Smith. About two weeks later David Willis and others, while trying to round up cattle in the neighborhood of the burned cabins, were fired upon by the Indians. They came in, organized a force of about fifty men, and on June 1 started out to recover the stock. They came upon the Indians near the Sierra La Sal Mountains, where a fight occurred in which about ten men were killed, but so far as can be learned there were no Indians killed.[47]

In 1886 an Indian on Bear Creek and his family were attacked by some white men who wanted the Indian's stock.[48] One squaw escaped by jumping down over a cliff—one of the men attempted to kill her with a rock—but the rest of the family were killed. This was cold-blooded murder on the part of the whites, perpetrated for the purpose of stealing stock, and in revenge the Indians burned the cabin of Mr. Gentner after killing him and wounding his wife. She and two children escaped. This is the first and last instance of Indians attacking settlements and burning cabins at night.

E. W. Camp, La Plata County [362-18].
Durango, January 16, 1934.

Interviewer: A. L. Soens.

I came to Durango June 26, 1883, and shortly after we built and moved into the house where we now reside.

There were no trees in Durango, with the exception of a few scattered pines. The trees were all planted later, and at that time Durango was covered with scrub oak, serviceberry, and wild currant bushes. Another very noticeable characteristic feature was the scarcity of women on the streets; one infrequently met a woman or an old man.

The Shaw Hotel at Animas City was quite a popular place. Mr. T. C. Graden, Mr. Porter, Joe Langley, and Frank Roberts boarded there. I have heard Mr. Camp tell about the mad rush to get at the table at mealtimes. This custom became so bad that Mr. Shaw allowed his steady customers to enter the dining room by a side door. The boarders generally had their special dishes, such as jellies or syrup, held aside. These were not a part of the bill of fare but were privately owned and subject to the call of the owner. There was no way of keeping food, and the butter was often rancid. Prices were high. Mr. Camp paid one dollar for a can of oysters, and they happened to be spoiled. I bought butter from Seth Sackett for which I paid fifty cents or more per pound. He often said that it was not worth making if he could not get fifty cents for it.

When Mr. John A. Porter came into this country, he carried a sack of coal on his saddle horse. He was examining engineer and was sent down to examine some property and report on it. He carried the coal in order to test the ores. When he came down Horse Gulch, he saw the coal outcropping and was so angry at having carried coal two hundred miles on horseback that he untied the sack and dumped the coal into the gulch. He then rode on up across Junction Creek, where he found Bob Dwyer plowing with a rifle strapped to plow handles.

At one time Mr. Henry M. Teller stopped at the Shaw Hotel.[49] He left early in the morning and failed to shut the door. A drunk came along and wandered into his room, lay down, and fell asleep. Shaw thought that Mr. Teller had changed his mind and decided to stay over for a while, so he allowed the sleeper to rest comfortably, undisturbed. On learning that Teller's horses were gone Mr. Shaw investigated and found that the slumbering drunk had perpetrated a hoax, so he proceeded to awaken and evict the sleeper. Indignation was high on both sides.

The stores carried very high grade stocks; the finest of imported jams, wines, cheeses, et cetera, could be purchased. Otto Mears said that he could buy in Durango the very finest groceries, and he brought his private car to Durango for supplies.[50] Venison, quail, and trout were plentiful.

The St. Julian was a very good restaurant. It was run by William Cau. It was located on Tenth Street across from the Gem Theatre and later became a Chinese restaurant. Mr. Elitch, who later opened Elitch's Garden in Denver, ran Elitch's Oyster House.[51]

There were kerosene streetlights, and two large cisterns furnished a supply for the town fire protective system. The fire department consisted of a horse-drawn steam pump, which could pump water from the cisterns in case of fire.

Dances were held in the DAC Hall, adjoining the present courthouse site, and were largely attended. There was also a fine skating rink located where the courthouse now stands. Everyone skated; it was a very popular amusement, and one could see people going to the skating rink at any time after nine o'clock in the morning. I still have my roller skates with my name engraved on them.

There were two extremes of social life. Mining engineers and managers, the official staff of the smelter, army people at Fort Lewis.[52] The Brooklyn Cattle Company brought out a group of wealthy and high-class easterners. Molyneaux was among them. These people were the type of men such as Theodore Roosevelt in his Dakota days. They were a cultured, well-educated, traveled class. The other extreme was the wild and woolly followers of the mining and lumber camps and the cattle ranges.

The reading club was organized in the fall of '83, and it is one of the oldest, if not the oldest organization of its kind in the state.

The first show I attended here was a circus. They had plenty of animals, including elephants. Many Indians came to town to see the circus; they were camped down across the street from where Graden's store is now located. They were gaudy in blankets, and when the parade came past with the elephants the entire band took to their horses and left as quickly as possible; they were afraid of the elephants.

Folsom's Mesa was platted and a racetrack was laid out. I attended races that were held there.

The Town Company set aside a block between Second and Third Avenues for public buildings, and in '91 or '92, when the new courthouse was built, the jail was moved up there from the south end of town. The jail was a steel cage inside a brick building. There were five or six prisoners in it, and the cage containing the prisoners was placed on wheels and hauled through the streets drawn by oxen. It moved very slowly, and there was quite a procession of small boys and others watching the proceedings. Judge Gary was very indignant at what he called the inhuman spectacle of prisoners "on a perambulating van."

Lazarus and Rapp ran a large clothing store, and J. E. Schutt built the house that is now owned by Dr. Ochsner, which he uses for his hospital. Mr. Weightman built the Monroe Fields house. Both of these men were very well-to-do, and about ready to retire when the panic of '93 came along and they lost their properties.[53] Among the business houses in '82 were Goodrich, Weightman, and Wilcox, groceries; I. Kruschke, clothing store; Adams and Bayley, hardware, later owned by Ferg Graham; Carter was running the Palace of Fashion, also a clothing store; Tom Rockwood was running the Grand Central Hotel, and the Leland Hotel was located where the Elks' building now stands.

Mary D. Hansen, La Plata County [362-22]. Durango, January 11, 1934.

Interviewer: A. L. Soens.

I was born in Fyen, Denmark, 1880. I was three years old when my parents brought us from Denmark in '83. We stopped in Chicago for some time, then came by rail to Ignacio. There was a fight between two big railroad lines, and our railroad fare from Chicago to Denver was a dollar each for adults.

I remember practically nothing of the trip across the continent, but I remember distinctly when we got off the train at Ignacio seeing "Nigger John" sitting on the bank fishing. He was the first Negro I ever saw.

The first thing that struck my mother was that when we came to Ignacio and had dinner there they had no butter. She said, "Oh well, we will have a cow on the farm." And Uncle Andrew, who had met us, said, "No. Although there are about fifty cattle, none of those Texas cattle can be milked."

My uncle Andrew Isacksen had taken up a homestead on Texas Creek.[54] My father homesteaded about two miles above what is now the middle bridge, about four miles north of Bayfield.

The first winter we were out there the house on the homestead was not built, and we lived in a cabin on the Lowell place. There was plaster between the logs, and we children could pull it out. There were only two rooms, one downstairs and a sort of attic upstairs reached from a ladder in the middle of the room. In the spring we moved to the homestead.

In '84 the Peeples sawmill people gave a dance in the dining room, where they were so often held in those days. The sawmill was several miles above Bayfield. The refreshments consisted of shortcake baked in great iron pans, each pan serving about fifty people. This cake would be split and filled with raspberries from gallon cans, served with whipped cream. Also coffee was served. The HD people, formerly Texas people, bought cattle from Texas cowboys who brought them in and sold them thirty-five hundred cattle, and actually delivered about three thousand. In delivering the cattle they put them in various gullies and recounted them many times. That night at the dance two of the Texas cowboys were talking about what they had done when the sheriff came into the dance. They knew it was for them and bolted for the window, broke the glass and went through and got away, and the HD people never did recover their loss, which just about broke them.

Chief Buckskin Charlie a number of times warned the white people of possible uprisings.[55] In about '84 one of the cowboys stole Indian cattle, and when the Indian came after his cattle the cowboy shot him dead. This caused much consternation among the Indians. Chief Buckskin Charlie warned all the white settlers. We all slept out on oak brush. Everybody went together so the men could protect their families if they needed to. It seemed the Indians would burn the houses but would not be likely to molest the people. I remember how angry the men were because my small brother kept asking questions about

"Why are we here?" and "Why don't we go home?" and the men were afraid of the noise letting the Indians know where we were. We slept out two nights. The Indians didn't cause trouble, but Charlie didn't know whether they could be held but wanted to run the white people out of their homes. My mother has a pair of moccasins Charlie gave her which his wife had made and beaded.

The only Indian uprisings seem to have been when white people did them wrong.

The first time Papa and Mama came into Durango, there was no bridge over the Pine River and we had to go down through the river and pull up a steep bank. Papa and my small brother were on the front spring seat, and Mama, my seven-month-old sister, and I were on the board seat put across the back of the wagon. Papa was urging the mules, trying to get them to pull up the hill, and didn't hear us shout when the board we were sitting on slipped out and we went into the river. The baby slipped out of Mama's lap and landed between two big rocks. Luckily it was in the fall of the year and the river was not very high. There was a board bridge at Ignacio, at that time.

I remember Mrs. John Petersen at Piedra told me they got seventy-five dollars a ton for their hay when the soldiers moved from Pagosa to Animas. They also stayed for a couple of days at the Petersen place.

In about '85 Mrs. Petersen came over and got me for a visit with them. Mrs. Mack came to the place horseback with Charlie riding in front of her and Edith in back. The little girl was raw in front from riding in back of the saddle. Mrs. Petersen said, "Oh, isn't that a shame?" Mrs. Mack said, "That's all right, no bones broken." Mrs. Mack used to ride after two or three hundred cattle with the two babies on her saddle. The babies couldn't be left in the house for fear of animals.

One night when Mamma and I were alone two lions were around all night and took three or four calves. We could hear the cattle howling but could do nothing about it.

In 1884, that winter we were blockaded, we had no sugar, nothing to eat but bread out of flour ground in coffee mills. We did not see anyone from the first of February until April 1, when Charlie Ayres came by with a six-oxen team pulling a log wagon and broke the road. The snow covered all the small sheds. The day before it stopped snowing it was about my father's height, six feet. You could go right out and get deer by the horns. The snow was so deep that they couldn't move. As the snow got deeper they kept coming down into the lower country. My father got eleven that winter on snowshoes without shooting. The meat we smoked and salted.

In about '85 Old Washington, a sub-chief, came and got Mama because his daughter-in-law was very sick. They usually didn't ask white people, but they saw she was going to die and were desperate. She died in childbirth in the tepee. Indians are supposed to have little feeling, but old Washington and his son suffered pitifully and tried so hard to do what they could for the pretty young girl.[56]

In about '85 there came a young man and his wife in a covered wagon drawn by oxen. He asked Mama to come help him, and their baby was born in the wagon with just he and Mama to take care of her. It was my mother's first experience at a birth, but both the mother and baby got along all right and in five or six days they started off again on their way.

At one of the early elections there was a bitter fight over the election, and somehow the election returns were lost in the Piedra River on the way to Durango, which turned the election.

One year Papa thought his calves were too small to butcher and so bought a portion of a calf from one of the neighbors. Some friends of ours had seen the butchering in the hills and later informed papa that he had bought a portion of his own calf.

One of the old-timers told my father that the only way to keep even was to know how many cattle he had, and one could usually tell about where they went, and the thing to do was wait your chance to take what was coming to you, and in that way try to keep about even as there was no chance to dare prosecute. Life was too cheap. One of the early settlers had killed seven men, all over cattle. A friend of ours, a really kind man, killed a man over a ditch.

In approximately '89 when we were at the big Schutz place, which my father later bought, an old bachelor, Tom Phillips, a good-natured old fellow, asked Williams, "When can you pay me the $2.50 you owe me?" Good-naturedly. Williams shot him dead. They were there waiting for the mail to come in. Phillips was sitting on the banister, and I remember he just fell backwards over the railing. Williams got seven years but got out in about three.

In about '91 I was riding with Mrs. Hensley and one of her boys. We heard something and rode off the road, and the cowboys were butchering there and told us to get off or they would shoot holes through us big enough to see the sun, moon, and stars through. That morning about twenty cattle had been stolen from the agency at Ignacio.

It seemed in those days that the outcome of trials was usually decided in some saloon or other.

One of the elections was not held because the judge didn't certify it in time, and the incumbent officers just held over.

Lars Hansen, a cousin of my mother's, had the job carrying mail between Pine River and Piedra, so I would ride horseback with him in front on the saddle. That hard ride would almost make me sick, but Mrs. Petersen on the Piedra treated me so well that I could go whenever I had the chance.[57] We moved to Durango in '86 and my father went to work at the smelter. We stayed in Durango until about '91 and then moved back near Bayfield on the old Johnson homestead. In about '92 one night all three candidates for sheriff—Democrat, Republican, and Populist—stayed overnight at our house. All electioneering was done on horseback.

In about '93 G. W. White started a cash-and-carry store and prospered just as the chain stores are doing today.[58]

In the early days they would invite seven or eight families to come for a dance. They would come up for supper, dance until about one o'clock, then lay blankets everywhere, floor, et cetera, and in the morning have bacon, biscuits, and fried eggs and coffee for breakfast before going home. Used to go eighteen or twenty miles horseback to a dance.

When I was about four and a half my father was working in the sawmill several miles away, so I walked two and a half miles to a cowboy camp of seven or eight cowboys and asked one cowboy to go to Durango for a doctor, and another went about six miles to get a neighbor woman to take care of my mother when my brother was born.

Carrie Smith Dunham, Montezuma County [360-103]. Dolores, July 28, 1934.

Interviewer: Anna Florence Robison.

I was born in Venango County, Pennsylvania, October 11, 1862. In 1882 I came to Telluride with my cousins. There were eleven of us in the party, and we intended to make Colorado our home. My cousin's husband had mining claims in the Telluride region, and we ran a confectionery store and boardinghouse.

When we came to Telluride, it was a relatively new camp.[59] There might have been about twenty-five families living there. But the miners from the camps in the basin around came in on Saturday nights and celebrated. There were thirteen saloons and two grocery stores in town at the time. All freight was brought by mule team from the nearest railroad point, which was then Montrose.[60]

The first funeral I attended was [in] a room sometimes used for a courtroom and located above the dance hall. As the principal character had died of smallpox, they left him outside in the wagon while his funeral was going on.

We had quite a trip from Montrose into Telluride. We had gone sightseeing in Montrose, and I got alkali mud on my dress and ruined that before we started. We hired a man with a buckboard to take us.

There was a train of freight mule teams stuck in the mud on the road ahead of us and we could not get around them so had to stay all night at the Dallas where Ridgeway now is. Usually six mules were used to a wagon on that haul, but they finally got the wagons through by hooking sixteen mules to a wagon to pull out of the mud hole there.[61]

In 1884 I went with my cousin to Rico, where we took over a mine boardinghouse. At that time Rico was pretty prosperous and probably had some fifty families living there as well as the miners.[62] The boardinghouse we had was at the C.H.C. Mine in the hills.[63]

When I met Mr. Dunham, he was taking care of a horse herd. But when he first came to Rico in 1881, he worked in the mines. But everyone had a saddle horse for summer use, and in winter they all sent their mounts out to winter range. Mr. Dunham and his half brother, William Dawson, took such horses together with those they owned themselves to their winter range on the Disappointment. Mr. Dunham and I were married in 1885. He took up a ranch there on the Disappointment and built a two-room house. We had to get our winter stock of supplies from Durango, over a hundred miles away.[64] One could not well get on without flour and coal oil at least. As a bride there I had the first real bedroom furniture in that whole country. The bureau and washstand were of the marble-topped variety. When spring came, I could not stay down there because the water was so bad. It was too much to try to haul that bedroom furniture about, so we traded it for two cows with calves. That was our first start in the cattle business right there. Then we went back to Rico and remained for two years, during which Mr. Dunham mined some and ran a livery stable.

Then, after a visit to our people back east, we moved down to Lone Dome on the Dolores River.[65] Mr. Dunham traded his horses for a ranch there. This was a place homesteaded by a brother of Jesse Robinson of Bear Creek on the Dolores. We lived there for ten years and had milk cows and raised quite a little bunch of cattle, over a hundred head. But we got our cattle little by little by trading, natural increase, et cetera. We then lived on the South place on the river near Dolores for ten more years. Then we bought the Moriarty place at Stoner, where we remained until we bought what is now the Lester King place, then known as the Abeln place, in the upper Montezuma Valley. Three years later still we moved to Dolores, where we have been ever since, and Mr. Dunham used it as a base from which to look after his interests, for he has in no sense retired.

We saw a good deal of the Indians in our first years here, but we had not the least trouble with them at any time. However, in the early days Mr. Dunham used to ride at night so as to escape their attention. One night he knew there was an Indian camp near and he meant to make a detour to avoid it. He took a steep trail to the top of a hill and was greeted at the top by some of the Indians he was trying to avoid. They took hold of his horse's bridle and detained him while Goodman, a sort of leader among the Indians, made him tell where he was going and why. He assured the Indians that he was alone, and presently they let him go away unmolested. Goodman used to visit us as a friend afterward. Later on he and two other Indians came to the place and wanted to stay the night, and my husband said they could sleep in the haystack. I got supper for them, and they scrubbed and scrubbed themselves in preparation for eating. When the main part of the supper was over, the Indians produced some watermelons which they had brought from McElmo Canyon to treat us. But the melons proved to be unanimously green, and the Indians were so disappointed.

The Indians called a spring on our place "Bob Water," and they would ask permission to camp there before doing so. Mr. Dunham's name is Robert, and he is known to all as "Bob" Dunham. Hence the Bob Water. Their leaders would never let them get off their horses until Mr. Dunham came. Then they would get off and come in and sit around waiting to be fed.

One time a man named George King wanted to trade a pony to the Indians for a pair of chaps and then stole the pony. All of the men down the Dolores River had gone to Rico and left the women and children alone there. An Indian came to our place and asked me if I had seen George King. He explained to me what King had done. I told the Indian they had better not kill George King, for when the cowboys returned, they would make him give back the pony to them. But the Indians chased King and shot at him. He jumped off the pony and let them get it without more trouble. Then the Indians came back and told me how the matter had been settled. This was about 1887, I should think. If such an episode had taken place a very few years earlier, it would probably have been the cause of someone else's being killed. Mr. Dunham thinks that in almost every case, Indian trouble around this part of the country could have been avoided if the white people had kept their heads instead of losing them. And he was here through the years in the eighties when the worst of it was going on.

I used to make buckskin gloves for the Indians with my glove pattern, and once they brought me a pair of lovely beaded moccasins. The cowboys would buy buckskin, and I would make gloves for them at a dollar a pair. The gloves were gauntlets, and I would do the stitching on them with blue and red silk. Jim Moore bought a ranch eight miles down the river that had belonged to a cat lover. It had fifty house cats on it. Mr. Moore had agreed to buy the ranch on condition that the man would kill all the cats. He did so, and Mr. Moore tanned the fifty hides and brought them to me to make into a robe. I used a government blanket to line the robe and took a good deal of pains to arrange the cat skins by size and color so that it would look as well as possible. It really made up nicely, but it wasn't the sort of thing I would personally want to have about, and I was afraid Mr. Moore would not care much for it. But he did. He was much pleased with his cat-robe. Some years later it was purchased by a tourist for fifty dollars.

Mr. Dunham was once cleaning ditch for the Lone Dome ranch, and he had his gun along. He was near a deer crossing, and he shot a deer. Presently an Indian came along and claimed the animal. Mr. Dunham suggested that the Indian should skin the deer and that they should divide the meat. The Indian wanted the hide, and it wound up by the Indian's taking the hide and Mr. Dunham the meat. The Indian was perfectly satisfied, and he used to come to see us each fall after that.

The Indians used to come to our place to buy potatoes in the fall. We had a great many chokecherries down there, and I made much chokecherry butter. The Indians called it coyote medicine and liked it very much. So I traded them coyote medicine for buckskin.

One Indian took a great fancy to my son Ralph, then a small child. He called Ralph his "Migo" and wanted to take him to the reservation.[66] He gave him a pony.

One time an Indian with his hair cut short came to the place when I happened to be curling my hair with an iron. He asked me to curl his hair, and I fixed him a few curls and let him look at himself. He then insisted upon having his entire head of hair curled up in style; I complied. He had noticed that Mr. Dunham's hair is curly, and he wanted to know if I curled it for him as I curled his.

Eva Adams House, Montezuma County [360-33]. Dolores, March 9, 1934.

Interviewer: Anna Florence Robison.

I was born on a farm near Bryan, Ohio, in 1860. In 1870 we moved to a farm near Rock Island, Illinois, and in 1874 to near Soldiers Grove, Wisconsin. There were eleven of us children. My twin sister, who still lives in Wisconsin, and I were the oldest. And among my earlier memories are soldiers passing. I know my parents were afraid my father would be drafted.

When I was eighteen I wanted to see something of the world. I went to visit my mother's sister in Cheyenne, Wyoming. My cousin had married Mr. A. W. Dillon in Illinois, and they had come out to Rico to live a short time before. My cousin wrote to me in Cheyenne and told me to come out and visit her. She thought I could get a good deal of sewing to do in Rico, and she said I could make my home with them. Mr. Dillon freighted between Rico and Durango, and it left her alone a good deal. I wanted some adventure; so I came. That was in 1878.

I came by way of Alamosa and Rockwood. which was near Electra Lake on the Durango-Silverton line. The stagecoach in which I rode was drawn by four horses. I made the trip alone. But after I got to Rico, I was very homesick. I would go down and sit on the riverbank and watch the water and cry. But I wouldn't give up and go home, because everyone would think I was acting like a baby. Rico was on the boom in those days. There was much going on. For amusement, we had dances and later Sunday school and church.

While living at Rico with the Dillons I met Calvin House, who was running a feed and grain store in Rico at the time. Mr. House had also a ranch down the Dolores River below the present site of McPhee. It is still called the House Ranch. We were married the spring of 1883, and we moved down onto his ranch that fall. Dolores was called the Big Bend then, and there weren't many houses there, but Mr. Ordway had the post office, and there was a log schoolhouse there and a store.[67]

There had been considerable Indian trouble a year or two before I was married, and I always used to be so afraid of the Indians. I would feel as if the blood were all going back into my heart whenever they were about. The Indians used always to pass our ranch on their way to and from the hills where they went to hunt. And they often stopped to ask for something to eat. We always fed them, and Mr. House never asked them into the house. But, afraid as I was of them and afraid as the children were, we never had any real experiences with them.

But when the cowboys killed a hunting party of Indians up at Beaver [Creek] and one got away so that the Indians killed a Mr. Gentner down in the Lakeview neighborhood and shot his wife in the shoulder for revenge, we later had a very bad fright.[68] After that for a while, Mr.

House kept a loaded gun in the house in case of need. My husband was out milking our cows and I was working in the kitchen. A kitten playing about the room ran up on the trigger of the gun and set it off with a loud report. It frightened me very much. Before I saw what had happened I thought the Indians were upon us. My daughter Winnie, then a six-months-old baby, screamed and screamed. Mr. House heard the shot and the screams and came running to the house. He ran so fast and was so frightened for us that he fell into the door when he got to the house. That was the extent of my adventures with the Indians, but that fright was terrible while it lasted even though nothing more dangerous than a kitten was the cause.

My oldest living child, Winnie, was eight years old when I first went back east to visit my family.

My daughters, Winnie, Edith, and Amy, went to rural school near the present McPhee. All three of them were married at our ranch home. Winnie married Joseph Akin, son of Mr. and Mrs. James Akin.[69] Edith married Oscar Trimble, and Amy married Roy Akin, a brother of Joseph. All live at Dolores at the present time.

I remember the first automobile that came down the river. Sam Johnson had horses rounded up for branding, and when they saw the car they ran in terror out toward Sage Hen, snorting and looking this way and that.

Since my husband's death, I have lived in Dolores to be near my daughters and their families.

Mary Lee Lamb, Montezuma County [360-108]. Mancos, August 1934.

Interviewer: Anna Florence Robison.

We first came from Utah to the Mancos in 1882. There was quite a large party of us, consisting of my mother, Mrs. Sarah C. Lee, known to all as "Grandma Lee"; my brother Charles, his wife and child; my other brothers, Robert E., Walter, and Ammon; my sister Sarah and her husband, and one child; John D. Young; my sister Josephine, then a child; John Hall and his wife, Rebekah; my husband, Charles M. Lamb, and myself with our two children, Ruby and Sadie, the last named born on the way. The Halls were old friends, not relatives. We originally intended to go to the Gila River in Arizona, where an older sister of mine, Mrs. Olive Norton, lived. We were unsettled in Utah, and only Mother had a home; so we persuaded her to dispose of her place and set out with us. We came through this way and stopped for a time.

We left Escalante February 26, 1882.[70] We had four or five wagons, the necessary horses, milk cows, and John Young had a four-ox team. My husband and I were well prepared for the road with a stove in the front part of our covered wagon and a bed with springs in the back. There were many friends to see us off on our long journey that February day. My second daughter, Sadie, was born ten or fifteen miles out of Escalante that same day. My mother was a doctor woman and took all of the care of me that was required.

We headed for Hall's Ferry on the Colorado, and we crossed over the river on March 19th or 20th when Sadie was three weeks old.[71] There the rocks are cut and blasted out so that a wagon can pass easily. The walls are slick and perpendicular, and the road down to the ferry between these walls is very steep, for it is said to drop seventeen hundred feet there in half a mile. There was a big ferryboat at the bottom to take us across the Colorado River. Our wagons were all that the boat could carry, and after we had driven them onto the ferry we had to swim the horses across. That was a frightening business, for we had a hard time to keep the stock from milling downstream into the canyon. One big, heavy horse reared up with his forefeet on another horse's back and rode across the river that way. All you could see was the animals' noses sticking out of the water. One man said he would swim with the horses, but the horse he was riding reared and he fell off. As he was himself no swimmer, he was towed over the river hanging onto the horse's tail. Eventually we got all of our horses, oxen, and milk cows across and were ready for the second lap of our journey. Fortunately, the road up from Hall's Ferry on this side is not so steep as the one we descended into it.

It was a terrible road—or lack of it—from the Colorado River to Bluff City, Utah. We got there about the first of April perhaps. We were a little short of food, and there was not much of a variety to what we did have. We used jerked meat cooked until tender and then gravy made with it. The Halls added much to the enjoyment of the rest of us on the trip, for they were very jolly. John Hall would say witty things to his wife, and she would pretend that she was angry for our entertainment.

We remained at Bluff City for a few days, then came on to Mancos. We came up the McElmo until we struck Montezuma Valley.[72] When we were traveling along somewhere east of the present site of Cortez, we saw a séance of some sort that has always remained a mystery to me. We were going along pretty well over toward the Mesa Verde and headed for the Mancos. We passed near a ranch with a little house and a stock corral where horses were rounded up. There were two men with saddle horses there, and the men were off the horses, running about in a peculiar manner, and acting strangely. A cloud of smoke began to rise from inside the corral just before one of the men came out of there. And out of the cloud of smoke came the most terrible and unearthly yells I ever heard. The two men got on the horses and started to ride away. Then, possibly because they noticed our party at a distance and knew we must be hearing those yells, they rode back and fired some shots into that smoke. The yells ceased. Whatever they had tied there they had killed, of course. Then they rode away again as fast as they could. We did not investigate, for we could see there was nothing we could do. We had no idea what might be the explanation of what we had seen and heard, and, being strangers in the country, we did not want to court trouble. But we never heard anything remotely concerning what we had seen that day.

We first got acquainted with Grandma and Grandpa Weston, and we cleared land for Andy Menefee at Mancos. Then we went to Durango and hauled freight by team to Rico. Finally we went to Rockwood and we women camped while the men were freighting.[73] We had a shelter of wagon sheets on poles. One night at our Rockwood camp, I heard a dreadful racket. So for protection, I got up and placed Mr. Lamb's needle gun beside my bed.[74] Next morning, Mother laughed when she saw the gun. "You fixed it nice and handy for them, didn't you, Daughter?" she said to me. I had placed the breech of the gun out so it would have been handier for an intruder than for me.

From Rockwood we went to the Gila River in Arizona, where my sister lived, and there we remained until 1888. We lived at Pima. On the road down, we were held up near Camp Apache because of Indian trouble.[75] On arrival, we developed malaria and had it for six months. One day I would have a chill, and Mr. Lamb would wait on me. The next day, he would have a chill, and I would take care of him. I got very white and thin. But when we got over the malaria, we liked the country very well. But we finally decided we liked Mancos better than any place we had ever seen, and we came back and homesteaded. We brought my sister Olive Norton with us. Halls remained in Arizona, and most of my relatives, including Mother, returned to Utah. But we have lived at Mancos ever since.

Mr. Lamb and I had eleven children: Ruby, deceased; Sadie, Mrs. Roy Parker of California, the daughter who was born on the way here; Ammon, Walter, Minnie Wheeler, Leona Wheeler, all of the Mancos country at present; two other grown daughters and one baby girl who are dead; Edmund Clyde, who was buried at sea during the war; and Kenneth, a boy of nineteen who died after a three-day illness nine months after Edmund was buried at sea. I went to France with the other Gold Star mothers in the 1931 pilgrimage.[76]

Mr. Lamb and I make our home just out of Mancos, but the place where we live is not our original homestead. We have taken a little girl,

Julia Heinz, whose father was tramping through the country and had no home for her. We will put her in school this fall.

My mother was a practical doctor. She never had another medical attendant for her family, and she had twelve children. I became a practical doctor myself when I realized the need. Aunt Hanna Perking used to be the doctor woman here. She was an Ellis by her first marriage and has two sons living here. There was a Dr. Winters at Parrott City, a wonderful doctor, and he came over when needed. But he died a drunkard, dope fiend, and a pauper. Once a Swede had a terribly injured hand which all others thought he must lose, but Dr. Winters, then in his last days, saved it. But for a while I was the only doctor on the Mancos, and I have ushered hundreds of babies into the world. After Dr. Trotter came, I worked with him and also nursed at his hospital.

A little more than a year and a half before I was born, I had a sister and brother killed by a house falling in at old Fort Harmony.[77] They were building New Harmony, and nearly everyone had moved there, and the rest were going soon. A neighbor asked two of my brothers to spend the night with her children before all moved out of the old fort. My mother was not one to let her children visit about away from home at night, but this once she consented that my brothers should go. That night my mother was carding and spinning, and suddenly she felt she absolutely must go out to get a bucket of water and some chips. She suggested it to Aunt Teresa, an old lady who was with her.

"The house is full of wood, and there is enough water," the old lady protested, and it was true. Mother had to empty the water bucket into the dishpan in order to get more space for water, but she felt somehow that she must go, and they went.

They heard a loud crash while they were out after the water and chips, and they knew it was some old house falling in. They had no idea until they tried to open the door of the house when they returned that it was their own dwelling that had fallen in. The door would not open. Through the window, Mother could see the baby buried to her neck in fallen adobe, but she could do nothing for her. The baby, eighteen months old, was Sarah Lee Young. In the cradle was a larger child, Margaret, dead and pinned by a beam through the back. She had lifted little Sarah out of her place in the cradle and got in there herself. Her time had come, and Sarah's had not. My oldest living sister, Olive Norton, had been knocked under the bed. Her leg was broken, but she was otherwise all right, and Mother managed to get her out of there. My brother George was just dying when Mother saw him first where he lay on the bed.

There was no one to help Mother get them out but one woman, two boys, and an old lady. She had to send twenty miles for help to get the children dug out.

My people owned Lee's Ferry at one time.[78] And when I went out to the dedication of the bridge there in 1930, it was the first time I had seen the place since I was a child.

My husband says that the so-called "Hole in the Rock" was between Lee's Ferry and Hall's Ferry. There was a road that way at one time, but when we came, the road to Hall's Ferry was the one they were using. Hall's Ferry was once known as the "Crossing of the Fathers" where the priests crossed the river in ancient days on their way to the Kayente country. There were big ruins there, and the Fathers lived in the ruins one winter in 16-something. The date was marked up in the ruin.[79]

In this country we have had to be pretty independent and learn to do many things. They come in handy sometimes to help others less fortunate than ourselves. When Wylie Sheek's baby was drowned recently, they sent for me because I knew them well and had helped them when I could before. It having been drowned accidentally, they had sent for the coroner, but he was away on a similar case elsewhere, and the deputy had to be sent for. The little thing was black from standing on its head in the water, and I worked with it and got it to looking better. I had them get some ice, and I packed the little body in it for them. Knowing as I did that they couldn't really afford the expense of a regulation funeral by the undertaker, I told them that if they liked I would explain to the coroner, who was also the undertaker, and then that some of us would help them with the baby ourselves. The parents told me to go ahead.

Archie Hays made the casket, and I helped to trim it. We got white terry cloth that gives almost the effect of velvet and covered the outside with that in such a way that the tacks we used were entirely covered. We padded the inside well with cotton and covered it with softly shirred white nainsook or long-cloth lining.[80] We tacked the lining on with white-headed tacks. We used finishing braid and lace to edge the top and made a pillow and put lace on that. It looked very dainty when it was finished and did not cost more than ten dollars all told. With the little casket which we neighbors helped to make and the wealth of flowers which could be obtained in summer from gardens, the little baby had as lovely a setting as could be wished.

Agnes Langkamp Lupke, Montezuma County [360-37]. Dolores, March 10, 1934.

Interviewer: Anna Florence Robison.

I was born July 16, 1860, near Osnabrück in the province of Hanover, Germany. When I was twenty-two years of age, I came to the United States in 1882 shortly after my father's death. I had relatives in Cincinnati where there was a German settlement, and there I worked for a long time as a servant girl and learned the language. I had a hard time doing that at first, but being among my own people, many of whom I had known in the old country, made it easier.

I had known Fred and Henry Lupke in Germany. They came to the United States in 1878. Before coming to Montezuma County two years before I arrived, they had spent two years in Minnesota. Each of them took up a homestead in the country south and west of the Big Bend, and they freighted from Durango to Rico and brought in supplies also to the Big Bend. So, in 1888, Fred Lupke sent me money to come out to Colorado to marry him. In a way, I was not coming to an entirely strange country, for my friends, the Roelkers, had already been here for six months. The Osterfelds came with me, and the Abelns a month after. We had known each other in Germany, and we were all good friends together in the new settlement near Big Bend. There was never any trouble, and on Sundays we would get together and have coffee and cakes and something to drink just as we had in Germany.

When I started from Cincinnati, I had the rheumatism so bad that I had to crawl on my hands and knees to get a drink of water on the train. But by the time I reached Durango, it left me. Mr. Lupke met me there with a team and a buggy he had hired from a liveryman in Cortez. He was to pay two dollars a day for the buggy. But when we got back and he found it was for a wedding journey, the livery stable proprietor wanted to charge Mr. Lupke twenty-five dollars, which was more than twice the price agreed upon. There was almost a shooting over it.

Almost everyone had log houses here then. But Mr. Lupke had hauled lumber from a mill near Mancos and built a frame house on his claim. There were many deer in the country then. I often saw them, and once a band of twenty-two went by our place. A man was hunting near us, and a frightened deer ran into the chicken house. There were many cattle running wild. And once when I went for our cows, I saw an animal I have since learned was a lynx.[81]

The Hartmans for whom Hartman Draw is named lived about a quarter of a mile from us.[82] Lillian Hartman Johnson married a lawyer, Charles Johnson, of Durango. And a brother of Lillian, Frank Hartman, edits a paper in Aztec, New Mexico.[83]

The Big Bend was our nearest town. Only the Morton place still stands there now. But then the Harris Brothers had a store there, and Mr. Ordway had the post office. I used to walk and carry my butter and eggs to sell at Harris's store. Sometimes they would bring fifty or sixty cents a dozen in winter. Flour had to be brought by packhorse from Durango in the winters then. People would go by wagon to Rico to sell their corn and fat hogs and vegetables and bring back a load of different supplies. Mr. Lupke crossed the Dolores as many as twenty-five times freighting to Rico. The Germans peddled vegetables in Big Bend, later in Dolores, and in Cortez too. Rico was by far the liveliest place hereabouts.

When we had been married seven years, Fred Lupke died. A team of mules had run away with him while he was working at Animas City before he came to Montezuma Valley, and he fell under the rake. That caused his illness which developed years later so that he was very bad a year and half before he died. He had to be lifted about, and we took him to the hospital at Durango for a while. That was after the trains came to Dolores.[84] But the nearest doctor was at Rico or Durango, whichever is the nearer. There were no telephones, so you had to send a messenger to bring back the doctor, and it cost thirty dollars a trip the few times we had him for Mr. Lupke. When he was gone, I was left with my little children.

A kind neighbor used to stay with the children while I went to town with my team and wagon to sell vegetables. I had to work very hard, but I made out to get along. There were very many bachelors about, and women were scarce. Eventually I married Mr. Lupke's brother, Henry, and we moved over to his homestead, a part of which we still own and live on. Both of my husbands worked with scoops and teams building the ditches for the irrigation system here.

The children went to school two and a half miles away at the old German schoolhouse that later burned down. The Germans built that one themselves for their children. They used to have three months of school there in the summertime, and there would be perhaps twenty-four or twenty-five children. Once there were thirty-six. The Osterfeld, Pomroy, and Ablen children were among those who went there. Mrs. Morton from Big Bend was the first teacher. I boarded seventeen teachers myself, in the course of the years. But back in those early days Louise Ordway, now Mrs. Harry Pyle, used to come out on a bicycle to teach at the German school.

The priest from Durango used to come over two or three times a year and say mass around in the various houses of the German settlement. Sometimes the children would walk five of six miles over to what is now the Kaylor place to receive religious instruction. The priest would stay at Wedell's or Osterfeld's each year for a while and instruct in religion. The children knew something about it then too.

But we amused ourselves mostly with hard work in the German settlement. We liked to see who could grow the best of everything and do everything the best way. We had great pride in what we did and in our homes. And on Sundays we got together at the home of one of us and had coffee and cakes and had a nice, quiet, friendly time. Among ourselves, it was just like Germany.

Alice Henderson Akin, Montezuma County [360-48]. March 13, 1934.

Interviewer: Anna Florence Robison.

Interviewer's note: Mr. and Mrs. Akin's children are Edward Akin, a ranchman up the Dolores River; Thomas Akin of Akin Mercantile Company of Dolores; Roy Akin, also of Dolores; Paul Akin, a ranchman of the Dolores Valley; and Mrs. John McKeever of Idaho Springs, Colorado. Joseph C. Akin and a daughter, Eula, are dead.[85]

I was born at Millville, Rust County, Texas, September 25, 1855. My early childhood was passed at Riley Springs, Texas. After the death of both of my parents, I went at the age of eleven years to live with my aunt at Cleburne, where, on July 2, 1874, I married James P. Akin from Hot Springs, Arkansas. After our marriage, Mr. Akin and I made our home at Cleburne, where he was marshal a part of the time. We had neither of us any near relatives in Texas. But Mr. Akin's mother and his married sister, Mrs. William Brumley, were already living on a ranch near Big Bend, and they kept writing for us to come to them. They said we could do fully as well in Colorado as in Texas and that the winter weather was marvelous. This was the winter of '83–'84, known since as the "winter of the big snow." That year there was a very mild, open winter until some date in February when it began to snow. Some say it snowed for forty days without really clearing off. Others say forty-eight. I do not suppose anyone knows exactly. Anyhow, Mr. Akin's relatives wrote before it began to snow so much. And my husband and I and our four little children—Ed, aged eight or nine, Tom, six or seven, Eula, and the baby Henrietta—started for Colorado late in March. It had probably been snowing here for six or more weeks then.

We were snowbound for a week or more three miles the other side of the section house on Cumbres Pass. There were quite a number on the train, and the only food with us was a few sacks of dried beans and some Limburger cheese.

During the time we were snowbound in the train, they brought food to us from the section house the three miles away on snowshoes. I was not well, but somehow I didn't mind it as I would have supposed. I wasn't sorry I came, and I didn't want to go back. There was one other woman on the train besides me, and everyone was kind and helpful.

The head man at Cumbres, a Mr. Leyden, I believe his name was, had a sled made to bring me and the children to the section house, where we could be more comfortable. I had a heavy and long winter coat which I had recently bought for my journey into Colorado. It was not suitable for plodding through such snow as there was on the pass. The character of the trail was such that I could not ride far, and then Mr. Leyden put his own coat on me and wrapped my feet well in gunny sacks. He took my arm and helped me to walk that snow trail. Before we left the snowbound train, the men got out our baggage and let me open my trunks and get out bedding. We even took my featherbed along to the section house. As we went along the trail, Mr. Leyden would point out to me stovepipes sticking out of the snow. That was all you could see of the houses. They had cut stair steps in the snow for us to go down into the section house from the trail. The snow was that deep.

They made us very comfortable in the section house, where we stayed another week before we could go on to Durango. There were about a hundred men at work cleaning snow off the tracks.

It was too high for me on Cumbres, and I had to sit up much of the time in order to breathe.[86] The brakeman made lineament for my husband to rub on my chest, and it helped much.

When we got to Durango, my husband decided to go on over to Brumley's on the Dolores River on snowshoes. It was early April. I remained with the children at a house in Durango where Miss Lizzie Allen and her sister were staying at the time. We had come to Durango on a freight train, and we stayed in the outskirts of town; so I took little notice of the place.

When the roads became good—perhaps it was the first of May, or anyway late April, W. H. Brumley, my husband's brother-in-law, came for the children and me and our things in a wagon. The water was very high everywhere on account of so much snow. The mountain roads with the deep cuts and the steep slopes on the outside edges frightened me. And when we came in sight of the greatly swollen Dolores—which, at the Billy May ranch above Big Bend, now William Ritter's place at the state bridge, formed a huge lake—it seemed that I had reached the "jumping-off place" indeed. We crossed the Dolores below the Morton place and stayed the first night with the Mortons at Big Bend.

We lived in a log cabin near W. H. Brumley's house across the river from Big Bend for several years after that. Mr. Akin worked with his brother-in-law's cattle. We did not get lonely, for Mr. Akin's mother was there with his sister, and Jim and John Brumley lived there too. There were enough of us that we did not need to be especially afraid of the Indians. The children went to school in Big Bend in the summers. The first two or three schools were held in a dugout. Then they built a log school building which was standing until a few years ago. My oldest boy, Ed, used to row Bill and John Brumley's children, Tom, Eula, and himself across the Dolores in a skiff to attend school. I used to be so uneasy about them, for the Dolores was so swift there.

At Big Bend we had plenty of vegetables and beef to eat because we could raise them ourselves. But all other groceries and other supplies we had to get from Mancos or Durango by wagon or packhorse. But we all managed to be quite comfortable nevertheless. We used to get vegetables from the German settlement.

Jim Trimble, the Moores, Mortons, Grandma and Grandpa Johnson, and Mr. Ordway were among our good neighbors in those days. A Miss Benson, who taught school at Big Bend, also started a Sunday school there. We had dances around at private places which were greatly enjoyed by all. They used to have the finest suppers at Nunn's down the river. Along about midnight everyone would gather around the big table, and it remained set all night so that anyone who was hungry could go and get more to eat. And some of the guests stayed until morning. Another diversion was horse races. Grandpa Johnson had some fine racehorses.

We lived across from Big Bend until the railroad came and the town was moved to its present site.[87] Paul Akin, my son, was the first baby born in present Dolores. We lived for a while in Dolores, then moved to the Burch place ten miles above town. Later we bought a place of our own where we lived until our return to Dolores nineteen years ago.

Joanna Spalding Todd, Montezuma County [360-105]. Cortez, August 1934.

Interviewer: Anna Florence Robison.

I was born in Pueblo the twelfth day of August 1866. My father, J. H. Spalding, took his family to the San Luis Valley a little later and lived there fifteen years. We came to the Dolores in June of 1885. My half brother, Sanford Bowen, who was eight years older than I, came here three or four years before that. And he persuaded my father, who was mining up at Silverton, to sell out and come over here. John Bowen, another half brother, had a trading post on the San Juan River below Fruitland, New Mexico.

We came into the country in wagons, and I drove four horses from Pagosa Springs to Dolores because my father had a broken hand. I could do it well enough, but it made my head and neck ache. We stopped for five weeks at Pagosa Springs and spent several days at Piedra. En route we passed through Agua Caliente, which is now Hot Springs, New Mexico. My brother, Sanford Bowen, came on from Pagosa because he had to be in the Disappointment country for the roundup.

When we reached the Dolores, we camped for a week while waiting for my brother to come over from the Disappointment to meet us. While we were waiting there, we saw signal fires of the Indians on Ute and Point Lookout on Mesa Verde.[88] When my brother came we started for Narraguenip Springs, where the cowboys had a camp.[89] We camped the first night between Beaver and the Dolores River. The following morning my father and brother started on with a four-horse team with the load of supplies. Mother and a little ten-year-old nephew and I were to remain in camp until later. We were then to come on in the light carriage.

When Father and my brother had gone ahead two or three miles, they found they would have to chop down a tree before they could go on, and had to return to the camp where Mother and I were to get an ax. Mother told Father that she was exceedingly uneasy at being left overnight in a strange country without any men about for protection. So he told her to hitch up the team and come on. We did as he said and so chanced to be camped on Beaver the night before the famous Indian episode of June 1885.

It also happened that our large tent looked very much like the tent of some surveyors who had been camped there the night before and for a while previously perhaps. But the surveyors had gone on elsewhere.

There was quite a party of Indians camped on Beaver at that time. The cattlemen believed that the Indians had been running off stock. They also had word from some source that these Indians were going to make a raid on their property. Mr. Todd, one of the cowmen, warned the Indians, but they paid no attention to the warning. The cowmen planned to wait until Mancos Jim, an Indian leader, and his party arrived the following morning and give the Indians a lesson.[90] So they sent a man to look over the country to see if any campers who might possibly be injured by accident were about. The cowboy reported that only the surveyors were camped anywhere near and that they, being all men, could care for themselves. He had mistaken our tent for theirs.

Next morning at daybreak we heard two or three shots. Mother called me to hurry about getting up, telling me that someone was out deer hunting already. Then we heard a whole volley of shots, and my brother said we must get away immediately, for it was almost sure to be an Indian fight. My brother snatched me up and put me on a horse just as I happened to be clad at the moment. He was going to put Mother on the other horse, but she would not have it. She said she didn't want to make a target of herself. Brother told me to ride to a cabin a mile and a half above. I did so. When I got there, I called and three men came out to see what I wanted. They were so utterly astonished to see a woman there in that unlikely spot that they stood and stared while

I explained. They asked me in, and presently Mother rode up too. We remained at the cabin until nine o'clock. While we were there, the cowboys from the raid came to the cabin. That was where I first met my future husband, Mr. Todd, who was the captain of the outfit and felt very sorry indeed that such a thing had taken place when there were women about to be frightened and endangered by it.

We moved on over to Narraquinnep Springs, where we spent the summer. Then we went to the mouth of the Disappointment for the winter. It was there that I was married to Sam Todd, January 10, 1886. We had been acquainted a little less than seven months. My father wanted us to wait at least until spring and promised me a real wedding dress as an inducement. But we saw no reason for the postponement.

My part of the preparations consisted in baking the wedding cake—a white one for the bride and a fruitcake—and lengthening down a black silk and wool dress which my sister had made for me in the San Luis Valley for a wedding outfit. It was rather short, and my husband-to-be thought it should be practically to the floor. So I lengthened it to his taste with material I had.

Sam Todd had to go from the mouth of the Disappointment to Durango to get the marriage license and some trunks of things he had stored over there, and other needful articles. It was the fore part of January, and the snow was very, very deep. What with the cold and the smelter smoke which he encountered in Durango, he was very ill the night after his arrival. It appeared that he had pneumonia. He told the doctor that he just couldn't be ill, for he had to be at the mouth of the Disappointment on January 10th because that was to be his wedding day. The doctor assured him he certainly would not be there to be married the tenth. Next morning Sam Todd told the man who was staying with him to go out to get his breakfast because he was feeling pretty well and would not mind staying alone. When the man was gone, he got up and dressed and went to the window to see if he could stand to breathe the outside air. He found he could. So he got out and took a delivery wagon standing nearby to take his trunks to the livery barn. There he arranged for a conveyance to take him home on to Mancos. From there he took them by packhorse to the mouth of the Disappointment. It was really just the smelter smoke which had caused his illness, and getting out of it was what helped him most. By the time he reached Mancos he had coughed up a good deal of it and was much better, and he was quite well again by the time he reached home, cold as it was on the way.

At the Bend, Judge Norton from Rico was waiting to go with him to perform the ceremony. He had with him a sealed envelope containing a note from Dr. Landon to the effect that the old gentleman was a great drinker and that on no account must Mr. Todd give him any liquor whatever if he hoped to get him to the mouth of the Disappointment to perform the wedding ceremony.

The judge was an old man and rather feeble. He felt the cold very much, and he kept saying to Mr. Todd that unless they were more than halfway to their destination, they had better go back to the Bend. Mr. Todd was obliged to assure him that the mouth of the Disappointment was the nearer in order to induce him to keep on. In his pocket, Mr. Todd had a couple bottles of apple brandy, and he wanted a drink to warm him, but he could not do so unseen, and he was mindful of Dr. Landon's warning. So he had to deny himself that comfort until they reached the double cabin of the summer camp on the upper Disappointment. There he stepped into the other room and mixed and drank a toddy. When he rejoined Judge Norton, the old gentleman smelled the liquor on his breath and asked if he could have some. Mr. Todd felt that he could hardly refuse him a mere toddy under the circumstances; so he mixed him one.

"That's very good," Judge Norton commented when he had finished drinking it, "but haven't you some of the raw material?" Mr. Todd admitted that he had, two bottles of apple brandy. The old gentleman asked him if he had the apple brandy with him while they were coming across that cold stretch of country, and Mr. Todd had to admit that too. So he told the old Judge about Dr. Landon's letter.

"Damn the man!" the old judge exclaimed. "I'll cut his heart out for that when I get back."

Judge Norton made up for his long dry spell after the wedding ceremony though. There was a great deal of peach brandy which was sent by relatives in the East to a consumptive neighbor, and which he contributed for the festivities. The judge had his share, or more, of that. And, for a fee for his services, Mr. Todd gave the old judge a hundred dollars. He realized that it had been rather a terrible trip for the old chap. Later on, Mr. Todd's son heard his father say something about the size of the wedding fee and asked, "Dad, was she worth it?"

At our cabin on the Disappointment, there was no decorating done for the wedding because there was nothing to decorate with. I prepared the wedding cakes myself, and a young butcher from Rico acted as master of ceremonies, helped with the cooking, and made Tom and Jerry.[91] We spread ourselves with that wedding dinner because it was the only way in which we could. We expected as guests twenty-five cowboys besides the family and connection. We prepared wild turkey and beef for the heavy part of the meal, and Jack Leslie suggested as a festive touch that we cut the wedding cake in part into squares, wrap the squares in tissue paper, and tie them with ribbons for the guests to sleep on. There were no flowers to be had from any source, nor could there be anything to represent them.

My wedding outfit was black with white accessories. I wore white stockings, white shoes, et cetera. My matron of honor was my sister-in-law, Mrs. John Bowen, and my brother John was best man. My father gave me away, and the wedding was conducted as conventionally as circumstances would permit.

After the ceremony, we had a big dinner with plenty to drink. The cowboys sang songs to the accompaniment of violin and banjo. We could not well dance because of small space and the scarcity of women for partners, but we had what was for that place and time a very festive affair.

Mr. Todd and I lived there with my parents that winter. We had a log cabin with a large and a small room at the mouth of the Disappointment. When spring came the river was high, and Mr. Todd was obliged to be on the other side of it for the roundup. So we moved up to the double cabin. There were logs on rocks across the river for a bridge. We had to carry our household goods across on those logs. We took the wagons across piecemeal after taking them apart. Then we swam the horses across, put the wagons back together, and made a road through the timber to the summer camp.

The Indians were rather hostile the summer of 1886; so a little later on Mr. Todd brought me out to the Dolores settlements, where we remained the winter of 1887 as well. We filed on a place in the valley a mile and a half due east of Cortez which was just starting. Mr. Saylor was almost our only neighbor, he and Mr. Dave Logenbaugh and Mr. Totten. The Simon family lived farther up the valley. We built a big pond later and stocked it with fish. My parents lived close to us always. They bought what is now known as the James place east of Cortez from a man named Royce. When we homesteaded our place, Cortez consisted of a few tents and Mr. Coffin's house; the MacHanna, Payson, and Turner places were ranches.

We lived on our homestead until 1924, when we sold out and went to California for Mr. Todd's health, and we were there until 1929. At that time we brought Mr. Todd back here, and he passed away. Lulu, my daughter, and I now make Cortez our home.

Our children are Mary, born in March 1887 and died the following year; Sarah Joanna, born August 24, 1888, now Mrs. C. J. Hanks of Steamboat Springs; John Edgar, born August 1, 1890, died March 1, 1900; Elizabeth, born October 8, 1892, now Mrs. Harley Longenbaugh of Cortez; George Leslie, born April 9, 1895, now of California; Lulu Esther, born June 26, 1902, of Cortez; and Francis Spalding, born April 16, 1905, of California.

My husband, Samuel George Todd, was born in Missouri in 1854. At the age of twenty-five he came to Colorado. He had tuberculosis and was not expected to live. He had been advised to remain with friends on that account. He had some cattle of his own and came to the Disappointment country in 1880 with them. He did not die of the tuberculosis by any means but grew strong and subsequently lived a very active life.

When the Chishum War was going on, Mr. Todd went down onto the San Juan to buy cattle with Jed Perce.[92] An old man and his wife had a little store down there, and while they were at the store a group of armed Mexicans came up and halted them.

Mr. Todd and Jed Perce called to the storekeeper and asked him the meaning of it all. The storekeeper said that a Mexican had been hanged down there and that the Mexicans were worked up over it. The Mexicans told Mr. Todd and his friend that they could go if they would give their guns into the care of the storekeeper. Mr. Todd told the Mexicans that he and Jed Perce would lay down their arms if the Mexicans would do the same. The Mexicans agreed, and so did they, as agreed. Then Mr. Todd took the Mexicans into the store and treated them.

Mr. Todd and Jed Perce found they could buy cattle satisfactorily but that the Mexicans would have only actual cash—no checks accepted. One of the two would have to go to Durango to get the necessary money. So they drew straws, and Jed was the one to go. So he got sick. He told Mr. Todd to take his horse and go.

When Mr. Todd told the officials at the bank that he must have the ten thousand or so dollars in cash, he was told that he couldn't even get out of town with such a sum of money, much less reach the San Juan with it. Mr. Todd said he must do so nevertheless, and he took it from the bank that night because he wished to make a very early start the following morning. He took the money to a store, and it was placed in the safe there. Later the storekeeper hid it for the night. In the morning, Mr. Todd took a pair of new overalls and put the money in one leg of them securely and tied it onto the saddle concealed in a slicker.

He started a little before sunrise from Durango and went down the

Animas River. There was another trail up on the mesa, and Mr. Todd thought he saw a man on horseback gallop along down below. He saw the man get off the horse and tie it in the thick brush. The man went to a big tree on the trail where Mr. Todd would have to pass and sat down there. It looked very much as if a holdup were in prospect. As he drew nearer, Mr. Todd saw that the man had a mask on in addition to being armed; but he recognized him in spite of it.

Mr. Todd rode up to him and said "Good morning." The man did not answer. He spoke again, and the man was still silent. So Mr. Todd rode on, keeping a sharp lookout and his hand on his gun until he was out of sight. Then he rode very fast for quite a long distance to keep the man from heading him off farther on. He did not see the man again and had no more trouble on the trip. He and Jed Perce got the cattle and went on to the Disappointment with them.

A week later, Mr. Todd was in the Durango bank. The banker asked if he had a gun and he said he had. The banker then told him he was expecting some money by express and wanted Mr. Todd to guard him to the bank with it. He said that "Any man who can ride up and face a desperado with all that money on him is a good man to guard me." The desperado must have told it on himself, for Mr. Todd certainly hadn't. That must have happened in 1883 or earlier.

Not so long before the above-mentioned incident took place, a couple of cowmen were returning from shipping cattle from Alamosa. That, of course, was before the railroad came to Durango in 1881.[93] The cowmen had a packhorse as well as their saddle stock, and the one in the rear on the trail led the pack animal. One morning the man ahead was held up. He had only pocket money with him so did not lose much. The man with the packhorse saw what happened, and while the holdup man was searching his partner he took the cattle money from where he carried it and threw it as far out into the brush as he could send it. The holdup man then came on and searched him and the pack and found nothing. When the desperado had departed without the money he was expecting to get, the men came back, found their several thousand dollars out in the brush, and came on west.

Mr. Todd was among the cowboys that trailed Mancos Jim's Indians in 1883 after they had raided some cow outfits out west and burned their chuck wagons. There were a good many cowboys with the soldiers in the pursuit, and when at last they caught sight of the Indians, they saw them breaking camp and packing to go on. The Indians had a lot of goats that kept right up with them and betrayed their whereabouts to some extent by bleating.

Finally the Indians got up on a rimrock with their goats and were more or less concealed. The narrow trail on which the white men had to pass lay just below the rimrock.

A cowboy and a government scout said they'd go up and find out what was up there before the rest of the party ventured on. They could hear the goats in the rimrock and they knew the Indians could not be far away. The Indians shot them but did not kill them outright. The cowboys and soldiers kept up a regular firing on the gap in the rock all day in the hope of being able to get the wounded men, or anyhow their bodies, from where they fell. But the Indians prevented that. Mancos Jim and others of the Indians mocked the dying men by shouting back at them such as "Oh, my God, men, give me some water," "My God, I'm suffering," and so on.

The white men saw the Indians taking the saddles and stripping the bodies. After staying the day in the hope of getting the bodies, they had to leave them after all, for they would surely have lost a number of men in any attempt to rescue them. I believe they were buried much later on by others.

The white men started back home. They had salty bacon and other dry food and no water. Pat O'Donnell got very ill on the way back. The soldiers had already gone off and left the cowboys, and Mr. Todd and Adam Lewey stayed with Mr. O'Donnell although he told them to go on. Mr. Todd had a crippled horse, due to the Indian skirmish, and it gave out. He knew where there was a cache of flour and coffee, and they got some of that and ate. Then Mr. Todd caught an unbroken mare and got on her and they started for the Dolores. They made a very rapid trip of it too.

Those are a few of the many experiences I have heard my husband tell. Though he came to the country for his health, he managed to live a fairly long life, about seventy-five years, and a very active life as well. He died the tenth of August in 1919.

There was a little trading post near, I believe, Navajo Springs—just a cabin and a corral. Mr. Todd was there one day, and the storekeeper was showing him a new gun he had. Mr. Todd asked if it were loaded, and the man said it was not.[94] There had been a good many inquiries on the part of the Indians as to when the white men were ready to fight. The cowboys had got all ready, but some of the cattle owners found it out and would not permit the cowboys to go to fight the Indians. So Mr. Todd, thinking the gun was empty, was fingering it and absently had it pointed in the direction of an Indian who was nearby. There was a cartridge in the gun after all, and it went off and the bullet struck between the Indian's feet. He naturally thought Mr. Todd had shot at him and leaped to his horse and rode away. That night the Indians set fire to the little trading post cabin, and the two men living there tied what they could snatch up in a handkerchief and got away. They rode into Mancos next morning at daybreak.

Sarah Elizabeth Walker Moore, Montezuma County [360-75]. June 12, 1934.

Interviewer: Anna Florence Robison.

Interviewer's note: Mrs. Moore's mother was Betsy Ann Wethers and her father was John Walker, who lived in Indiana before coming to Iowa. Betsy Ann Wethers's mother was a Hanks girl, and according to Mrs.

> Moore, a sister, either of Abraham Lincoln's mother or of his grandmother, Lucy Hanks. Anyhow, Betsy Ann Wethers was named for an aunt, Elizabeth (called Betsy) Hanks. I do not have much idea how reliable this family tradition may be, but all else Mrs. Moore told me seems reliable.[95]

I was born on February 4, 1859, in Iowa. There were nine of us children, and I had a twin brother to whom I was much attached. All but three of us children were born in Indiana, and I had an older brother who was in the first regiment that left our section of Iowa during the Civil War. I was exceedingly proud of him, as I remember. When I was ten years old we moved to Missouri and settled at Harrisonville, Cass County, where I grew to womanhood. The day my twin brother and I were twenty-two years old, my mother was buried. My brother was at that time cook at the Eureka House at Robinson's Camp north of Denver. So, after Mother's death, I came to Colorado to be with him. I arrived at Robinson's Camp in 1880 and spent that winter there. Robinson had a mine and hotel there, and the camp took its name from him. There was a great deal of claim jumping in those days, and guards had to be posted about on that account. Robinson was killed by one of his own guards, who mistook him, because he did not think to speak, for a claim jumper.[96]

Early in 1881 I married George P. Moore, a miner. Shortly afterward, my husband and I went to Pitkin in Gunnison County, where he had to do assessment work on a mine.[97] While there I paid a dollar for a dozen eggs and found only two of the eggs fit to use. It was too high there for me, and, on the doctor's advice, my husband sent me back to Longton, Elk County, Kansas, to an older sister. He sold the mine and went to work at Leadville for a time. He had a brother at Socorro, New Mexico, who ran a meat market. He was ill and sent for my husband to come down there and run his market until he recovered. He remained in New Mexico until in May, when he bought a buggy and drove up to

Antonito, Colorado.[98] He went on to Pueblo, where he bought a span of mules and a camp outfit and bargained with a young man to drive it for him to Antonito in return for being taken on to Durango. This was in the spring of 1882.

In the meantime, my daughter Della had been born on November 13, 1881, at my sister's home at Longton, Kansas. We made the trip from Antonito here in a covered wagon when she was a little over five months old. My husband knew Nathan Dickerson, who was already in this country, and he had made up his mind he wanted to take up a ranch on the Dolores River. But the water was so high with the usual spring flood that we could not hope to go down the Dolores at the time of our arrival. We camped at the H. M. Smith place at Mancos for a while. Also we were at the Simon place before we went to Durango on our way to Silverton, where my husband teamed all summer. He did well, too. When we left there in October to came to the Dolores Valley to find a home, we had eight hundred dollars, which was good for those days.

Speaking of the Simon family, Mr. Louis Simon was the father-in-law of my husband's friend Nathan Dickerson, who had married his daughter Rachel. Mr. Simon had a place in Montezuma Valley at what is since known as Simon's Draw in the Lakeview neighborhood. But at this time he lived on the Dolores River not far from Mr. Dickerson. I suppose you have heard how when Mr. and Mrs. Simons' silver wedding anniversary arrived, one daughter came from Rico and another from Durango, and the Saylors, a young couple with one little child, who lived nearby in the direction of where Cortez now stands, were there for the dinner. Afterwards when the Saylors got home, they found that the Indians had ransacked their house while they were gone and had taken even some of the baby's clothes, not to mention everything eatable. [The] Saylors returned to Simons' that night.

When we came to the Dolores Valley in October 1882, my husband selected a ranch at Lone Dome about sixteen miles down the Dolores River from here.[99] Dolores, the new town. A young man named Charley

Salter had taken it up, but he was young and homesick and wanted to get away. The place had a good cabin on it and a ditch that would carry water for fifty acres of land completed. It had been rented the summer before, and the renter had raised a splendid crop and had the cellar full of produce. My husband bought out Charley Salter, and they went to Durango to fix up the papers and the filing. We had to live on it five years to prove up, and we kept that ranch, which was a good one, until 1916, when we sold it and our cattle. That first winter, the man who had had it rented lived with us. We furnished such groceries as we had to buy, and he furnished the vegetables.

We were very comfortable on our place at Lone Dome. Some of our neighbors were the Barnes family; Gene Salter, a brother of Charley; Jim Trimble; some English people; a bit later, the Dillons; and later still the Bradfields. Every family had log cabins to live in and just what housekeeping paraphernalia they could haul in their wagons, except the family of Charles Johnson, who lived where McPhee now is.[100] They had moved into their new adobe house about three months before we came. They had nice furniture and lived very comfortably indeed.

At Lone Dome we ranched and ran cattle, and after I got over being afraid of the Indians I liked pioneer life very much. We did very well too, with our ranch. My children I always brought up to Dolores—the present town it was, by the time they were ready for school—for the winter. We built this house, in which we still live, for that purpose.

Rico was our market in those days. When the weather was suitable, we took produce up there in wagons. Sometimes we took it on packhorses. At one time I sent up eighty dozen eggs at a single trip. My husband put up ice so that in summer I had ice to pack my butter in for the trip. That way it arrived in good condition so that the merchants would be willing to buy it in summer. I have sent as much as thirty dollars' worth of butter to Rico at one time. We used to get fifty cents a dozen for our eggs and fifty cents a pound for our butter there before the railroad came.[101]

The winter of '84 was almost as nice as the winter of 1933–34 until the last of February. Then it began to snow, and for twenty-two days we could not see the sun. The snow was so deep that they could not break a road. Mr. Trimble from below us thought he had to go to Big Bend for mail. He got above our place when his horse gave out and he had to give up the attempt. Finally they drove cattle over the trail and broke a road in course of time so that people could come up to Big Bend on horseback. Many people down the river got very short on food, but we were fortunate enough not to run short on anything but coal oil. At our place the snow was far over the height of the well curb, and our dog, running across the snow, fell into the well. My husband had to fish out the dog and then dip out all of the water and clean the well as a result. Fortunately, it was not a deep well. In later years we piped water to the house from a spring on the hillside.

Although there was so much snow the spring of '84, it did not take it long to go, for the snow was not packed. The Dolores River surely roared for a long time.

The highest water we ever had here at Dolores was October 5, 1911. The water was all over Dolores deep enough to swim a cow or a horse. It washed hay from one end of a field to the other on our ranch. It washed a lot of squashes from the Vasco Bradfield ranch down onto our field. There had been a great deal of rain all summer, and it came to a climax in the flood.

When we first came here, everyone was much afraid of the Indians. When we were new here, my husband had to go to Durango for a lot of supplies, and he had Mr. Nathan Dickerson go with him to help him haul them over. I naturally did not want to remain on our ranch with him away all nights, so I went up to stay with Mrs. Dickerson. That night we had an Indian scare. I was lying on the bed asleep, and Mrs. Dickerson was reading. I woke up to hear her asking who was at the door. The man who had the place rented opened it and told us the Indians were on the warpath and that we had better go immediately up to her father's place for the night. Mr. Simon lived about a mile away. We were very much frightened, and we got dressed to go right away. The man who had notified us went on up the river telling people. There were a good many living on the river at that time, and most of the ones below us took time to bury their belongings to keep the Indians from finding them so easily. Mrs. Simon and Mrs. Dickerson wanted Mr. Simon to take them up to Grandpa Johnson's at once. Johnson's house stood in an open place where the Indians could not well ambush the settlers. That was why everyone was going there. Dave Johnson and a man known as Jesse Williams came by Simons' on a wagon. They had their guns all ready to shoot in case an Indian should appear. I got on the wagon with them and went on up to Johnsons', and when we got there, no one of the family was at home except Mr. Johnson's mother. We put the horses in the big corral, and everyone else who came did likewise. There was a large crowd of neighbors there. At about four o'clock in the afternoon, after the warning was given, Al Nunn and Chick Porter arrived. Both married daughters of Grandpa Johnson and worked for him as well. They were hungry and were wishing the Johnsons would come on home so that the crowd might be fed.

Mrs. Dickerson was acquainted with Johnsons, but I had never met any of them up to that time. Mrs. Dickerson told Al Nunn that if he would show us where to find things, we would get dinner. Johnsons had a lot of their provisions down in the basement and did part of their cooking down there. Mrs. Dickerson told me to go down in the basement and make biscuits. I did as she directed and was busy cutting out biscuits to bake when Johnsons came home. I felt so embarrassed there in a strange woman's kitchen cooking up her flour and lard and things without her permission that way. But Mrs. Johnson didn't mind. She knew how it all was and made me forget at once how foolish I felt. After that, we all had a splendid time getting acquainted before everyone decided it was safe to leave Johnsons'!

When my husband and Mr. Dickerson got back from Durango, we

went down to our ranch again, and we found the people from down below us, who had been at Johnsons' previously, at our place because it was open too and could not be ambushed.

Much later on when the Indian troubles were over, my husband used to hire Indians to help bring in the hay and to dig potatoes. When I got used to them, I wasn't afraid of them at all. But when we first came here, there was reason to be afraid.

And of course the Gentner killing disturbed us all a good deal. Some cowmen that had cattle on the mesa went to an Indian camp and killed all but one squaw. She crawled on her hands and knees and somehow got away through the brush and made her way to the reservation. A little later, some of the Indians went to Gentner's, and when he came out to see what was going on they shot and killed him. They shot Mrs. Gentner through the shoulder. She took the children and started for the nearest neighbors, which was Wooleys. They were in their nightclothes and barefooted. She said the Almighty must have directed her to where Doug Wooley was out in the sagebrush asleep. His father was away from home, and he was alone. The Indians had been at the Wooley place that day; so he had taken his gun and gone out in the brush to sleep so they would not be so likely to find him in the night if they came back. Being just a youngster, he had fallen asleep in spite of the circumstances, and Mrs. Gentner had her boy slip up and remove his guns out of his reach before wakening him. When he understood the situation, he helped the Gentners on to Simons', for Mrs. Gentner was getting chilled since her wounded shoulder had bled so much on her nightgown.

On the way to Simons' they thought they heard horses approaching, but no horses came. When they arrived and Mrs. Simon saw them, she fainted with fright. Doug Wooley went on to the Dolores Valley and gave the alarm. Next day the party of men from Big Bend who had come over in response to Doug Wooley's call put a bed in a wagon and took Mrs. Gentner and the children back with them. They made up money later and took her on to Durango, and the government later did something for her. I believe the government gave her a deed to the place without their having to live on it longer, too. Her brother came from California and took her and her children back with him.

My husband and I have four children: Alice Adella, born at Longton, Kansas, November 13, 1881, now married to Edward Moore (no relation, though the same name). And with two living children, Ada Clark of Durango, and Earl Moore who runs a dairy near McPhee; Charles Alonzo (Lonnie), born May 7, 1888, who lives down the Dolores at the ranger's station and has no children; Joseph S., born April 11, 1890, who lives at Littleton, Colorado, and has no children; Georgia Frances (Mrs. Tim Lynch), born June 9, 1894, who lives in Dolores and has three children, Arveda, Bertha, and George. My husband and I were married at Robinson, Colorado, March 14, 1881. He was from Ellsworth, Maine.

I can remember as a little girl when the message came to our town that Lincoln was shot. We were at church at the time. The messenger entered and gave a paper to the minister, who read it. Tears began running down his cheeks. He turned to the congregation and said to us that there would be no church services that day because we had lost our president. I felt so very sorry for my mother that day because Lincoln meant so much personally to her.

We—my husband and I—have been living at our home in the town of Dolores since 1916. At present my husband is running a restaurant here.

Dora Provis Pedersen, Montezuma County [360-53]. Dolores, March 30, 1934.

Interviewer: Anna Florence Robison.

My maiden name was Dora Provis. I was born in Vermont the spring of 1879. When I was five or six years of age, my mother, a widow, came with my baby sister and me to Durango, where my married aunt, my grandmother, and two young uncles, perhaps sixteen and eighteen, then lived. My aunt was Mrs. Hechtman. She had lived in Parrott City, and she and her husband, my uncle Henry, who was a lawyer, had been very good friends of William Franklin Ordway.[102] My grandmother was Mary Ann Holston, who later moved to a claim about four miles east of Cortez. I spent a good deal of time with her.

My mother was a teacher. At first most of the schools were three-month terms and conducted in summer. Among other places, my mother taught at La Plata City; Aztec, New Mexico; and the present main building at Lakeview in Montezuma Valley.[103] She was the first to hold school in the last-named building. I would go to school to Mother where she taught and spend the rest of my time with Grandmother. I went a short time to the Cortez schools.

Even a schoolchild in those days recognized that he had to get busy in the short time he had at his disposal and learn something. The books were just any books he could get hold of. There was nothing in the least uniform about them. And the furnishings of the little pioneer schools were largely homemade.

I remember the time when the cowboys massacred those Indians at Beaver Creek. The white people were much afraid of what the Indians might do after the Gentner killing. They would gather in groups of several families at some house which could be fairly well defended every night for a while. They would keep everything dark, and the men would watch. I was just a little child then, and I had a bad habit of sucking my thumb of which Mother had been unable to break me. But when we went to spend the nights so semi-publicly as we did in those days after the Gentner killing, I was ashamed for the neighbors to see me sucking my thumb like a little baby that I abandoned the habit at once.

The story of the Gentner affair in my paper is as it was always told by my uncle Henry Hechtman.[104] I believe—you must remember that I was very small then—that Uncle Henry was Mrs. Gentner's legal representative in an attempt to get some recompense from the government for her for her loss at the hands of the Indians. Uncle Henry's story of the affair differed from the one most old-timers tell, and there will be a great deal of argument if my repetition of his account should ever come before the public in any way. But it seems to me that under the circumstances Uncle Henry had an opportunity to know the story correctly.

At eighteen I took the teachers' examination and began teaching. Among other places, I taught at Mildred, Beulah, two years at a school down the Dolores River, and a school which used to be conducted at a place east of the Cortez Cemetery.

At twenty-nine years of age I married Hans Peter Andrew Pedersen, a Danish sailor whose ship was in San Francisco harbor when he heard of the gold excitement in the Blue Mountains. He and some more sailors left the ship, came here, bought burros and a pack outfit, and went. They didn't make anything out of it though. He took a ranch here and ran cattle. We still live on that place.

I must tell you one other thing. There was a little romance which grew out of the Indian "scare" following the Gentner killing and the Beaver Massacre. Sam Todd was a cowboy at a cow camp in the hills. His present wife's family were rather isolated, and they sent her on horseback to the cow camp to appeal for help and protection from the cowboys there. Sam Todd was sent to help them protect their place.[105] That is how Sam Todd and his wife chanced to meet and later to marry.

Mary Alverda Estes Taylor, Montezuma County [360-34]. Dolores, March 9, 1934.

Interviewer: Anna Florence Robison.

I was born somewhere in New Mexico, May 1, 1879. My parents had gone there from the family home in Estes Park a short time before with my grandparents Joel and Patsy Estes. Grandmother Estes had begun to find the park home too high for her, and Grandfather traded the beautiful tract of land which he had discovered and improved for a team of oxen to take her south in search of health. Even so, she outlived her adventurous husband and died later at the home of a daughter in Iowa.[106]

My father, Joel Estes, had a place in New Mexico which included the present site of Aztec. He raised cattle, and when he and his sons returned from a few years spent in Texas and Arkansas they came in covered wagons, driving their cattle before them. My father, the younger Joel Estes, Grandfather's thirteenth child, was a cowboy in his younger days. When the family lived at Estes Park, he went to school in pioneer Denver. The Estes men used to hunt and fish and take their game into Denver to sell or buy groceries.

In 1880, some years after Grandfather's death, my father, the younger Joel Estes, moved his family to a place three miles east of Durango, Colorado. I was about a year old then. We moved in wagons. My mother had not been very well a little while before, but her condition was not considered serious. Then one night on the road between Pagosa and Durango, Mother died very suddenly. My two oldest sisters, Mrs. Cora Myler and Mrs. Lena Nash, were old enough to understand something of what her death meant. They were so frightened that they ran into the woods screaming. My father's party had to hunt for them all night before they finally found them. And that night the Indians stole my father's best team. He never saw the horses again.

There was an old man in the party who took pity on us children and tried to take Mother's place in caring for us. I cannot remember his name. But I can never forget his kindness though I was myself too young to know.

My father lived on the ranch east of Durango for a good while. Then we moved to Animas City above Durango, and I went to school in the old brick schoolhouse which is still there. I can remember the horse-drawn streetcars rattling along in Durango so well.

When I was nine years old, my father went over to the Disappointment Valley. I used to spend summers there and go to school in Rico in the winters of '90 and '91 later on. I stayed for two years there with my sister Cora, Mrs. William I. Myler, and went to school in the old brick schoolhouse there. In those days six hundred children attended there. Rico was a busy, lively town. They worked two shifts at the mines, and swarms of men could be seen morning and evening when shifts changed. My brother-in-law, Mr. Myler, had a burro train which brought ore from the mines to the town.

The railroad had come by then, I know. I had the whooping cough, and they sent me to my father at Durango for fear I would catch pneumonia in the high altitude. I remember going by train to Durango, and I thought it a very ambitious trip.

Later [the] Mylers moved from Rico to the homestead near the present town of Dolores. I went to school at the Lakeview school for two years and finished the eighth grade there.[107] The school was about three and a half miles from my brother-in-law's place. The same schoolhouse still stands there; my children went to it also. And last year my granddaughter finished her common school training in that same building.

Before the railroad came this far, there was no town where Dolores now stands. But a settlement—known as the Bend because at that point the Dolores River makes a large bend—was located a short distance west of the present town. There was very little of the Bend, but what there was surely was lively. The Bend was a supply center in a cattle country, and the early cowmen surely were go-getters. I was in and out of the Bend many times when a child. I remember once when they had a dance in an upstairs room there, the floor swayed and rocked. I was very much frightened because I thought the building would come down.

Harris Brothers had a store in the Bend, and Ordway, who died just this winter [1933–34], had the post office. There was a log school building. There was a road from the Disappointment country to the Bend, and provisions were freighted in from Durango in the fall for those who wintered over there. There was no bridge over the Dolores River, and wagons coming from Durango were often left on the other side while their occupants rode across on the horses. It used to frighten me to ford the Dolores because the water came up so far on the horses that I thought they might be knocked down by the current or that I would be swept away.

The Hammond place on the River near the site of the Bend used to belong to Jim Lavender.

There was trouble between the cowmen and Indians too, back in the eighties. The Indians used to hunt up the Dolores River, among other places. And they began killing the cattle whenever they wanted that sort of meat. They would cut out the loin from a fine fat animal and leave the rest. That made the cowmen furious after a while. So Jim Nash and his father and some other cowmen who came upon a good-sized camp of Indians at Beaver decided to give them a lesson. The Indians were camped down low, and the cowmen were up above on higher ground. They fired down into the Indians' camp and killed nine or ten. One buck ran out holding up a baby to let them know that there were women and children in camp. Both were killed. The cowmen did not know that any Indians survived at the time, but a squaw escaped and made her way down through the Montezuma Valley to her people after a while. That made the Indians hostile.

A family named Gentner lived near Totten's Lake in the Lakeview neighborhood of Montezuma Valley.[108] The Indians shot Mr. Gentner, wounded his wife in the shoulder, and burned their house. Mrs. Gentner took her little children and managed to reach the Simon place for shelter. She eventually recovered. The Gentner affair was almost certainly a result of what had happened at Beaver, and the white people were very much afraid of the Indians for a long time afterwards.

I was at Beaver Camp with small children a few years later. There were no men about, and an Indian jumped suddenly up from somewhere. He got a gun and pointed it at me. I suppose he wanted merely to frighten me. But afterward my sister always had some of the men stay about near camp all of the time.

After the Gentner affair, they required Indians to have passes to go through the country. They were supposed to show their passes to whoever asked to see them. Two came by our place and showed their passes. On one pass was written: "This is a pretty good Indian. He's all right." On the other pass it said: "This is a damned son of a bitch. Look out for him." I suppose someone was trying to be clever.

In 1896 I married Frank Ritter, not himself a pioneer, and we lived for the next five years on a place in the Lakeview neighborhood south and west of the school. Then we moved to my husband's father's place to make our permanent home. My father-in-law was Henry Ritter, who came to this country eleven years before my husband. Henry Ritter was a stone mason and farmed a little between working at his trade. My husband farmed and ran cattle for years and built up the ranch which became his. Later he ran sheep. His death and that of our son, Leslie, occurred the fall of 1918. His place is now in the hands of my daughter and son-in-law, Mr. and Mrs. Oscar Schlegel.

I married George D. Taylor of Dolores February 13, 1921, and we make our home on our ranch just above that town. Mr. Taylor is president of the Harris Bank in Dolores and also has a hardware store there.

Lucy Catherine Brumley-McConnell, Montezuma County [360-72]. Dolores, June 11, 1934.

Interviewer: Anna Florence Robison.

Interviewer's note: Mrs. McConnell has been recommended to me as unusually reliable, and her memory is remarkable for events of long ago. Her account of the Gentner affair is the best I have secured for completeness, and she has the advantage of knowing almost at first hand concerning it. See account by Mr. Fred Taylor, also highly recommended for reliability, for supplementary details.[109]

I was born at Stephenville, Texas, on February 5, 1859. My husband, Samuel Milton McConnell, was born in Gordon County in Georgia in 1846. We were married November 13, 1878, at Cleburne, Johnson County, Texas, where as girls Mrs. Alice Akin and I were friends. In 1880 my husband and I came to Trinidad, Colorado, for my health. My father had been to the state previously, and he felt sure that the climate here would be splendid for me, which it was. We also spent some time in New Mexico. We returned to Texas and went on to Georgia after that. But we liked Colorado, and in the winter of 1884 we set out for the Big Bend of the Dolores River, where my brothers were.

The Akins, coming from Texas, arrived at Pueblo just a day ahead of us coming from Georgia, but there was such a storm that that one day's difference prevented us from being in the big blockade on Cumbres Pass with their family. The railroad officials would not let us go on because we could not get through, so we went to Trinidad where I had sisters living, and there we remained until July. We arrived at the Big Bend of the Dolores River on the first day that the river could be forded after the famous high water of '84, but we did not ford. We crossed the Dolores in a boat. People told us that during that heavy snow the spring of '84 food was short so that men had to go by snowshoes to Durango and pull sacks of flour home—nearly sixty miles, I believe—on hand sleds to share with their neighbors who had less than they.

We built a house at Big Bend in '85. It was about where Bill Ritter's large cellar now is, just above the ditch. When we left Big Bend to go out to the Lewis neighborhood, the ditch men took our house. My husband worked with the LC cattle while we lived at the Bend. These cattle belonged to my sister, Mrs. Lacy. There were ten thousand head of them which had been driven from Vermejo, New Mexico, and turned loose here. We lived at Big Bend three years. And my son Henry went to school there to Miss Lulu Swenk the last year we were living at the Bend.

In 1885 there was a log schoolhouse at Big Bend. It had homemade desks and benches in it, and there the Akin children, the children of

John, William, and Jim Brumley, Ernie, Stella Adams and, perhaps Burt Morton besides my own young son went to school. They often had dances at the schoolhouse too, and the cowboys would often drink a good deal and get in fights, so that it would get pretty lively. There was not so much more drinking then than there is now at dances, but there was a good deal of shooting at that time which we do not have in these days. A lot of the men were well educated and only got tough when they were drunk. When sober, many of them were very fine and would do anything to help anyone in need. People out here weren't so selfish in those days. They depended more upon one another and looked out for one another, and the cowboys would go fifty or sixty miles to get a doctor and help to sit up with the sick.

There were three saloons and a boardinghouse at Big Bend. Mortons had a little store and a post office and kept a few boarders. Miss Lulu Swenk boarded there before she boarded with me, and I believe Miss Lizzie Allen lived with the Mortons at one time also when she taught at the Bend. The Morton family consisted of Walter Pearl, son of Mrs. Morton by her first husband; Stella Adams, daughter of Mrs. Morton by her second husband, who was known as Stella Morton; Elmer, aged twenty-one or twenty-two, Burt, aged eighteen or nineteen years, and Ernie, aged about sixteen years when we came to the Bend, all sons of George N. Morton by his first wife. Mr. and Mrs. Morton had no children in common, however.

We had preachers to come in now and then and hold services. A Baptist minister—from Denver, I think—walked into Bob Brown's saloon at Big Bend and laid his hands on the shoulders of some of the boys playing cards there. He asked them nicely to leave their cards and come over to the schoolhouse and listen to him for a while. The card players left their cards where they lay and went with him and listened as gentlemanly as you please. Another time a Methodist minister named Needham came to Big Bend to hold services, and Adam Lewey shot over his head for a joke. The Methodist minister told Mrs. Lockett about it: "Cousin Lottie, they shot at me."

"Cousin Needham, they took you for a fly-up-the-creek," she explained to him.

Afterwards Adam Lewey went over to the schoolhouse and put around the candles and arranged the seats for the service that the Rev. Needham held. That Methodist minister thought Adam Lewey was great after that.

George Bauer of Mancos opened a store at Big Bend, a branch of his establishment in Mancos, and Mr. Ordway ran it. Later Mr. Bauer sold out to the Harris Brothers.

When the ditch was being built, it was rather "wild and woolly" at Big Bend.[110] On the night of March 10th when one of my babies was born and I was very sick, the doctor looked out of the window and saw a group of men coming. They all had guns and they had been drinking. The doctor called my husband, who had just lain down for a rest, and together they went out to the gate to see what they wanted. My husband asked them to be quiet, and they did. It appeared that there had been a fight up at the tunnel that day, and they were looking for a man who had knocked another man out. The armed party accompanied my husband to look over all of the men sleeping in the outbuildings. They searched all around but did not find him anywhere at the Bend. When the searching party had gone, the fugitive came out of hiding and started to Durango on foot. He had been hidden up under the roof of the icehouse behind one of the saloons, and as he had plenty of guns, he could have put up quite a defense from there if they had found him.

On Thursday in June before Mr. Gentner was killed on Saturday night, my husband and I, my sister-in-law, Mrs. J. H. Brumley, and Richard Lockett, a young cowboy, went down to Gentners' to get some cows the cowboys had left there for us. The Gentners were from Tennessee. We had dinner with them, and they had new potatoes and peas on the table that day. As we came back to the Bend driving the cattle, we heard a yell and looked back and saw an Indian behind us. An Indian pony had joined our cows and insisted upon going along with them. The Indian told us as best he could that the pony had been up on Beaver on fine grass and wanted to go back. It was on Beaver that the white men killed the Indians, which inspired the killing of Mr. Gentner for revenge. It was running away.

On Saturday night it was some of the same Indians that had been in the Beaver country that killed Gentner. That day Mr. Gentner had walked to Dolores River from his ranch out near what is now Totten Lake in the Lakeview neighborhood of Montezuma Valley to get his mail at Big Bend. He took his mail and walked home again. It was June and very warm for a walk of so many miles—fourteen or more, counting both ways. He was tired and lay down on the bed to read the mail that evening. His wife, who was undressed and in her night dress, barefooted, sat by the bed reading also. The three older children—a boy eight or ten years old, a girl, and a smaller child which I believe was a boy—were upstairs asleep. The baby, a boy about a year old, perhaps, was asleep in the room with its parents.

Mrs. Gentner saw a light flicker and looked out and saw that the house was on fire. She told her husband, and he ran out with a bucket. The Indians shot him at once. Mrs. Gentner ran to him, and the Indians shot her through the shoulder, not breaking any bones. She did not see any of the Indians, however.

"I'm killed!" Mr. Gentner told her. "Go back into the house to the children."

"I'm shot too," she told him.

She reentered the burning house where the children were. She told them what had happened and asked them if they should stay and burn up with the house or try to get away with Indians all around. The children wanted to make the attempt to get away. So she took the baby on her sound arm and with the hand on the side of the injured shoulder she led the next-youngest child.

The dog had been shot too, and before she left it came into the house and dropped dead at Mrs. Gentner's feet. All in their nightclothes, without shoes, the remains of the family fled from the burning house. The two older children followed their mother leading and carrying the two younger ones.

Mrs. Gentner saw no Indians that night, but the next day the men saw where they had stood to shoot. Certainly no Indian helped her to get away that night, as some have said. But on the other hand, no Indian trailed her and her children. Probably they had done all of the damage they cared to do already, for the Gentners, both husband and wife, were utterly innocent of harm to the Indians.

In a canyon, Mrs. Gentner and the children came upon Doug Wooley, a young neighbor, who was sleeping out in the brush for fear of the Indians. He told her that there were Indians all around and to lie down on the ground for safety. After a time, she told him she would have to get somewhere even if the Indians would be likely to kill her in the attempt. So Doug Wooley helped her with the children, and they came on to Simons' ranch for help.

Doug Wooley came on to the Dolores Valley and arrived at Mays' about sunup to report the Gentner killing. George May came over and told us about the killing and that the men at Big Bend were going down into the valley at once to investigate. George May hated Indians. His brother Dick had been killed by them out near the Utah line before we came to the country. Every man on the river left and went to the valley that Sunday except my husband. He had been going to go to a roundup down in the Montezuma Valley that day according to previous plan. And the rest of our family and Cora Estes, who lived in our home, and the Mays were going fishing and having a picnic. Such was the plan until Doug Wooley brought the news about the Gentners. When I knew that all of the men would be away, leaving only a lot of unprotected women and children at Big Bend, I begged my husband to stay with us, and he did. No one knew but what the Indians would see the men going toward Gentners' and seize their chance to come down from the valley and kill us all, for the Gentners had had nothing in the world to do with the killing of the Indians on Beaver, and neither had we. And of course, although we had the dinner all prepared, the picnic and fishing on Lost Canyon Creek had to be given up.[111]

The men from Big Bend took a wagon and brought Mrs. Gentner and the children over to Mortons'. My sister-in-law, Mrs. Brumley, took care of the baby until the mother was able to go on to Durango. Dr. Winters came from Durango to attend Mrs. Gentner, and though I saw her while she was ill, I did not talk to her about the affair myself. I got this story straight from those who did. I feel that it is one happening in those early times which I am in a position to know the straight of. She often said it seemed terrible to her to go away with the children and leave Mr. Gentner lying there, but he told her he was killed, and she looked back and saw that he did not move again. There was nothing she could do for him, but she might save the children.

When Mrs. Gentner was able to travel, she and the children went to Durango, and I believe the government did something for her. Later, I think the Gentners went to California, but the boy returned here later and lived on the old place.

We moved to a ranch in what is now the Lewis neighborhood in about 1887. We preempted and proved up on 160 acres and then homesteaded a place adjoining. Our home was a mile south of Lewis. Del Raplee, a miner who now lives at Bluff City, Utah, had the place that the Lewis from whom the place takes its name later on bought. John Brumley had a place next to ours, and the Bob Brown ranch was nearby. There were not many out there when we first moved there. But a school was opened right away in a little house on the place where Mr. Burnett, a minister, lived, and he taught the children of John and Bill Brumley and our children that year. Later they built a schoolhouse nearer our place, and Will Ormiston—his widow still lives at Mancos—taught here.[112] He was a splendid teacher. Later a school was built at the present site of the Lewis school. Our children went to school at Dolores in the winter later on. The two older ones boarded in Dolores while attending school, but when it came time for the two younger ones to go, I came in to town with them and Mr. McConnell remained on the ranch.

We had some hard winters back in those days. One winter the snow was so deep we could not get feed for our horses. Often the snow was over the tops of the fences. We always laid in the supplies for winter in the fall, and often we ran pretty low before spring. In the first years we bought them at Durango and brought them a two-day—or one day and a half—trip home. Later we bought the supplies at Dolores. Once my husband and Charley Hosea took four horses and started to break roads to haul some beef we had killed into Dolores. The distance was ten miles and took two days.

There was no post office at Lewis when we lived there. Our address was Dolores, and the mail carrier to Monticello, Utah, used to bring out our mail.[113]

We lived at Lewis twenty-seven years and moved in to Dolores where we have since lived.

Cora Estes Myler lived with us at Big Bend for four years. She was sixteen when she first came from Durango and a very fine girl in every way. It was at Big Bend that she met Mr. Myler. She stayed for six months with Mrs. H. F. Morgan at the sawmill on Lost Canyon Creek and returned to my house where she was married. There was a large crowd assembled for her wedding, and we had a big dance that night. After the wedding, she and Mr. Myler went up to Rico, where he had a packtrain and carried ore.

Marie Simon, now Mrs. Fred Taylor of Cortez, worked for me when I ran a boardinghouse at Big Bend.

Our children are Henry McConnell, now marshal at Dolores, who has three children and one grandchild; Homo McConnell Johnson, wife of James Johnson, who is the son of Charles Johnson Jr., long deceased, son of Grandpa Charles Johnson, who once owned the site of McPhee—whose son, Chester, has two children; Ada, now Mrs.

Frank Morgan, who has a son with two children; Callie, now Mrs. Harry Morgan, who has one daughter with two children. Then there are two of our daughters who are dead.

Mrs. Hattie Johnson Porter, Montezuma County [360-47]. Dolores, March 26, 1934.

Interviewer: Anna Florence Robison.

My father, Charles Johnson, was born in New York in about 1823 or 1824. His father had been killed by Indians before his birth. My father lived in Wisconsin, in Iowa, and in Nebraska before he came to Colorado. With his family, he lived for several years at the foot of the Greenhorn Mountains about thirty miles southwest of Pueblo near what is now Rye. Then he moved on to Los Pinos and had the Pine River post office near present Bayfield. He furnished cattle for the Indians on a government contract for so many per week delivered, and he made good money at it. He had thoroughbred Hereford cattle and fine racehorses from Kentucky. Once some thieves stole some of his racers, and he and his men went after them and got the horses back. One, however, had been injured too badly to be taken home to Pine River and had to be left in the care of a rancher. All of the racers, totally unused to such hard treatment as they had had from the horse thieves during the pursuit, were bedraggled and out of condition.

After my father had had the store and post office at Pine River for several years, he wanted to move on. Grass was getting scarce, for there were too many cattle and horses in proportion to the size of the range. He came over to the Dolores Valley and bought land for a ranch from Billy May. He also took up some land. Then he put a great many improvements on his new place. There was a fourteen- or fifteen-room adobe brick house built for him by some men from Durango. It was painted brick color on the outside and the bricks outlined with white so that it appeared like a building of regulation brick. It was canvassed and papered on the inside and very comfortable indeed. But the builders had not put a stone foundation under it as they should have done. For that reason we never planted flowers on shrubbery of any sort against the house wall. When we left the house in charge of a caretaker in later years, flowers were planted against the walls and disintegration began with the necessary watering. It progressed until the house fell, many years before such a thing need have happened otherwise. The big stone barn, built by the same men, was also defective in its construction and fell in later years before the site was converted into the present McPhee.

This stone barn with its windows high along the sides was somewhat fortress-like. It was also situated so that no one could approach very near it without being seen. For that reason when the Indians had killed Gentner and the word came to the people along the river, they gathered at our place to defend themselves against the attack they feared and expected. We were returning from a funeral of a man killed as a result of a fall from a horse. The funeral was at the old graveyard. We were driving along and saw a horseman riding toward us in high excitement. We knew instinctively that something was wrong, though we denied it to one another. He told us we'd better get home quickly because the Indians had risen and were killing everyone.

When we reached our ranch, the yard was full of people cooking and making camp. We had a large basement under our house and did our cooking there in summer. Mrs. George Moore was in the basement cooking tin after tin of biscuit. She was preparing for a siege. She said they thought they had better feed their men before the Indians came, for there might not be time later.[114]

There were people sleeping all over the yard for the next two or three days. But no Indians appeared, and the neighbors went home again.

That Indian affair at Beaver was not a thing to talk of in those days. Fear of the Indians and fear of the action of the government on the part of those connected with it played a part in keeping it out of conversation. Fear of the Indians greatly influenced even those of us who had had no connection, however remote, with the unfortunate affair. Tales of how those dead Indians lay up there all swelled up and flyblown got about, and the thought was very distressing. The Indians themselves finally came up and buried them, I believe. But for a long while they were afraid themselves to go near the spot.

This was an isolated country in those days. We came here in December of 1880. My married brother, Charles, was living in a little house below us a short distance, and we could not visit freely for fear of being shot by Indians. The May of '81 was rather a fearsome time, for Dick May, our neighbor from up the river, Thurman, and Smith were killed then.

My brother Charles was not very well one day and quite ill the next. You might say he had been really ill only a few hours when he died on May 16, 1881. There had not been even time to send for a doctor before he was gone. I feel sure now that it was appendicitis, but we had no idea at the time what the nature of his illness might be. Mother worried and worried over it. She thought she could feel reconciled if only she could know what Charles died of. Worry made her so ill that Father took a wagon when Charles had been dead three or four weeks and went to Durango to get two doctors to perform an autopsy. He brought the two doctors, and the men took up my brother for the examination. They examined him and gave as their verdict that he had died of pneumonia. That satisfied Mother and set her mind at rest. But the rest of us had our doubts, for we had not very much confidence in the doctors in question. The autopsy fee was a thousand dollars.

We ran horses and cattle. My father used to take his racehorses east each summer, and sometimes he made money on it, and sometimes it was not so profitable. He would take his horses to such places as Saratoga, Coney Island, and Sheepshead Bay. He had all of the horse-racing paraphernalia imaginable. Once Mother and I went on to Chicago where he was training his horses and accompanied him to Saratoga and Sheepshead Bay and elsewhere. We had a grand time that summer. There was plenty of money with which to enjoy ourselves. I used to bet on the races. If I lost, I went to Father for more money so that I could go on betting.

My father died in 1904 at a ripe old age. He had eight children, six of whom were girls. My brother Sam had a ranch below McPhee and ran cattle until his death about nine years ago. Charles had died many years ago, as mentioned above. One of my sisters was the mother of Arthur Waldron, whose widow is county clerk and recorder of Montezuma County.

Mrs. Matt Hammond, Montezuma County [360-36]. Dolores, March 27, 1934.

Interviewer: Anna Florence Robison.

Interviewer's note: Read at the Old Timers' Reunion, Cortez, September 8, 1909. From a manuscript in possession of the secretary of the Montezuma County Old Timers' Association.

MY EARLY RECOLLECTIONS OF MONTEZUMA COUNTY

I came to the Dolores River with my parents July 11, 1881. Durango was then less than a year old, and Montezuma Valley was La Plata County. We camped all night on the old Phelps ranch in Lost Canyon where the roundup was being held. The river valley was pretty well settled. Besides the many men which you always find in a new country, there were eleven women. Isaac Denby, a settler, was shot and killed by Owen Bean a few days after our arrival.

The fall of '81, Grandpa Johnson and family moved here from Pine River, bringing with them hundreds of cattle and horses. This made him the largest—or one of the largest—cattleman in these parts. Mr.

Johnson's family spent the winter in a log cabin and the next summer built the adobe house which is still standing on the old place. The new house was the largest and strongest on the river and was built where the canyon had widened out so that the approach of any Indians could be seen. When the rumor of another Indian raid was brought to the people, they came to Mr. Johnson's. But no Indians came, so the people went back home.

In the fall of '82, Ben Quick was thrown from a horse and had his hand injured. Dr. Fields of Mancos was sent for, but it was too late, as blood poison had set in which caused his death. Mr. Quick was the first person buried in the Dolores Cemetery.

The first ranch in Montezuma Valley was taken up by John Brewer, followed by William Wooley and Louis C. Simon. Mr. Brewer attempted to dig an artesian well but was not successful so abandoned his homestead.

The first silver wedding celebrated in the valley was that of Mr. and Mrs. Louis C. Simon. Among the guests were Mr. and Mrs. D. H. Saylor and family. While the Saylors were gone, the Indians went through their house and took everything they wanted, including every particle of food. Mr. Saylor's family returned to Mr. Simon's, where they spent the night and then went on to Durango.

There were very few if any pigs on the river and none in the valley, so one of the ranchers made arrangements with a man on the La Plata who had pigs for sale to bring the pigs to Durango and leave them in the care of the proprietor of a short-order restaurant who was to give the money for the pigs. Now there were to be three pigs and each was to weigh ten pounds and to cost ten dollars apiece. But when the pigs were brought home, the three only weighed about ten pounds. So he had paid about three dollars a pound for his pigs.

The first lumber used in the building of our county seat was hauled here by Nick Krone and Matt Hammond. It was on Christmas Day 1886. The roads were not laid out as well as they are now, and the townsite was not very plain. So they found it very hard to locate our present thriving county seat.

The road going to Rico was not very good either. It is said it crossed the Dolores River fifty-six times, and the distance was only fifty miles. The winter of '84 is known as the winter of the big snow when it snowed sixteen days and nights continuously, completely blockading the passes through the mountains. Ask our worthy citizen, J. P. Akin. He knows because he was coming to the "sunny Montezuma" and was blockaded on Cumbres Range twenty-one days and had to stay there until the road was opened. The old-timers reckon time as before or after the high water of '84. But now we can say the year of the "big rain."[115]

The Indians were always a source of uneasiness. When we came here the people were still talking about the killing of Dick May, John Thurman, and Byron Smith. Mr. Thurman and J. H. Anderson owned a band of fine horses. Mr. May and Mr. Smith went out to buy horses. The news was taken to Mancos, and a party of men went out and buried Thurman and May. But Smith's body was never found, unless a skeleton recently found in a draw near a spring on the other side of Monument was his.[116] The same year, Willis and Melvin were killed in the Sierra La Sal Mountains. Cal House, Hi Barber, and Mrs. Willis went out and found their bodies and brought them in for burial.

In 1882 there was no one killed, but Dan Williams's cabin on the Dolores was burned and the Indians fired at him. In '83 there were many horses and cattle killed and driven off, but no persons were killed or injured. In '84 Hank Sharp and Dolph Lusk while driving cattle were fired at by the Indians. Sharp was slightly wounded, and Lusk's horse was killed and he himself was reported dead. Sharp rescued him, however, managed to get him on his own horse, and took him to a place of safety. He was severely injured and was taken to Fort Lewis for medical attention, where he soon regained his health.[117] A company of soldiers was sent after the Indians, but nothing was accomplished.

Washing, a scout, and "Roudy" Wilson, a cowboy, who accompanied the expedition, were killed.

On June 22, 1885, some white men killed a small band of Indians on the head of Beaver Creek. One squaw escaped, and a day and a night later the Indians attacked the Gentner home. Mr. Gentner had received the mail that day, and he and his wife were sitting up late reading. Mr. Gentner smelled smoke and went out to see what was on fire and immediately returned and told his wife that the house was on fire and he thought there were Indians around. He tried to put out the fire and was shot and killed. Mrs. Gentner and her four children, one a baby less than a year old, escaped. This baby was the first white child born in Montezuma Valley. Mrs. Gentner was shot, the bullet breaking her collarbone. Carrying the baby and helping the other children, she made her way to Mr. Simon's place. In crossing an arroyo, she saw Doug Wooley. He frightened her again because she thought it was another Indian. But it was only Doug Wooley, who had taken some bedding and was sleeping out away from the house to lessen the chances of the Indians' finding him. The next morning, Doug went to the Big Bend for help, and a party of men went up to the valley and buried Gentner.

In '86 William Ball was killed near Piute Springs, where he is buried.[118] Mr. Ball was the last man killed by the Indians.

Each year as we meet, we miss some of the old, familiar faces, and among those who have passed to the Great Beyond never to return since our last meeting are Mike O'Donnell, Mr. Honaker, Mrs. Augusta Hosea, William Wooley, Grandma Johnson, and Herman Mitchell.

In the days that are yet to come let us not get discouraged or give up, but rather let us stand firm and true as befitting "Pioneers of the Great West."

Appendix

The Correspondence of Anna Florence Robison and LeRoy Hafen

I have always been interested in doing something of this sort in this very region where we live but have never had the time and opportunity together. I can assure you it would be a "labor of love" on my part as well as a task done in order to earn again if you could possibly let me have a share in this project. . . . I want so much to work at anything I can do to keep my poor tiny mother from hardship.

Anna Florence Robison

Anna Florence Robison, the field-worker for Montezuma County in 1934, corresponded frequently with LeRoy Hafen, curator at the Colorado Historical Society in Denver and the project director for the fieldwork being done across the state. Although Anna Robison need not be seen as necessarily representative of field-workers in general, certainly her correspondence sheds light on her own life as a field-worker, her reasons for working, her background, her interest in the project, and the day-to-day details of carrying out such a project.

Anna Robison was born in Edmond, Oklahoma, on December 29, 1899, the only child of William H. R. Robison and Mary Eleanor Belt Robison. The family moved to Colorado and bought a house on forty acres just outside the community of Dolores. Robison attended Fort Lewis College in Durango and Western State College in Gunnison.

She earned a Bachelor of Arts degree, a Master of Arts degree (both in English), and in 1927 and 1928 she attended the School of Journalism at Columbia University in New York. She taught for a year in North Dakota (1930–31), after which her position was eliminated and she returned to her parents' farm in Dolores. Her mother, born about 1858, survived Anna's father, who died in the early 1930s.

In 1934 Robison applied for a job with the Civil Works Administration (CWA). She worked for several months (off and on) under the Federal Emergency Relief Administration (FERA), which replaced the CWA in mid-March 1934. After September 1934, her correspondence stops abruptly. Although the historical survey project was supposed to have been continued under what Hafen calls "Professional Projects," it is not clear whether or not Anna participated. There are no later letters to or from Robison in the Hafen correspondence.

According to Alice Odell of Mancos, Colorado, Anna played the piano and preferred Campbell's soup to other cooking. After her mother's death in the late 1930s, Anna married Clyde Everett Jewel, a millworker, miner, and mechanic. In the late 1940s the couple moved to Grand Junction, Colorado, where Anna became active in the Mormon Church. She died in the summer of 1970, a year after her husband's death. She left her Grand Junction property to the Mormon Church.

In addition to the Montezuma County narratives that Robison recorded and submitted as a part of the historical project, the letters she wrote to Hafen are testimony to her enthusiasm for the project and her integrity in carrying it out. Because she is a near-contemporary of the children of the women whose histories she collected and preserved, the account of her own career complements the narratives of the pioneer women. The narrative of her career suggested by the correspondence answers western women historians' call for suggestions about "how the story turned out."[1]

The letters are reprinted courtesy of the Colorado Historical Society, repository and owner of the records. Hafen's letters are unsigned copies, whereas Robison's are the signed originals.

R.R. No. 1, Box 51,
Dolores, Colorado
January 2, 1934

The Secretary
Colorado State Historical Society,
Denver, Colorado

My dear Sir:

I have just been informed that your organization has funds from the CWA to put a certain number of persons to work throughout the state gathering historical data and stories of pioneers. I know nothing definite about the arrangements for this. But if at all possible, I should like to be considered for some of this work in this region.

I shall ask the Employment Bureau at Columbia University to send you my credentials in case there might be a possible and much needed opportunity for me here. I believe I am fully qualified to do this work since, in addition an AB and an AM in English, I have finished the two-year course in the School of Journalism at Columbia, and have therefore had occasion to interview all sorts of people. In addition, I have always been interested in doing something of this sort in this very region where we live but have never had the time and opportunity together. I can assure you it would be a "labor of love" on my part as well as a task done in order to earn again if you could possibly let me have a share in this project.

I am an unemployed college instructor and have had no chance to earn since the spring of 1931 when the depression eliminated my position in a college in North Dakota. As I had taught just one year since finishing my course at Columbia, you can see that I was none too affluent even then, even for a college instructor. Since that time, I have lived on a ranch with my aged parents and tried to earn my keep with such chores as abound on ranches.[2] Now my father is dead, and my mother and I have not the size nor the strength to run the place by ourselves. Mother is seventy-five and tiny. She was never strong enough for really rough work. Her savings are in a bank here which has little prospect of paying its deposits at any future date. I am small and physically inadequate to do a man's work in running the place which is our one resource. But my health is good. I am thirty-four, and it seems as if I ought to be good for something, even though no college is likely to be able to hire me for many a long day. But, though I majored in English, I have never taught anything but art, and art is a "frill." I want so much to work at anything I can do to keep my poor tiny mother from hardship.

Should you care to know more of me, I refer you to Dr. E. E. Johnson, of Cortez, who has known me since I was a child, and Eliza Needham, Principal of the Durango (Colorado) high school, who has known me a similar length of time. As I mentioned above, I shall have the Columbia University Employment Bureau send you my credentials.

If it happens that you can consider me for some of this work in this region, I shall be deeply grateful. And I shall do all in my power to merit being chosen. It would be heavenly to have work again, even for a little while.

Very Respectfully yours, Anna Florence Robison

P.S. Dr. E. E. Johnson's address is Cortez, Colorado.

January 11, 1934
Miss Anna Robison
R.R. No. 1, Box 51
Dolores, Colo.

Dear Miss Robison:

In response to your letter of January 2nd will say that all the field workers in our Historical Survey project have been selected, and we are not permitted to make changes or substitutions.

If the Project is renewed on its termination, February 15th, we might possibly be able to avail ourselves of your services which I should like very much to do. We shall keep you in mind in case anything develops that would enable us to employ you.

Sincerely yours,
Historian and Curator of History

January 18, 1934

My dear Mr. Hafen:

I received your kind letter in reply to my application for work in collecting historical data and was glad to hear that there might be some remote possibility of an extension of the work which might conceivably result in an employment opportunity for me.

I sincerely hope so, and I shall be infinitely obliged if you will be so good as to employ me if you can. With that possibility in mind, I am enclosing the letter which one of my Columbia University professors sent for me to send to you.[3] I should have greatly preferred for him to send it direct, but he did not because he had no individual's name for the address.

Very respectfully yours, Anna Florence Robison

March 31, 1934

My Dear Mr. Hafen:

I am sending you what material I have that is complete and signed either to-night or by the next mail, which will be Monday morning's. The rest I shall probably send by express as soon as I finish copying the remainder (on my own time as I understand perfectly) and get it signed. The getting it signed is the thing which makes great delays. But I shall make what haste I can. I got a large volume of material this week because I wanted you to feel I had given you good measure, and I have not as yet taken time to write it all up. I have two very long interviews which I haven't touched at all and some shorter ones.

I have not more than scratched the surface of the material which there is here in the county and which ought to be gathered before it is too late. I have scarcely touched Mancos and as yet done only little with Cortez, but I have been at it all of the time, and could have planned so much better had I had a suspicion how short my time was to be. But I certainly have enjoyed the work and thank you for your part in securing it for me.

Very truly yours, Anna Florence Robison

April 20, 1934

My dear Mr. Hafen:

By express am sending to you to-day the rest of the material which I have on hand. There are eight interviews or other documents in the express package and a ninth, which I hope to have signed in Dolores to-day, in this letter. I had written early in March to one pioneer family which should be included for material, and I held the rest of this material in the hope that I should receive what they were writing up for me before too much time went by. I have just heard that, while the daughter is working on it, it is not ready; so I am sending this without it. If I receive the reminiscences of these people later, I shall forward them to you.

If any of the others who have spoken of writing up something for you, preferring to do it that way, turn in what they offered, I shall send that on also, for I am sure they would be disappointed if I did not. However, I do not promise this, for those who volunteered to write their reminiscences may not have the time so to do after all. The chances are that they will not get around to it. But many of them are anxious that the material shall be preserved, and the majority of pioneers whom I asked were willing to cooperate beyond my most optimistic expectations.

Regarding certain old magazines which I mentioned to you, I shall still send in a copy if I can get one with which the owner is willing to part.

Again I want to thank you for permitting me to do this work so far as it has gone. And, should you in future have the funds to go on with it, I hope you will consider me as a suitable person to complete the historical survey which I have begun. I assure you that I have and shall continue to have an interest in so doing which transcends the remuneration, much as I need that also. And, if I could afford such an indulgence at this time, I should go on collecting the portion of the material most likely to escape in a short time "on my own." But unfortunately that costs too much gas and oil and time for my present situation.

With best regards, I am
Yours respectfully,
Anna Florence Robison

April 24, 1934

Dear Miss Robison:

I am delighted with the material received from you today. Have not been able yet to read the stories as I am preparing to leave town this afternoon for a week's trip.

We hope to continue the Historical Project in some of the Counties as a Work-Relief project. You might see your County Administrator and see if it is possible for you to do this work there. We would be delighted if you could continue with it.

Sincerely yours,

May 1, 1934

My dear Mr. Hafen:

I received your letter of April 24, 1934. I am glad you were pleased with the material I sent in.

Regarding the suggestion you made that I see our County Administrator,

Mr. Harry Kauffman of Dolores, about the possibility of continuing the project under Work Relief, I shall do so as soon as I can find Mr. Kauffman. He was just confirmed in his appointment last Wednesday, April 25th, I am told. Mr. Phlegar, who was one of the office men for the CWA projects and is to be in a similar position under the new "set-up," has made these suggestions to me. (How appropriate they are, I do not know, but I follow them for what they are worth, trusting that Mr. Phlegar knows whereof he speaks even though he does not speak for the head man.)

Mr. Phlegar says he will have Mr. Kauffman call me up the first time he comes to town. And in the meantime, Mr. Phlegar suggests that *you* should write personally to Mr. Kauffman about the continuation of my work as a work relief project. That, *in addition to* my seeing Mr. Kauffman myself of course. Mr. Phlegar says that he thinks Mr. Kauffman would see no objection to my going on with that work provided it had the approval from your end. Mr. Phlegar said, if I correctly understood him, that you should have the approval of Mr. Shauver (Is that the name?) on the project freshly made out. If the Denver office approves the continuation in some counties, he thinks Mr. Kauffman will do so in this, provided he understands that and that *you* want me to go on with it here. I believe that is right.

I shall write to Mr. Kauffman unless he gets in touch with me to-day. He is not yet established in his regular office, and he has no telephone since he lives up the Dolores River. And I should appreciate your writing to him too, which might make things far clearer than I could unaided as regards the work I have been and wish to continue to do. His address is:

Harry Kauffman, County Administrator, Dolores, Colorado.

Thanking you, I am
Sincerely yours,
Anna Florence Robison

May 26, 1934

My dear Mr. Hafen:

The first of the week County Administrator Harry Kauffman called me up and told me he had an application for the historical project for me in this county. He told me it was signed up and ready with exception of the signature of the chairman of the county commissioners, Edward Porter by name, of Lewis, Colorado. Mr. Kauffman suggested that I should call up Mr. Porter and ask him to drop in at the office at Dolores with a view to signing the application. As I doubted my ability to explain the historical project to him over the telephone, I wrote Mr. Porter a letter, explaining the work I had done already, the incompleteness of the project and need for its being done soon, together with my need of work.

I have just called up Mr. Kauffman to learn if Mr. Porter had been in and signed it. Mr. Kauffman tells me that he (Mr. K.) was out when Mr. Porter came in and *that the application cannot at present be found*. Mr. Kauffman thinks that, *as he himself had already signed the application for the historical project*, his office help may have sent it in to the Denver office with some other papers. Mr. Kauffman seems quite distressed about the error, and he made this suggestion to me in order that time in getting it settled may be saved: He asked me to write to you at once.

He asks that *you* check up with the Denver office to see whether the application signed by him for the historical project in this county has been received there with other papers. If so, and if it is really necessary (He thinks *perhaps* it may not be.) to have the signature of Mr. Porter upon it, he asks that you see it is returned to his office (Mr. K's.) at once in order that that signature may be put on it.

If the application for the historical project has not been sent to the Denver office as he thinks, Mr. Kauffman asks that you will please be so kind as to make out a duplicate application for that work here and send it to him as soon as conveniently possible. Both he and I are distressed that such a mix-up should have occurred, and are sorry to put you to bother. But we want the project, very much.

Regarding Mr. Porter, Mr. Kauffman gave me the impression that he was considered for the place Mr. K. now holds as County Administrator. He says Mr. Porter would probably not read my letter when he saw that it referred to Mr. K's. work and jurisdiction. He thought Mr. Porter would just turn it over to him for his attention unless he was asked in person. However, he did come to Mr. Kauffman's office and leave a letter for me, the contents of which I have no idea as yet since I have not been to the office since it was left. As Mr. Kauffman was not in when Mr. Porter called, he did not talk with him.

Now I do not know whether I am to read between the lines of that and suppose that Mr. Porter was hurt at not being made County Administrator and so inclined to be "difficult" about signing things or not. If it should prove that he is, perhaps a note from you on the subject of the project would be helpful, if it would not be too much bother. His address is *Edward Porter, Lewis, Colorado.* If, after reading his letter to me at the office and talking with Mr. Kauffman, I believe it will be desirable to write such a letter, I shall indicate as much in a postscript.

I want to thank you for all you have done, and what I hope you will do, most sincerely. And I am surely sorry that a mix-up should have so delayed the settling of the affair of the project. I am hoping you will pardon the error Mr. Kauffman's office help seems to have made and assist in rectifying it as soon as possible in order that the project may be approved.

Hoping to hear soon and favorably, and thanking you again, I am
Very sincerely yours,
Anna Florence Robison

(So you will not have to look up the address.)
Harry Kauffman, County Administrator, Dolores, Colorado.

P.S. The letter Mr. Porter left at the office was the one I wrote to *him*. Mr. Kauffman was not in, but the rest of the office staff got the impression he had meant to refer the matter to Mr. Kauffman for decision, not knowing that Mr. K. already had approved it. The staff believes Mr. Porter will approve when he gets hold of the application. And the staff feels sure the partly signed project went to Denver with another which was completely signed. Anyhow, the Denver office can tell you whether it arrived or no.[4]

A. F. R.

May 29, 1934

Dear Miss Robison:

Upon receiving your letter of the 26th I inquired of the State office and learned that the Historical Project from your County was returned to the office here OK.

Everything is apparently ready for you to begin work. Continue the work as you did under the CWA, except that you may not be paid for so much time as under the old setup. Your County Administrator is to determine the number of hours you are to be allowed to work each week. Your pay also comes from his office. Report to him at once and get your directions.

We want your completed interviews and articles sent to me as formerly.

With best wishes,
Yours sincerely,
Historian

June 1, 1934

My dear Mr. Hafen:

This is to report: I received your letter yesterday and also interviewed Mr. Kauffman. He told me that, according to the project, I was to have 360 hours of work at seventy-five cents an hour. He directed me to work six hours a day six days a week and to make him a weekly diary report when I turn in my time. I am starting work to-day. I thought of making duplicate diary reports and sending you one and Mr. Kauffman one.[5]

Mr. Kauffman asks me to inquire whether you have had a field representative working in Dolores County. He told me of some material collected here locally years ago from persons now dead which he thought might possibly overlap a little in places on what a Dolores County field representative might have been gathering. I have not seen this material yet myself—nor has Mr. Kauffman, I understand, for a long time. But when I get to it, I want to be able to work on it without duplication of someone else's efforts.

The point is that a majority of the early settlers in Montezuma County came out here first to the Rico mining boom and then drifted on down here when the boom deflated or for some other reason. So the early history of the two sections is pretty well interwoven, and one cannot tell of one without mentioning the other.

I want to thank you for arranging it so that I can go on with this, to me, thrillingly interesting project. Aside from the very real financial help, it bids fair to be to me, I have also the satisfaction of doing a thing I love to do. I hereby promise to do my very best at it.

I shall probably send some material by mail and, when I have enough, some by express as I did before. Thanking you again, I am

Yours very sincerely,

June 7, 1934

My dear Mr. Hafen:

I am enclosing some completed material which does not in the nature of things require signatures to let you know that I am back at work again.

Report: I have worked three hours each morning and three each afternoon this week, thus getting in my six hours a day. My time has been occupied in writing letters to absent pioneers or other authorities on local history, or to those who live at such a distance that it is desirable to make an appointment before calling on them; in a little interviewing in the afternoons, and in writing up material I have obtained.

It seems impossible to get original copies of old papers because the papers are kept only because they are treasured by the owners. But they are willing to let me make copies of the articles for which the papers were saved. Mrs. Mary Williams, daughter of Mrs. Agnes Lupke with whom I had an interview in March, has made her treasured papers and a magazine, which you tell me you do not have on file, available to me for copying purposes. It is the material from them that I send in to-day.

The paper—one of them, that is—is an old *Dolores Star* of August 1902 which gives an interesting picture of the town at that time. The other is a Montezuma County Edition of *Lillian Hartman's Colorado* published in 1909.[6]

When discounted the proper number of percent for the boom era psychology and the habitual rose-colored spectacles of the editor, it gives a comprehensive picture of the county at that time. My family finds the magazine so absorbing that they have to read it from cover to cover.

I have an article in prospect, to be written by the daughter of a teacher in this region in the early eighties, the daughter herself having attended the pioneer schools. I asked her to describe them comprehensively for you, and she seems most happy to do so, preferring to write the article herself.

I have asked a number of persons who signified their willingness to do so to collect old letters which they have which deal with pioneer times or later local history.

Very sincerely yours,
Anna Florence Robison

June 15, 1934

Dear Miss Robison:

Please pardon my delay in acknowledging your letter and report of the 7th. This is good material you sent in.

In answer to a question in your letter of the 1st will say that we have had no historical worker in Dolores County in the last ten years, and I think none at any time. So you need fear no duplication. Anything you can obtain for that County would be very welcome.

Sincerely yours,

June 15, 1934

My dear Mr. Hafen:

I shall not be able to get the signatures on the rest of the work which I have done with economy of time just yet, so I am sending on what is signed and some more material from *Lillian Hartman's Colorado* which Mrs. Williams has permitted me to use for a little while. I shall do all of the material in that magazine because it is interesting in showing how things were in Montezuma County's best period. But I am doing part of it on *my own time* because I want it personally but am making you a copy too. I do not want you to think I am taking the easy way because I am using so much of it and so want you to know I am doing a large share of it on my own time.

Two of my best sets of material this time come from persons at the farthest ends of the Valley, and as no one else lives on the way there and as I do not find it at all satisfactory in town for signatures and any corrections or additions there may be. Another of my "interviewees" has promised to have more for me when she can collect her thoughts further, etc. Shall hope to send some of those in next week's installment. In haste,

Very sincerely yours,
Anna Florence Robison

June 22, 1934

My dear Mr. Hafen:

I am sending you another installment as you will see. I wish I might send in the series of letters I have been working on, but I do not want to send it until I have it completed to my satisfaction. The people from whom I borrowed these letters are the sort that save them all, and want to see if they can't find me the letters describing a number of the important events of the eighties which I have not as yet. I feel sure such letters were written, and, as they have simply oceans of them, it seems likely that they may have the ones I want. They would be splendid to fix dates accurately, for one thing. And the writers of the letters are unusually fine letter-writers. Reliable people, all around. Both the man and the wife of the family which has the letters had mothers who wrote unusually well and much. The wife's father also wrote the same way. And they are more than accommodating to me in this work.

The forester at Mancos tells me that the material of which I told you is in his office and that I may use it freely there. No more of my interviews are signed up as yet. But I have been interviewing, arranging for interviews, and typing my six hours per day six days a week *and then some*, for there are some things I get which I am not sure are absolutely essential *which I type out on my own time*, but *I make you a copy* for the files, suitably labeled, anyhow.

I haven't had time to look over the forestry office material as yet. It is there and can be seen and worked over when someone I wish to interview is not available at the moment.

I wish to get this in the morning's mail if possible.

Sincerely yours,
Anna Florence Robison

June 25, 1934

Dear Miss Robison:

Your letters of June 15th and 22nd were duly received, together with the excellent manuscripts submitted. The interviews contain good material and preserve interesting details of history.

Sincerely yours,

July 23, 1934

My dear Mr. Hafen:

I hoped to have an envelope full of material approved to send to you this morning. But I haven't been able to find my interviewees in time, and I have nothing on hand but interviews right now. Some of these men are very hard to find at home, and there are so few phones in the country that one cannot check up in advance. One of the interviews—the hardest to have approved, I am afraid, because of the activities of the man who gave it—is positively the best I have obtained for reliability, amount, and the fact that it covers material no one else available has at first hand.

When convenient, let me know if any other field worker interviewed Frank Taylor of Boulder, *who was a pioneer in this section in the late seventies and early eighties*, won't you please? I am sure his interview belongs in this section of Colorado, but, he being elsewhere, someone else may have seen him personally. I can write to him for information, but most of these would never be able to tell much on paper; so what I shall get will probably be a disappointment even though I am positive he could tell me a great deal if I could talk with him.

Here is something else: Would you please be so kind as to make the arrangements *from your end* (I am sure it would be better than for me to attempt making them from mine.) for me to attend this year's meeting of the Montezuma County Pioneer Association which occurs in August sometime? I am sure it would be somewhat valuable to the Historical Society for me to do so, and individual pioneers speak as though they expected me to be there. But these pioneers are exceedingly jealous of their pioneership and unless my presence were *thoroughly official*, there is no telling how some one or two of them might take the notion to react to it. Now I want my association with every one of them to be absolutely cordial; so I should like to be armed with plenty of credentials and to be *invited locally besides*, so that the affair might go off pleasantly for all concerned. These pioneers are surely on guard, tooth and nail, against intrusion, fancied as well as real.

Now, though many of them have spoken as though they expected me to be there, *I have no idea that it will occur to a one of them to invite me.* Those who think I will be there as a matter of course will suppose that I will either take it for granted I am welcome (A thing I couldn't think of doing.), that some one else has invited me, or that you will have arranged it. Those who are especially "touchy" might, if I went without the full credentials I speak of, create some of the scenes they have in the past created *for no good reason.* And I am not so constituted that I can consider the source of an embarrassing public rebuff and proceed to do my best work immediately after. Of course only a very few of the pioneers would dream of acting so; but there are some, and *I should want my right to be present as your representative unquestionable.*

Mrs. Mabel Waldron, Secretary of the Montezuma County Pioneer Association, *Cortez, Colorado*, could arrange for an invitation to be extended locally to me and further things a great deal, if you would be so kind as to write to her concerning it. And I feel sure she would do so unless factors of which I am ignorant prevent. I am told you have had representatives at that Pioneer Association meeting before. Only, a total outsider would not require the amount of credentials that I would, because, not living here at all, one would have to be very unreasonable to fancy such a person was trying to "force the way in" to an organization to which he had no right as I might possibly be because we have lived in Colorado a good while.

The mail with your letter has just come. I am glad you met and liked Mr. Kauffman. I agree with your estimate of him most heartily. . . .

Very truly yours,
Anna Florence Robison

July 27, 1934

Dear Miss Robison:

In response to your letter of the 23rd I am writing to Mrs. Waldron as per enclosed copy. I trust this will clear the way for you to attend their meeting.

I do not find any material from Frank Taylor in the Boulder Collection, so should be glad to have you get from him what data you can pertaining to your section of the State.

Sincerely yours,

July 28, 1934

My dear Mr. Hafen:

I have been able to get this much of my material approved.

I shall be writing in a few days regarding some pictures which the owners are willing to let you copy. Please let me know whether there could be extra copies of some of these pictures printed at the same time. The local Pioneer Association will probably want some, and so I should like to know whether you could have an extra copy or so printed and the price.

Sincerely yours,
Anna Florence Robison

July 30, 1934

Dear Miss Robison:

Was pleased today to receive the two envelopes full of historical material from you. Am glad you are to have something from the Mancos region. Will you get something from the Mormon settlers there? You wrote once of getting a story from a daughter of John D. Lee, but I do not remember receiving it.

I was glad to meet your County Administrator the other day. He appears to be a fine man.

Sincerely yours,

Aug. 1, 1934

Dear Miss Robison:

Thanks for your letter of the 28th and accompanying manuscripts. You have some very excellent material this week. . . . *Sincerely yours,*

August 3, 1934

My dear Mr. Hafen:

Mr. Kauffman called me up to tell me that, due to having a great number of new cases on relief and no extra money for August, my project would have to be suspended for the month. He added that "with a more ample allotment for September, it is probable that the project can be reopened."

I imagine it would be more than well if you would write to Mr. Kauffman toward the last of August reminding him of the desirability of so doing, for there is a great deal of work here yet which I have not yet had time to do though I have put in my time thus far to good advantage. Mancos has a vast deal of material which I have not had time yet to obtain, not counting the days' works which await me at the forestry office and the newspaper office.

I have a number of interviews which lack the signatures only, which I will try to have ready to send in a few days or less. Of course, due to the expense of running a car, I shall try to combine the getting of the approvals with trips which we must make for ourselves. I think there are about seventy to ninety pages thereof altogether. Getting the signature to one of the best would involve a trip of thirty miles over quite terrible roads. The man does not come to town, and we have no occasion to go down that way otherwise; so I may have to hold that interview until the project is reopened. It is the best interview I have too, and I am anxious to send it in.

I am sorry for the interruption, but that is the way it is. I hope to write again soon.

Sincerely,
Anna Florence Robison

P.S. The differential in our old car requires some expensive repairs before I can go anywhere and get any approvals, as it turns out. I shall do so as soon as we get the repairs and get it fixed up, which we hope will be in a week or ten days. The repairs have to be ordered from away—hence the long delay. I am sending the two interviews which I have had approved. But will have to hold the rest for those repairs to be made before I can combine them with even our family errands.

A. F. R.

August 13, 1934

Dear Miss Robison:

Thanks for your letter and the manuscript. Am sorry to learn of the interruption of the project and hope that it may be renewed next month.

Sincerely yours,

September 4, 1934

My dear Mr. Hafen:

Here is the long-delayed batch of interviews at last signed up for you. I have one more to which the subject added a good deal when I went to have it approved and another which has long required merely the signature. But the latter requires a thirty-mile trip to obtain. I shall send those two as soon as possible. Both are long—21 and 15 or more pages.

I have interviewed the woman mentioned in your letter of July 20th after all. I told you at the time that I did not know such a person was in this country now, but I later found that she was and had an interview. Naturally she did not tell me who her father was, the circumstances being what they are, but you will be able to identify the interview as hers by names contained therein. She is one of the most charming women I have ever met, incidentally, and decidedly a leader in the community. She was identified to me by a woman who knew her and her mother back in 1882 when they first came into this country. The one who told me about her would not rest easy henceforth if she supposed I told you more plainly than this lest it should somehow leak out and she get into trouble for telling me. I trust you understand. . . .

I do not know whether Mrs. Mabel Waldron, Secretary of the Montezuma County Pioneer's Association, told you in reply to your letter that the board of that organization decided that it would make hard feelings if they invited me to their annual celebration because this year they were not allowing members to bring any visitors whatever. That was the decision. They are growing exceedingly strict the last three or four years. In years past members might bring any guests they thought might be interested in going. This year it was to be almost as secret as a lodge. From tales I have heard, it is possibly a good thing the board decided against inviting me, for Mrs. Waldron promised me a copy of the program anyhow, and it would be bad policy for me to be—no matter how innocently—the cause of any ill-feeling in any quarter. Some of the pioneers are very quarrelsome, I am told, about what persons are strictly entitled to attend and belong. Mrs. Waldron herself is a pioneer by marriage only, and she did her best to get permission for me to be present.

Mr. Kauffman was able to allow me to work the last six and two-thirds working days of this month. I still have seventy-five hours of my allowance on the project yet to work. And there is work enough in Mancos alone to put in that seventy-five hours. That material at the forestry office is splendid and much of it cannot be obtained elsewhere at this late date. Then there are a good many interviews which I have not been able to get there as yet. Mr. Kauffman said he would try to let me work some this month and some next month on it according to the money he would have, just as he did in August. *If you could give him a little encouragement in this, it would be a help too.* That Mancos material is some of the best in the whole county, and I do not want any of it to get away. I have a number of letters out after material too, and the persons have promised to send it but haven't done so yet. I do so want to give you good measure and to have you feel that I have done so.

I have the pictures to send in for you to have copied, but the pioneer Association *might* like to have copies made of some of them if this is permissible and would like to know what they cost if ordered from you.

You might be interested in the book, just published: *Desert Wife*, by Hilda Faunce, Little, Brown & Co., I believe. I understand that Ruth Wattles, the friend who helped and encouraged Mrs. Faunce to write the book, is a relative of T. W. Wattles mentioned in early Mancos tales. I haven't seen the book myself.[7]

Very sincerely yours,
Anna Florence Robison

Sept. 19, 1934

Dear Miss Robison:

Upon returning to the office after a vacation trip I was pleased to find your letter of the 4th and the two envelopes full of manuscripts. They look good and give evidence that you have been doing real work. No, Mrs. Waldron did not reply to my letter so far as I know. The policy of the pioneer society over there appears very strange to me.

Prints from our negatives run about 25 cents, depending on the size.

I hope Mr. Kauffman will keep you at work as you are doing exceedingly well.

Sincerely yours,

September 26, 1934

My dear Mr. Hafen:

I was so glad to hear from you and to know that those two envelopes of interviews were safely in your possession. I knew you must be on your vacation; so I did not send on the two interviews here enclosed as soon as I got them signed.

I wish you would write and tell Mr. Kauffman regarding my work what you have told me and encourage him to have me go back to work and get the rest of the material I have not yet been able to cover. I can hereby assure you that there is fine material in Mancos which I have not yet touched, due to lack of time thus far. This is a large territory, and there is much running about in the car to do in gathering the material. Mr. Kauffman is likely to think that perhaps I have been "padding my material" or stretching the work because I told him I was not through by a considerable. He, not knowing how much interested I am in the work I am doing *entirely aside from the pay*, might suppose I would pad it. But I fancy few people in this county who have FERA projects are doing work which they love *for its own sake* as I do this, and he could hardly be expected to know, seeing me the few times that he has, that I am one of that few. On my project as approved, I have seventy-four (74) hours yet *uncompleted*. I believe it would take it all to finish up Mancos too. I have tried to give full measure of work on this project, and *if you feel that I have*, I would appreciate it if you would encourage Mr. Kauffman in keeping me busy by telling him as much. I have quite a bit of unfinished work yet out.

Thank you for the price quotations. I shall see the secretary of the Pioneer Association regarding pictures so that I can send in these I have.

The local Pioneer Association has some pictures which I wish you could have. I have been promised that the owner will bring you the most interesting one if she goes to Denver this fall. She will not trust it to the express company. These pioneers are exceedingly jealous of their pioneership. They quarrel fiercely over dates of arrival in the country and injure one another's feelings with gusto. And you would be astonished to know how many intend to write a book about either their own experiences or the settlement of the country and are afraid that giving me an interview may possibly "injure their copyright." Probably not so many of them will ever write their book, but they all think they will since Louisa Wade Wetherill's "Traders to the Navajos" or the "Wetherill's of Kayente" appeared.[8] I have always got the interview, thus far, but I have had to promise them all I would not write a history of the county with their material for commercial purposes. Then some of them are afraid they might tell me something about the Mormons which would bring down upon their heads the wrath of the progeny of some of Brigham Young's "Avenging Angels" which are supposed to reside in these parts. I shall find out all I can about the Mormon settlement at Mancos if I am continued in this work. But it will be difficult to do on account of this same fear to speak on the part of the non-Mormons who are old-timers and the scarcity of the older Mormons themselves.

I have heard much of the Mormons who came to this country through the so-called Hole-in-the-Rock through which they are said to have poked their wagons, wheel by wheel and board by board. But so far I have not found anyone who could name a pioneer who actually came in that way. Charles Lamb of Mancos, who came here in 1882, said he had heard of that route, but that it was disused when he came and that he did not know of anyone who came that way. I had been confidently assured that Lambs came that way. Mrs. Lamb did not even know what the Hole-in-the-Rock was. Maybe some day I shall find one who actually did come through it.

I have some more material in addition to this, but it is not entirely ready to send. I had been hoping for work from Mr. Kauffman to go ahead again, but I do not believe it is coming this month; so I am writing to you instead. In the meantime, I am helping with our little apple crop—very little one.

I trust Mrs. Menefee's interview is not a duplicate. She said some one interviewed her last spring for some organization. She did *not* believe it was for the Historical Society, and the name was Sowens [Soens].[9] I thought it might have been a worker from Durango, however, but I went ahead with her anyhow because she is one of the very oldest pioneers, and the incidents she told me might not be the same in any case.

Mr. Fred Taylor is regarded by most pioneers as very accurate, and confidence in his story is such on the part of practically everyone that his word should take precedence over that of other witnesses in cases of disagreement where he spoke of events he knew.

Hoping to be back at work for you soon, I am
Very sincerely yours,
Anna Florence Robison

October 2, 1934

Dear Miss Robison:

I was glad to have your letter of the 26th and the accompanying replies for pioneers.

We are planning to replace, in the near future, our existing projects under the Relief Administration by substituting Professional Projects, newly provided for. We are asking for a worker in your County under this set-up and shall communicate soon with Mr. Kauffman respecting this and asking for your appointment to this work.

With best wishes, I am
Yours sincerely,
Historian and Curator

Notes

Introduction

1. Riley argues that although there were certainly fearful women in the West, "Sheer numbers of women who lived, worked, and played in nature disprove the notion of female fear of Western landscapes" ("Myth of Female Fear," 34).

2. Riley, *A Place to Grow*, 197–209.

3. Wyckoff corroborates the assertions of these narrators, pointing out that "Landslides, earthquakes, blizzards, cyclical droughts, floods, firestorms, and insects made life in the West eternally tenuous" (*Creating Colorado*, 11).

4. For a general overview of schooling, see Kaufman, *Women Teachers on the Frontier*. There are several studies of the history of regional frontier schools for counties in Colorado, and although the specifics vary from region to region, much applies to frontier schools in Colorado generally. For the Uncompahgre Valley see Hemstrom, *Slates, Chalk, and Inkwells*; for Custer County see Francis, *One-Room Schoolhouses*; for Routt County see Leslie, *Routt County Rural Schools*; for the southwestern counties see Spinning, *Clapboards, School Boards, and Blackboards*; and for Boulder County see Dyni, *Back to the Basics*.

5. For an account of some of the Colorado towns that did not survive into the twentieth century, see Eberhart, *Ghosts of the Colorado Plains*.

6. Riley points out that "the majority of Western women coped and eventually conquered their 'wilderness' milieus" ("Myth of Female Fear," 34).

7. Jameson and Armitage, *Writing the Range*, 3.

8. For general overviews of Colorado history, see Abbott, *Colorado*, and Ubbelohde, Benson, and Smith, *A Colorado History*; see also Hafen, *Colorado and Its People*.

9. Hopkins, *Spending to Save*, 116. For book-length studies of the programs see Schwartz, *Civil Works Administration*, and Rose, *Put to Work*.

10. LeRoy Hafen, editorial, *Colorado Magazine* 11, no. 1 (1934): 39.

11. Hafen, Civil Works Administration, MSS 2591, Stephen H. Hart Library, Colorado Historical Society.

12. Undated letter from Hafen, Hafen Collection, MSS 1458, Stephen H. Hart Library, Colorado Historical Society.

13. Hafen, editorial, 39.

14. Robison to Hafen, June 1, 1934, Correspondence, Hafen Collection. See the appendix for the Robison-Hafen correspondence.

15. For an overview of how the land affected settlement in Colorado, see Wyckoff, *Creating Colorado*, and Worster, *Rivers of Empire*, esp. "In the Shadow of the Rockies," 83–96. See also Chronic and Chronic, *Prairie, Peak, and Plateau*; Huber, *Colorado*; Lamm and McCarthy, *The Angry West*; and Riley, *Women and Nature.*

16. See Wyckoff, *Creating Colorado*, 157–61. For a thorough overview of the Colorado geography, see Mutel and Emerick, *From Grassland to Glacier.*

17. These accounts bear out what most historians have noted. According to Danz, the "Southern Herd [of American Bison] . . . was basically wiped out between 1870–1874. The Northern Herd . . . was systematically destroyed between 1876 and 1883" (*Of Bison and Man* 112).

18. Wilkinson offers an overview of the geography of the plateau region in *Fire on the Plateau.*

19. A good overview of the gold rush in Colorado is West, *Contested Plains*; see also Cochran, *Miners, Merchants, and Missionaries*, and Wickersheim and LeBaron, *Mine Owners and Mines.*

20. The south-central town of San Luis, not established until 1851, for instance, boasts that it is the earliest permanent European American settlement in what is now Colorado.

21. For a detailed account of the gold rush and its impact on Native Americans, see West, *Contested Plains.* Other important accounts are Riley, *Women and Indians*, and Tate, *Indians and Emigrants.* For general histories of Native Americans in and around Colorado, see Crum, *People of the Red Earth*, and Hughes, *American Indians in Colorado.*

22. Iverson, "Discoverers, Pioneers, and Settlers," 7.

23. For accounts specific to the Utes, see Emmitt, *The Last War Trail*; Pettit, *Utes*; Marsh, *People of the Shining Mountains*; and V. M. Simmons, *Ute Indians.*

24. Riley, *Women and Indians*, 184.

25. Riley, *Women and Indians*, 202.

26. Garceau-Hagen, *Portraits*, x.

27. Several collections of women's voices exist for the West and for western

states. Allen collects 194 women's accounts in *Traveling West*, for example. See also Butruille, *Women's Voices*. In *Prairie Voices*, Riley edits a sampling of women's writings from Iowa. Lindgren investigates the experiences of women who filed claims in North Dakota in *Land in Her Own Name*, and Foote relies primarily on first-person accounts to describe pioneer settlement in New Mexico in *Women of the New Mexico Frontier*. Similarly for Oklahoma, Reese offers *Women of Oklahoma*, and for Kansas one can turn to Stratton's *Pioneer Women*. Riley's *Frontierswomen* offers narratives from Iowa, and Fischer edits a collection of narratives from mostly California and Arizona, *Let Them Speak for Themselves*. Schissel's *Women's Diaries of the Westward Journey* and Holmes's *Covered Wagon Women* offer interpretations of the texts of women's diaries. Several studies focus on Colorado, but none with the scope and particular time period offered by the narratives in this collection. Jones-Eddy collects the narratives of forty-five women (taken in the 1980s) in *Homesteading Women*. In another compilation of narratives, *In Other Words*, Rodgers provides excerpts from 182 selections, some only one sentence long. In *Long Vistas*, Harris writes a history based on interviews from 1975 and 1982, providing an account of northeastern Colorado women pioneers. None of these, however, provides firsthand accounts of the actual pioneering by the pioneers themselves from essentially all the geographical regions of Colorado

28. For a brief but solid overview of western women's history see Armitage, "Turner's Ghost."

29. Johnson, "'A memory sweet to soldiers,'" 495.

30. Lerner, "Placing Women in History," 359.

31. Jeffrey, *Frontier Women*, xii.

32. Jameson and Armitage, *Writing the Range*, 3, 4.

33. Armitage and Gluck, "Reflections on Women's Oral History," 7.

34. Carter et al., *Unsettled Pasts*, 4.

35. Jameson and McManns, *One Step over the Line*, 3.

36. Friedman, *Mappings*, 202.

37. Schissel, Ruiz, and Monk, *Western Women*, 1988.

38. Schissel, Gibbens, and Hampsten, *Far from Home*, xvi.

39. Garceau-Hagen, *Portraits*, 1; Schlissel, Ruiz, and Monk, *Western Women*, 5; Jameson and Armitage, *Writing the Range*, 5.

40. Jameson and McManns, *One Step over the Line*, 1.

41. Friedman, *Mappings*, 200.

42. Sigerman, *Land of Many Hands*, 9.

43. See Stoeltje, "A Helpmate for Man Indeed," 26, 41.

44. Prescott, *Gender and Generation*, 15, 3.

45. Pascoe, "Western Women," 46; Jensen and Miller, "The Gentle Tamers Revisited," 16, 35.

46. Armitage, "Through Women's Eyes," 14.

47. Sigerman, *Land of Many Hands*, 10. Armitage, Banfield, and Jacobus make a similar point in "Black Women and Their Communities in Colorado."

48. Riley and Etulain, *By Grit and Grace*, xi.

49. Garceau-Hagen, *Portraits*, 3.

50. Deutsch, *No Separate Refuge*, 13.

51. Rosaldo, *Culture and Truth*, 19.

52. Pascoe, "Western Women," 46.

53. Armitage and Jameson, *The Women's West*, 5.

54. Armitage, "Through Women's Eyes," 16.

55. Armitage, "Turner's Ghost," 138.

1. The Northwest Plateau

1. For a general overview of the settling of this northwestern corner of Colorado, see Wyckoff, *Creating Colorado*, esp. 243–52.

2. For a full account of the battle and its results, see Miller, *Hollow Victory*.

3. The Navajos and Utes have a long history of both trade and conflict. The nomadic Utes, living a sophisticated horse culture, often raided settlements of the more sedentary Navajos on their farm settlements. Such raids and kidnappings were common between the tribes.

4. Dan'els refers here to a slingshot war club, made with rawhide or horsehair.

5. The Uintah Utes lived south of the Great Salt Lake and occupied the Great Basin area east of the lake. After what is known as the Black Hawk War in 1861, Tabby (Tabby-to-Kwana, Child of the Sun) became an influential and important chief of the Uintahs; he led the starving group to the Uintah Reservation in 1869.

6. Kit Carson (1809–68) did serve as an Indian agent, but in New Mexico, not Utah, from 1853 through 1861. He had, however, earlier established a fort near Whiterocks, Utah, in the winter of 1832–33, roughly a decade before the narrator was born.

7. With many different names, a Sun Dance has been practiced by many different, mostly Plains, tribes, including Lakota, Dakota, and Nakota of the Sioux.

8. According to Marsh, *People of the Shining Mountains*, the Utes have both a Tea Dance and a Deer Dance. The Tea Dance evidently is "an adaptation of the strange rites the Indians observed while watching the white man's dances at trading posts and mining camps." An herbal tea or other refreshment was commonly served. According to Marsh, the Deer Dance, which Mrs. Dan'els refers to, "seems

to have died out with the coming of the white man. But, from early reports, it resembled 'ring around the rosie.'" (154). According to tradition, the Bear Dance is the oldest of Ute ceremonies. When bears wake, it is time to visit, to play with, and to mourn those gone; it is also time to welcome new members of the tribe; the dance is in imitation of the bear as he steps forward from the winter den (150, 152; see also Pettit, *Utes*, 85–86).

9. Provo and Spanish Fork were Mormon settlements on the east side of Utah Lake. Whiterocks, a small community in northeastern Utah, fifteen miles west of Vernal, served as the Uintah Agency until 1886.

10. Fort Bridger in southwestern Wyoming was an important trading post; established in the 1830s, it was used by the military until 1890.

11. Red Jacket Jane (Uintah) was enslaved in Tabby's lodge after the death of her parents; she often ran away, and in 1857 she was sold to the wealthy William A. Carter at Fort Bridger. She married a man named Pauvitz of the White River Band, and she got employment in the Meeker household in the 1870s. She died in 1908. The "trouble" Dan'els refers to here is the battle at Milk Creek and the Meeker Massacre of 1879. See Sprague, *Massacre*, 150–58.

12. If the narrator refers to a former Confederate soldier when she calls Bynum Lane a "rebel," she was probably sold in about 1866, which would suggest she was born in the early 1850s, and thus about eighty-three when she is narrating, rather than the "past ninety" she begins with.

13. Mormon leader Brigham Young (1801–77) directed the mass migration of Mormons to Utah in 1847 and served as governor of the Utah Territory from 1849 to 1857. He was removed as governor because he practiced polygamy, but he retained great influence among the Mormons.

14. Tintic (or Tintick) Junction, just south of Utah Lake, between the East and West Tintic Mountains, is named for the Goshute leader Tintick. See Van Cott, *Utah Place Names*.

15. With its headwaters in Flaming Gorge, the Green River flows south through eastern Utah, joining the Colorado in Canyonlands. Cub Creek is one of its tributaries.

16. Lucerne is another name for alfalfa, an important hay-feed crop throughout the West.

17. The Uintah Reservation was established in 1861 for the Utah Utes, but after the battle at Milk Creek 1879 the White River Utes were also forced to take up residence there. As stipulated by the Dawes Act (1887), each enrolled member of the reservation tribe was allotted a piece of land (up to 160 acres) on which to settle. Unclaimed lands became available for non-Indian settlers.

18. Beginning in 1878 with Richard Pratt's Carlisle Indian School in Pennsylvania, based on the belief that assimilation was appropriate, it became United States policy to take Native American children from their homes and "board" them in order to "educate" them. They were not allowed to speak their own languages and, given Pratt's slogan, "Kill the Indian, save the man," were taught that all things "Indian" were bad. The system thrived until about 1930, by which time more than one hundred thousand Indians in some five hundred different schools had attended.

19. John J. Critchlow was the appointed agent of the Uintah Reservation from 1871 to 1883; he argued that the future of the Utes was in farming.

20. According to the interviewer, Mrs. Harris amends the first statement about her birth: "I was not born in Brown's Park. I was born farther up Green River. We moved to Brown's Park when I was a little girl. I remember when we moved, so I must have been about seven or eight years old. Father was running cattle in Brown's Park at the time of the Meeker Massacre [1879]." Brown's Park is a long, narrow upland basin surrounded by mountains extending from southwestern Wyoming, through Colorado, and into northeastern Utah.

21. West Boone Draw drains into Vermillion Creek just to the east of the Green River in the extreme northwestern corner of the state. A few miles to the east, East Boone Draw drains into the Little Snake River.

22. Fort Davy Crockett was built in Brown's Park in 1837.

23. Harris amends the account of her great-uncle Sambo's name: "My great-uncle was called Washambo, and the Indians generally called him Sambo for short. He was half French and half Scotch. He was called Scott, but I do not know whether that was his first or last name. That chimney-and-rock foundation east of Whiterocks that you thought might be the ruins of Fort Robideux was built by my father and his uncle." Fort Robideux, named for Antoine Robideux, a fur trapper, was established in 1832 near present-day Whiterocks, Utah. It was the first year-round white settlement in Utah. Powell and Frémont visited it during their explorations. It burned in 1844.

24. Here Harris probably refers to Thomas Jonathan ("Stonewall") Jackson (1824–63), the Confederate general who gained fame in the battle of Bull Run in 1861.

25. Fort Benton, also known as Benton Station, near the Nevada-California line, served as Pony Express station and later as depot for the Carson and Colorado Railroad. Fort Bridger, in the southwestern corner of Wyoming, was on the 1860–61 Pony Express route.

26. Major John Wesley Powell (1834–1902) explored the Green and Colorado

Rivers in 1869. As director of the Bureau of Ethnology, he collected American Indian materials for the Smithsonian Institution. Powell lost his right arm in the Civil War Battle of Shiloh in 1862.

27. If Harris's father died six years before the interview, which would be in 1928, as she says, it seems unlikely that he was born as early as 1811.

28. By "Gosho" Harris refers to the Gosiute (or Goshute) tribe, a Shoshone-speaking nation from the Great Basin area of Utah. The Gosiutes' traditional territory extended from eastern Nevada to the Wasatch Range in central Utah.

29. Bear River has its headwaters in northeastern Utah, flows north through Wyoming, into Idaho, and then sweeps south again, reentering Utah near Logan.

30. Captain Jack is most likely a reference to the self-appointed leader of the White River Utes. Raised in a non-Indian household in Salt Lake City, he left to join the White River Band. He was killed by U.S. soldiers on April 29, 1882. Persune, of the White River Band, was involved in the Meeker Massacre and the abduction of Josie Meeker and the other women and children. Douglas (Quinkent) was longtime leader of the White River Band and lived at Meeker. In 1880 he was held in prison for nearly a year without formal charges and was finally released without explanation. He died in 1885.

31. The portion of the river upstream from the confluence of the Colorado and Green Rivers in eastern Utah, what is now the Colorado River, was called the Grand; by a 1921 act of Congress, the upper Colorado got its present name. Located due north of Glenwood Springs, the mining community of Carbonate Camp (Carbonate Town Camp) lies at eleven thousand feet and was established in 1883. By the end of 1884 the last resident left, and the town was abandoned. In Eagle County, Dotsero was established in 1880 and had a post office of its own from 1882 through 1948.

32. North Elk flows from south to north and empties into the White River just to the east of Meeker. A tributary of the White River, Piceance Creek flows south to north just west of Meeker.

33. New Castle, earlier Chapman, a stop on Post Road no. 29, at the junction of Elk Creek and the Grand River (Colorado River), is mentioned in 1885. See Gulliford, *The First Hundred Years*.

34. The Denver and Rio Grande Railroad completed a line from Glenwood Springs to Rifle Creek in October 1889. The line from Red Cliff at the foot of Tennessee Pass to Rifle Creek was completed in 1890.

35. In 1887, Colorow, with a small band of hunters, was attacked by a game warden and his posse. Before a full-fledged battle could develop, the militia was called out to escort the Utes back to the reservation in Utah.

36. The Meeker bank robbery took place in mid-October 1896 when three men held up the Hugus retail store and bank in Meeker. All three robbers were shot and killed before they were able to mount their horses and ride out of town. One of the three was never identified.

37. According to field-worker Monaghan, Madeline and Jennie are "daughters of Jim Baker." In a letter to LeRoy Hafen (March 30, 1934, Hafen Collection), Monaghan describes the two women: "Those girls do not speak anything but English, but they are Indians to the core. They are very pleasant and very hard to get anything out of. Having made their acquaintance, they might be easier to talk to now." According to Leighton Baker, Madeline Baker was born to Meeteese (Mary), a Shoshone woman (Jim Baker's second wife), on July 15, 1859. Jennie was also born in 1859, to Mary's younger sister, Janetse (Eliza) on October 6. Thus the two women are half sisters as well as cousins. Jennie married August Reschke in 1881. She died on December 12, 1937. See L. L. Baker, *Jim Baker*, 85–86, 90, 99.

38. The Little Snake River, rather than the Snake River, flows south and southwest from Wyoming into the Yampa River in Colorado.

39. Dixon lies just north of the Colorado border in Wyoming.

40. Nolie Mumey's *The Life of Jim Baker, 1818–1898* was published in 1931, just three years before this interview took place.

41. The narrators here seem to be correct. According to Miller, "Merritt spoke with Joe Rankin about the Milk Creek situation. Rankin advised Merritt to hire Jim Baker to help out when they got to Snake River. Merritt agreed. An old-time guide and trapper, Baker's knowledge of the country and the Indians was second to none" (*Hollow Victory*, 129–30).

42. Monaghan, the field-worker, notes that "The gun is a breech loader, with set trigger and the slide action of an 1848 Sharps. It has an extra heavy hexagonal barrel. The forearm has been made out of elk horn and the rifle has a sling strap. The caliber is fifty or more."

2. The Mountains and Foothills

1. For overviews of mining and the gold rush in Colorado, see Dorset, *The New Eldorado*; Wolle, *Stampede to Timberline*; Zanjani, *A Mine of Her Own*; and Wickersheim and LeBaron, *Mine Owners and Mines*. See also Moynihan, Armitage, and Dichamp's collection *So Much to Be Done*. In *All That Glitters*, Jameson examines class and gender roles in the mining community of Cripple Creek.

2. Scharff, "Mobility, Women, and the West," 161.

3. The Denver and Rio Grande Railroad arrived in Pueblo first from the north via Colorado Springs on June 15, 1872. For an overview of mountain rail history

see Robertson, *Encyclopedia of Western Railroad History*, vol. 2, *The Mountain States*. See also Wilkins, *Colorado Railroads*.

4. The rail line from Durango to Silverton was completed on July 8, 1882.

5. An abbreviation for centum weight (hundredweight), cwt means 100 pounds.

6. Ouray (1833–80), a powerful and influential leader of the Uncompaghre band of Utes, was much respected as a peacemaker by whites and other Utes alike.

7. As noted above, the Meeker Massacre took place in October 1879.

8. The Gunnison boom began in 1883 when gold was discovered in the vicinity. The town was named for Captain John W. Gunnison, who traveled through the area in September 1853. The community had a post office beginning in October 1876. Lime Kiln Gulch, in the Black Canyon of the Gunnison River, is quite a distance from Gunnison; Grafflin Gulch, however, is just a few miles west of Gunnison on Tomich Creek. Tenderfoot Mountain rises from the southeast edge of town. The La Veta Hotel opened on April 15, 1884, and was advertised as "Gunnison's Pride." The palatial building was demolished in 1943.

9. Vulcan, due south of Gunnison, was still rich with chimney mines as late as 1895, when the post office was established, and had a large population; as many as five hundred people were there for several years. The Vulcan post office was discontinued in 1912.

10. Sugar Creek flows northward into the Gunnison River, just to the east of the town of Vulcan.

11. Central City, established in 1859, the first year of the Colorado gold rush, was the hub of mining activity in the Gilpin County area and thus appropriately named.

12. At least five mines in Colorado are called Bobtail. The reference here is to a mine on Bobtail Hill just south of Black Hawk. Cold Spring mentioned here may survive in name only as Cold Springs Campground, just to the north of Blackhawk, at the junction of current State Highways 46 and 119.

13. Gregory Road (between Green and Flagstaff Mountains in Boulder County) was the result of one of several early attempts during the 1860s to connect Boulder and the Central City mines. Complete with a couple of hoisting stations along the way, Gregory Road did enable wagons to make a very difficult trek between Black Hawk and Boulder. By 1866 the road through Boulder Canyon was opened to wagon traffic and the other, more difficult routes became obsolete.

14. Petersburgh, in Arapahoe County, had a post office off and on between 1876 and 1907, but the locale no longer appears on maps.

15. Charles N. Hockaday (1837–1910) served as county sheriff from 1875 to 1877.

16. The Rio Grande County townsite was first named Lariat (with a post office

from 1881 to 1884) and was renamed Henry after a land speculator, Theodore C. Henry (with a post office from 1884 to 1886). Ultimately renamed for its view of the nearby mountain, Monte Vista was incorporated in 1886.

17. Of the forty named canals and irrigation ditches in Rio Blanco County, of which Del Norte is the county seat, none is called Saguache. By "the Rio Grande and Saguache Canal" the narrator may intend the Rio Grande Canal, which flows to the northwest out of the Rio Grande (river) at Del Norte.

18. Conceived in October 1883, the College of the Southwest was officially opened on September 10, 1884, with a class of thirty students. George Darley was instrumental in getting the college going. The first faculty consisted of President Dr. Willis Lord from the College of Wooster and his recent graduates F. N. Notestein and Miss Amanda Flattery. No mention is made of a Rev. Goodell. See Bender, "A College Where One Ought to Be."

19. Under the headline "Woman Knocks Gun Down and Threatens to Spank Young Thug," the following account of Anna Lee Fulcher Clarkson appeared in the *Denver Post* on January 19, 1934, one month after the interview presented here: "In case a point of etiquette on how to meet a stickup man bothers you, it might be well to consult Mrs. A. L. Clarkson, 66 of 1602 South Emerson Street. Mrs. Clarkson has very positive convictions on how such riff-raff should be handled, and she demonstrated Wednesday night that her ideas on the subject are practical. As she waited for a street car at East Tennessee Avenue and South Pearl Street, she related to police, a young man approached and pushed a gun against her side, demanding money. First, Mrs. Clarkson knocked the gun from the hands of the aspiring robber with the firm remark, 'I'll not give you my purse young man.' This little detail out of the way, Mrs. Clarkson then gave the amazed fellow a piece of her mind. 'You ought to be ashamed of yourself—a big, strong fellow like you—trying to hold up poor women who haven't any money,' she said. 'Now you get away from here and get away quick, before I take you over my knee and spank you.' The holdup paused only long enough to snatch his gun from the ground and then fled."

20. Valmont, named for the nearby buttes and laid out in 1865, was a leading community, larger than neighboring Boulder in the early years. The community had its own post office from 1865 to 1901.

21. White Rock, seven miles east of Boulder, was on the Colorado and Southern Railway between Longmont and Jefferson County. The community could be found on maps from 1892 to 1916, but it had no post office.

22. Wayside was established in 1876, and Alamosa (meaning "full of cottonwoods") was established in 1878. The Denver and Rio Grande actually reached Alamosa via La Veta in June 1878.

23. Fulcher here perhaps refers to Hans Johannsen, who came from Germany in 1867, made his home in Conejos County, and became a successful grain and stock rancher. See *Portrait and Biographical Record of the State of Colorado*, 1049. Fulcher is, of course, a reference to her own family.

24. Also known as "rocking" or "the largo," single-footing refers to a smooth cadence at different gaits, in which the horse moves with one foot on the ground at a time.

25. La Jara, once known as La Jara Station, took its name from La Jara Creek. Developed around a railroad station, it was built a short distance from an older Hispanic settlement also called La Jara. The settlement established a post office in 1884. Wayside was an early name for the community that became Alamosa.

26. Hattie (Dorris) Mullins was the second wife of William "Billy" Adams, governor of Colorado from 1927 to 1933. She died in 1918, two years after the marriage.

27. Denver had a population of roughly 5,000 in 1860; by 1870 the population was perhaps a bit lower, 4,759. The Clarksons came through in 1872.

28. William H. Adams (1861–1954), a future three-term governor of Colorado (1927–33), was originally from Wisconsin. He had moved to Colorado in 1871 and to Alamosa in 1878, where he worked as a ranch hand.

29. California Gulch, near Leadville and prosperous as early as 1859, was one of the first rich mining areas in Colorado.

30. From Kansas City the railroad reached only as far west as Topeka in 1866.

31. Albert Gallatin Boone (1806–84) was a grandson of Daniel Boone and a friend of William Bent.

32. By the "Little Arkansas Fort" and "Little Fort, Arkansas" (in the following paragraph) the narrator might mean Station Little Arkansas, the trading post and breastwork where the Santa Fe Trail crossed the Little Arkansas River, 229 miles west of Independence, Missouri, in central Kansas, a mile south of present-day Lyons, Kansas. Bent's original trading post, or Bent's Old Fort, twelve miles west of the confluence of the Purgatorie and Arkansas Rivers in Colorado, served as a haven and trading post for trappers, Indians, and immigrants, and was used by the military as well. Although it was burned in 1849—perhaps by William Bent himself—and abandoned, by 1861 it was functioning again as a stage station. Bent's New Fort, built in 1853, was situated thirty-eight miles downstream from the original fort.

33. Fort Larned, earlier known as Camp Alert, was established in 1859 on the Pawnee River just above its confluence with the Arkansas in central Kansas. Fort Dodge, established in 1865, served as another guard center and military fort. It

stood near the intersection of the "dry" and "wet" routes along the Santa Fe Trail where Indians frequently crossed the river. One dry route crossed the Cimarron Desert, Cimarron Cut-off Dry Route, and by its name travelers referred to its fifty to sixty miles without a reliable water hole.

34. Felicia Dorothea Browne Hemans (1793–1835), a British poet, was one of the most popular female poets of the nineteenth century.

35. By Bovino, Harrington must mean Carlos Beaubien, whose daughter Maria married Lucien Bonaparte Maxwell. At Beaubien's death in 1864, the Maxwells bought the claims of all Maria's siblings and thereby became sole owners of the immense tract of land, known as the Maxwell Grant. In 1870 they sold to Jerome Chaffee.

36. Solomon Young (ca. 1816–92) was a freighter who according to some sources was no relation to the Mormon Brigham Young, but the two did know each other.

37. Brigham Young (1801–77), Mormon leader, was the governor and superintendent of Indian affairs in Utah Territory from 1851 to 1858.

38. Boone, established in 1860, lies about twenty miles east of Pueblo.

39. John A. Thatcher (1836–1913), from Pennsylvania, opened the First National Bank of Pueblo in 1871 and was a successful businessman. Oliver Hazard Perry Baxter (b. 1835) came to Colorado in search of gold in 1858 and remained. He settled in Pueblo in 1866 after having participated as a volunteer in the Sand Creek Massacre. He was involved in state and local politics and was the first president of American National Bank in Pueblo. According to an 1899 biographical record, "During the Civil War, when the Indians committed ceaseless depredations in Colorado, Mr. Baxter raised Company G, of the Third Colorado Cavalry, and was made its captain. The company bore an active part in the battle of Sand Creek, and remained in service until the regiment was mustered out. . . . The high regard in which he is held by his fellow-townsmen shows that he has been successful in his endeavor to discharge every duty of life with honesty and fidelity." *Portrait and Biographical Record*, 126, 127.

40. Dayton, first county seat for Lake County, was built in the 1860s on the present site of Twin Lakes south of Leadville at the foot of Independence Pass.

41. Granite, formerly known as Dayton, had a post office established on November 30, 1868.

42. Georgia Bar, a mining camp in Chafee County, was established in 1860, two miles south of Granite, also established in 1860.

43. The Denver and Rio Grande Railroad reached Leadville from Canyon City in 1880.

44. Centerville, also spelled Centreville, in Lake and then Chaffee County, had a post office from 1868 to 1930.

45. The Uncompahgre, from *ankapagarits* ("red lake"), was a Ute band of west-central Colorado.

46. A. Cameron Hunt was territorial governor from 1867 to 1869.

47. Shavano (Blue Flower), of the Tabeguache band of Utes, was killed on the street in front of a store at Ouray, Utah, in 1886.

48. The parenthetical material is in original.

49. The Cleora post office was established in December 1876 and was discontinued in 1882.

50. Poncha Springs, in Lake and then Chaffee County (created in 1879), had its post office established in 1877; the townsite became Poncha Springs in 1924. Salida, formerly named Arkansas, had a post office established in 1881. Cleora actually predates Poncha Springs.

51. James True (born 1848 in New York) laid out the town of Poncha in 1877 and prospered there as a banker and merchandiser. See *Illustrated History of Arkansas Valley, Colorado*, 537.

52. Poncha Springs experienced several major fires. In 1874 a fire destroyed much of the town. Buildings were lost to fires again in 1880 and 1881. In 1882 twenty buildings were destroyed by fire.

53. Jeremiah Rusk (1830–93), the Republican governor of Wisconsin from 1882 to 1889, was actually the second secretary of agriculture. Grover Cleveland had appointed Norman J. Coleman to the newly created position in February. Some three weeks later, Benjamin Harrison, who had just taken office, appointed Rusk (March 6, 1889).

54. By the "green hide" law Goff may refer to the 1893 statute making it unlawful for any railway company, express company, stage line, or private person to transport animals or hides. As early as 1887 the Colorado legislature stipulated that only those deer (elk and antelope as well) that had horns could be hunted and killed. In 1893 the law was modified to include a ban on transporting, and a limited hunting season, from August 1 through November 1. There was also the explicit statement that deer could be killed for food purposes only.

55. Colorow ("the Red," also called Colorado, ca. 1810–88), an Apache man adopted by the Utes, led a small band on a hunting expedition into Colorado from the Uintah Reservation in Utah in 1887. The game warden accused him and the other members of the hunting party of poaching and forced them to return to the reservation. Later, Colorow settled on the Southern Ute Reservation in Colorado, where he lived until his death in 1888.

56. Chipeta (1843–1924), a Tabeguache Ute, married Ouray in 1859; in 1880 she traveled to Washington DC on behalf of her people. Some five thousand people attended her burial in 1924.

57. There were two toll gates on La Veta Pass, one on each side. Wagon Wheel Gap, established in 1872, supposedly took its name from a large wheel left there in 1861. Lake City, established in 1875, took its name from Lake San Cristobal. It remains the only community in Hinsdale County.

58. Fort Garland, named for John Garland, a military commander, was established in 1858. The fort was abandoned in 1883, but the settlement retained the name.

59. The Ute leader Washington was a delegate to the Brunot Treaty Conference of 1873. One story has it that when approached by some illegal prospectors, Washington raised his hand as a sign of peace and showed a card with his name and the message "This is a good Indian."

60. Littleton, on the South Platte River, now a suburb less than ten miles south of downtown Denver, was established in 1872.

61. The Cripple Creek boom actually began in 1891 after Winfield Stratton staked his Independence claim, which he eventually sold to a London company for ten million dollars. Even as late as 1917 over ten million dollars' worth of gold was mined from the Cripple Creek area in a single year.

62. The Silver Cliff mines were at their peak in 1878, the same year the Silver Cliff, Custer County, post office was established.

63. La Sauces, in Conejos County, had a post office from 1890 to 1895. From 1895 until 1920 the post office was known as Lasauses.

3. The South

1. See, for example, Fry, *Smelters of Pueblo*. For a general history of the county, see League of Women Voters, *This Is Pueblo County*. Another overview of Pueblo history is Dodds, *They All Came to Pueblo*.

2. Ten years after the interview recorded here, Marion Russell published accounts of her experiences traveling overland and settling; the account here, recorded by her daughter-in-law Mrs. Hal Russell, was first printed in the *Colorado Magazine* (1943 and 1944), and a much fuller account was published as a book in 1954. In 1981 the University of New Mexico Press published a facsimile edition, *Land of Enchantment: Memoirs of Marian Russell along the Santa Fe Trail*. In an afterword to the facsimile, Marc Simmons writes that the printers misspell her name: "Surviving family papers as well as her tombstone give the correct spelling, Marion" (162).

3. The Cimarron Route of the Santa Fe Trail offered a shortcut from the Mountain or Northern Route, which followed the Arkansas valley and then traversed Raton Pass, but the Cimarron Route included roughly fifty dry miles between the last fording of the Arkansas River and the Cimarron River in southwestern Kansas. Along that river it traveled southwest toward Santa Fe.

4. Stonewall is the site of the settlers' rebellion against the Maxwell Company's attempt to displace them in the summer of 1888 when about two hundred settlers gathered to resist company agents. Russell's husband, Richard, was killed in the standoff.

5. The Maxwell Grant—bordered on the north by the Arkansas River, on the east by the Purgatorie River, and on the west by the San Juan Mountains—is one of several huge tracts of land of southern Colorado and northern New Mexico that Mexican governor Manual Armijo granted; in this case he awarded lands to Carlos Beaubien and Guadalupe Miranda. As a result of the Mexican-American War (1846–48), Miranda sold his lands to Lucien Bonaparte Maxwell, Beaubien's son-in-law. With the death of Beaubien in 1864, the Maxwells became sole owners, then sold to the investors Jerome B. Chaffee and Stephen Elkins in 1870. While the tract itself changed hands several times in the next two decades, homesteaders and miners settled and made their claims regardless of the actual ownership of the Maxwell Land Grant. Hence, disputes arose that resulted in occasional guerrilla wars and general disagreement as to ownership. For a detailed study, see Keleher, *Maxwell Land Grant*.

6. In an attempt to depoliticize the land claims issue, the United States Congress established the Court of Private Land Claims in 1891. Of the more than thirty-five million acres at stake, however, Hispanic claimants were awarded barely two million acres of their land. According to Deutsch in *No Separate Refuge*, the court rejected claims "which were over one hundred years old and without previous dispute" (20). This reassigned land was then made available to railroad companies and Anglo homesteaders.

7. William Hill Sloan (ca. 1843–1917) served with the Union in the Civil War and then became a missionary first in Rangoon, Burma (Myanmar), and then twice in Mexico, 1884–88 and 1893–1907. See the afterword to Russell's *The Land of Enchantment*, 160–61.

8. Fort Crawford on the Mississippi River in what is now Prairie du Chien, Wisconsin, was built in 1816 as a military and staging outpost for the West. Established in 1819 at the confluence of the Mississippi and Minnesota Rivers First and first called Fort St. Anthony, Fort Snelling was completed and so named in 1825.

9. St. Jo is a reference to St. Joseph, Missouri, and the "government train" is a train of covered wagons pulled by oxen.

10. Jesse James (1847–82) was a Confederate outlaw who—despite being a robber and murderer—was, and still is, revered throughout the West as a hero.

11. Fort Mackay, just west of Fort Dodge in Kansas, went by several names, including Camp Mackay in 1850 and Fort Atkinson after 1851.

12. Canadian-born Francis Xavier Aubrey (1824–54), a well-known Santa Fe freighter and trader, had ridden from Santa Fe to Independence (850 miles) in just over five and a half days to win a ten-thousand-dollar bet. Richard Hanson Weightman (1816–61) did indeed print an uncomplimentary account of Aubrey, and Aubrey promised revenge. The two men met in a bar, and when Weightman proposed a toast to Aubrey's horseback-riding skills, which had been the subject of the satirical news article, Aubrey drew on him. Before Aubrey could shoot, however, Weightman stabbed him. Weightman was tried for murder and found "not guilty."

13. Colonel Edwin Vose Sumner (1797–1863) of the U.S. First Cavalry led campaigns against the Plains Indians as early as 1857. See West, *Contested Plains*, 1–6.

14. Westport Landing on the Missouri River, at Kansas City, was a major starting point of the Santa Fe Trail as early as the 1830s.

15. As mentioned in note 3 above, the so-called Northern Route followed the Arkansas River as far as La Junta before turning to the southwest toward Trinidad and Raton Pass.

16. Eugene W. Crittenden (d. 1874) was a major in the Fifth Calvary.

17. Trinidad, first called Río de Las Animas and later Santísima Trinidad (Most Holy Trinity), was established in 1859.

18. The convent was begun in 1852 when a group of nuns arrived from St. Louis, the Academy of Our Lady of Light (Loretto), in which case the young Marion would have been among the school's first pupils.

19. Established in 1851, Fort Union was situated near the junction of the Mountain and Cimarron branches of the Santa Fe Trail, about thirty miles north of Las Vegas, New Mexico. In 1891 the military abandoned it, but it is preserved as a National Monument. James H. Carleton (1814–73) was known as an Indian fighter, especially for campaigns against the Apaches and Navahos.

20. Colonel Chas T. Alexander (d. 1878) was also known for his service against Indians.

21. Kit Carson (1809–68) worked as an Indian scout, served in the military fighting against the Apaches, Navajos, and Kiowas, and, ironically, later became an Indian agent. On June 1, 1865, he established Camp Nichols, near Wheeless on the Colorado-Oklahoma border in the extreme western portion of the Oklahoma panhandle. Accompanying him was Pfeiffer, who had fought with him in Arizona

the previous year. The fort was abandoned in September of the same year. See Roberts, *A Newer World*, 265–68, and M. Simmons, *Kit Carson*, 125.

22. In her book-length account, *Land of Enchantment*, Russell describes her impression of the area she and her husband settled: "Suddenly we came to a gap in the towering wall and drove through a natural gateway. God, it seemed, had decided to let us into the Garden. . . . We camped that night in the loveliest spot I had ever seen" (129). Russell devotes only the last chapter to settling and building a home in Colorado. In the earlier chapters she describes crossing the plains and settling in New Mexico.

23. St. John Valley is evidently Russell's translation of the Spanish El Valle de Gutiérrez. Established in 1867, the town was first called Stoner's Wall after its first settler, James Stoner; the post office was established in 1878 when the name was changed to Stonewall.

24. J. E. Coe (perhaps J. P. Coe) may well be the son of the J. P. Coe who worked the hotel at Stonewall.

25. Robert R. Poole ran the hotel in Stonewall, which was a summer resort. The J. P. Coe family was in charge of the resort syndicate. José Luís Torres participated in the battle against the Maxwell Grant deputies.

26. In *Land of Enchantment*, Russell writes that her husband "was shot while carrying a flag of truce and attempting to negotiate with the deputies who barricaded themselves in the Coe Hotel" (139). For a treatment of the conflict see Taylor, *Maxwell Land Grant Conflict*, esp. "The Stonewall War," 211–25.

27. Colorado City, established in 1859, was the original seat of El Paso County, but because the railroad chose Colorado Springs, Colorado City declined in importance and was annexed to Colorado Springs in 1917. Settlers built the Colorado City Fort in 1864 for protection against Indians; it was abandoned in 1868. (This original townsite is not to be confused with present-day Colorado City in southwestern Pueblo County.)

28. Conflicts between the settlers and the Plains tribes were commonplace throughout the 1860s; most deadly was the Sand Creek Massacre on November 29, 1864. Afterward, travel across the plains was interrupted as a result of retaliatory strikes by the Cheyennes.

29. According to a newspaper report, the Indians killed "two little lads, aged respectively eight and twelve, the sons of Mr. Robbins," and Charlie Everhart, age seventeen. Judge Baldwin is identified as having been shot and left for dead, but not scalped or killed. *Colorado Springs Gazette*, August 8, 1874.

30. Initially known as Brown's Spring, Rosita in Custer County was early one of Colorado's most populous towns, with several very successful mines, including

Pocahontas and Humbolt. A post office was established in 1874 and was discontinued only in 1966. See Wickersheim and LeBaron, *Lost Cities of Colorado*, 88; and Dallas, *Colorado Ghost Towns*, 168–70.

31. The Colorado Midland Railroad operated from Colorado Springs to Buena Vista by the summer of 1887.

32. Mary Fandall-Hindman, a granddaughter of Sara Chivington Pollock, submitted Nellie Pollock Snyder's narrative for the Colorado History Essay Contest of the Colorado Federation of Women's Clubs in June 1933. The judges awarded it first prize in Denver the following month. Civil Works Administration interviewer Anna Florence Robison copied the document, noting that she secured the essay "through courtesy of Edna Dillon-Longenbaugh, Cortez, Colorado in March, 1934."

33. Jefferson Territory, established in October 1859, was essentially a squatter's territory until February 1861, when Congress voted in the territory of Colorado.

34. Nicknamed the "Fighting Parson," John Chivington (1821–94) was honored for his role in forcing the Confederate army out of New Mexico in the battle of Glorieta (1862). He was later condemned for leading a surprise dawn attack and massacre against the peaceful Arapahos and Cheyennes at Sand Creek in 1864. He resigned from the army in 1865 and spent the rest of his life trying to escape the stigma of his role in the massacre.

35. Howbert defends Chivington's actions, writing that Howbert and the other soldiers involved in the massacre returned to their homes "convinced that we had done a good work and that it needed only a little further punishment of the savages permanently to settle the Indian troubles." Further, he contends, "a large majority of the members of the Third Colorado Cavalry were high-class men, whatever might be said to the contrary" (*Indians of the Pike's Peak Region*, 113, 115). Howbert does not detail that these "high-class men" wore the body parts of the women they massacred as decorations on their hats and belts. Perhaps Snyder was unaware of the details of the massacre. Dunn offers another defense of Chivington, "*I Stand by Sand Creek*."

36. Baker's Park is a six-mile-long mountain basin named for Captain Charles Baker, whose exploratory party of fifteen men entered the valley in 1860 in search of gold.

37. Cascade Creek flows southward from its headwaters on Rolling Mountain for ten to twelve miles before joining the Animas River. There are no surviving communities on the creek.

38. John Charles Frémont married Jessie Benton in 1841.

39. In the fall of 1860, George Steele came to Denver supposedly to challenge

the editor of the *Rocky Mountain News* for having misrepresented him in print. He was shot at Bradford's Corner, now Sixteenth and Larimer Streets.

40. Silverton was established in 1874 and named the following year. Nearby Howardsville had been settled in 1869.

41. Pinkerton-in-the-Pines was near Durango and had no post office.

42. According to her obituary in the *Pueblo Chieftain* (June 13, 1918), "Mrs. Hayden was born in Des Moines, Iowa, Nov. 22, 1841. When she was three years old her parents removed from Iowa to Kansas, settling later in what was then Westport, Missouri (now Kansas City). Mrs. Hayden crossed the plains from Missouri to Colorado in 1863, coming to Pueblo. In the same year she was married to Daniel G. Hayden, the ceremony taking place at the Old Bent's Fort. The couple decided to make Pueblo their home, and took up their residence in a house then located on what is now the west side of Santa Fe Avenue between Third and Fourth Streets. In 1868, the year of the founding of the *Chieftain*, Mr. and Mrs. Hayden moved out to the Huerfano River where Mr. Hayden established a flour mill. The family home on the Huerfano was retained until 1884 when the family moved to Walsenburg. Mr. Hayden died at Walsenburg in 1903. During most of the years since her husband's death Mrs. Hayden had resided in Pueblo." Bent's Fort was originally built by Charles Bent at the confluence of the Timpas and Arkansas Rivers. After it burned in 1849, Bent rebuilt about thirty-eight miles down the Arkansas. (For a detailed account of the history of Bent's Old Fort see Arps, "From Trading Post to Melted Adobe, 1849–1920.") Later, Fort Lyon (initially named Fort Wise) was established just to the west. Fort Lyon no. 2 was built at the confluence of the Purgatorie and Arkansas Rivers. Pretty (or Pleasant) Encampment was located about four miles east of the Kansas-Colorado line and thus more than thirty miles east of Bent's New Fort. As Scott notes, the "locations of many stage stations, road ranches (built to provide needs of travelers) and ghost towns are not well known because available records provide few detailed maps. . . . Many features were abandoned before the land was surveyed. . . . After stage lines were abandoned, the station buildings were almost immediately torn down and scavenged as material for constricting buildings elsewhere" ("Historical Trail Map of Lamar"). See also Spurr and Spurr, *Historic Forts of Colorado*, and Beckner, *Old Forts of Southern Colorado*; more generally, see Frazer, *Forts of the West*.

43. Council Grove in eastern Kansas is roughly halfway between Independence, Missouri, and Fort Larned. Fort Larned, on the Arkansas River, is northeast of Fort Dodge and was established on the Santa Fe Trail in 1859.

44. John Smith was an interpreter for and trader with the Cheyennes and Southern Arapahos in the 1860s. Serving as an interpreter, he traveled to Washington DC and met with Lincoln. See Coel, *Chief Left Hand*, 166–67, 273–77.

45. Cow Creek was a way station along the trail, situated 249 miles west of Independence, Missouri.

46. Hayden probably means Great Bend, also called the North Bend, where the Santa Fe Trail joins the Arkansas just north of Fort Larned.

47. Left Hand, also known as Niwot (born ca. 1840), of the Southern Arapahos, died in 1864 from wounds received during the Sand Creek Massacre. He is reputed to have stood in front of his tepee during the fighting with his arms crossed, unwilling to fight and break the established truce. The friendly Indians whom Hayden sees here were very likely those massacred a few months later at Sand Creek. During the spring and summer of 1864 there were numerous raids along the overland trails in eastern Colorado, "hostilities which brought ever more serious problems to the territory" (Ubbelohde, Benson, and Smith, *A Colorado History*, 105.)

48. Chicosa Creek flows into the Arkansas at the eastern edge of Pueblo County and is said to have gotten its name from a plant commonly called "rabbit thorn."

49. From Bent's Old Fort (functioning as a stage station) to Fort Lyon no. 1 was about twenty miles, and thus a good day's travel.

50. Mary E. Hayden might be referring specifically to the June 11, 1864, killing of Nathan Hungate and his wife and two children on a ranch about twenty-five miles south of Denver.

51. Of these named men I find reference only to Hinsdale, whose given name was Governor. He was a lawyer in Pueblo in the 1860s and 1870s and had aspirations to be governor, but was never elected. See *Pueblo Chieftain*, June 1, 1868.

52. A loaded wagon train typically made about fifteen miles a day.

53. Greenhorn Creek flows from west to east through Rye and Colorado City, where it turns north toward the Arkansas. Four miles upstream would put her at the Pueblo County line in the Wet Mountains.

54. Crow, in Pueblo County, had a post office from 1885 to 1891 and again in 1896. It was discontinued in 1907, and the town is no longer on the maps.

55. Barbed wire, first mass-produced in 1874, made the fencing of large tracts of homesteaded prairie land relatively easy and affordable, and thus it ultimately meant the end of the cowboys' open-range cattle industry.

56. Smelting, refining the crude to final metals, flourished at both the Philadelphia Smelting and Refining Company and at the Colorado Coal and Iron Company in Pueblo during the 1880s.

57. Pueblo was incorporated on November 15, 1885.

58. A. T. King was mayor from 1895 to 1897. Benjamin B. Brown did not take the mayor's office until 1902; he served until 1905.

59. The flood of 1921 devastated the city; high water at the Union Depot building was eleven feet.

60. The Missouri Pacific Railroad extension west to Pueblo was completed on December 15, 1887.

61. John Lambert (b. 1837) was quartermaster at Fort Reynolds, east of Pueblo, until he took over the *Pueblo Chieftain* in 1870. He turned the paper into a daily and remained owner until 1903.

62. West Abriendo is a Pueblo street just to the southwest of the Arkansas River.

63. The Grand Hotel opened on September 3, 1887, and had a reputation for being as nice on the fourth floor as on the first.

4. The Northeast

1. See Porterfield, *Homestead Act of 1862*.

2. For a general overview of Weld County history, see Schwayder, *Weld County Old and New*; see also Smith, *First Hundred Years*. In 1938, just a few years after these interviews took place, Mary Geffs published a county history: *Under Ten Flags*.

3. From a circular in the *New York Tribune*, April 12, 1870, quoted in Willard, *Union Colony at Greeley*, 165.

4. Wyckoff, *Creating Colorado*, 3; Limerick, *Legacy of Conquest*, 42; Georgi-Findlay, *Frontiers of Women's Writing*, ix–x.

5. Left Hand (Niwot), one of leaders of the Southern Arapahos, was born about 1840 and died from wounds he received at the Sand Creek Massacre in 1864.

6. John Q. A. Rollins established Rollinsville in Gilpin County in 1861.

7. The fort at La Porte was established in 1859, but after a flood in 1864 it was relocated to Fort Collins. The post office at Flemings Ranch in Weld County was established in 1863. This office was discontinued in 1875. Flemings Ranch also served as a stage station.

8. Johnstown is between twelve and fifteen miles southwest of Greeley.

9. First called Modoc, the town of Niwot was established in 1872 and named in honor of the Arapaho chief Niwot (Left Hand).

10. Grace Brush Mayne refers to her father, William, and her uncle Jared Brush, a cattleman, for whom the town of Brush was named.

11. Johnstown was not established until 1902. The Millikin post office was established in 1909.

12. By 1869 the Denver Pacific had its first railroad line into Colorado, from Cheyenne City, Wyoming, through Greeley to Evans. The Denver Pacific line published its first timetable on January 3, 1870, from Cheyenne City to Greeley and Evans.

13. Eaton, just north of Greeley, was established in 1888 in Weld County and was named for Benjamin H. Eaton, the fourth governor of Colorado (1885–87).

14. General Robert A. Cameron served as the original vice-president of Union Colony. William E. Paber was an original member of the colony and wrote its first history in 1871. Both left the colony in 1873. See this chapter's headnote for brief biography of Nathan Meeker (1817–79), founder of Union Colony.

15. General Charles Adams, along with Ouray and his brother-in-law Sapawanero (neither of whom had been involved in the battle), negotiated for the release of Meeker's wife, Arvilla; her daughter Josephine; and Flora Ellen Price and her two children. The women were released in October 1879, twenty-three days after their kidnapping on the day of the massacre. The women returned to Greeley, where they had lived before having moved to the White River Agency.

16. During the first year, a qualified Union Colony settler could obtain land in proportion to the amount paid in membership fees. After July 1871 and the incorporation of Greeley as a town, land was auctioned, available to anyone interested. For a general overview see Hibbard, *History of Public Land Policies.*

17. Latham, formerly named Cherokee City, just south of Greeley, served as seat of Weld County from 1868 to 1870 and had a post office as early as November 1863 through October 22, 1864, when it was moved to Evans.

18. Completed in 1869, the transcontinental line followed the South Platte valley briefly, dipping into extreme northeastern Colorado before turning northwest at Julesberg toward Sidney, Nebraska, and Cheyenne, Wyoming.

19. The Colorado Central Rail Road Company first operated from Julesberg, through Sterling to LaSalle just south of Greeley in 1880–81. The Colorado Central was consolidated into the Union Pacific in 1890.

20. According to a park history brochure (Sterling City Hall), the Cheairs family donated land (sometime before 1920) that became Cheairs Playground, later named Cheairs Park, located at South Third and Columbine Streets. It was the city's first park. In 1920 the Cheairs Investment Company sold a larger track of land (about sixteen acres) that the family had lived on to the city for twenty thousand dollars. This land became Columbine Park.

21. Haxton (in present-day Phillips County) is thirty miles due east of Sterling, Colorado, in the northeastern corner of Colorado.

22. Holyoke is forty-seven miles due east of Sterling, Colorado.

23. In this context, "breaking" probably refers to breaking or turning up sod in order to cultivate the land, growing crops being a requirement of the Homestead Act.

24. "We looked upon a world unknown" is from John Greenleaf Whittier's

poem "Snow-Bound" (1865). Elizabeth Akers Allen (1832–1911) is credited with the ballad "Rock Me to Sleep" (1860).

25. From Edgar A. Guest (1881–1959), "A Man Must Want," in *The Passing Throng* (1923).

26. Fort Morgan, established in 1884 on the South Platte River, was named for Colonel Christopher A. Morgan of the U.S. Volunteers. Walter Gresham was appointed postmaster general by Chester Arthur on April 3, 1883, and served until October 1884.

27. Belle Case La Follette (1859–1931), wife of Wisconsin governor Robert La Follette, was a women's suffrage activist.

28. The *Greeley Tribune* was established in 1870.

29. Ansel Kellogg (1832–86), considered the father of the newspaper syndicate for his first use of "patent insides," was editor and publisher in Wisconsin.

30. Clatworthy refers to Lyluph, Sixth Earl of Airlie (1861–1947), and his father, David Ogilvy, Fifth Earl of Airlie (1826–88).

31. Although the post office at Fort Morgan was initially established as early as 1866, it was reestablished in 1884.

32. Clatworthy's statement is not clear. There is an Ensign in southwestern Kansas, but the Burlington and Colorado Railroad Company operated from Wray to Denver through Brush and Fort Morgan from 1892 to 1908. The earlier Burlington and Missouri River Railroad Company operated from 1870 through 1880 before selling to the Chicago, Burlington and Quincy Railroad Company in 1880.

33. The first issue of the *Fort Morgan Times* actually appeared one month later, on September 4, 1884.

34. In Weld County, the community of Otis was established in 1883. There is no record of its ever having had a post office.

35. Fort Morgan was incorporated in 1887, not 1888 as Clatworthy remembers. According to Bright, the "former military post was first known as Camp Tyler, but in 1865 was renamed Fort Wardwell. The following year substantial buildings were erected, and the name was changed again to its present one" (*Colorado Place Names*, 55).

5. The Eastern Prairie

1. Wyckoff provides a good overview of the climate, geography, and settlement of eastern Colorado in chapter 5 of his *Creating Colorado*, "Hinterlands: Eastern Plains, 1860–1920," 154–90.

2. For an overview, see *History of Kit Carson County, Colorado* by the Kit Carson Historical Book Committee.

3. The Rock Island Railroad was completed as far as Burlington by June 23, 1888, and the town was platted at that time.

4. Although she is clearly referring to land in present-day Colorado, Lengel might here refer to the Arapahoe County of Kansas Territory, established in 1855 and named in honor of the Native American residents who were soon dispossessed. Arapahoe County in Colorado, which originally extended east from Denver to the Colorado state line (north of Washington County), never included the area that became Kit Carson County, which was established in 1889 with Burlington as its seat. The area that became Kit Carson County was carved out of the original Douglas County, which had been divided into Greenwood (1870–74) and Elbert (1874).

5. Cheyenne Wells, in Cheyenne County, is thirty-eight miles due south of Burlington. The Landsman post office was established on March 27, 1883.

6. Compare Lengel's account of Munsinger with that of Anna Homm later in this chapter.

7. Emerson Ditch, getting its water directly from the South Fork Republican River, was dug as a canal for irrigating alfalfa, corn, and other corps.

8. Old Burlington got its name because, according to Benson in *1001 Colorado Place Names*, "For a short time in 1887 two townsites existed side by side: Lowell, named for the man who platted it, and *Burlington*, named by settlers for their former homes of Burlington, Kansas, and Burlington, Iowa. After Lowell was abandoned, *Burlington* residents moved a mile or so east and replatted the townsite, keeping the name *Burlington*. In 1889, the New Burlington addition was platted to the west, where the Rock Island railroad had placed a depot; consequently Lowell/Burlington became known as *Old Burlington*" (28).

9. According to Bright, the beaver "gives its name to twenty-seven streams in Colorado" (*Colorado Place Names*, 12). Around Burlington, for example, there is Little Beaver Creek to the north, Beaver Creek to the west, and Little Middle Beaver Creek to the southeast.

10. Cheyenne Wells is about thirty-five miles due south of Burlington.

11. The Chicago, Rock Island, and Pacific Railroad came through Limon and reached Colorado Springs on November 5, 1888.

12. Lansing was a small community on the wagon road, about ten miles northeast of present-day Idalia. The post office was in operation from 1886 through 1910.

13. Arapahoe County, the Colorado Territory's first county, was established in 1861 and stretched from Denver to the eastern border of the state. Elbert County was actually formed from Douglas (which also originally extended from the South Platte River to the state's eastern border) and Greenwood Counties in 1874.

14. Old Columbia was platted in 1888 next to the Rock Island Railroad right-of-way, but it never had a post office. Claremont was platted in 1888 and was renamed Stratton in 1906.

15. That first passenger train to Denver on the Chicago, Union, and Nebraska line came through on November 5, 1888.

16. Claremont could boast three weekly newspapers in 1888, all short lived: the *Claremont Star* (1888–89), *Crystal Springs Register* (1888–89), and *Claremont Journal* (1888–91).

17. A walking boss was the foreman on the crew.

18. Flagler, named for millionaire railroad magnate Henry M. Flagler, was established in 1887 and had a post office by October 1888.

19. The Union Pacific had established a line into eastern Colorado through Cheyenne Wells and Hugo en route to Denver by 1885.

20. Blackleg, a bacterial infection affecting young cattle, causes blood poisoning, darkening of the muscles (hence the name), and rapid death.

21. Cane, or sorghum, was one of early Colorado's important prairie crops, both for cereal and livestock feed.

22. The present-day southern half of Yuma County, organized in 1902, was formerly part of Arapahoe County.

23. About forty miles due north of Burlington, Wray had a post office, established in May 1883.

24. Two hundred years ago, gray wolves were more widely distributed than any other mammal across North America, including the prairies. They have been exterminated in the continental United States except in Minnesota and the far western states.

25. The township of Friend was established in 1886 and had a post office from 1887 to 1901.

26. Peconic Siding was a whistle-stop on the Rock Island line, six miles northeast of Burlington. It was still on the maps as late as 1968. Two miles further northeast, Carlisle had a post office from 1887 through 1890.

27. Kanorado, which was indeed first called Lamborn, had a post office as early as 1889, and train service in 1888. The town was not incorporated, however, until 1907.

28. Established in 1888, Cope is on the Arikaree River and lies just over the line in Washington County. The post office moved from Gray in 1889.

29. Hoyt in Elbert County is not to be confused with the town of Hoyt in Morgan County. Hoyt in Elbert County had a post office only from March 27 through November 1888, after which time it was discontinued.

30. The old fort may have been on the South Fork Republican River (northeast of present-day Seibert) and would thus not have been a part of the Santa Fe Trail, which followed the Arkansas valley to the south. The Republican River, however, did mark a major travel route, followed as early as 1843 by Frémont as he explored the eastern part of the state. Later it served as a main stagecoach line through Seibert to Willow Springs and then on to towns on the Front Range.

31. In *1001 Colorado Place Names*, Benson writes: "In the late 1880s, the Burlington Railroad asked Jonathan C[alvin] Cope to establish a terminal point for a proposed line. Cope agreed, but said that he would stay only if trees could be grown in the area. The forest that Cope nurtured became known as *Cope's Grove*, the site evolved into the town of Cope, and 'Daddy Cope,' as he was fondly known, remained in the area until his death in 1921 at age eighty-six" (46).

32. The *Diamond Telescope* was a weekly newspaper out of Cope, Washington County, published from 1888 to 1890.

33. The Newton post office, in Arapahoe County, then Adams County, then Yuma County, was established on August 6, 1889, and was discontinued in 1918.

34. See note 20 above.

35. See Elizabeth Gutting Lengel's account earlier in this chapter.

36. Limon, formerly called Limon Station, or just Station on some maps, is the point where the Chicago, Rock Island, and Pacific Railroad crossed the Union Pacific line. Limon had rail service by 1888.

37. Tuttle, no longer on the maps, in Elbert and then Kit Carson County, was School District 39 and had a post office from March 1883 through July 31, 1918.

38. In this context, a relinquishment was a piece of land abandoned by someone who could not or would not prove up or pay for the acreage.

39. Just southwest of the Burlington area (a few miles north of the township of Kit Carson) there is a Big Spring, at the site of the ruins of Fort Big Spring.

40. Hale in Arapahoe County, then Adams County, then Yuma County, had a post office from May 17, 1890; it was discontinued in 1894 but reestablished and again in operation from 1900 through 1984.

41. Given the description, the "bugs" Merrill refers to could well be grasshoppers, *Arphia pseudonietana*, whose habitat is the open prairie: the size and color match her description: bright, deep red forewings, gray body, 30 millimeters (about 1.2 inches) long.

42. Wolf Creek flows northward into the Arkansas at Granada.

43. On the Arkansas River, Granada is about ninety-five miles due south of Burlington. In *1001 Colorado Place Names*, Benson notes that "*Granada* was initially the end of the track town for the Atchison, Topeka, and Santa Fe, which arrived

on July 4, 1873. . . . [A] new townsite platted a few miles west in the mid-1880s survived as homesteaders came into the area" (87).

44. Boulder, first called Boulder City, formed early in 1859 as one of the first mining outposts, named, of course, for the large boulders in the area. I find no corroboration for the assertion that Jones named Boulder, nor do I find anything to refute it.

45. The stepmother referred to here, the second wife of Robert Todd, was Elizabeth "Betsey" Humphreys (ca. 1800–1874); she married Robert Todd in 1826. According to biographer Jean Baker in *Mary Todd Lincoln*, "Betsey Todd's niece shared a room with Mary for six years" (33).

46. Perhaps Merrill refers to Caleb H. Norris, an Ohio Supreme Court justice born ca. 1850. He is listed in the 1910 U.S. Census as still living in Marion, Ohio.

47. The *Granada Exponent* was a weekly newspaper that ran from 1886 through 1890.

6. The Southwest

1. Parrott City, built on the La Plata River just to the northwest of present-day Durango, was the first county seat of La Plata County, from 1874 to 1881, and it had a post office until 1896. The town essentially disappeared after it was abandoned. In the late 1940s, shortly after these narratives were recorded, there was still a Parrott ranch, and between the towns of La Plata and Mayday there is still Parrott Peak, and a Parrott Creek flows into the La Plata River just south of Mayday.

2. For a thorough history see Freeman, *A History of Montezuma County*; a more recent account is Chavis and Morris, *Fire on the Mesa*.

3. Although a U.S. geological team led by John Moss did explore and survey the Mesa Verde area as early as the 1860s, the large Grand Palace ruins were not widely known to European American settlers until 1888, when three cowboys in search of stray cattle glimpsed them from an opposite ridge. Mesa Verde National Park was established in 1906.

4. McIntyre is not listed as ever having been a post office in Colorado. The first post office in Mancos was established in 1877.

5. The Denver and Rio Grande Railroad had reached Alamosa via La Veta and Garland by June 26, 1878, and had reached Durango via Chama, New Mexico, by July 27, 1881. The Rio Grande Southern line ran twelve miles north of Cortez through Dolores from Rico to Durango by 1891.

6. Thompson's Park on the Rio Mancos is noted in the *Rocky Mountain News* as early as October 8, 1874, as "a lovely series of groves of immense pines with an unbroken carpet of turf underneath." But there is no mention of the letter carrier's death.

7. Named for Denver businessman William McPhee, the site of the original community is now underwater in the McPhee Recreation Area Reservoir, and the name survives only in the names of the reservoir and a nearby park.

8. On McElmo Creek, which flows from west to east, the town of McElmo in Montezuma County had a post office from March 11, 1892, through March 15, 1911, and again from March 16, 1912, through February 29, 1932. Toltec in La Plata County gets its name from the Aztec word *tolteca*, meaning people of the tules or reeds; it had a post office from January 26, 1886, until November 21, 1887. The Cortez post office was established on June 21, 1887.

9. Durango is roughly forty-four miles east of Cortez, so the trip would have been a difficult forty miles each way through the La Plata Mountains just west of Durango.

10. Mildred in Montezuma County had a post office from March 18, 1895, until May 30, 1903.

11. The "trouble" referred to, the shooting at Beaver Creek, occurred in 1885, not 1886.

12. This could be Pedersen's version of "Queen Mary's Prayer," popular at the time: "May we put away all pretense and meet each other, face to face, without self-pity and without prejudice. . . . Teach us to put in action our better impulses—straight forward and unafraid."

13. Aztec, New Mexico, about thirty-five miles due south of Durango, was first settled in 1879 and was named in 1890 by settlers evidently thinking the Anasazi ruins in the area were Aztecan.

14. Wolf Creek Pass and Wolf Creek seem to have been named for the timber wolves that were once common in the area, rather than for the man who was shot and buried there.

15. Pagosa Springs was established in 1883; the name refers to *pagósa*, the sulfurous odor of the springs in the area.

16. Del Norte, established in 1872, gets its name from the river Rio Grande del Norte.

17. The Florida River, from its headwaters on the continental divide about forty-five miles northeast of Durango, flows generally south paralleling the Animas, which it joins just north of the New Mexico state line.

18. La Plata County was designated a county in 1874.

19. The 1843 land grant to Correli Vigil and Ceran St. Vrain covered four million acres; it was bordered by the Arkansas on the north, the Purgatorie on the east, and the Sangre de Cristo Mountains on the west.

20. Ignacio, a leader of the Weeminuches, called the Ute Mountain Utes, was

instrumental in their refusal to accept family land allotments in 1895. As a result of this refusal, they received common land in the extreme western portion of the Southern Ute Reservation.

21. Pinkerton Springs, New Mexico, was established on the site of present-day Wagon Mound. European American immigrants settled there as early as 1836, making it a post on the Santa Fe Trail. Animas City—named for the river Río de las Animas Perdidas (River of the Lost Souls)—was settled as early as 1861 by miners, but it was abandoned by September of the same year and later resettled. The community was essentially absorbed by Durango in 1880.

22. The land in Taos Valley was part of the one and one-half million acres that the Mexican governor Manuel Armijo gave to Carlos Beaubien and Guadalupe Miranda. In 1864 Lucien Maxwell and his wife bought the entire area, which thus came to be known as the Maxwell Grant.

23. Trinidad, an important early trading center, was called Santísima Trinidad (Most Holy Trinity). If this is the case, it is not clear what Bohlick means by saying it was named after her mother's cousin.

24. It is unlikely that Menefee traveled anywhere near the site of the Mountain Meadows Massacre on her Washington-bound journey, since it took place in extreme southwestern Utah. The massacre occurred when a group of Mormons, disguised as Indians, along with several Paiutes, attacked and killed about 120 members of the California-bound Fancher Company emigrants on September 11, 1857. At the time of the massacre the emigrants were traveling under a flag of truce and with were under the Mormons' escort.

25. I find no reference for a Touchet River, nor for a Tumbleum River, mentioned in the next paragraph, in eastern Washington. Menefee might be referring to the Tucannon River, a tributary of the Snake that fits her description, flowing north of Walla Walla, east of Dayton, Washington.

26. Menefee might mean Little Blackfoot, Idaho, north of Salt Lake City, conceivably on the route between southern Washington and Denver, through Salt Lake City.

27. The Mancos River, from its headwaters in the La Plata Mountains about fifteen miles northwest of Durango, flows south and west toward New Mexico.

28. Pine River, which flows north to south paralleling the Florida River, refers to Los Pinos; the names were essentially interchangeable. Johnson is referred to frequently in the narratives; people would go to his home during an Indian scare.

29. Junction Creek flows into the Animas River at Durango. Parrott City was located on the La Plata River just south of the present-day town of La Plata. Cottonwood Creek flows out of Cottonwood Canyon into Cherry Creek (in

present-day La Plata County) about ten miles west of Durango, or about six miles east of the travelers' destination, Mancos. Starvation Creek just to east also flows into Cherry Creek from the north.

30. Red Jacket is mentioned in the 1885 Southern Ute census as being forty-five years old and having three sons: Edward, eighteen; James, sixteen; and Peter, fourteen.

31. Mariana was a close associate of Ignacio of the Weeminuche Band.

32. Named for the Weeminuche chief, Ignacio was established in 1877 and has since served as the agency for the Southern Ute Reservation.

33. Mancos Jim was a Paiute with the reputation of having killed many cowboys and prospectors, but he seems peaceful enough in Menefee's account.

34. Ouray, a Tabeguache leader, born ca. 1833, died in 1880 after an extended illness, suffering from nephritis. Menefee's is the only source I know of that attributes his death to poisoning.

35. Bluff City (later shortened to Bluff), Utah, named for the high bluffs along the San Juan River, was established in 1880.

36. Parrott City had a post office as early as May 5, 1876. The Mancos post office was not established until February 19, 1887. There is no listing for a Thompson's Park post office, although the area itself, just to the east of Mancos, is identified by name at the very western edge of La Plata County. Although Freeman mentions this death of a letter carrier in his *History of Montezuma County*, I find little additional published information other than what Menefee provides here. Clara Ormiston and Dora Pedersen (later in this chapter) make brief mention of the incident in their narratives.

37. The Denver and Rio Grande Railroad extended from Garland to Alamosa by June 26, 1878.

38. Armago, New Mexico, established in 1881, was named for the bitter taste of the water to be had there. The town was renamed Lumberton in 1894. Before being built over the Colorado passes, the railroad looped through northern New Mexico to as far as Armago.

39. Arboles, Colorado, is on the San Juan River just north of the New Mexico state line.

40. The railroad line from Chama, New Mexico, reached Durango on July 27, 1881.

41. The Florida divide is ten miles southeast of Durango, between the Animas and Florida Rivers.

42. This awkward phrasing is in the original.

43. William Quantrill, a Confederate guerrilla leader, burned and plundered Lawrence, Kansas, on August 21, 1863.

44. The only newspaper in Durango in 1884 was the *Southwest*, published from 1882 to 1884.

45. According to the *Durango Record* (April 26, 1881), the Stockton-Eskridge-Garrett party, "altogether with their aiders and abettors, have left Durango for good. The motive for leaving was that the Farmington party had gotten out indictments against them, and a requisition for them; rather than fall into the hands of the law." According to one contemporary report, Stockton sold his partner out, "had himself deputized and arrested for which he received $2,500. Wilkerson was lynched and Stockton was killed later for his part in the affair." See John Melton, Civil Works Administration, interview, March 8, 1934, Colorado Historical Society Library, Denver. According to the *Aspen Weekly Times* (May 21, 1881), there was a $500 reward offered for Isaac (Ike) Stockton and $250 each for James Garrett and Hargo Eskridge. Stockton was killed on January 4, 1881. For a detailed account of the Stockton-Eskridge history, see Rasch, "Feuding at Farmington."

46. Joe Wormington, a government scout, was killed on July 15, 1884, as an expedition of about 120 cavalrymen and cowboys pursued a small band of Utes into Utah Territory.

47. Suspected of killing Mays and Thurman (and Smith too, though his body was never recovered), the Indians were pursued into Utah Territory by a posse without legal authority. In a sandy wash near the La Sal Mountains, formerly called the Elk Mountains, the posse was trapped and nine or ten of its members were killed.

48. By "Bear Creek," Ormiston probably means Beaver Creek, the site of the massacre she relates.

49. Henry Moore Teller (1830–1914), involved in real estate and railroad development, was a United States senator from Colorado from 1876 to 1882 and from 1885 to 1909. He was President Chester Arthur's secretary of the interior from 1882 to 1885.

50. Otto Mears, born in Russia, became a builder of mountain toll roads, a United States mail contractor, and a railroad engineer; he was instrumental in finding ways through the Colorado mountains, especially in the southwestern part of the state. He died in California in 1931.

51. John Elitch came to Denver from San Francisco in 1880 and started a restaurant called the Tortoni. On May 1, 1890, he opened the amusement park in Denver, first called Elitch's Zoological Gardens.

52. Fort Lewis at Pagosa Springs was established in 1877, meant to protect settlers from Indians, to safeguard the terms of the Brunot Treaty, and prevent warfare over cattle trespasses. In 1880 it was relocated to Durango and abandoned in 1891.

53. The panic of 1893 came about when silver prices fell from eighty-three to sixty-two cents an ounce. The fall threatened to shut down the mines. Banks closed throughout the state, and the livelihoods of twenty thousand silver miners were threatened. At the same time, farmers in the eastern part of the state were experiencing the worst drought in the short history of the immigrants' prairie settlements.

54. Texas Creek flows from the west into the Los Pinos River about seven miles north of Bayfield.

55. Buckskin Charlie (Chief Sapiah, of the Moache Band) was an important leader of the Southern Utes, essentially taking over as representative of Ute interests after the death of Ouray in 1880. Sapiah died in 1936.

56. [George] Washington (born ca. 1834) is named in the Southern Ute censuses of both 1885 and 1900.

57. Piedra had a post office as early as 1875, which was discontinued in 1878 and then reestablished in January 1880. A post office was established in Pine River (later Pineriver) in 1878.

58. Hansen may be referring to George W. White (b. 1853) and his son Earle (born 1892). W. Earle White founded the White Stores chain in 1930 in Clinton, Oklahoma, a chain that by the 1960s had more than five hundred stores in fourteen states.

59. Telluride, founded as Columbia in 1878, takes its name from the element tellurium, often found with gold.

60. The Denver and Rio Grande Western Railroad reached Montrose from Gunnison on September 8, 1882, and reached Grand Junction in November of the same year. Tracks on the Rio Grande Southern did not reach Telluride until November 21, 1890.

61. There was a stagecoach line between Montrose and Telluride over Dallas Pass.

62. Rico, from the Spanish for "rich," was established in 1879.

63. According to Engel, "In 1879 Charles H. Carpenter staked a claim on the west face of Telescope Mountain and named it the C.H.C." (91).

64. Disappointment Creek, from its headwaters in the La Plata Mountains almost due north of Durango, flows northwesterly and into the Dolores River in San Miguel County, near the Utah state line.

65. Lone Dome in Montezuma County had a post office only from 1893 through 1894.

66. "Migo" is likely a shortened form of the Spanish *amigo*, friend.

67. Dolores post office was established on April 5, 1878. In 1001 *Colorado Place*

Names, Benson writes that "*Dolores* was established on the Dolores River after Rio Grande Southern Railroad bypassed Big Bend, a few miles downstream, in 1891" (57). The Dolores River was named perhaps as early as 1776 by Domínguez-Escalante, El Río de Nuestra Senora de Dolores (The River of Our Lady of Sorrows).

68. That the Utes' motive was revenge for the Beaver Creek massacre is, of course, conjecture on the part of the settlers. As several narrators make clear, Gentner himself had nothing directly to do with the attack thirty-six hours earlier.

69. See Alice Akin's narrative below.

70. Escalante, in south-central Utah, due west of Mancos, was named for the eighteenth-century explorer Silvestre Velez de Escalante by one of Powell's company in the late 1860s or early 1870s.

71. Late in 1879 the Mormon Hole-in-the-Rock expedition camped near Dark Hall Rock awaiting safe crossing of the Colorado River. Hall settled thirty-five miles to the north at the mouth of Hall's Creek in 1882, and he ran a ferry crossing; there was a settlement there from 1881 to 1883.

72. McElmo Creek drains westward out of the valley. Bluff City is now Bluff, Utah.

73. Rockwood is a small community near Electra Lake on the Durango-Silverton Stage line on the Animas River a few miles north of Durango.

74. A Dreyse rifle, a single-shot breechloader, is named for its inventor, Johann Nikolaus von Dreyse (1787–1867), and is nicknamed a "needle gun" owing to its long, sharp firing pin.

75. Camp Apache, known as Fort Apache after 1879, was constructed in 1870 at the confluence of the Black and White Mountain Rivers in east-central Arizona. It served as a military outpost for controlling the White Mountain Apaches and other Indians.

76. Between 1930 and 1933, the American War Mothers Organization, founded in 1917, sponsored (in conjunction with the War Department) the pilgrimage to France for women who had lost their sons or husbands during World War I.

77. Fort Harmony, Utah, was named for Harmony, Pennsylvania, by the Mormon founders.

78. Lee's Ferry, established and run by John D. Lee, an outlaw of the Mountain Meadows Massacre, crossed the Colorado at the mouth of the Paria River.

79. Kayente country is probably a reference to Silverstre Father Vélez de Escalante who, along with Francisco Atanasio Domínguez and others, explored southwestern Colorado and southern Utah, following the Dolores River in 1776, not in "16-something" as Mary Lee Lamb here suggests.

80. Nainsook, a fine, usually white soft cotton fabric on which there was quite a premium, was often used for lingerie and infants' wear.

81. Though there is some controversy concerning the extent of native lynx habitat in Colorado, this sighting suggests that these small wild cats were as far south and west as Montezuma County as late as the 1890s.

82. Hartman Draw flows south into McElmo Creek just west and south of Cortez.

83. Lillian Hartman Johnson, journalist and poet, published a magazine called *Lillian Hartman's Colorado* in 1909.

84. The Rio Grande Southern came through Dolores to Muldoon in 1891.

85. According to the interviewer, Anna Florence Robison, Akin was killed in a skirmish with the Paiutes while a member of a posse from Montezuma County called to near Bluff City, Utah, in February of 1915." For a contemporary account of the battle, see the *Mancos Times-Tribune*, February 26, 1915.

86. The elevation at the Cumbres Pass summit in south central Colorado on the New Mexico state line is just over 10,000 feet (about 3,054 meters) above sea level. The Denver Rio Grande completed the route from Alamosa over Cumbres Pass to Durango in July 1881.

87. The Rio Grande and Southern Railroad from Rico to Durango came to Dolores in 1890.

88. This Ute Peak (one of at least three so-named peaks in Colorado) is about ten miles southwest of Cortez and rises above McElmo Canyon.

89. Narraguinnep Springs was named from the Ute word *náragwinap*, meaning battleground. There is a Narraquinnep Reservoir and wildlife area just north of Cortez, as well as a Narraquinnep Canyon. See Bright, *Colorado Place Names*, 101..

90. Mancos Jim (d. ca. 1930), a Paiute, had the reputation of having killed many cowboys and prospectors.

91. A Tom and Jerry is a hot beverage consisting of egg, milk or water, spices, and liquor, typically rum.

92. The "Chishum War" may refer to the skirmishes and shootings having to do with John Chisum's struggles over mercantile interests in the cattle industry. Cattle king Chisum (1824–84) got into serious debt in the 1870s, and several men lost their lives in disputes related to these debts.

93. The Denver and Rio Grande Western Railroad opened its line between Chama, New Mexico, and Durango on July 27, 1881.

94. Navajo Springs in Montezuma County had a post office first in December 24, 1910. Five years later it was moved to Towaoc.

95. Abraham Lincoln was shot in April 1865, when the narrator would have

been six years old. Lincoln's maternal grandmother's family, the Hankses, included Betsy Hanks (sister of Lucy Hanks, Lincoln's grandmother), who raised Nancy Hanks, Lincoln's mother.

96. Formerly named Ten Mile, the community of Robinson in Summit County had a post office from February 17, 1881, through January 1883. According to Benson in *1001 Colorado Place Names*, "Leadville businessman George B. Robinson grubstaked prospectors in 1878 who struck paydirt north of Leadville. Soon the Robinson Mine and the nearby camp, known variously as Ten Mile City, Summit, and Summit City as well as Robinson, were prospering, but Robinson himself . . . shortly after his election as lieutenant governor . . . was accidentally killed by one of his own men during a property dispute" in November 1880 (181).

97. Pitkin the township, initially named Quartzville, was established in 1879 and incorporated the next year. The name had been changed to honor Governor Frederick W. Pitkin (1837–86).

98. Antonio was initially San Antonio Junction; the name was changed to Antonito, Spanish for Little Anthony.

99. Lone Dome, a community just north of Dolores, had a post office from 1893 to 1894.

100. McPhee, near Lone Dome, supposedly named for a Denver lumber baron, had a post office from 1924 to 1948; the name survives in the reservoir and park.

101. The Rio Grande Railroad came to Rico through Dolores in 1891.

102. William F. Ordway came to the Dolores Valley in June 1881; he built a store in Big Bend, and in 1886 he became postmaster of Big Bend.

103. Although there is no record of a Lakeview in Colorado, there was a Lake Vista which had a post office later, from 1914 through 1918.

104. Dora Pedersen's paper on the history of Montezuma County is included in the introduction to the Montezuma County narratives above.

105. It is not clear from Pedersen's account whether Sam Todd was involved in the massacre. Mary Alverda Estes Taylor, whose narrative follows this one, names "Jim Nash and his father and some other cowboys" as the ones involved in the massacre. According to Parkhill, Agent Stollsteimer claimed that the "perpetrators of this foul murder have not been discovered" (*Last of the Indian Wars*, 38). In Joanna Todd's account, however, the narrator clearly identifies the "captain of the outfit" as Sam Todd, the man who became her husband.

106. Though Joel Estes had settled there in 1859, Estes Park (known earlier as Estes Park Village) was not established until 1905.

107. As noted above, by Lakeview the narrators are most likely referring to Lake Vista, a community in Montezuma County with a post office from 1914 through 1918 only.

108. Totten Lake, now Totten Reservoir, is just east of Cortez.

109. According to Fred Taylor's account of the Beaver Creek affair, "Gentners were new settlers in the country, and the Indians killed Mr. Gentner in revenge for the Beaver affair. It could not possibly have been anything he had personally done to the Indians, for Gentners lived off the trail they traveled, and very possibly the Indians that did the killing were the first Indians the Gentners had seen. Their house was south of where T. C. Bennett has lived in recent years and over the hill. The evening of the killing, Mr. Gentner heard the Indians outside and went to the door where they shot him. They shot Mrs. Gentner in the shoulder, but she took her children and went to the Simon place. The Indians set the Gentner house on fire. My wife's young sister Sarah went over there and pulled Gentner's body out away from the smoldering house. She burned her face. They came over from Dolores next day and took Mrs. Gentner over to Big Bend with her children. Dr. Winters came over from Durango and a veterinary doctor, a good young one, Dan Drake by name, came from Cross Canon and helped to fix the shoulder. Dan Drake was a good surgeon but didn't like it and turned cowboy. Mrs. Gentner got well and later went to California." Howard Porter adds this to the account: "About that Indian trouble on Beaver, those Indians were good Indians and the cowboys did not have anything against them particularly. The Indians had written permission from their agent to hunt there, and they thought they were all right. They had been at our store trading before they went up to Beaver, and they were behaving themselves. The cowboys fired into their camp because they felt that if they let one bunch of Indians come onto the forbidden territory, they would have to let others. So they fired into the Indian camp and started all of the trouble." Taylor' and Porter's accounts are part of the Civil Works Administration interviews for Montezuma County (Pamphlet 360-86).

110. Beginning in 1887, the irrigation and water ditch was being built from Dolores to Cortez in the Montezuma Valley. The first water from the system came to the Montezuma Valley in 1889.

111. Flowing eastward from the San Juan Mountains, Lost Canyon Creek has its confluence with the Dolores River at the town of Dolores.

112. See Clara Morris Ormiston's account earlier in this chapter.

113. The Lewis post office was established in 1909 and named for R. W. Lewis, who bought the townsite.

114. Compare Porter's account here with that by Sarah Elizabeth Walker Moore (earlier in this chapter) of the same biscuit-baking episode.

115. For the account of being stuck at Cumbres Pass during this storm, see Alice Henderson Akin's account earlier in this chapter. The year of the "big rain" was probably 1909, when the Dolores flooded.

116. According to most accounts, a band of Paiutes killed Smith, Thurman, and May in May 1881. Evidence against the Indians is circumstantial, and no body identified as Smith's was ever found.

117. Fort Lewis was established in 1877 on the site of present-day Pagosa Springs, but was moved twelve miles south in 1880. The fort was abandoned a few years later.

118. Piute Springs, Utah, is near Monticello, near the Colorado border.

Appendix

1. Armitage, "Through Women's Eyes," 16.

2. The Robisons' forty-acre homestead consisted of ten acres of fruit orchards (mostly apples, but also cherries, plums, peaches, and apricots), six acres of hay, and pasture for milk cows and pigs.

3. That enclosure is not a part of the correspondence manuscripts.

4. This postscript was handwritten and followed the typed letter.

5. I have been unable to locate these diary reports in the Hafen Collection.

6. *Lillian Hartman's Colorado* was a women's periodical published by the poet and journalist Lillian Hartman Johnson.

7. Hilda Faunce's *Desert Wife* (copyrighted in 1928 and 1934) is an account of the author's experiences among the Navajos based on the letters she wrote to Mrs. Wattles.

8. First published in 1934, *Traders to the Navajos: The Story of the Wetherills of Kayenta*, coauthored by Frances Gillmor and Louisa Wade Wetherill (1877–1945), who lived in Mancos, was a popular account of the experiences of the Wetherill family as they pioneered in Navajo country beginning in the last quarter of the nineteenth century. The book was reprinted by Kessinger in 2007.

9. A. L. Soens, the field-worker for La Plata County, does include a narrative by Sarah Ann Menefee (see chapter 6).

Bibliography

Archival Sources

Civil Works Administration, MSS 2591, Stephen H. Hart Library, Colorado Historical Society, Denver.

Hafen Collection, MSS 1458, Stephen H. Hart Library, Colorado Historical Society, Denver.

Published Sources

Abbott, Carl S. *Colorado: A History of the Centennial State*. Niwot: University of Colorado Press, 1994.

Allen, Martha Mitten. *Traveling West: Nineteenth-Century Women on the Overland Routes*. El Paso: Texas Western Press, 1987.

Armitage, Susan. "Through Women's Eyes: A New View of the West." In *The Women's West*, ed. Susan Armitage and Elizabeth Jameson, 9–18. Norman: University of Oklahoma Press, 1987.

———. "Turner's Ghost: A Personal Retrospective on Western Women's History." In *The Practice of U.S. Women's History: Narratives, Intersections, and Dialogues*, ed. S. Jay Kleinberg, Eileen Boris, and Vicki L. Ruiz, 126–45. New Brunswick: Rutgers University Press, 2007.

Armitage, Sue, Theresa Banfield, and Sarah Jacobus. "Black Women and Their Communities in Colorado." *Frontiers: A Journal of Women Studies* 2, no. 2 (1977): 45–51.

Armitage, Susan, and Sherna Berger Gluck. "Reflections on Women's Oral History: An Exchange." *Frontiers: A Journal of Women Studies* 19, no. 3 (1998): 1–11.

Armitage, Susan, and Elizabeth Jameson, eds. *The Women's West*. Norman: University of Oklahoma Press, 1987.

Arps, Louisa Ward. "From Trading Post to Melted Adobe, 1849–1920." *Colorado Historical Magazine* 45 (Fall 1977): 29–55.

Baker, Jean H. *Mary Todd Lincoln: A Biography*. New York: Norton, 2008.

Baker, Leighton L. *Jim Baker: The Redheaded Shoshoni*. Denver: Colorado Historical Society, n.d. Rpt. Tavares FL: Golden Lifestyles' Books, 1993.

Bauer, William H., James L. Ozment, and John H. Willard. *Colorado Post Offices*. Golden: Colorado Railroad Museum, 1990.

Beckner, Raymond M. *Old Forts of Southern Colorado*. Pueblo: O'Brien Printing, 1975.

Bender, Norman J. "A College Where One Ought to Be." *Colorado Magazine* 49, no. 3 (1972): 196–218.

Benson, Maxine. *1001 Colorado Place Names*. Lawrence: University Press of Kansas, 1994.

———. "A Centennial Legacy." *Colorado Magazine* 57, nos. 1–4 (1980): 1–80.

Bright, William. *Colorado Place Names*. Boulder: Johnson, 1993.

Bromwell, Henrietta E., ed. *Colorado Portrait and Biography Index*. 5 vols. N.p.: Colorado Historical Society, n.d.

Brown, Dee. *The Gentle Tamers: Women of the Old Wild West*. New York: Putnam, 1958.

Butler, Anne M., and Ona Siporin. *Uncommon Common Women: Ordinary Lives of the West*. Logan: Utah State University Press, 1996.

Butruille, Susan G. *Women's Voices from the Western Frontier*. Boise: Tamarack Books, 1995.

Carter, Sarah, Lesley Erickson, Patricia Roome, and Char Smith, eds. *Unsettled Pasts: Reconceiving the West through Women's History*. Calgary: University of Calgary Press, 2005.

Chavis, Tracey L., and William R. Morris. *Fire on the Mesa*. Durango CO: Durango Herald Small Press, 2006.

Chronic, John, and Halka Chronic. *Prairie, Peak, and Plateau: A Guide to the Geology of Colorado*. Denver: Colorado Geological Survey, 1972.

Cochran, Alice Cowan. *Miners, Merchants, and Missionaries: The Roles of Missionaries and Pioneer Churches in the Colorado Gold Rush and Its Aftermath, 1858–1870*. Metuchen NJ: Scarecrow Press: American Theological Library Association, 1980.

Coel, Margaret. *Chief Left Hand: Southern Arapaho*. Norman: University of Oklahoma Press, 1981.

Crum, Sally. *People of the Red Earth: American Indians of Colorado*. Santa Fe NM: Ancient City Press, 1996.

Dallas, Sandra. *Colorado Ghost Towns and Mining Camps*. Norman: University of Oklahoma Press, 1984.

Danz, Harold P. *Of Bison and Man*. Niwot: University Press of Colorado, 1997.

Deutsch, Sarah. *No Separate Refuge: Culture, Class, and Gender on an Anglo-Hispanic Frontier in the American Southwest, 1880–1940*. New York: Oxford University Press, 1987.

Dodds, Joanne West. *They All Came to Pueblo: A Social History*. Virginia Beach VA: Donning, 1994.

Dorset, Phyllis Flanders. *The New Eldorado: The Story of Colorado's Gold and Silver Rushes*. New York: Macmillan, 1970.

Dunn, William R., Lt. Col. *"I Stand by Sand Creek": A Defense of Colonel John M. Chivington and the Third Colorado Cavalry*. Fort Collins CO: Old Army Press, 1985.

Dyni, Anne Quinby. *Back to the Basics: The Frontier Schools of Boulder County, Colorado, 1860–1960*. Boulder: Book Lode, 1991.

Eberhart, Perry. *Ghosts of the Colorado Plains*. Athens: Swallow Press, Ohio University Press, 1986.

Elliott, Donald R., comp. *Place Names of Colorado: A Genealogical and Historical Guide to Colorado Sites*. Ed. Doris L. (Salmen) Eliott. Denver: Council of Genealogical Societies, 1999.

Emmitt, Robert. *The Last War Trail: The Utes and the Settlement of Colorado*. Boulder: University Press of Colorado, 2000.

Engel, Charles M. "Rico, Colorado: A Century of Historic Adventures in Mining." In *Guidebook of San Juan—San Miguel—La Plata Region, New Mexico and Colorado: Nineteenth Field Conference*, ed. John Shomaker, 88–92. N.p.: New Mexico Geological Society, 1968.

Faragher, John Mack. *Women and Men on the Overland Trail*. New Haven: Yale University Press, 1979.

Federal Civil Works Administration. *Rules and Regulations*. Washington DC: United States Government, 1933.

Fischer, Christiane, ed. *Let Them Speak for Themselves: Women in the American West, 1840–1900*. Hamden CT: Archon, 1977.

Foote, Cheryl J. *Women of the New Mexico Frontier, 1846–1912*. 1990. Rpt. Albuquerque: University of New Mexico Press, 2005.

Fowler, William W. *Woman on the American Frontier*. Hartford: Scranton, 1880.

Francis, Irene. *One-Room Schoolhouses, Custer County, Colorado*. Westcliffe CO: Frontier Pathways Scenic and Historic Byway, 2001.

Frazer, Robert. *Forts of the West*. Norman: University Press of Oklahoma, 1963.

Freeman, Ira S. *A History of Montezuma County, Colorado*. Boulder: Johnson, 1958.

Friedman, Susan Stanford. *Mappings: Feminism and the Cultural Geographies of Encounter*. Princeton NJ: Princeton University Press, 1998.

Fry, Eleanor. *Smelters of Pueblo*. Pueblo: Pueblo County Historical Society, 2000.

Garceau-Hagen, Dee, ed. *Portraits of Women in the American West*. New York: Routledge, 2005.

Geffs, Mary L. *Under Ten Flags: A History of Weld County, Colorado*. Greeley: n.p., 1938.

Georgi-Findlay, Brigitte. *The Frontiers of Women's Writing: Women's Narratives and the Rhetoric of Westward Expansion*. Tucson: University of Arizona Press, 1996.

Gillmor, Frances, and Louisa Wade Wetherill. *Traders to the Navajos: The Wetherills of Kayenta*. 1934. Rpt. Whitefish MT: Kessinger Publishing, 2007.

Gulliford, Andrew. *The First Hundred Years, 1883–1983*. [Garfield County, Colorado, University of Colorado Boulder, Western History Archives. Pamphlet.] Boulder: Grand River Museum Alliance, n.d.

Hafen, LeRoy. *Colorado and Its People: A Narrative and Topical History of the Centennial State*. 2 vols. New York: Lewis Historical Publishing Company, 1948.

Harris, Katherine. *Long Vistas: Women and Families on Colorado Homesteads*. Niwot: University Press of Colorado, 1993.

Hemstrom, Greta. *Slates, Chalk, and Inkwells: A History of Schools in Colorado's Uncompahgre Valley*. Montrose CO: Lifetime Chronicle Press, 2008.

Hibbard, Benjamin Horace. *A History of the Public Land Policies*. Madison: University of Wisconsin Press, 1965.

Holmes, Kenneth, ed. *Covered Wagon Women: Diaries and Letters from the Western Trails, 1854–1860*. Lincoln: University of Nebraska Press, 1993.

Hopkins, Harry L. *Spending to Save: The Complete Story of Relief*. 1936. Rpt. Seattle: University of Washington Press, 1976.

Howbert, Irving. *The Indians of the Pike's Peak Region*. 1914. Rpt. Glorieta NM: Rio Grande Press, 1970.

Huber, Thomas P. *Colorado: The Place of Nature, the Nature of Place*. Niwot: University Press of Colorado, 1993.

Hughes, J. Donald. *American Indians in Colorado*. Boulder: Pruett, 1977.

Illustrated History of Arkansas Valley, Colorado. N.p., 1881.

Iverson, Peter. "Discoverers, Pioneers, and Settlers: Toward a More Inclusive History of the American West." *Western Historical Quarterly* 37, no. 1 (2006): 5–19.

Jameson, Elizabeth. *All That Glitters: Class, Conflict, and Community in Cripple Creek*. Urbana: University of Illinois Press, 1998.

Jameson, Elizabeth, and Susan Armitage, eds. *Writing the Range: Race, Class, and Culture in the Women's West*. Norman: University of Oklahoma Press, 1997.

Jameson, Elizabeth, and Shelia McManns, eds. *One Step over the Line: Toward a History of Women in the North American Wests*. Edmonton: University of Alberta Press, 2008.

Jeffrey, Julie Roy. *Frontier Women: The Trans-Mississippi West, 1840–1880*. New York: Hill and Wang, 1979.

Jensen, Joan, and Darlis A. Miller. "The Gentle Tamers Revisited: New Approaches to the History of Women in the American West." *Pacific Historical Review* 49 (May 1980): 173–213. Rpt. in *Women and Gender in the West*, ed. Mary Ann Irwin and James Brooks, 9–36. Albuquerque: University of New Mexico Press, 2004.

Johnson, Susan Lee. "'A memory sweet to soldiers': The Significance of Gender in the History of the 'American West.'" *Western Historical Quarterly* 24 (November 1993): 495–517.

Jones-Eddy, Julie. *Homesteading Women: An Oral History of Colorado, 1890–1950*. New York: Twayne, 1992.

Kaufman, Polly Welts. *Women Teachers on the Frontier*. New Haven: Yale University Press, 1984.

Keleher, William. *Maxwell Land Grant: A New Mexico Item*. Santa Fe NM: Gannon, 1975.

Kit Carson County Historical Book Committee. *History of Kit Carson County, Colorado*. Dallas: Curtis Media Corporation, 1988.

Lamm, Richard D., and Michael McCarthy. *The Angry West: A Vulnerable Land and Its Future*. Boston: Houghton Mifflin, 1982.

League of Women Voters. *This Is Pueblo County*. Pueblo: Congressional Times Press, 1965.

Lerner, Gerda. "Placing Women in History: A 1975 Perspective." In *Liberating Women's History: Theoretical and Critical Essays*, ed. Berenice A. Carroll, 357–67. Urbana: University of Illinois Press, 1976.

Leslie, Jan. *Routt County Rural Schools, 1883–1960: Windows to Yesterday*. Steamboat Springs CO: Legacy Books and Resources, 1998.

Limerick, Patricia Nelson. *The Legacy of Conquest: The Unbroken Past of the American West*. New York: Norton, 1987.

Lindgren, H. Elaine. *Land in Her Own Name: Women as Homesteaders in North Dakota*. Fargo: North Dakota Institute for Regional Studies, 1991.

Marsh, Charles S. *People of the Shining Mountains: The Utes of Colorado*. Boulder: Pruett, 1982.

Miller, Mark E. *Hollow Victory: The White River Expedition of 1879 and the Battle of Milk Creek*. Niwot: University Press of Colorado, 1997.

Moynihan, Ruth B., Susan Armitage, and Christiane Fischer Dichamp, eds. *So Much to Be Done: Women Settlers on the Mining and Ranching Frontier*. Lincoln: University of Nebraska Press, 1990.

Mumey, Nolie. *The Life of Jim Baker, 1818–1898*. Denver: World Press, 1931.

Mutel, Cornelia Fleischer, and John C. Emerick. *From Grassland to Glacier: The Natural History of Colorado and the Surrounding Region*. Boulder: Johnson, 1992.

Noel, Thomas J., Paul F. Mahoney, and Richard E. Stevens. *Historical Atlas of Colorado*. Norman: University of Oklahoma Press, 1993.

Parkhill, Forbes. *The Last of the Indian Wars*. New York: Collier, 1961.

Pascoe, Peggy. "Western Women at the Cultural Crossroads." In *Trails: Toward a New Western History*, ed. Patricia Nelson Limerick, Clyde A. Milner II, and Charles E. Rankin, 40–58. Lawrence: University Press of Kansas, 1991.

Pettit, Jan. *Utes: The Mountain People*. Boulder: Johnson, 1990.

Porterfield, Jason. *The Homestead Act of 1862: A Primary Source History of the Settlement of the American Heartland in the Late 19th Century*. New York: Rosen Publishing Group, 2005.

Portrait and Biographical Record of the State of Colorado. Chicago: Chapman, 1899.

Prescott, Cynthia. *Gender and Generation on the Far Western Frontier*. Tucson: University of Arizona Press, 2007.

Rasch, Philip J. "Feuding at Farmington." *New Mexico Historical Review* 40, no. 3 (1965): 215–32.

Reese, Linda Williams. *Women of Oklahoma, 1890–1920*. Norman: University of Oklahoma Press, 1997.

Riley, Glenda. *Frontierswomen: The Iowa Experience*. Ames: Iowa State University Press, 1981.

———. "The Myth of Female Fear of Western Landscapes." *Journal of the West* 37, no. 2 (1998): 33–41.

———. *A Place to Grow: Women in the American West*. Arlington Heights IL: Harlan Davidson, 1992.

———, ed. *Prairie Voices: Iowa's Pioneer Women*. Ames: Iowa State University Press, 1996.

———. *Women and Indians on the Frontier, 1825–1915*. Albuquerque: University of New Mexico Press, 1984.

———. *Women and Nature: Saving the "Wild" West*. Lincoln: University of Nebraska Press, 1999.

Riley, Glenda, and Richard Etulain, eds. *By Grit and Grace: Eleven Women Who Shaped the American West*. Golden CO: Fulcrum Press, 1997.

Roberts, David. *A Newer World: Kit Carson, John C. Frémont, and the Claiming of the American West*. New York: Simon and Schuster, 2002.

Robertson, Donald B. *Encyclopedia of Western Railroad History*. Vol. 2, *The Mountain States*. Dallas: Taylor, 1991.

Rodgers, Maria M. *In Other Words: Oral Histories of the Colorado Frontier*. Golden CO: Fulcrum Press, 1993.

Rosaldo, Renato. *Culture and Truth: The Remaking of Social Analysis*. Boston: Beacon, 1989.

Rose, Nancy E. *Put to Work: Relief Programs in the Great Depression*. New York: Monthly Review, 1994.

Russell, Marian. *Land of Enchantment: Memoirs of Marian Russell along the Santa Fe Trail As Dictated to Mrs. Hal Russell*. 1954. Rpt. edited by Marc Simmons. Albuquerque: University of New Mexico Press, 1981.

Scharff, Virginia. "Mobility, Women, and the West." In *Over the Edge: Remapping the American West*, ed. Valerie Matsumoto and Blake Allmendinger, 160–71. Berkeley: University of California Press, 1999.

Schissel, Lillian, ed. *Women's Diaries of the Westward Journey*. 1982. Rpt. New York: Schocken, 2005.

Schissel, Lillian, Byrd Gibbens, and Elizabeth Hampsten. *Far from Home: Families of the Westward Journey*. 1989. Rpt. Lincoln: University of Nebraska Press, 2002.

Schlissel, Lillian, Vicki Ruiz, and Janice Monk, eds. *Western Women: Their Land, Their Lives*. Albuquerque: University of New Mexico Press, 1988.

Schwartz, Bonnie Fox. *The Civil Works Administration, 1933–1934: The Business of Emergency Employment in the New Deal*. Princeton NJ: Princeton University Press, 1984.

Schwayder, Carol Rein. *Weld County Old and New: An Historical Gazetteer of Weld County, Colorado, 1836–1981*. Greeley: Unicorn Press, 1982.

Scott, Glen. "Historical Trail Map of Lamar, Colorado." Lamar Quad, USGS, 1995.

Sigerman, Harriet. *Land of Many Hands: Women in the American West*. New York: Oxford University Press, 1997.

Simmons, Marc. *Kit Carson and His Three Wives: A Family History*. Albuquerque: University of New Mexico Press, 2003.

Simmons, Virginia McConnell. *The Ute Indians of Utah, Colorado, and New Mexico*. Niwot: University of Press of Colorado, 2000.

Smith, Barbara. *The First Hundred Years: Greeley, Colorado, 1870–1970*. Greeley: Greater Greeley Centennial Commission, 1970.

Spinning, Bruce. *Clapboards, School Boards, and Blackboards: A History of the Florida Area Rural County Schools, 1875–1959*. N.p.: Florida Schools Association, 1993.

Sprague, Marshall. *Massacre: The Tragedy at White River*. Boston: Little, Brown, 1957.

Spurr, Dick, and Wendy Spurr. *Historic Forts of Colorado*. Denver: Colorado Historical Society, 1994.

Stoeltje, Beverley J. "A Helpmate for Man Indeed: The Image of the Frontier Woman." *Journal of American Folklore* 88, no. 347 (1975): 25–41.

Stratton, Joanna L. *Pioneer Women: Voices from the Kansas Frontier*. New York: Simon and Schuster, 1981.

Tate, Michael L. *Indians and Emigrants: Encounters on the Overland Trails*. Norman: University of Oklahoma Press, 2006.

Taylor, Morris F. *O. P. McMains and the Maxwell Land Grant Conflict*. Tucson: University of Arizona Press, 1979.

Ubbelohde, Carl, Maxine Benson, and Duane A. Smith. *A Colorado History*. 8th ed. Boulder: Pruett, 2001.

Van Cott, John. *Utah Place Names*. Salt Lake City: University of Utah Press, 1990.

West, Elliott. *The Contested Plains: Indians, Goldseekers, and the Rush to Colorado*. Lawrence: University Press of Kansas, 1998.

Wickersheim, Laurel Michele, and Rawlene LeBaron. *The Lost Cities of Colorado*. Bowie MD: Heritage Books, 2002.

———. *Mine Owners and Mines of the Colorado Gold Rush*. Westminster MD: Heritage Books, 2005.

Wilkins, Tivis E. *Colorado Railroads Chronological Development*. Boulder: Pruett, 1974.

Wilkinson, Charles. *Fire on the Plateau: Conflict and Endurance in the American Southwest*. Washington DC: Island Press, 1999.

Willard, James F., ed. *The Union Colony at Greeley*. Denver: Robinson, 1918.

Wolle, Muriel Sibel. *Stampede to Timberline: The Ghost and Mining Camps of Colorado*. 1949. Rpt. Chicago: Sage, 1974.

Worster, Donald. *Rivers of Empire: Water, Aridity, and the Growth of the American West*. New York: Pantheon, 1985.

Wyckoff, William. *Creating Colorado: The Making of a Western American Landscape, 1860–1940*. New Haven: Yale University Press, 1999.

Zanjani, Sally. *A Mine of Her Own: Women Prospectors in the American West, 1850–1950*. Lincoln: University of Nebraska Press, 1997.

Index

Page numbers in italic refer to illustrations.

Unless otherwise indicated, all cities and towns listed in the index are located in Colorado.

www.ingramcontent.com/pod-product-compliance
Lightning Source LLC
Chambersburg PA
CBHW031929110726
47902CB00001B/100

* 9 7 8 0 8 0 3 2 3 5 1 5 1 *